ANABAPTISTS &
POSTMODERNITY

The C. Henry Smith series is edited by J. Denny Weaver. As will likely be true of many future books in the CHS series, Volumes 1 through 4 are being published by Pandora Press U.S. (the original name of Cascadia Publishing House) and copublished by Herald Press in cooperation with Bluffton College and Mennonite Historical Society. Bluffton College, in consultation with the publishers, is primarily responsible for content of the studies.

1. Anabaptists and Postmodernity
   Edited by Susan Biesecker-Mast and Gerald Biesecker-Mast, 2000
2. Anabaptist Theology in Face of Postmodernity:
   A Proposal for the Third Millennium
   By J. Denny Weaver, 2000
3. Fractured Dance:
   Gadamer and a Mennonite Conflict over Homosexuality
   By Michael A. King, 2001
4. Fixing Tradition: Joseph W. Yoder, Amish American
   By Julia Kasdorf, 2002

ANABAPTISTS & POSTMODERNITY

Edited by
Susan Biesecker-Mast *and*
Gerald Biesecker-Mast

Foreword by
J. Denny Weaver

The C. Henry Smith Series
Volume 1

Pandora Press U.S.
Telford, Pennsylvania

Copublished with
Herald Press
Scottdale, Pennsylvania

Pandora Press U.S. orders, information, reprint permissions:
pandoraus@netreach.net
1-215-723-9125
126 Klingerman Road, Telford PA 18969
www.PandoraPressUS.com

Anabaptists and Postmodernity
Copyright © 2000 by Pandora Press U.S., Telford, PA 18969
All rights reserved
Co-published with Herald Press, Scottdale, PA; Waterloo, ON
Printed in the United States by G. B. Printing, Logan Township, NJ
Library of Congress Catalog Number: 00-026150
International Standard Book Number: 0-9665021-2-4
Book and cover design by Pandora Press U.S. in collaboration with Christine Siemens Lautt, whose design for the 1998 Bluffton College Anabaptists and Postmodernity conference influenced this book's design; cover photo of the Münster Anabaptist cages is by Susan Biesecker-Mast.

The paper used in this publication is recycled and meets the minimum requirements of American National Standard for Information Sciences—Permanence of Paper for Printed Library Materials, ANSI Z39.48-1984.

All Bible quotations are used by permission, all rights reserved and except when otherwise indicated are from the *New Revised Standard Version Bible*, copyright 1989, by the Division of Christian Education of the National Council of the Churches of Christ in the USA; RSV from the *Revised Standard Version of the Bible*, copyright 1946, 1952, 1971 by the Division of Christian Education of the National Council of the Churches of Christ in the USA.

Grateful acknowledgment is made to the following for permission to reprint, all rights reserved: to Turnstone Press for "at Basil's," reprinted in ch. 8, and "nonresistance, or love Mennonite style," reprinted in ch. 9, from *Agnes in the sky*, copyright © 1990 Di Brandt; to Rosemary Nixon for "Mennonite Your Way," *Conrad Grebel Review* 15 (1997), 141-42, reprinted in ch. 8; to Dallas Wiebe for excerpts from *Our Asian Journey* (MLR Editions Canada, 1997), reprinted in ch. 9.

Library of Congress Cataloguing-in-Publication Data
Anabaptists and Postmodernity / edited by Susan Biesecker-Mast and Gerald Biesecker-Mast ; foreword by J. Denny Weaver.
    p. cm. -- (C. Henry Smith Series ; v. 1)
    Includes bibliographical references and index.
    ISBN 0-9665021-2-4 (alk. paper)
    1. Anabaptists. 2. Postmodernism. I. Biesecker-Mast, Susan, 1964- II. Biesecker-Mast, Gerald, 1965- III. Series.
BX4931.2 .A496 2000
284'.3--dc21

00-026150

10 09 08 07 06 05 04   10 9 8 7 6

*To Lee Snyder,
for work and hope*

CONTENTS

The C. Henry Smith Series 11
Foreword by J. Denny Weaver 12
Editors' Preface, by Gerald and Susan Biesecker-Mast 15
Introduction: Anabaptists and Postmodernity: A Risky/Risqué Proposition, by
  Susan Biesecker-Mast 19

PART I: RADICAL CHRISTIANITY AND POSTMODERN THEORY
Chapter 1 The Christian Difference: or Surviving Postmodernism
       Stanley Hauerwas • 41

Chapter 2 Foucault, Genealogy, Anabaptism: Confessions of An Errant Postmodernist
       Peter C. Blum • 60

Chapter 3 "Universal Truths": Should Anabaptist Theologians Seek
       to Articulate Them?
       Thomas Finger • 75

PART II: ANABAPTIST STORYTELLING AND HISTORICAL MEMORY
Chapter 4 Valuing the Story of Power and Telling a Grander One: Anabaptism
       and Power Postmodernism in Mutually Enlarging Conversation
       Michael A. King • 91

Chapter 5 Postmodern Practice and Parody: Dallas Wiebe's *Our Asian Journey*
       Paul Tiessen • 106

Chapter 6 Context, Conflict, and Community: South German Mennonites at the
       Threshold of Modernity, 1750-1850
       John D. Roth • 120

PART III: MARGINAL VOICES AND CHURCH POLITY
Chapter 7 When Bloch Pointed to the Cages Outside the Cathedral
       Scott Holland • 147

Chapter 8 Mennonite Literature and Postmodernism: Writing the
       'In-Between' Space
       Hildi Froese Tiessen • 160

Chapter 9 (In)visible Cities, (F)acts of Power, (Hmm)ility, Fathers and (M)others: Anabaptism, Postmodernity, and Mennonite Writing
       Jeff Gundy • 175

PART IV: PRACTICAL DISCIPLESHIP AND LITURGICAL RENEWAL

Chapter 10 Recovering the Anabaptist Body (To Separate It for the World)
Gerald Biesecker-Mast • 193

Chapter 11 *Leitourgia* Beyond Altar and Sacrifice: How Then Shall We Worship/Serve God?
John Richard Burkholder • 214

Chapter 12 The Lord is Still My Shepherd When I Sing: Experiencing God in Postmodern Anabaptist Worship
Marlene Kropf • 233

PART V: RELIGIOUS PARTICULARITY AND SOCIAL IDENTITY

Chapter 13 Nicaea, Womanist Theology, and Anabaptist Particularity
J. Denny Weaver • 251

Chapter 14 Anabaptist Autonomy, Evangelical Engulfment, and Mennonite *Mestizaje*: Three Postmodern Options
Douglas Jacobsen • 280

Chapter 15 The Vow of Stability: A Premodern Way through a Hypermodern World
Gerald W. Schlabach • 301

PART VI: PEACE WITNESS AND POLITICAL COMMITMENT

Chapter 16 Sticks and Stones, Words and Bones: The Body of Christ and the Gospel of Peace
John Stahl-Wert • 327

Chapter 17 Christian Pacifism as Friendship with God: MacIntyre, Mennonites, and the Genealogical Tradition
Chris K. Huebner • 339

Chapter 18 Anabaptists and Postmodernity: Two Visions of Hope
Thomas Heilke • 356

PART VII: CULTURAL CAPTIVITY AND CHRISTIAN FREEDOM

Chapter 19 Postmodern Experiments: Blips or New Revolution?
Leo Driedger • 285

Chapter 20 Following Christ in a Postmodern World
J. Lawrence Burkholder • 406

Select Bibliography 415
Index 429
The Contributors 437
The Editors 440

SERIES PREFACE

C. Henry Smith began teaching at Goshen College, 1903-1913, then taught history at Bluffton College, 1913-1948, except for 1922-1923 at Bethel College. The first Mennonite in North America to earn a Ph.D. and remain in the Mennonite church, Smith was the premier North American Mennonite historian of his era. He wrote many articles for Mennonite periodicals and was a central figure in planning the *Mennonite Encyclopedia*. He had published five major works over thirty-five years, more full-length works than any other Mennonite historian of his time. Also a church leader, Smith was on the publication board of the General Conference Mennonite Church and the Peace Committee of Middle District.

Producing the C. Henry Smith Series (CHS) with cosponsorship of the Mennonite Historical Society is one dimension of the service Bluffton College seeks to provide the Mennonite Church as well as Anabaptists at large. Smith's historical expertise, staunch commitment to pacifism and nonresistance, commitment to the church, and wide-ranging interests beyond the discipline of history all represent the values and interests that characterize the series bearing his name. Naming the series for an individual of multiple interests and talents signals a vision to publish works that use a variety of disciplines and modes of inquiry to serve Anabaptist and Mennonite churches.

Works in the CHS Series reflect the assumption that a peace church worldview holds potential to shape discussion of any issue. These books present no consensus view, however, since none exists. Instead, they address aspects of Anabaptist and Mennonite studies pertinent to the future of these churches. Precisely that future dimension compels CHS publication.

FOREWORD

Bluffton College, in cooperation with the Mennonite Historical Society, is pleased to inaugurate the new C. Henry Smith Series with *Anabaptists and Postmodernity*.

Several factors make this an auspicious time to launch such an open-ended project. This first volume appears in the centennial year of Bluffton College and thus christens the college's second century. For the Western world, the appearance of the series marks the turn to the third millennium—every volume will carry a publication date of 2000 or later. And since the C. Henry Smith Series appears as a parallel to the time-honored Studies in Anabaptist and Mennonite History, it makes a major contribution to the vision of the Mennonite Historical Society to provide leadership in the ever-widening range of Mennonite studies.

Most important, this series arrives at a time of particular significance for the future character—the future faithfulness—of Anabaptists and of the Mennonite churches. Standing on the doorstep of the third millennium, Anabaptists and Mennonites face a greater variety of influences and challenges than at any previous time of their sojourn in North America. Such challenges run the gamut from assimilation and loss of identity for those in tune with North American culture to being turned into commodities by the tourist industry for those who resist North American culture.

A current dimension of these challenges is the need to respond to the impact of the loss in wider society of a sense of common truth. The last two centuries of the demise of Western Christendom involved arguments about whether the supposed foundation of the "universal truth" of Western civilization is or should be located in the Christian tradition or on supposedly universal, rational principles identifiable outside of Christian tradition. In the twentieth century the demise came to include loss of the idea that a common narrative or a common truth might exist. This demise of Christendom and loss of the sense of a common truth, accompanied by a rising tide of pluralism and relativism, have come to be known as postmodernity.

Anabaptist intellectuals are responding in a variety of ways to such challenges, and Mennonite as well as other Anabaptist churches are affected by them, often without specific awareness of that impact. The series of books projected for the C. Henry Smith Series is not about postmodernity or the series of conditions and challenges of early-twenty-first-century North American culture per se. Rather, the series will specifically address theological, cultural, social, and historical issues raised for Anabaptists by the ferment in North American and Western society.

Anabaptists and Postmodernity is an appropriate volume to inaugurate the series. The essays reflect multiple disciplines and modes of inquiry: literature, theology, rhetoric, history, philosophy, and sociology are among the prominent ones. As such it foreshadows the variety of volumes to follow.

For the volume in hand, the introduction and twenty essays constitute a microcosm of the condition called postmodernity as well as the debate about it and the response to it that is occurring in the Anabaptist churches. There is no grand narrative or universal consensus on the character of postmodernity, nor does this volume attempt one. In fact, the authors of these essays understand postmodernity in different and conflicting ways; they make both positive and negative claims about its potential contribution to Anabaptist thought and about the Anabaptist response to it. But in this cacophony of voices readers will begin to discover the diverse and multifaceted character of the phenomenon called postmodernity.

The essays published in *Anabaptists and Postmodernity* were selected from some thirty-six presentations made at the conference "Anabaptists and Postmodernity" that was held at Bluffton College, August 6-8, 1998. Gerald and Susan Biesecker-Mast originated the vision for that conference and made it happen in a masterful way. It was only fitting, therefore, that Gerald and Susan edit this volume of papers emerging from that conference.

Susan's opening essay provides a superb introduction both to the subject of postmodernity and to the individual printed essays. As the series editor, I am deeply grateful to Gerald and Susan for their excellent and unstinting work in organizing the conference and now in editing this volume. Readers will certainly appreciate their efforts.

The development of the C. Henry Smith Series owes much to Michael A. King, editor and publisher, Pandora Press U.S. He supported the concept of the series since its inception. And it has been a pleasure working with Michael as editor and publisher of this volume, which bodes well for the future of the C. Henry Smith Series.

Without the warm support of scholarship in service of the church and the generous commitment of institutional resources by Bluffton College, President Lee Snyder, and Academic Dean John Kampen, neither the conference on Anabaptists and postmodernity nor the series that *Anabaptists and Postmodernity* inaugurates would have happened. Those who will produce the C. Henry Smith Series and those who read the volumes will be ever grateful.

—*J. Denny Weaver, CHS Editor*
Bluffton College

EDITORS' PREFACE

The conference from which the essays in this collection are drawn had a multitude of origins and was indebted to many sources of encouragement, inspiration, and serendipity, not all of which can be named or even recognized.

One place we might start, however, is with the whirlwind of ideas, events, and people associated with Anabaptist communities in Pittsburgh while we were in that city completing our graduate work at the University of Pittsburgh during the early 1990s. We recall challenging conversations and difficult dreams shared with Scott Holland, pastor at the Monroeville Church of the Brethren, and John and Milonica Stahl-Wert, then pastors at Pittsburgh Mennonite Church.

Our brotherly and sisterly exchanges bore much fruit, including one apple that seemed rotten at first: plans for a conference in Pittsburgh on "Anabaptist Radicalism and Postmodern Publics" that never happened due to lack of registration. Fortunately, John D. Roth, editor of *Mennonite Quarterly Review*, consented to publish the presentations prepared for that conference in a special issue devoted to the subject of "Mennonites and Postmodernity" in April 1997, thus advancing and broadening discussion of the agenda slated for the "failed" Pittsburgh conference.

As we attended churchwide gatherings in the following years, we discovered that more and more church leaders and academics in Anabaptist-identified communities were dealing with concerns that tend to fall under the rubric of "postmodernity." Particularly significant was a consultation on "Anabaptists in Conversation: Mennonite and Brethren Interactions with

Twentieth-Century Theologies," planned by Theron Schlabach and hosted by the Young Center for the Study of Anabaptist and Pietist Groups at Elizabethtown College June 19-21, 1997. Discussion after discussion at this event turned from the impact of modern religious thinkers like Barth, the Niehburs, Bonfhoeffer, and Troeltsch to disturbing questions raised by such postmodern writers as Foucault, Derrida, Lyotard, and Gadamer. This consultation inspired us to consider the possibility that a conference such as we had helped to envision at Pittsburgh might now generate enough interest to transpire at Bluffton College, where we were now employed.

On our way home from the Elizabethtown consultation we discussed this prospect with our Bluffton College colleagues J. Denny Weaver and Gerald Schlabach. They were enthusiastic about the idea and subsequently agreed to serve on a planning committee with us for a projected conference on Anabaptists and postmodernity. Fortunately, our planning committee convened in the forward-looking and intellectually inspiring climate of the Bluffton College campus, where an atmosphere of mutual encouragement prevails among faculty and administrators. Such an environment helped confirm for us that what had been postponed in Pittsburgh was now possible at Bluffton.

In the end, the conference on "Anabaptists and Postmodernity" that took place August 8-10, 1998, exceeded our highest expectations. The call for papers received so many exceptional responses that we had to revise and extend our program. The goal of getting at least thirty and as many as sixty people to attend the conference was replaced by the struggle to manage the nearly 200 registrations that poured in.

The spirit and intellect present at that conference was the most immediate source of inspiration for the work of editing a collection such as this. We have sought in the selection and organization of the essays to capture at least some of the wisdom and delight we experienced during those three intense days of presentation, dialogue, argument, and worship.

We owe a great debt of gratitude to the C. Henry Smith Series Editor, J. Denny Weaver, for his painstaking review and correction of our work and for his many helpful suggestions during the process of gathering and polishing these essays into a book. Denny's greatest gift to us, though, has been his untiring devotion to rigorous and principled scholarship on behalf of the church, a lifework that has profoundly shaped our own aspirations and commitments.

Michael A. King, of Pandora Press U.S., was enthusiastic about this book from the beginning and shepherded us through territory unfamiliar to us as first-time editors. He provided substantial assistance in framing the revisions for which we asked and gave us considerable latitude in shaping the schedule by which we worked.

We are thankful for the financial, institutional, and intellectual support provided by Bluffton College for this project. Wesley Richard, Chair of the Communication and Theatre Department in which we hold our appointments, and John Kampen, Vice President and Dean of Academic Affairs, were both forthcoming with resources—including student assistance and computer equipment—that were crucial. Whitney Lehman, who served as a research assistant to the Communication and Theatre Department while we were completing the book, assisted with numerous word processing tasks and compiled the select bibliography and the index for the book. By accepting the book into the C. Henry Smith Series, the college contributed a sizable subsidy to the publisher associated with that series—thus keeping the book's price as modest as possible.

Finally, as president of Bluffton College, Lee Snyder has led the way in making the college a hospitable community for hopeful dreams and visions of all kinds, such as those which led to the "Anabaptists and Postmodernity" conference. Her personal interest and support for both the conference and this book demonstrates an ingenious administrative craft that is concerned with both programs and people, with both bottom lines and blossoming vines, and with both strategic plans and intellectual inquiries. We dedicate this book to her.

—Gerald Biesecker-Mast
Susan Biesecker-Mast
Bluffton, Ohio

INTRODUCTION
Anabaptists and Postmodernity: A Risky/*Risqué* Proposition

Susan Biesecker-Mast

CONSIDERING AN ANACHRONISM

The title of this book was intended simply to bring together two concerns: Anabaptist identity on the one hand and our postmodern cultural moment on the other. Thus the purpose of the book was to inquire about the relationship between the two. The aim was to seek answers to such questions as what it means to be an Anabaptist today, the extent to which postmodernity presents problems and possibilities for Anabaptists, and how Anabaptists ought to live out their faith in the contemporary context.

However, in bringing together Anabaptists and postmodernity, the title also raised an important question about their very pairing—namely, does *Anabaptists and Postmodernity* speak an anachronism? By what logic, if any, can we link with our cultural moment the Anabaptists who struggled (too often until death) for a believers baptism, the separation of church and state, the visible church, and pacifism? Today (in the United States, at least) few care whether we baptize or dedicate babies; the highest law of the land guarantees freedom of religion; the most visible among us (the Amish) are a major tourist attraction; and young men have not been drafted since Jimmy Carter was president.

One afternoon last summer when Gerald (my spouse) and I, as well as twenty-three other Mennonites, were enjoying another in a string of days packed with awe-inspiring historical sights on our European Heritage Tour, tour guide John Ruth put me on the track of a possible answer to the question of whether we dare fruitfully link Anabaptists and contemporary culture. While we were stopped somewhere in the Palatinate, John retrieved from the belly of the bus a copy of the *Martyrs Mirror*. Later, once we were underway, he read us the author's invocation. There Thieleman van Braght confesses,

> Ah! how often did I wish to have been a partaker with them [the martyrs]; my soul went with them, so to speak, into prison; I encouraged them in the tribunal, to bear patiently, without gainsaying or flinching, their sentence of death. It seemed to me as though I accompanied them to the place of execution . . . saying to them in their extremity, Fight valiantly dear brethren and sisters; the crown of life awaits you. I almost fancied that I had died with them; so inseparably was my love bound up with them; for Thy holy name's sake.[1]

As I have read that passage repeatedly since, I have wondered whether those of us who would call ourselves Anabaptists (or even spiritual descendants of the Anabaptists) would be capable of such a confession. Could we presume a relationship of such strong identification with the sixteenth-century Anabaptists as van Braght apparently did? Indeed, could we, like van Braght, wish actually to have been a partaker with them? Moreover, even if we could honestly say that we wished to suffer for our faith as they did, could such a wish (however genuine) ever have integrity as long as we live in times in which our cultural distinctives and faith commitments seem only to register as tourist attractions when they register at all? Or would such a wish at the beginning of this third millennium merely romanticize what it once meant to be called Anabaptist?

Is *Anabaptists and Postmodernity* anachronistic? To put the answer simply, yes. And before we rush to lament that disjuncture, we ought first to appreciate all the gifts it makes possible for us. Indeed, we ought to thank God for the gap between us and our spiritual forebears.

We should thank God for the movement of history by which the sixteenth century gave way to the seventeenth, the Thirty Years War to Reason, monarchies to democracies, religious persecution to tolerance, and the Middle Ages (in the West at least) to modernity. We Anabaptists in the West have been blessed by modernity and the emergence of nation-states and political ideologies that have rendered state-sanctioned burnings at the stake nonsensical. We should be mindful of the rights, benefits, and privileges we enjoy as subjects after modernity, lest we be tempted to view premodernity through a nostalgia that erases the suffering and thus the courage we admire in our forebears.

To pair Anabaptists and postmodernity, then, is anachronistic insofar as the pairing seeks to bridge an impossible chasm between two very different times. However, admitting that chasm does not necessarily oblige us also to say that the Anabaptists are irrelevant to us. On the contrary, such an admission makes the sixteenth-century Anabaptists all the more relevant to those of us who aspire to become early twenty-first-century Anabaptists.

If we were simply to assume our relationship to sixteenth-century Anabaptists (whether by a logic of blood or cause), in what sense could we call ourselves faithful? In what sense could we be full of faith to Anabaptism, not to mention Christ, if we were to depend on some historical or biological continuity for our commitments which we inherit apart from our choosing?[2]

Whenever we engage the sixteenth-century Anabaptists through a presumption of continuity, whether of cause or blood, I think we do so in error. Whenever we assume that the story of the Anabaptists is our story, then try to relive it, we make a mistake. This is so for several reasons. For one, both the presumption of continuity and the effort at imitation ignore the historical chasm that separates us from the sixteenth century—a chasm that accounts for our rights and comforts. In addition, and more importantly, both reduce our faith to a historical accident. We experience the truth of this claim whenever we in the North American context look into the faces of our youth and worry that their commitments are more an accident of birth than an outgrowth of faith.

Rather than begin from the presumption of continuity, then, I think we should begin from the presumption of difference both between the sixteenth century and the present as well as between the Anabaptists and ourselves. When we pay attention to the differences between the sixteenth century and our own, we become capable of resisting the temptation to romanticize from a safe distance a horrible time in which the powers that were could not see their way through to religious tolerance.

Further, when we recognize differences between the Anabaptists and us, we can appreciate that our heritage is not a given but a gift. Indeed, only from the presumption of difference can we see that the Anabaptists were so very much unlike us—antagonists that they were, preferring not to but ultimately being willing to be tortured and martyred for their faith.[3] Moreover, only from the presumption of difference can they teach us. For what would we have to learn from them if, in fact, they were just like us? My point is perhaps subtle, but I hope also significant—that the condition of possibility for our leap of faith is the studied recognition that there is, indeed, a gap.

Minding the Gap

Whatever differences there were among sixteenth-century Anabaptists—and apparently there were many—it seems fair to say that they shared a common problem: they were intolerable in their time.[4] Of course, theirs was a tumultuous era, coming as it did between two rather different historical moments. On the one side was premodernity. This was a period in which the Catholic Church enjoyed orderly control of its religious subjects and territories. Feudal lords exercised profitable and paternal rule over illiterate peasants and inherited lands.

On the other side was modernity, a time in which "the people" revolted against the rule of monarchs and wrote their God-given rights into declarations of independence for individual property owners. In between was the time of the Anabaptists, when capitalism was emerging in the context of feudalism, when a mercantile class and wage laborers were coming to replace serfs, when peasants were starting to understand themselves as individuals, when printing presses and commerce created a need for literacy, when civic authorities were starting to think like nation-states.[5]

In this in-between time—between the one church and nation-states—the question that had to be answered was this: What was to be the relationship between church and state? For Catholics and Reformers, the best answer was that it would be a cooperative one. The Catholic preference was for a church that retained its headship by legitimating the relatively autonomous workings of the state. The Protestant envisioned a church able to enjoy the protection of the state as long as it gave civic matters over to the state. Whether from the Catholic or Protestant perspective, then, the relationship between church and state was to be a relationship of complementarity.

Not so for the Anabaptists. For the Anabaptists the church was to be an alternative, even an antagonist, to the state. It was to be other than the world. The church was not only to aspire to be, but actually to dare to live, as if it were the kingdom of God on earth. As John Howard Yoder summed up this view so well, for the Anabaptists, the church "combine[d] the defenselessness of the church under the cross with the persistence of a prophetic critique which refuse[d] to be stilled by the claimed moral autonomy of the political realm."⁶

Neither Catholic nor Protestant leaders could tolerate the Anabaptist view of the church and the state because that view did not presume, as both of theirs did, that the church and the state ought to exist in a cooperative relationship. The threat posed by the Anabaptist view of the church and state was, of course, made most concrete in the Anabaptists' believers baptism. Indeed, so well did adult baptism exemplify the antagonistic separation between the church and state that it became the epithet by which the Anabaptists (re-baptizers) were popularly known.

Ours is a decidedly different problem shaped by an altogether different time. Living as we do on the other side of modernity, or what has been called postmodernity, our problem is not that we are intolerable but, rather, that we are adorable. Of course the point is not to antagonize the world for its own sake. On the contrary, if we are to antagonize, we must do it for Christ's sake. But suppose we believe, as John Howard Yoder has insisted, that as a people we are "called today to be what the world is called to be ultimately."⁷ Suppose we are convinced that the full reign of God is not yet here. Then it seems to me we ought to differ—and differ significantly.

But to differ significantly these days is one of the hardest things anyone can set out to do. That is because we live in a moment characterized by late capitalism. Now economic growth apparently depends less on the production of the assembly line worker (as in industrial capitalism) and more on the consumption of the Wal-Mart shopper. Thus Gretchen Morgensen, in the business pages of the *New York Times*, writes matter-of-factly that "Retail spending, after all, accounts for two-thirds of the output of the United States." Moreover, she goes on to say, not only do American consumers now account for most of the production in the United States, they are also becoming increasingly important to production in other, especially Asian, countries.⁸

To keep the U.S. economy growing and to buoy economies of other nations as well, then, American consumers must keep buying. But with all those storage units filling up, one has to wonder what more we could possibly need. For the white, middle-class (or better) shopper who is the target of unsightly numbers of marketing dollars, nothing really is needed.⁹ Indeed, for these shoppers it is not a question of need. Rather, consumption is a matter of desire. "Where do you want to go today?" Microsoft asks. Not surprisingly, the greatest desire of all among the consuming citizens of a global village dominated by Coca Cola, Nike, and CNN is to be unique.

However, the consumer economy alone is not what makes differing significantly so hard. The consumer economy and its capacity to reiterate every difference ad infinitum may help create our insatiable desire for uniqueness. But it is the media culture that has hitched that desire for uniqueness back to the consumption of every emerging difference.

For example, for some time Nike ruled the "athleisure" (athletic shoes for leisure wear) shoe market with its high-tech, high-performance casual shoes. But with that market domination also came the problem of consumer boredom, especially among youth. American youth, a crucial sector of the athleisure shoe market, grew tired of Nike's approach through the nineties. Thus emerged Airwalk, an athleisure shoe manufacturer that linked casual athletic shoes to a countercultural youth—the urban, slacker, skateboarder against whom villages and city councils write ordinances to keep Main Street sidewalks and shopping center parking ramps clear of them.

Airwalk's strategy, however, was not so much to market their shoes to these skateboarders, though that was part of it. Rather, it was to create an identification between Airwalk shoes and a certain countercultural identity, on the one hand, and millions of youth looking for a difference, on the other. To buy the shoe, went the logic of the marketing approach, was to link with that countercultural identity. Apparently, American youth liked the link Airwalk offered between something like the edge of culture and their identities. The shoes sold like mad. Indeed, in the first five years of this marketing approach, Airwalk made more than $750 million worth of sales.

Now, however, Airwalk has its own problem. Airwalk's success in achieving a large market share threatens the viability of its claim to sell a shoe that marks the distinctiveness of a countercultural identity. Thus Airwalk finds itself caught in an interesting tension between its strategic link to a counterculture and its placement on the shelves of upscale department shoe stores.[10]

What this brief example suggests is that it is hard to maintain a distinction even when, like Airwalk, that is precisely what you must do to survive. The example also indicates how easy it is for countercultural identity, like that of skateboarder, to be co-opted by a marketing strategy. When differences seem no longer to be the necessary effects of secure essences but, rather, issue from the play of differences in a system of arbitrary (though interested) signs, any difference (however countercultural initially) can apparently be linked to any thing, or person, or appeal. And in these days in which marketers are well aware of our desire to be unique, we can be sure they will be looking to hitch their wares to any difference that has potential for significance.

If differences are co-opted so easily, and if cultural difference is one of consumer/media culture's best marketing strategies, then how can anyone (not to mention us would-be twenty-first century Anabaptists) even hope to differ significantly? Put another way, how can we aspire to be a visible church in a context in which countercultural difference is one of our consumer/media culture's best marketing strategies?

A *RISQUÉ* PROPOSITION

> "You are the salt of the earth; but if salt has lost its taste, how can its saltiness be restored? It is no longer good for anything, but is thrown out and trampled underfoot." (Matt. 5: 13, NRSV)

> "By this counsel we are all taught . . . that we must not love the world and things therein, nor conform to the world; that we through faith must die to our evil flesh and conquer the devil, lead an upright, irreproachable, pious life through faith, and in all things act according to the will of the Lord." (Menno Simons)[11]

To escape the welcomed yet distracting e-mail inquiries about the conference that inspired this collection, Gerald and I slipped out of Bluffton to finish our conference presentations. Fortunately, our need to leave Bluffton coincided with a meeting in Goshen for another upcoming conference. Unfortunately, all the hotels in picturesque settings around Goshen had no vacancies. So we settled for a room at the Holiday Inn Express just across U.S. route 33 from a Goshen Wal-Mart. As I wrote by the window, I could see Wal-Mart across the highway, the semis loaded with campers and manufactured homes traveling down route 33, and the Amish buggies turning off the highway and into the Wal-Mart parking lot. I could not have asked for a better setting to inspire meditation on Anabaptists and postmodernity.

There they were, the Amish, our spiritual and historical kin, differing in all the ways we can imagine—horses, buggies, plain clothes, four-hour Sunday worship services—and pulling into a Wal-Mart only too happy to provide them with special parking accommodations, including a garage on the edge of the parking lot where up to six buggies and horses can be hitched under a protective roof.[12] So there the Amish park their buggies and, once inside Wal-Mart, there the Amish shop in their favored way—frugally. They shop Wal-Mart, the store that "sells for less," because therein the Amish can buy "more with less."

In these ways, then, postmodernity's consumer culture and the Amish simple life fit like the beautifully dovetailed corners of an Amish-made pie safe. Thus I witnessed postmodernity's seamless accommodation of difference for our consumer economy's profit, as I peered over my laptop and across U.S. 33.

But if the Amish dovetail with postmodernity so well, whether by shopping at its discount superstores or, perhaps, even more significantly, by serving as proof to middle-American tourists that it is still possible to differ significantly in our global village, then why did a network voice in postmodernity's consumer/media culture take an apparently hostile stance against the Amish? In February 1997, during sweeps week, ABC's *20/20* aired a dramatic exposé of "the dark side of Amish life"[13] in Holmes County, Ohio. *20/20* contrasted the Amish as "an ideal image of [a] gentle, God-fearing people" who seek "simplicity in their daily lives [as they] reject many of the conveniences of the modern world, such as electricity and telephones," with "case after case of . . . violent and sometimes brutal punishment." In brief, what *20/20* "revealed" was that the Amish "live lives of secrecy" in which "petty rules" (*Ordnung*), forced ignorance (education limited to the eighth grade), and physical abuse are not only tolerated but may even be encouraged as sanctioned forms of obedience training.

To offer visual evidence for the underside of Amish life, *20/20* used a variety of video techniques, including slow-motion shots of Amish walking in a group that encouraged viewers to see the adults as pulling the children down the street. They also cast youth, telling stories of childhood abuse, into dark shadows "for their own protection" and for our entertainment.

But the most dramatic video/exposé moments in the show came with the story of George Edwards, the nonethnic but former Amish man who was trying to "rescue" his two children from their allegedly abusive ethnic Amish mother. In exchange for *20/20*'s financial backing, Edwards invited *20/20* cameras to videotape his farm-to-farm search for his children. When Edwards finally learned of their location, the television audience was treated to a backseat view of his highway chase of the mother's buggy. Once the van overtook the buggy, viewers witnessed up-close the face of the stoic mother as the sheriff pulled the screaming children from the buggy. But if that scene disturbed the audience, later close-ups of the little girl's delighted face during her very first telephone conversation were certainly designed to please viewers—average middle-American viewers, that is.

20/20's exposé of the Amish upset Amish and Mennonites in Holmes County and elsewhere because of its selective and dramatic treatment of

Amish life. These communities were right to be upset with *20/20's* representation of the Amish as well as *20/20's* tactics for getting the story they wanted to tell. However, by reconsidering this *20/20* piece not from the perspective of what it "does" to the Amish but for the purpose of discerning what kind of ideological work it can be read as doing on behalf of middle Americans, we may gain some clues toward a visible church that matters.

The *20/20* segment claims to "reveal" to middle Americans that the otherness of the Amish, however seemingly charming or inspiring, is, above all else, a "secret." Thus Amish otherness not only enables coercion and abuse of children but also encourages it. The segment seeks to persuade its audience that the simple and communal life of the Amish, which may be alluring to middle-American tourists of Amish country is, in fact, a front for cultural pathologies and criminal behavior.

Second, the segment lets the viewing public "see for ourselves" that such secrets can be brought to the light of day with the help of technology—those advances in gizmo know-how that the Amish tend to eschew. In this way the audience "learns" that surveillance cameras (whether found at ATM machines, department store dressing rooms, or convenience store checkout counters) are, in fact, for all our protection, even the protection of Amish children who would one day commit themselves to a subculture that rejects them.

Finally and most importantly, this segment "teaches" its viewers that those who appear to be otherwise—that is, who seem, in *20/20's* words, to be "an ideal of a gentle, God-fearing people"—are, in fact, no better than any typical middle-class American. For when we look closely at the "rescued" little girl who is neither fully Amish (she is too young to have been thoroughly indoctrinated) nor fully middle-American (she is too new to middle-American life to have been influenced by it), what we discover is that she loves telephones, video games, and television.

As a pre-ideological subject this child "proves" to us (like no middle-American child could) that American life with all its technological wonders is what any one of us would choose naturally. "Resistance is futile," to borrow a phrase from Star Trek, not because we are incapable of resisting but (*20/20* is arguing) because we would always prefer not to resist at all.

The *20/20* exposé of the Amish, then, "teaches" Americans that the Amish are not separate and charming but secret and criminal, that technology does not obstruct good family and community relations but instead enables us to catch others who would harm them, and that our desires for technology are not cultural inventions but are rather perfectly natural. This ideological work is important for our consumer/media culture. It props up the fiction of readily available and meaningful choice, which is central to consumption. Then it simultaneously sustains the idea that consumption and technology are natural choices in the context of any alternative that might inspire us to abandon both.

The ideological work *20/20* is doing is also important for us because, when we read it against the grain, it tells us Amish distinctives are significant. If they were not, then it would not make sense for *20/20* to run an exposé of those differences. It would make no sense for *20/20* to attempt to convince middle Americans that the Amish are "just like us" (to quote the segment's closing line) if, in fact, middle Americans were not tempted by Amish people's critical engagement with and thoughtful rejection of technology. Indeed, I suspect that *20/20* aired a story on the Amish during ratings week precisely because its producers recognized that many middle Americans are at least intrigued by the cultural critique that the Amish perform in their daily practices.

So again, as disturbing as this *20/20* segment is on a number of levels, it helpfully reminds us that the Amish do differ significantly. The elegance of their simple life and their thoughtful resistance to the seemingly inevitable influx of technologies of communicative speed contest the twin propositions that consumption is a meaningful expression of choice and that technological advances are either necessary or desirable.

My point is not that we should reject technology. My point is rather that it is possible, though admittedly difficult, to differ significantly. My point is also that we may learn something about how to differ from our Amish brothers and sisters whose cultural indecency in an age of cultural indifference is inspiring. Truly theirs is an "indecent" life, as the most conservative Amish walk around daily with no shoes on, seeing no need (as I certainly do) for taking a shower every day, and making their way through the world with not so much as a telephone in the house, not to mention an answering machine, caller ID gizmo, television, VCR, cable hook-up, computer, e-mail server, satellite dish.

Amish indecency calls us to consider, among other things, which postmodern technologies we have decided are necessary, natural, and/or desirable. What of their costs do we fail to count? I am thinking of the call that disrupts dinner, the television commercials that encourage our children to cry out from the grocery cart for some sugar-coated cereal, or the e-mail messages that a few years ago were not even a part of our existence but now are so commanding of my attention that I sometimes feel compelled to leave town to ignore them. Indeed, I cannot help but wonder whether the *20/20* segment functions much as do the cages still hanging in St. Lamberti's Church in Münster, left over from an earlier indecent Anabaptist experiment: a reminder to nonconformists that they risk an unseemly end.

A RISKY PROPOSITION

> Then Job answered the Lord: "I know that you can do all things, and that no purpose of yours can be thwarted. . . . I have uttered what I did not understand, things too wonderful for me, which I did not know. . . . I had heard of you by the hearing of the ear, but now my eye sees you; therefore I despise myself, and repent in dust and ashes." (Job 42: 1-6, NRSV)

> "If we do not desire willfully to oppose the Holy Ghost and reject the grace of God, it is impossible to believe that a true faith can be without regeneration and without obedience, and that this obedience can be without promise."[14] (Menno Simons)

As I have said, I am not arguing for a wholesale rejection of technology. The Amish in their wisdom do not even do that because they know that meaningful resistance is not about reaction. My point has to do with agency, choice, decision. The point is not to turn away from the world, since after all we must live in it. It is about seeking ways to be in the world but otherwise, according to the teachings of Jesus.

What I am calling for is for us to get serious about empowering our own agency in the world in which we live. Given the principalities and powers of these days (especially the consumer/media culture), we can begin by reading critically those media texts we do watch or technological wonders we do take into our lives. We can stop ignoring texts as if they were merely entertainment or using technologies as if they simply made life easier. We can start to read them as a primary mode of creating and preserving the troubled and complicated world in which we live. Then we begin to diminish their power over us and start to assert our agency or power with them.

When we subject media texts to that kind of engagement, we can learn from them, against the grain of their ideological workings, that our times are relativistic largely to the extent that our consumer/media culture seeks to make them so. The media encourage the proliferation of ultimately meaningless differences because in so doing they create an insatiable desire in us for a difference that matters. For our consumer/media culture, the difficulty of the difference is just fine. And its short shelf life is even better since, as I have argued, that is precisely the condition of possibility for our return to the mall.

When we read our consumer/media culture critically and learn that all differences are not necessarily the same but are made the same largely for the marketing purposes of that same consumer/media culture, then something remarkable becomes possible. For perhaps the first time we become open to hearing what our consumer/media culture would prefer to keep silent—namely, the voices of the others of that consumer/media culture that might dare, like the Amish, to witness to another way.

But if it is difference we are really after, then we should be aware of the risk we are taking. If we begin to listen to such others, there is no telling in advance what else we may do. As Jacques Derrida argues in his close reading of Kierkegaard's interpretation of the story of Abraham and Isaac, every other is of God, because God is wholly other. Thus to come to the other is also to come to God. And to come to God is always to avail oneself to God, to give oneself over to God and, thereby, to risk oneself before God. Hence, whenever we seek out the other, even the other voice of a media text, we seek God and put ourselves in God's hands. Finally, precisely because God is wholly other, totally not us, we cannot know God's purpose or God's plan. Thus, we can never know in advance what will become of us. That is the very serious risk of seeking the other.

If we do take on this project of engaging our consumer/media culture critically to hear its other, we should do so defenselessly—that is, not to try to find the answers we are looking for but rather to make ourselves available to unexpected challenges and surprising contestations to who we are and who we have been. Although I have not argued that we should "kill our televisions," I also cannot promise that when we have spent some time critically engaging, say, the various media representations of the Amish from the *20/20* segment, front-page articles on cocaine-selling Amish youth, or films like *For Richer or Poorer*, we will not, in fact, find ourselves throwing out our televisions.

As I said at the outset, I believe the relationship between the sixteenth-century Anabaptists and postmodernity is an anachronism. The two do not mix. We will not get them to synthesize. Like the Anabaptists, the Amish are significantly different from us too. Unlike us, they have figured out a way of living that offers a visible witness to our consumer/media culture's preferred view. We could take (and many of us have taken) these relations of significant difference to mean that neither the sixteenth-century Anabaptists nor the Amish have much to say to us. Thus we could (and many do) put them aside. But if we did that, we would forfeit the chance to consider the possibility, however unlikely, that precisely in their otherness breathes the Spirit of our transformation toward that wholly other who is God.

Throughout this introduction, I have been seeking to warn against taking either of two familiar yet unhelpful postures in relation to sixteenth-century Anabaptists. Early on I argued that we should not presume continuity by history or blood with sixteenth-century Anabaptists since doing so undercuts the condition of possibility for faith. Then I suggested that we should also not presume that, because of their differences from us, the Anabaptists of the sixteenth century have little or nothing to teach us.

Instead I am inviting us to take another more difficult approach: studying the gap between us. By investigating the gap that stretches between the sixteenth century and the beginning of the twenty-first, we learn that our Anabaptist forebears inspire us to differ significantly. By studying the gap between the Amish and ourselves, our contemporary brothers and sisters teach us that it is possible to differ significantly. Whether and how we will aim to differ significantly, or to witness, will be our question of faith.

These essays seek in their various ways to answer that question of faith and its accompanying questions. Shall we seek to differ? What would it mean for us to do so? Should we endeavor to antagonize? And if so, what or whom? If we should try either to differ or to antagonize, how? What type of differing could serve as a witness these days? What should our witness say?

A RADICAL CHORUS?

Shortly before the conference from which these essays came was convened, a letter to the editor appeared in the Mennonite press.[15] The letter suggested that the people gathering for the Bluffton conference were really not very radical. Indeed, the writer indicated that watching Seinfeld reruns would probably be more productive than attending the conference.

I do not wish to discount watching *Seinfeld* reruns, especially given the case I have just made on behalf of a critical engagement with consumer/media culture. And most conference presenters and participants would probably acknowledge that they have not yet become adequately radical as Christians. Yet I am not willing to concede altogether the point that gathering at the conference was insignificant.

I doubt that, taken individually, the participants at this conference were especially radical. Certainly we were no more radical than the participants of most such conferences. But gathered together as historians and poets, pastors and chemists, parents and administrators, rhetoricians and philosophers, we were at the very least two or three come together in Jesus' name for the purpose of thinking through what it might mean to be a visible church in these times. Moreover, in these days in which gathering face-to-face seems to become ever harder amid ever more pressing demands for speed and efficiency, that familiar gospel claim seems only to turn more radical with time.

In that spirit of gathering, we have brought together in this collection some of the voices of that conference. These chapters speak from a variety of disciplines, generations, and perspectives. Each endeavors to help us discern a meaningful difference and to make a significant witness in these times. But given their differences, it is no surprise that there are gaps in and between these essays, just as there are gaps between ourselves and our Anabaptist forebears. It is our hope that these gaps will inspire further questions and conversations.

The essays collected here have been arranged into seven parts plus this introduction. Part one, "Radical Christianity and Postmodern Theory," takes up directly the question as to what posture radical Christianity ought to adopt with respect to postmodern theories. Thus with this section the reader is invited to plunge right in to the theological and theoretical complexities of the question this book pursues.

In the opening essay of that section, Stanley Hauerwas argues that postmodern theory is best understood not as a radical departure from a modern thinking that rendered God irrelevant but as the cultural logic or handmaiden of an advanced capitalism that has ruled God out of order as well. As a discourse suspicious of all grand narratives and constitutive of fragmented subjects, postmodern theory, Hauerwas continues, is no friend of Christianity and makes excellent consumers for a global market. Yet, Hauerwas further argues, the church may not only survive but flourish in this global market if the church learns to be an international community speaking from a position of moral authority insofar as it gives voice to local people.

In the second essay of this section, Peter Blum alerts us to a problem of Truth, which is its tendency to coerce assent and underwrite programs of violence. However, by way of a productive dialogue between the work of Michel Foucault and John Howard Yoder, Blum urges us to resist the temptation to respond to this problem of Truth with apathy. He invites us instead to engage our world through the particular and noncoercive witness of the gospel.

The first section of the book closes with Thomas Finger's contribution, which addresses the problem of Truth from the question of whether Anabaptists ought to make universal truth-claims. Finger recognizes the relevance of postmodern critiques of the practice of making universal truth-claims. However, by way of a philosophical and theological analysis of certain universal truth-claims in Christianity, Finger argues that Anabaptists are obliged to deal in universal truths conceptualized not as epistemological foundations but as eschatological goals.

In part two, "Anabaptist Storytelling and Historical Memory," we turn our attention to stories, whether of the gospel, on the one hand, or of Mennonite experiences, on the other. We ask how stories function as well as how they might be told amid postmodern theories and exigencies.

This section begins with Michael A. King's essay in which he, also engaging the work of Foucault, asks whether Foucault's theorization of power, according to which our Anabaptist stories are effects of power, is the story we want to tell. Determining that though the Anabaptist story can benefit from Foucault yet dare not become thoroughly Foucauldian, King urges us not to seek a return to a modern view that truth and knowledge are outside power. Rather, he invites us to consider with Gadamer that the truths we have received through time, while not objective, can still be affirmed as true.

With Paul Tiessen's essay we encounter a close reading of Dallas Wiebe's story (in *Our Asian Journey*) of a small group of nineteenth-century Russian Mennonites who traveled to Central Asia to meet the returning Christ. Tiessen's reading of Wiebe's novel teaches us much, not only about postmodern novels in their formal and stylistic features, but also about the power of stories to constitute identities, to dismiss the other as unworthy, to violate the history of those who would be forgotten, and also (and perhaps most importantly) to subvert the "proper" stories by engendering regard for the indecent actions of dreamers and visionaries.

John D. Roth's essay closes out part two and gives us a glimpse of a historiography emerging among some historians through which stories are told with an ear not only to continuities but also to discontinuities between times. In Roth's telling of the stories of the South German Mennonites at the turn of the nineteenth century, we learn of the tensions and struggles through which these Mennonites forged their identity and their practices in a moment of transition between premodernity and modernity.

Part three, "Marginal Voices and Church Polity," invites us to hear the dissonant voices of past, present, and beyond for the disturbances they may speak into the way we have been the church. Thus Scott Holland asks us to heed Ernst Bloch's call that we do theology from the cages in which the Anabaptists of Münster were punished for their heretical attempt to bring forth the reign of God into the here and now. From these cages—places of delegitimation from which Anabaptists since Menno Simons have been running—Holland argues, we may speak of and for the underside of Christendom wherein God dwells.

Seeking the underside of both Mennonite "experience" and Canadian culture, Hildi Froese Tiessen's essay directs our attention to some Mennonite writing that employs "postmodern irony"—the use and misuse of dominant modes of understanding on behalf of alternative understandings—for the purpose of productively interrogating "proper" culture, be it Mennonite or mainstream. Through her readings of works by Di Brandt and Rudy Wiebe, Tiessen introduces us to spaces between Mennonite tradition and postmodern fragmentation wherein destiny gives way to possibility.

With Jeff Gundy's essay we return to the problem or, rather, possibility that comes with the question of Truth. If Truth is a problem—if we humans cannot settle on an absolute Truth—Gundy reasons, then a great opening is made in the discourses we have inherited for all the many voices so far silenced. If these voices are to speak to our heritage meaningfully and into the silences artfully, then they will bring us both good and bad news but news, in any case, by which we may work out our peoplehood together.

In part four, "Practical Discipleship and Liturgical Renewal," contributors ask us to re-examine the ways we live our faith in our daily and worship practices, often encouraging us to discover "new" ways of making "old" practices witness to our troubled world and local communities. In his essay, Gerald Biesecker-Mast takes contemporary sensitivity to the limits of Platonism as an occasion to outstrip dualisms like word and deed for a nonresistant "discipleship of performance." By way of such a discipleship that is otherworldly in its defiance of violence done in either word or deed, he hopes, we may bring forth audaciously and lovingly the reign of God.

Concerned that urgent calls for meaningful Mennonite distinctives cannot fully be answered by either systematic theology or high church liturgy, John Richard Burkholder offers a theology of worship that seeks to transgress traditional Christian demands for the altar and sacrifice. Burkholder takes our postmodern condition (which, he argues, frees us from having to ground a theology of worship in philosophical foundations) as an opportunity to think worship beyond the conventional logic of Christ as scapegoat. He makes the case (via René Girard) for a theology of worship (as service, work, ministry, and praise) according to which worship is not a cultic dying but instead a living and self-offering discipleship.

Also seeking to transform traditional conceptions of worship, in particular those conceptions that have obscured the extent to which singing forms faith, Marlene Kropf lets us hear the testimonies of numerous Mennonites who say their experience of singing is sacramental. In these postmodern times, Kropf argues, in which so many of us are seeking multi-sensory engagements with God, singing has the potential to become all the more significant and powerful as a kind of sacrament.

Part five, "Religious Particularity and Social Identity," offers three strategies for re-constituting Anabaptist-Mennonite identity now that no single origin or story can persuasively function as its secure anchor. J. Denny Weaver's strategy is to write a theology grounded in the teachings of Jesus according to which a peace witness is constitutive of the Christian community. Such theology remains marginal but could disrupt Christendom hegemony, Weaver argues, if Anabaptist-Mennonites would take seriously the particularity of their and Christendom's theology, thus risking a choice between a church of the common ground and a church for the culturally disenfranchised. For Weaver, the choice could neither be more obvious nor more difficult.

Douglas Jacobsen approaches the question of Mennonite particularity from a suspicion of the so-called possibilities of postmodern pluralism for Mennonite community. Unconvinced that postmodernity bodes well for particularity, Jacobsen argues on behalf of a hybrid (or *mestizaje*) vision by which Mennonites might accept and even celebrate, rather than resist or ignore, the diversity among Mennonites and others through a politics of compassion and an ethics of forgiveness.

Seeing similar perils between the would-be faithful of medieval and hypermodern times, Gerald Schlabach, in the third essay of this section, urges us to become Catholic Mennonites who resist the speed and consumerism of these days by making a vow of stability. By this vow, he argues, we would resist contemporary trappings of endless and repetitive desires for the new with the freedom that accompanies self-conscious slowness, long-suffering patience, and uncoerced obedience, which are of God, our saving rock.

Part six, "Peace Witness and Political Commitment," consists of three essays that take the peace witness so seriously as to consider what it would mean for social relations and political commitments if we were to become dedicated to it. In his meditations on the gospel of peace, John Stahl-Wert urges us to welcome the new millennium with a renewed commitment to the truth of Jesus as enfleshed, a truth that undoes all our hatred of flesh, whether ours or someone else's. For if we were ever to live by that commitment, that incarnation of peace, that affirmation by God of God's love for all, then, Stahl-Wert muses, we would through our fleshly lives begin to create a new world.

Chris Huebner's essay works us through three key theological arguments from Alisdair MacIntyre, Jacques Derrida, and John Milbank. He contends that these three thinkers, in their departure from or theorizations of our relationship to God via friendship, tend to reproduce dualistic conceptions of our relationship to God as either aesthetic or concrete. Written out of the notion that the church is the body of the forgiving and suffering Christ, Huebner argues, Mennonite theology enables us to participate in the very life of God as it unites rather than opposes aesthetics and reality. Such theology calls us toward a following that does not merely repeat Jesus' life, as well as toward acts of reconciliation and forgiveness that transgress violence.

Finally, Thomas Heilke compares modern, postmodern, and Anabaptist discourses on politics at the level of their eschatologies to inquire into their differing visions of hope. Modern articulations of the political order always aim for a specific and concrete outcome, and postmodern versions give up all concrete forms of hope through politics. Against such tendencies, Heilke argues, an Anabaptist counter-vision of hope sees in the potent remainder of all political aspirations a space in which God's grace and peace may come. Thus, according to Heilke, although politics are not irrelevant (since at their best they may serve as the space in which the message of salvation may be proclaimed and heard), they are also not our salvation. Rather, our salvation is in remaining faithful to God's reign of grace and peace in this world.

The book closes in part seven, "Cultural Captivity and Christian Freedom," with two critical inquiries into the possibilities in postmodernity for Christian freedom. Leo Driedger surveys characterizations of postmodernity as compared to premodernity and modernity as well as discusses thinking being done by postmodern theorists. Driedger argues that postmodernity, when understood against the backdrop of modernity, does mark a departure from modernity's "iron cages" and opens the possibility for a new Mennonitism that might embrace new communities, experiences, art forms, and ways of knowing.

For J. Lawrence Burkholder, postmodernity also presents a possibility. The freedom it makes available versus its suspicion of, for instance, categorical imperatives, may enable us to be disciples of Jesus and responsible inhabitants of the larger social order at the same time. So far, Mennonites have taken the freedom of postmodernity as an opportunity to conform to the world. However, such freedom might as easily enable a nonconformity by which we could become socially responsible disciples of Jesus through freely chosen and thus generously offered self-sacrifice. The test of our success, he challenges, will be precisely the extent to which such self-sacrifice becomes a reality.

Despite their differences in disciplinary approaches, Anabaptist perspectives, and generational concerns, all the chapters in this book, I believe, challenge us to think through difficult questions toward a meaningful Anabaptist witness for these times. We hope that the differences and gaps in and between these essays will inspire productive thinking and energetic conversation on the issues (whether or not best understood through the rubric of postmodernity and postmodernism) that we face.

Notes

1. Thieleman J. van Braght, *The Bloody Theater or Martyrs Mirror of the Defenseless Christians* (Scottdale, Pa.: Herald Press, 1997), 5.

2. For the persuasive and eloquent development of this argument, from which these claims are borrowed, see Jacques Derrida, *The Gift of Death*, trans. David Willis (Chicago: University of Chicago Press, 1995).

3. The *Martyrs Mirror* often recounts the gladness with which Anabaptists faced their executioners. To us this may seem strange, even oddly masochistic. But another reading of their stories is available. What their stories do say is that the Anabaptists resisted their pursuers when they could by fleeing towns and living in hiding. Thus they did not seek out martyrdom. However, once they determined that their deaths were near, they typically greeted them gladly as potent witnesses to their faith. Importantly, nothing maddened the powers that were more than to hear Anabaptists singing on their way to the stake or praying on behalf of the executioners. So infuriated did the executioners become in the face of this Anabaptist refusal to let their persecutors have the last terrible word that executioners often took to cutting the Anabaptists' tongues out or screwing them to the top of their mouths.

4. I am, of course, referring here to the polygenesis thesis according to which the origins of the Anabaptists are considered to be so diverse as to disable the unity once claimed in the work of such church historians as Harold S. Bender. For a recent critique of the polygenesis thesis, see Abraham Friesen, *Erasmus, the Anabaptists, and the Great Commission* (Grand Rapids, Mich.: Eerdmans, 1998), and Gerald Biesecker-Mast, "Anabaptist Separation and Arguments against the Sword in the Schleitheim *Brotherly Union*," *Mennonite Quarterly Review*, forthcoming issue.

5. This is a very brief summary of Stephen Toulmin's characterization of the shift from premodernity to modernity in *Cosmopolis: The Hidden Agenda of Modernity* (New

York: Free Press, 1990).

6. John Howard Yoder, "'Anabaptists and the Sword' Revisited: Systematic Historiography and Undogmatic Nonresistants," *Zeitschrift für Kirchengeschichte* 85.2 (1974), 139.

7. John Howard Yoder, *Body Politics* (Nashville: Discipleship Resources, 1994), ix.

8. On this point, Morgensen writes the following: "Everybody knows that the American consumer has been the high-octane fuel behind the nation's decade-long economic boom. Retail spending, after all, accounts for two-thirds of the output of the United States. But it is becoming increasingly apparent that American shoppers are also fueling the recoveries just starting to be charted in depressed economies overseas." Gretchen Morgenson, "U.S. Shoppers Shoulder the Weight of the World," *New York Times*, June 20, 1999, sec. 3, p. 1.

9. Of course, there are plenty of people in need in the United States. But those in need tend not to be the "targeted shopper" about whom I am speaking here. Indeed, the shopper most energetically sought after is the (especially male) middle-class (or more affluent) shopper between the ages of 18 and 49.

10. This example has been developed from the following article: Gary Strauss, "Battle's afoot: Airwalk tries not to trip," *USA Today*, July 31, 1998, 1B-2B.

11. Menno Simons, "The New Birth," *The Complete Writings of Menno Simons* (Scottdale, Pa.: Herald Press, 1984), 101.

12. According to John D. Roth, that garage was actually a cooperative effort between Wal-Mart and the Amish around Goshen.

13. All quotations from this *20/20* segment were taken from an ABC News videotape of the February 21, 1997, broadcast of *20/20*, produced by Ene Riisna and Frank Mastropolo.

14. Menno Simons, "Christian Baptism," *The Complete Writings of Menno Simons*, 265.

15. D. R. Yoder, Letter to the Editor, *Mennonite Weekly Review*, July 16, 1998.

PART ONE

RADICAL CHRISTIANITY AND POSTMODERN THEORY

ONE

THE CHRISTIAN DIFFERENCE:
Or Surviving Postmodernism

Stanley Hauerwas

CAN POSTMODERNISM HAVE A HISTORY?
"Post-Modernism is the pessimism of an obsolescent class—the salaried official intelligentsia—whose fate is closely bound up with that of the declining nation-state."[1] This may sound like a particularly harsh judgment made by Nicholas Boyle in his extraordinary book, *Who Are We Now?: Christian Humanism and the Global Market from Hegel to Heaney*. Yet I think Boyle is right to so judge postmodernism. That I agree with Boyle may surprise some who have grouped me with the nihilistic, relativistic, barbarian hordes who threaten all we hold dear—values such as objectivity and the family. I confess I have at times taken great pleasure watching postmodernists dismantle the pretensions of modernism. But it is still the case that being an enemy of my enemy does not and should not necessarily make me a friend of postmodernism.

Before I elaborate on and defend Boyle's judgment, however, I need to prepare a case for why his understanding of postmodernism is important for those of us who, in an allegedly postmodern time, attempt to do Christian theology. That some may have mistaken me as a sympathetic supporter of postmodernism is understandable. After all, I have playfully used postmodern playfulness to remind Christians that we are in a life-and-death struggle with the world.[2] I have thought the playful use of postmodernism justified because I have found it difficult to take postmodernism seriously as an intellectual position. However, if Boyle is right to interpret postmodernism as the position of those who would make our time the end of history, then it is a serious mistake not to take postmodernism seriously.

That I have not taken postmodernism seriously does not mean I have not taken seriously the work of people like Michel Foucault. Indeed, as David Toole has shown in his remarkable book, *Waiting for Godot in Sarajevo: Theological Reflections on Nihilism, Tragedy, and Apocalypse*, Christians, particularly Christians committed to Christian nonviolence, cannot afford to ignore Foucault's extraordinary work.[3] This is particularly true, as Toole makes clear, for those influenced by the equally remarkable work of John Howard Yoder.

Toole observes that where Foucault's work meets a Yoder-like reading of the New Testament, both step into the glow of a new light that is the product of their convergence. This is particularly the case when considering how similar Foucault's account of power is to that of the "principalities and powers" in the New Testament. Toole rightly defends Foucault against those who suggest he provides no alternative of resistance to the powers.

Toole additionally argues, however, that it is the cross, as Yoder directs our attention, that gives the hope—a hope Foucault cannot make intelligible—necessary for such a struggle. Responding to his own question of how to characterize the difference between Foucault's tragic politics and Yoder's apocalyptic alternative, Toole observes, drawing on Beckett's *Godot*:

> For Vladimir and Estragon the difference is that Godot will finally arrive. For Nietzsche, the difference lies between Dionysus and the Crucified. John Howard Yoder sums up this difference in a word: Jesus, the slain lamb, the one who took up the cross and not the crown. Of course what this means for Vladimir and Estragon is not only that Godot will arrive one day, perhaps one day soon, but that he has already come and that they can, therefore, wait with confidence and patience; it means that even in Sarajevo they can protest their suffering with dignity.[4]

If Toole is right (and I certainly think he is), Christian intellectuals face an enormous challenge which Yoder's work only signals. In short, we theologians must provide an account of our situation that is at least as radical and imaginative as the one Foucault was attempting. In other words, we must challenge the knowledges currently enshrined in the academic disciplines dominating the modern university. Such knowledges provide the theodical accounts necessary to convince us that the way things are is the way things have to be—which is one reason I have had difficulty taking postmodernism seriously. The problem in brief is that postmodernism is a far too comforting story for alienated intellectuals.

Of course, it can be objected that I am being unfair to postmodernism. After all, most postmodern thinkers style themselves radicals. As a style of thought, postmodernism is allegedly suspicious "of classical notions of truth, reason, identity and objectivity, of the idea of universal progress or emancipation, of single frameworks, grand narratives or ultimate grounds of explanation."[5] Postmodernism seems, in other words, to call into question the Enlightenment project. Surely that is a good thing. Yet I am not convinced that postmodernism, either as an intellectual position or as a cultural style, is post-anything.[6]

For example, Boyle observes that many postmodernists deny or at least remain agnostic about whether "post-modern" is a chronological term at all. Lyotard, according to Boyle, seems to assume that postmodernism runs in parallel with modernism or is even a permanent possibility of the human spirit. Thus Montaigne, in the sixteenth century, is postmodern, but the brothers Schlegel, in the 1800s, are only modern. Boyle notes that the denial of chronology is an understandable ploy for postmodernists just to the extent that modernity depends on some opposition between the present and the past. Thus for the postmodernist, all architectural styles are always simultaneously available.[7]

The Christian difference—why we are not postmodernist—is revealed at this point. Christians have a stake in history, which as Boyle (appealing to Hegel) observes, is the collective self-understanding of modern Europeans who thought the history of the world, or at least of their "states," inseparable from Christianity. They so saw themselves not because of some continuity between institutions, but just to the extent history, understood as the "meaningful interconnection of *all* events, each of which is invested both with individual uniqueness and absolute importance," is in the bounds of a Christian world.[8] Christians must be able to narrate postmodernism more powerfully than postmodernism cannot narrate Christianity. Or more adequately: we must show how Christianity provides the resources for a critique of its own mistakes that modernity or postmodernity cannot provide.

Such narration will require Christians to develop accounts, as I suggested above, that are more powerful than either modernist or postmodernist can muster. Indeed, one illusion of postmodernism is to give a far too intelligible and thus comforting account of where we are. Our world and our lives are far too fragmentary and disordered to know where we are, but at least Christians owe it to themselves and their neighbors to confess that such disorder is but a reflection of the failure of the churches to be faithful. Modernity and its bastard offspring, postmodernity, are but reflections of the Christian attempt to make God a god available without the mediation of the church.[9] Such a god cannot help but become some "timeless thing" necessary to insure the assumed truth of Christianity in service to the growth of secular power.

Postmodernism, in short, is the outworking of mistakes in Christian theology correlative to the attempt to make Christianity "true" apart from faithful witness. This is undoubtedly a strong thesis, but one I think we are beginning increasingly to appreciate thanks to that extraordinary group of theologians currently clustered at or around Cambridge University. For example, Philip Blond, with the confidence we have come to associate with this theological style, observes that the crucial moment in the surrender of theology to secular reason's account of nature and corresponding understanding of natural theology occurred in England between the time of Henry of Ghent (1217-1293) and Duns Scotus (1266-1308).[10]

Blond notes that Henry maintained that any knowledge of a created thing by the human intellect was also knowledge of God. In creatures, however, being was determinable; but God's being is indeterminable. For Scotus the distinction between knowing God in himself and knowing him in a creature was not important. For this reason, according to Blond, when considering the universal science of metaphysics, Scotus elevated being (*ens*) to a higher station over God in order that being could be distributed both to God and his creatures. Scotus did this because God could not be known naturally unless being is univocal (*univocum*) to the created and uncreated.[11]

The univocity of God and creature, according to Blond, marks the time when theology itself became idolatrous. Theologians disregarded what they should have learned from Aquinas, namely, that nothing can be predicated univocally of God and other things. Thus in Aquinas's contention, that which can be predicated of God can only be participated in by finite creatures via analogy. "This analogical mode, whilst it accepts that we only come to have knowledge via His effects, understands that the reality of these effects belongs by priority to God, even though we only uncover God as the source of these effects after having experienced such effects without initially recognizing their antecedent cause."[12]

I am painfully aware that the introduction of these rather obscure remarks about how Christian theologians came to understand God's relation to creation cannot help but appear as unrelated to issues raised by postmodernism. I am convinced, however, that to grasp the challenge of postmodernism—as Robert Jenson puts it, how "the world lost its story"—we must understand how modernity and postmodernity are the result of mistakes in Christian theology.[13] This means, as suggested above, that Christians must challenge any postmodern narrative that simply forgets Christianity has had anything to do with the world in which we now find ourselves.

I am not suggesting we need to remind postmodernists that Christianity once was capable of producing cultural and political effects. It is not a question of getting our historical due as Christians, though that is not entirely irrelevant, but rather of our ability to maintain for ourselves an account of the world in which the God we worship matters. The attempt to make God knowable separate from how God has made himself known through Scripture makes a world without God thinkable. God could not help but become another "thing" amid other metaphysical possibilities. Accordingly, Christians robbed the world of its story.

Boyle observes, for example, that Dante's *Divine Comedy* differs in its very manner from non-Christian poetry because, like the Bible, the *Comedy* is about the world of grace and also about the world of history. Dante's poem is about real, datable men and women who at particular times accepted or rejected the grace of God offered them thirteen centuries earlier through the bodily life, death, and resurrection of Christ.

For Dante, and for the world in which his poem was written, the earthly passing over of the incarnate Word was what constitutes history,

> that gives direction and purpose to the time which leads up to Christ and an eschatological expectation to the time after him; that divides the ages into a pre-Christian period of signs and figures and a Christian period of fulfillment; that provides the temporal point of reference by which years are dated and people and their activities made singular and unrepeatable. For Dante it is only in relation to Christ that human doings are part of history, and only as part of history that human doings become the subject-matter of his poem.[14]

Postmodernism, then, names not only the end of the time when poetry like Dante's is possible, but it names a time when such poetry has become unintelligible. Modernity, drawing on the metaphysics of a transcendent god, was the attempt to be historical without Christ. Postmodernity, facing the agony of living in history with no end, is the denial of history.[15] In the wake of such a denial, the only remaining comfort is the shopping mall, which gives us the illusion of creating histories through choice, thus hiding from us the reality that none of us can avoid having our lives determined by money.[16] Money, in modernity, is the institutionalization of univocity of being that Scotus thought necessary to insure the unmediated knowledge of God.[17]

POSTMODERNISM AND THE GLOBAL MARKET

I began by agreeing with Boyle's extraordinary definition of postmodernism; his claim is one I think I can defend. He is right to suggest that postmodernism is "the pessimism of an obsolescent class." I would emphasize that the most determinative representatives of his "salaried official intelligentsia" are to be found in the universities. That the fate of such an intelligentsia is "closely bound up with that of the declining nation-state" should not be surprising given that universities as we know them were formed to produce and reproduce the knowledges to sustain the ruling classes in turn necessary to maintain the nation-state system. That that system is currently under stress by the developments of global capitalism is reflected in the confusions trumpeted about the universities in the name of postmodernism.

I do not wish to be misunderstood. I am not suggesting that postmodernism is nothing but smoke and mirrors. Rather, I believe that Fredric Jameson rightly identified postmodernism with the cultural logic of advanced capitalism in which the production of culture has been integrated into commodity production, thus creating the urgency of producing ever fresh waves of novelty.[18] As David Harvey observes, "whatever else we do with the concept, we should not read postmodernism as some autonomous artistic current. Its rootedness in daily life is one of its most patently transparent features."[19]

The everyday life in which we are rooted, however, is not easily known, particularly by intellectuals. Indeed, intellectuals (who like to believe their "work" is free from the market) have a stake in hiding from themselves the material factors that make their existence possible. Thus the illusions of a genealogist can be thought to be quite compelling until, as Boyle observes, "the funding dries up and it becomes apparent that the nation no longer has an omnipotent monarch commanding the propagation of Enlightenment (that is, the critique of Church and the bourgeoisie) 'for its own sake' (that is, in the interests of the state.)"[20] What the university intellectual cannot face is the socioeconomic truth that in a global market we have all become the proletariat.

It is hard to imagine an intellectual alternative better suited for the elites of a global capitalism than postmodernism.[21] Capitalism is, after all, the ultimate form of deconstruction. How better to keep the laborer under the control of capital than through the scarcity produced through innovation? Capitalism, as David Harvey observes, is necessarily innovative, not because of the myth of the innovative entrepreneur, but because of the coercive laws of competition and the conditions of class struggle endemic to capitalism. Of course the effects of such innovation are to make past investments of labor skills valueless.[22]

Obviously such a system produces a self that is fragmented if not multiple. The difficulty in the description of the loss of the unified self by postmodernists is their failure to see that such a self is the result of social and economic developments. Such a causal connection, however, is precisely

> what "genealogical" deconstructive thinking not only cannot represent—it denies it exists. In so doing it plays the game precisely as the global market wants it played. For the fiction by which the global market commends itself to us and encourages our participation in it is that the human self is purely a consumer. . . . The self is little more than a formality, the name we give to the principle that consumes options, the transient locus of interpretation. There is nothing outside the text, just as there is nothing outside the market.[23]

The belief that there is no single truth or world but only a multiplicity of mutually untranslatable perspectives, Boyle observes, is strangely analogous to the belief that the market is a boundless medium of perfect competition among an infinite number of ever-expanding commercial identities.[24] It is no wonder that, confronted with such a system, intellectuals discard the idea of totality.

> For in a period when no very far-reaching political action seems really feasible, when so-called micropolitics seems the order of the day, it is relieving to convert this necessity into a virtue—to persuade oneself that one's political limits have, as it were, a solid ontological grounding, in the fact that social totality is in any case a chimera.[25]

The recent example of Richard Rorty is surely good evidence for the inability of postmodernism to mount any politics worthy of the name. In *Achieving Our Country*, Rorty confirms an earlier description of his own position by Terry Eagleton. That is, since all conventions are arbitrary, one might as well conform to those of the Free World.[26] "For purposes of thinking about how to achieve our country," Rorty asserts, "we do not need to worry about the correspondence theory of truth, the grounds of normativity, the impossibility of justice, or the infinite distance which separates us from the other. For those purposes," asserts Rorty, "we can give both religion and philosophy a pass. We can just get on with trying to solve what Dewey called 'the problems of men.'"[27]

According to Rorty, that means we must continue to support the nation-state as the only "agent capable of making any real difference in the amount of selfishness and sadism inflicted on Americans."[28] We must do so from Rorty's perspective because, since 1909, the only dividing line between the American left and the American right is the former's presumption that the state must make itself responsible for redistributive policies.[29] The cultural left must therefore shed its "semi-conscious anti-Americanism" to get back "into the business of piecemeal reform in the framework of a market economy."[30]

Rorty's book, which bears the subtitle *Leftist Thought in Twentieth-Century America*, is surely the tombstone that confirms the death of the left in America. His call for a renewed loyalty to the nation-state, at least the nation-state called America, comes just at the time the nation-state, other than as an agency to insure prosperity,[31] is increasingly undermined by the global market.[32] His "social vision," like that of so many postmodernists, turns out to be but another form of liberalism. That is, the "just state is one neutral in respect of any particular conception of the good life, confining its jurisdiction to furnishing the conditions in which individuals may discover themselves."[33]

I realize that it may be quite unjust to tar postmodernism with Rorty's brush, but too often postmodernists turn out to be liberals in their ethics and politics who no longer believe in the conceits of liberalism but have nowhere else to go.[34] If you want a way to test whether this is true, try to engage a postmodernist in a discussion about abortion or so-called assisted suicide. Eagleton rightly credits postmodernism for putting on the political agenda issues of sexuality, gender, and ethnicity but fears that these concerns can become a substitute for classical forms of radical politics that deal with class, state, ideology, revolution, and the material modes of production. Questions of sexuality are no doubt political, but they can also be a form of forgetfulness for questions about why some people do not get enough to eat. Eagleton notes that perhaps one reason feminism and ethnicity are popular is because they are not necessarily anticapitalist and so fit well with a postradical age.[35]

Indeed I fear that a reason postmodernism has become such an attractive alternative for many in the contemporary university is because serious work is no longer expected there. The fragmentation of the curriculum into disciplines that are unintelligible even to themselves is surely the breeding ground for postmodernism. The more fractured the university becomes, moreover, the more it is able to act as the institution capable of confirming the postmodernist description of the world. As a result the university becomes a useful place to sequester people who might otherwise get into trouble. But then that is exactly what we should expect, given Boyle's judgment that postmodernism is the pessimism of an obsolete class.

THE CHRISTIAN DIFFERENCE

Obviously I think it would be a profound mistake for Christians to side with the postmodernists, although even to think that Christians have a choice to be for or against postmodernism seems a far too optimistic account of our situation. If the analysis of postmodernism I have provided is close to being right, it is not a question of choice. Rather, Christians are faced—along with our non-Christian sisters and brothers—with the challenge of surviving postmodernism. To survive, moreover, means we must have skills of resistance. I believe God has given us all we need not only to survive but to flourish. But as I suggested above, theologically we have only begun to imagine the knowledges necessary for the task.

To survive will require us to develop practices and habits that make our worship of God an unavoidable witness to the world. By unavoidable I mean that we must help the world discover that it is of course unintelligible just to the extent that it does not acknowledge the God we worship. That God "is whoever raised Jesus from the dead, having before raised Israel from Egypt."[36] That God, having created all that is, can be known only by analogy—which is how we name the metaphysical implications that God wills to care for his creation through calling into existence a faithful people.

Commenting on the apocalyptic character of Ezekiel, Daniel, Mark, and John of Patmos, John Howard Yoder observes that these texts are not either about pie in the sky or the Russians in Mesopotamia. "They are about how the crucified Jesus is a more adequate key to understanding what God is about in the real world of empires and armies and markets than is the ruler in Rome, with all his supporting military, commercial, and sacerdotal networks."[37] Postmodernists cannot help but think such a claim to be the grandest of grand narratives, but I cannot imagine Christians saying anything less. Not only saying it, but also thinking it true.

For example, consider Yoder's claim that the point apocalyptic makes is not that people who use violence in the name of fostering justice are not as strong as they think, though that is true, but rather

> it is that people who bear crosses are working with the grain of the universe. One does not come to that belief by reducing social process to mechanical and statistical models, nor by winning some of one's battles for the control of one's corner of the fallen world. One comes to it by sharing the life of those who sing about the resurrection of the slain Lamb.[38]

"Working with the grain of the universe" is not a confessional claim peculiar to Christians, but rather a metaphysical claim about the way things are.

Contrary to the oft-made assertion that Yoder-like claims require Christians to withdraw from the world, the opposite (as Yoder constantly stressed) is the case.[39] Indeed, I think it is important for Mennonites particularly, as well as their fellow travelers—that is, people like myself and John Paul II—to deny they seek only to be a prophetic minority in the wider church or world. Rather, we seek to provide an alternative by which the world can see that we are not condemned to anarchy and violence. Rather than withdrawing from the world, even a postmodern world, we are better off siding with those who would "take over" the world.

Gerald Schlabach, a Mennonite theologian who teaches at Bluffton College, recently sent me criticisms of my thought that another Mennonite had posted on an e-mail forum. The critic had argued that my work was far too Catholic and thus incompatible with an Anabaptist perspective: "Hauerwas has a Constantinian fear of Christian liberty. He wants the clergy to tell us the story and the church to have the sanctions to enforce it." In his response, Schlabach agreed that this is an accurate (although insufficiently nuanced) summary of my views, but defended my position nonetheless. As Schlabach put it,

> Hauerwas has discovered a dirty little secret—Anabaptists who reject historic Christendom may not actually be rejecting the vision of Christendom as a society in which all of life is integrated under the Lordship of Christ. On this reading, Christendom may in fact be a vision of shalom, and our argument with Constantinians is not over the vision so much as the sinful effort to grasp at its fullness through violence, before its eschatological time. Hauerwas is quite consistent once you see that he does want to create a Christian society (*polis, societas*)—a community and way of life shaped fully by Christian convictions. He rejects Constantinianism because "the world" cannot be this society and we only distract ourselves from building a truly Christian society by trying to make our nation into that society, rather than be content with living as a community-in-exile. So Hauerwas wants Catholics to be more Anabap-

tist, and Anabaptists to be more Catholic, and Protestants to be both, and the only way he can put this together in terms of his own ecclesial location is to be a "Catholic" Methodist in roughly the way that some Episcopalians are Anglo-Catholic.[40]

Schlabach's presentation of my own position says what I have been trying to say better than I have said it. More importantly, I hope, his suggestion points a way forward if we are not only to survive but to find ways to resist global capitalism. It should surprise no one to discover that I believe that any response Christians have to the challenge of the global market will be ecclesial. In particular, I think Christians must find ways to be Catholic in a world in which the church is but another international agency—and one that is probably less effective than the many that exist already and the many more that are sure to be created.

Let me try to explain these obscure remarks by returning again to some observations by Boyle, who describes himself as a Catholic humanist,[41] about the international character of the church. He suggests that the international character of the church (and I assume he means the Roman Catholic Church) is likely to be more problematic in the future than it has been for many centuries. In the era of nation-states the international character of the church was one of its most significant features, just to the extent the church offered an alternative to the loyalties bred through nationalism. Though the church often failed to challenge nationalism, its very existence at least provided the material possibility for mounting a challenge to the state's pretension to rule over minds and bodies.

Yet in the new global order, Boyle suggests, the church's universality may be a more serious temptation than that of nationalism's since the Reformation. For the new order is a kind of universality whose ambition is to rule minds and bodies just as nations did so effectively in the past. The church may be tempted to collaborate with these worldly powers, celebrating that they have adopted the church's global perspective. But as Boyle notes, the worldly powers have their own purposes, "and if one is disturbed when a papal tour becomes a media event it is because it is becoming unclear in such a case who is using, or paying homage, to whom."[42]

That the church has often imitated the secular rule of its day is no great surprise. In feudalism the popes became feudal lords, absolute monarchs in the age of absolutism, and in the age of nation-states something like presidents for life of a kind of international state. Thus in the First Vatican Council the church battened down the hatches to face the totalitarian pretensions of the state in the era of unrestrained nationalism. So in an international age the church, according to Boyle, cannot help but act as one global agency among others, and we should be glad that it does so—just as Christians in the past were glad the church had the strength and presence to speak to the state when men and women were often at odds with their country and had no friend other than the church.

However, the moral authority the church derived from its past internationalism will have to be drawn from elsewhere if the church in this new age is to continue to be unassimilated to the secular world. Boyle suggests that such a church will "need to draw its moral strength not from its international presence but from its claim to represent people as they are locally and distinct from the worldwide ramifications of their existence as participants in the global market."[43] Grand narratives continue,

> but the little narratives of the victims of the grand process, the stories of what the big new world is squeezing out or ignoring, they will be told on the small scale, and full of details which the new world will dismiss as superficial and inessential. In terms of church structure, the little narratives will be told at diocesan, parochial, or base-community level.[44]

The church capable of such little narratives will need all the resources it can muster—particularly those resources from the past that give us the confidence in the face of the universal market to claim universally that Jesus of Nazareth was raised from the dead. The worship of such a God surely requires that the church not forget those who have become expendable, too poor even to be debtors, and therefore, from the market's perspective, "non-persons."[45] The worship of such a God means that we must pray and pray fervently for the reconciliation of Catholics and Protestants, as our very division wounds not only ourselves but the world itself.[46]

Such a church is surely necessary if, as Boyle puts it, we are to learn to see God in the world in which we find ourselves, and not only in some past golden age, such as the Catacombs or the Middle Ages. Rather, we must be at least as courageous and inventive as those Christians who made the Middle Ages possible by living in catacombs. To be such a people in this time we must be sustained by our worship of God who wills himself known in Christ and so known can safeguard "us from self-worship and maintain us in the conviction that nothing we know in this world is ultimate—not the media of communication, nor the system of signs, not even the end of history."[47] Through the faithful worship of a God so known, Christians can not only survive postmodernism but even flourish.[48]

NOTES

1. Nicholas Boyle, *Who Are We Now?: Christian Humanism and the Global Market from Hegel to Heaney* (Notre Dame: University of Notre Dame Press, 1998), 318. I have followed Boyle's use of capitalization and hyphenation of Post-Modernism in this quote, but when I am writing in my own voice I will use neither.

2. That I have been associated with the postmodernist has always seemed to me a mistake deriving from those who fail to understand Wittgenstein's influence for how I work. Stanley Fish is certainly a friend, and I have learned from his work, but I have no idea what it would mean to say that Fish is a postmodernist. Philosophically I have learned more from Alasdair MacIntyre who, exactly because of his appreciation of Nietzsche, is anything but a postmodernist. I suppose my attack on the National Association of Scholars in *After Christendom?* (Nashville: Abingdon Press, 1991), 140-152, may have led some to think I am a "relativist," but even if I were a relativist, which I am not, that would not make me a postmodernist. If MacIntyre is a nonfoundationalist, I suppose I must also be such, but again a MacIntyrian nonfoundationalism does not entail the kind of skepticism thought to be at the heart of postmodernism. For a defense of "postmodernism" in theology with which I am in large agreement, see Nancey Murphy and James McClendon, "Distinguishing Modern from Postmodern Theology," *Modern Theology* 5 (April 1989): 191-214.

By a "playful use of postmodernism," I mean how I have used the "atheism" of postmodernism against the humanism of modernism: for I assume that postmodernism is the only atheism modernity could produce. Modernism is the rejection of God, or at least a parody of the Christian God, in the interest of a kind of divinization of the human. Postmodernists, seeking to be thorough in their atheism, deny such humanism. See, for example, Chapter 11, "No Enemy, No Christianity," in my book *Sanctify Them in the Truth: Holiness Exemplified* (Edinburgh: T & T Clark, 1998), 191-200. For a powerful account of modernity as a project to build "the city of man," see Pierre Manent, *The City of Man*, trans. Marc Le Pain (Princeton: Princeton University Press, 1998). Like Boyle, Manent locates modernity with the discovery of "history" and, in particular, how such history is displayed through the sociolgoical and economic viewpoints.

3. David Toole, *Waiting for Godot in Sarajevo: Theological Reflections on Nihilism, Tragedy, and Apocalypse* (Boulder, Colo.: Westview Press, 1998).

4. Ibid., 269-270.

5. Terry Eagleton, *The Illusions of Postmodernism* (Oxford: Basil Blackwell, 1996), vii. Eagleton's account of postmodernism as a general intellectual style is, I think, about as good a characterization as one can get. I confess, however, that I remain extremely suspicious of whether any coherent postmodern position exists.

6. Eagleton notes that postmodernism as a style of culture allegedly reflects an epochal change characterized by "a deathless, decentred, ungrounded, self-reflexive, playful, derivative, eclectic, pluralistic art which blurs the boundaries between 'high' and 'popular' culture, as well as between art and everyday experience. How dominant or pervasive this culture is—'whether it goes all the way down, or figures just as one

particular region within contemporary life'—is a matter of argument" (ibid., vii-viii). How to understand the relation between postmodernism as an intellectual position and as a cultural movement is not clear to me.

7. Boyle, *Who Are We Now*, 82. The problem, I think, is not that postmodernism might not have been present in earlier times, but that the unclarity about what postmodernity is makes such judgments arbitrary. Significant thinkers are bound to be ambiguous in terms of "periodizations." Thus Descartes is increasingly read as a late medieval thinker and Kant, or at least the Kant of the third *Critique*, as a harbinger of Romanticism.

8. Boyle, *Who Are We Now*, 290.

9. Michael Gillespie observes that "nihilism is not the result of the death of God but the consequence of the birth or rebirth of a different kind of God, an omnipotent god of will who calls into question all of reason and nature and thus overturns all eternal standards of truth and justice, and good and evil. This idea of God came to predominance in the fourteenth century and shattered the medieval synthesis of philosophy and theology, catapulting man into a new way of thinking and being, a *via moderna* essentially at odds with the *via antiqua*. This new way was in turn the foundation for modernity as the realm of human self-assertion" (*Nihilism before Nietzsche* [Chicago: University of Chicago Press, 1995], xii-xiii).

10. Philip Blond, "Introduction: Theology Before Philosophy," in *Post-Secular Philosophy: Between Philosophy and Theology*, ed. Philip Blond (London: Routledge, 1998), 6. Blond notes prior to this observation that modern theologians and philosophers who have attempted to resist skepticism in theology have done so by means of natural theology, that is, they have "attempted to discern, or infer, the nature of God from a secular construal of the nature of the world" (ibid., 5). To do this, a correspondence between cause and effect necessitated that some term be given due proportion to both creatures and Creator because it was assumed that mutual knowledge depends on the classical notion that "like knows like."

11. For a much more detailed account of Scotus's position as well as critique, see Catherine Pickstock, *After Writing: On the Liturgical Consummation of Philosophy* (Oxford: Basil Blackwell, 1998), 121-140. Pickstock's book is an extraordinary account of the theological and philosophical developments that created the possibility of modernity and postmodernity correlated with social and political developments. Anyone acquainted with her work will recognize how much I have learned from her as well as her and Blond's teacher, John Milbank.

12. Blond, *Post-Secular Philosophy*, 6. When "being" is assumed to be univocal, analogical predication becomes a "theory." Thus the importance of David Burrell's work in freeing Aquinas from those who falsely assume the centrality of analogy in Aquinas means that Aquinas must have had a theory of analogy.

13. Robert Jenson, "How the World Lost Its Story," *First Things* 36 (October 1993), 19-24.

14. Boyle, *Who Are We Now*, 289-90.

15. Boyle suggests that in postmodernity a history that refers to the past has come to an end in favor of history that only names an unrealized future (ibid., 81). Boyle argues

that Heidegger is the great representative of this understanding of history just to the extent he believed so firmly in our power to make our future that he made that power the source of our historicity. "We make the continuity, and so the history, of our existence by choosing our hero, choosing a tradition and inheritance that we have in common with others. We create our past in the image of our future, of the projection of our existence forward to its limit in death. We have a fate (*Schicksal*) because, like Nietzsche, we are a fate. Out of the contingencies of that 'fate' Existence chooses its particular destiny (*Geschick*), the events it willingly shares with 'its collectivity, its people.' The flaw in this account is its ignoring of the extent to which our 'destiny,' the historicity of our existence (and indeed of existence itself), is a gift from others, and the extent therefore to which the temporality of existence derives from pastness as well as futurity" (ibid., 223).

Boyle, I believe rightly, identifies Heidegger's denial of the past with his refusal to understand our existence as the result of an act of love. "Behind Heidegger's reluctance to see historicity as a gift, and not only a construct, lies a general" but, as his analysis of the presuppositions of selfhood shows, not necessarily fundamental" hostility to givenness" (ibid., 198).

16. Boyle, *Who Are We Now*, 80-81. Boyle's use of the shopping mall as the image for postmodernism is anticipated by James Edwards in his *The Plain Sense of Things: The Fate of Religion in an Age of Normal Nihilism* (University Park, Pa: Pennsylvania State University Press, 1997), 47-50.

17. Marx no doubt deserves the credit for the discovery of the significance of money for the transformation of the market. David Harvey provides a wonderfully clear and incisive account of Marx's analysis of money in his *The Condition of Postmodernity* (Oxford: Blackwell, 1990), 99-105. Harvey observes how Marx saw that with the advent of a money economy, the bonds and relations of traditional communities could not help but be dissolved so that money becomes the real community. This creates the "fetishism of commodities" just to the extent money "masks" the social relations between things. Boyle also emphasizes the significance of money for the transition to modernity. But he credits Max Weber, not Marx, with the discovery that the true revolution was not with the invention of capitalist modes of production, but with the invention of money as the means to define capital itself (ibid., 104-105).

18. Fredric Jameson, *Postmodernism, or, The Cultural Logic of Late Capitalism* (Durham, N.C.: Duke University, 1991), 1-55. I have changed "late" to "advanced" to indicate my sense that, at least as far as capitalism is concerned, it is not clear how late his "late" is.

19. Harvey, *The Condition of Postmodernity*, 63.

20. Boyle, *Who Are We Now*, 234.

21. Terry Eagleton observes that capitalism deconstructs the difference between system and transgression because capitalism is the mind-bending paradox of a system whose margins are installed at its center (Eagleton, *The Illusions of Postmodernism*, 62).

22. Harvey, *The Condition of Postmodernity*, 105.

23. Boyle, *Who Are We Now*, 153-154.

24. Ibid., 152.

25. Eagleton, *The Illusions of Postmodernism*, 9. I am not sure what connection, if any, there may be between the rise of postmodernism as a movement in university cultures and the end of the cold war, but I think the loss of a clear "enemy" must have some relation to the lack of seriousness on the part of many intellectuals.

26. Eagleton, *The Illusions of Postmodernism*, 27. For Rorty's book, see *Achieving Our Country* (Cambridge: Harvard University Press, 1998).

27. Rorty, *Achieving Our Country*, 97. One of the few things about which Rorty is adamant is that any future politics must leave Christianity behind and, in particular, any "vocabulary built around the notion of sin" (ibid., 32). I confess it is unclear to me on what basis he can be so dogmatic, but I find his dislike for Christianity rather charming. He has not, however, given up entirely on religion, urging us to not discard the hope shared by Alison, Bloom, and Matthew Arnold—the hope for a religion of literature, in which works of the secular imagination replace Scripture as the principal source of inspiration and hope for a new generation" (ibid., 136).

Rorty identifies this religion of literature with Whitman's and Dewey's hope that America, which is a term convertible with democracy, would be the place where people come to see the ultimate significance of the finite, human, historical project. They both hoped America would be where a religion of love would replace a religion of fear, where the traditional link between the religious impulse to stand in awe of something greater than oneself and the infantile need for security would be broken. They wanted to put hope for a casteless and classless America in the place of the will of God. "They wanted that utopian America to replace God as the unconditional object of desire" (ibid., 17-18).

Rorty, I suppose, is to be commended for being so candid about his faith in America. Interestingly enough, he criticizes the theories of Hegel and Marx, as well as the "rationalizations of hopelessness like Foucault's and Lacan's," for attempting to satisfy the urges that theology used to satisfy. Such urges, according to Rorty, are what Dewey hoped Americans might cease to feel (ibid., 38).

28. Rorty, *Achieving Our Country*, 98.

29. Ibid., 48.

30. Ibid., 105. In some ways Rorty's book is an extended attack on Fred Jameson. But his criticism of Jameson, I fear, is at best inept and at worst stupid.

31. Foucault provides an extraordinary account of the development of this understanding of the state's function in his extremely important article, "Governmentality," in *The Foucault Effect: Studies in Governmentality*, edited by Graham Burchell, Colin Gordon, and Peter Miller (Chicago: University of Chicago Press, 1991), 87-104. Foucault distinguishes the governmentality of the modern state from sovereignty by noting that the former has no interest in disposing things to lead to the common good, but rather, the role of government is "to ensure that the greatest possible quantity of wealth is produced, that the people are provided with sufficient means of subsistence, that the population is enabled to multiply, etc." (ibid., 95). Crucial for the development of this understanding of government is the displacement of the family as the analogical paradigm for government in favor of that new entity called population. "Governmentality" does not mean that the state is any less inclined to go to war, but, rather, that wars

fought by such states, as Hegel says, become ends in themselves. That is, war having no end other than itself becomes the reason for the state to exist.

These are extremely complex matters, obviously, given Boyle's understanding that the effects of globalization are uneven. Globalization compliments the workings of a strong state like the United States which is also still captured by the myth of being a savior nation. States such as France and Germany more perfectly fit Foucault's understanding of governmentality. It is, for example, quite interesting to wonder if such states could now initiate a war in the name of their self-interest, whether such interest be understood in terms of honor or economic well-being. Wars, at least in Europe, increasingly will be police actions initiated by regional alliances. I am indebted to Ken Surin and Reinhard Hütter for pressing me on this point.

32. This contradiction, of course, Rorty shares with people like Mrs. Thatcher, who failed to see that nations are growing obsolete not as a matter of fashion but as the result of the operation of the same economic trends she otherwise endorsed. Boyle wonderfully analyzes this contradiction in the first chapter of his book, entitled "After Thatcherism," in *Who Are We Now*, 13-67. Rorty acknowledges the tension between concern with the inequality of wealth between nations and thinking one's responsibility is to the least advantaged in one's own nation. He confesses he has no idea how this dilemma is to be resolved *(Achieving Our Country*, 88-89).

In an interesting manner Martha Nussbaum exemplifies the same tension in her book, *Cultivating Humanity: A Classical Defense of Reform in Liberal Education* (Cambridge: Harvard University Press, 1997). Nussbaum, who would usually be considered on the other side of the postmodern divide than Rorty, at once wants to train students locally as well as for world citizenship. This works well as long as she is thinking of white males, but proves embarrassing once she turns to African Americans. Should African Americans, in the interest of being world citizens, a citizenship of nowhere, become, as she recommends, "philosophical exiles from our (their) own way of life?" (ibid., 58). It is hard to be politically correct and a universalist at the same time. Nussbaum does not feel the tension since, like Rorty, she is confident that education for world citizenship has been most fully embraced in the United States (ibid., 9).

33. Eagleton, *The Illusions of Postmodernism*, 76.

34. Actually, a place where they have to go is the university, which has become for them a safe haven that serves as well as a quasi-church. Indeed, Rorty favorably quotes Eisenach's observation that "Progressive intellectuals turned American universities into what he calls something like a national 'church,' the main repository and protector of common American values, common American meanings, and common American identities" *(Achieving Our Country*, 50).

35. Eagleton, *The Illusions of Postmodernism*, 22-25. In this respect, Boyle makes some fascinating remarks about the gay movement. He credits the movement with teaching us to abandon the puritan pretense that social affections can be anything other than erotic in form. But he denies that identity, and particularly sexual identity, can be a matter of our own affective preferences. When sexual preferences are detached from the process of bodily reproduction, we lose touch with the constraints necessary for discovering that our bodies are not only for consumption but also for production. "If

marriage is redefined as a long-term affective partnership, so that it may be either homosexual or heterosexual, the essential reproductive nature of male and female bodies is no longer given institutional (and therefore political) expression" *(Who Are We Now,* 59).

36. Robert Jenson, *Systematic Theology: The Triune God,* vol. 1 (New York: Oxford University Press, 1997), 63.

37. John Howard Yoder, *The Politics of Jesus: Vicit Agnus Noster,* 2d ed. (Grand Rapids, Mich.: Eerdmans, 1994), 246.

38. John Howard Yoder, "Armaments and Eschatology," *Studies in Christian Ethics,* 1 (1998): 43-61.

39. See, for example, Yoder's "Firstfruits: The Paradigmatic Public Role of God's People," which now is the first chapter in his *For the Nations: Essays Public and Evangelical* (Grand Rapids, Mich.: Eerdmans, 1997), 15-36. Commenting on Barth, Yoder notes that "the order of the faith community constitutes a public offer to the entire society" (ibid., 27). I have no doubt such a characterization describes Yoder's own views.

40. I am extremely grateful to Professor Schlabach for his permission to use his characterization of my position. Schlabach's account, however, does raise some interesting questions about the differences between Yoder and myself. Yoder in style and substance was always more willing to work within the world as he found it than I have been. For example, I will polemically try to expose what I take to be the contradictions in a position by forcing, for instance, those that would defend just war theory in the name of democracies to see that they cannot do so with consistency. In contrast, Yoder would assume it is a good thing to believe that war should be limited and try to help those with that belief to live accordingly. The difference may be a matter of style, but I believe it may also be due to what might be described as my lingering longing for Christendom. For example, the strategy of argument I use in this paper, I suspect, would be quite foreign to Yoder's way of thinking about postmodernism.

41. Boyle, *Who Are We Now,* 8.

42. Ibid., 91.

43. Ibid., 91-92.

44. Ibid., 92. For this reason Boyle thinks that the moral authority of the church in the future will lie more with the College of Bishops than the papacy. For it will be the bishops who will have the authority to challenge the claim of the global market to express and exhaust the human world. Already the church has produced the glorious examples of the martyred Bishops Oscar Romero and Juan Geraldi Conedera, who could understand what was going on in their little countries of El Salvador and Guatemala much better than could John Paul II (hindered as he has been by his Polish fear of communism, though now we've seen him changing as to Cuba). I owe this Central American reminder to Sarah Freedman.

45. Dan Bell makes this observation in his remarkable dissertation, "The Refusal to Cease Suffering: the Crucified People and the Liberation of Desire" (Duke University, 1998).

46. See, for example, Ephraim Radner's extraordinary account of the effects of our

division on the church in his *The End of the Church: A Pneumatology of Christian Division in the West* (Grand Rapids, Mich.: Eerdmans, 1998). It would be fascinating to compare Boyle's more Hegelian account of history with that of Radner's. Both maintain that Christians owe the world an account of the history of the world, but Radner argues such an account can never lose its "figural," that is, biblical, character. According to Radner, the division of the sixteenth century resulted in a limitation on pneumatic accounts of history that requires repentance. As a result, "modern historical consciousness" was created which was but the cultural adaptation of a straitened Christian consciousness due to the incapacitation of the figural reading of history by multiple ecclesial referents (ibid., 301).

47. Boyle, *Who Are We Now*, 93. The careful reader who checks my use of this quote from Boyle will discover that I did not follow Boyle's appeal that began the quote to the "Catholic belief that we are but creatures, and the creatures of a wholly unknowable God," which he believes safeguards us from self-worship. I do not know whether Boyle and I are in fundamental disagreement on the matter of knowledge of God, but it is clear to me, as Blond puts it, that "negative theology requires a positive discourse about God, if, that is, this form of negation is to be recognizably about God at all" *(Post-Secular Philosophy*, 5).

48. Besides those mentioned earlier, I am indebted to Abraham Nussbaum, Joel Shuman, and Michael Cartwright for their criticisms and, as usual, to Jim Fodor.

CHAPTER TWO

FOUCAULT, GENEALOGY, ANABAPTISM: Confessions of an Errant Postmodernist

Peter C. Blum

Whoever fights monsters should see to it that in the process he does not become a monster. —Nietzsche¹

PROBLEMATIC TERMS

My purpose in this chapter is to share my experience, as a self-identified Anabaptist Christian, of reading some so-called postmodern social thought, especially that of Michel Foucault. I would like to begin, however, with some comments on problematic terms in my title.

I have little interest in clarifying exactly what postmodernism is, partly because I simply find that project uninteresting and partly because I don't believe postmodernism is anything, exactly. It seems fair, nonetheless, to allow that there are postmodernists, inasmuch as there are scholarly folk nowadays who refer to themselves as such. The situation here seems to me analogous, in fact, to that of the term *Christianity*. I'm often inclined to think that there isn't anything that Christianity is exactly, yet there are, and have been, numerous folk who refer to themselves as Christians, including myself. Indeed, many people who are not greatly concerned about whether they are Christian are routinely categorized as such because of the places they go, the books they read, the habits they exhibit, or the people they sup with. It is in this manner, roughly, that I sometimes find myself being thought of, or even thinking of myself, as a postmodernist.

The sense in which I am an *errant* postmodernist is a bit more complicated. I am errant theoretically, inasmuch as I am inclined *not* to commit to postmodernism precisely as "ism." The thinkers who inspire me, who are often called postmodernist, seem to me consistently to question the very possibility of a full-fledged "ism." Nietzsche wrote that "the will to a system is a lack of integrity,"[2] and I strongly suspect that he was right about this (among other things). When I look at various attempts to articulate postmodernism as an "ism," as the systematic avoidance of system, as a theory that undermines all theories, I suspect there is a joke being circulated. Nietzsche gets the joke, and so do Derrida and Foucault, as far as I can tell. The funny thing is that many who try to tell the joke do not seem to get it. If I treat my postmodernism as an "ism," then I have not gotten the joke either.[3]

Now, one might suggest that my anti-"ism"-ism is exactly what makes me a real, genuine, certified postmodernist. Rather than pursue the laughter that lies in that direction, I will simply move on for now. I will note, in passing, that there are other senses in which I am errant. I believe there are no absolute foundations, yet I constantly fight the temptation to make of this very insight an absolute foundation. I am aware of the circularity of human understanding, yet I tirelessly seek noncircular ways to enlighten others of this very idea. I know that the Enlightenment has run off its road—into a different ditch, perhaps, than that of which Lessing wrote. Still, the old Enlightenment clearly remains one of the armies at war in my intellectual members.

I should also note that my semantic puzzlement does not subside when we turn to the word *Anabaptist*. With the increasing credence given to so-called "polygenesis" by historians of Anabaptism, along with increasing recognition of the "theology-ladenness" of various attempts to define Anabaptism,[4] we may at least consider the possibility that there is not anything in particular that Anabaptism *is*. Being neither a historian nor a theologian, but only a social theorist, I have the luxury of leaving this matter aside as beyond my expertise. This implies, of course, that I otherwise speak within my expertise, and I hope readers will not take that implication too seriously.

One more problematic term: *confessions*. Here is a term I am probably misusing rather badly. What I intend to convey is not that my comments carry some special sort of intellectual or spiritual weight (like Rousseau's or Augustine's), nor that you can expect anything embarrassingly steamy or aberrant (as in "Confessions of an Amish Cocaine Dealer"). Rather, I intend to convey that my remarks about Foucault and Anabaptism arise from very personal ruminations. I have chosen to present them as such rather than placing myself at some rhetorical remove from the matters at hand.

Whether this approach is premodern, modern, postmodern, hypermodern, or whatever else, I will leave for others to decide (if they care). As Foucault writes: "Do not ask who I am and do not ask me to remain the same: leave it to our bureaucrats and our police to see that our papers are in order. At least spare us their morality when we write."[5]

Whether my comments are in any sense "Anabaptist" is, in the end, probably the issue of greater concern to me. "Confession" here carries this sense as well: I may adopt a playful postmodern tone herein, but I do not wish thereby simply to distance myself from accountability.

FOUCAULT AS ANTITHEORIST

What has drawn me to the work of Michel Foucault, more than anything else, is his stubborn refusal to be a Theorist. The initial capital letter is important here. I do not advance the wildly implausible claim that there is no theory in Foucault's writings in any sense. In stating that Foucault is not a Theorist, I am drawing attention to his obstinate avoidance of overarching or all-encompassing theoretical consistency, and especially to his evasion of the role of intellectual guru or "expert." Among the more putatively vicious elements of Foucault's supposed "relativism" is his unwillingness (or inability) to outline positive alternatives to the discursive and institutional frameworks that are undermined by his historical critiques. To many readers, the dark, unremittingly deconstructive tone of Foucault's thought appears inimical to any Christian outlook, including an Anabaptist one. My own reading of Foucault, however, has led me to conclude that this appearance is only superficial.

As I have been reading and teaching Foucault[6] for the last several years, I have been struck by how the idea of *particularity* provides a good pedagogical fulcrum for beginning to understand him. I choose this word, *particularity*, rather than *relativism* or *contextualism*, because I think it more effectively conveys some central Nietzschean motivations behind Foucault's avoidance of Theory. It will also help me articulate how I have come upon Foucault and at least some Anabaptist thinkers, apparently making camp at the same site.

Lest I sound as if I am trying to make a deep theoretical comparison (or even worse, a *synthesis*) of "Foucault's Thought" and "Anabaptist Thought," I want to be clear that I am focusing on particular texts. For Foucault's most explicit ruminations regarding genealogy as an enterprise, and more specifically its insistence on the primacy of particularity, I rely here mainly on two essays: "What is Enlightenment?"[7] and "Nietzsche, Genealogy, History."[8] I begin with Foucault and will identify my Anabaptist texts of choice presently.[9]

Foucault is clear in his insistence that genealogy does not amount to a theoretical outlook nor to a methodological doctrine in any standard sense. Yet he is also clear that a genealogical approach to inquiry involves adopting a certain stance—a stance which, he argues, is in continuity with the central Enlightenment theme of freedom and maturity, of liberation from authority:

> The critical ontology of ourselves has to be considered not, certainly, as a theory, a doctrine, nor even as a permanent body of knowledge that is accumulating; it has to be conceived as an attitude, an ethos, a philosophical life in which the critique of what we are is at one and the same time the historical analysis of the limits that are imposed on us and an experiment with the possibility of going beyond them.[10]

Foucault is also clear in his insistence that genealogy must eschew the universal in favor of the particular. It is "gray, meticulous, and patiently documentary,"[11] seeking the disjunctive irregularities of emergence (*Entstehung*) and descent (*Herkunft*), rather than the monolithic ultimacy of origin (*Ursprung*).[12] Rather than seeking a grand historical narrative that frames the present as an unavoidable *telos*, genealogy "maintain[s] passing events in their proper dispersion."[13] Indeed, as so often becomes a central issue in discussions of Foucault, genealogy refuses to accept the Platonic finality of Truth:

> Truth is undoubtedly the sort of error that cannot be refuted because it has hardened into an unalterable form in the long baking process of history. Moreover, the very question of truth, the right it appropriates to refute error and oppose itself to appearance, the manner in which it developed (initially made available to the wise, then withdrawn by men of piety to an unattainable world where it was given the double role of con-

solation and imperative, finally rejected as a useless notion, superfluous and contradicted on all sides)—does this not form a history, the history of an error we call truth?[14]

Now both Nietzsche and Foucault are frequently read as advancing a truth-claim to the effect that there is no truth, to the endless delight of self-referential incoherence detectives. I take for granted here that neither of them may be dismissed as making simplistically self-refuting claims. As is becoming increasingly appreciated in the secondary literature, Foucault joins Nietzsche not in arguing that there is no truth of any sort, but in asking why we are so insistent on the primacy of Truth, why it is of such momentous import.[15] Consider the following possible reply to this Nietzschean question:

> We want what we say not only to be understandable, credible, meaningful.... We hanker for patterns of argument which will not be subject to reasonable doubt.... To say it another way, *the hunger for validation is a hunger for power*. We want people to *have* to believe what we say.

The writer of this passage is neither Foucault nor Nietzsche, but John Howard Yoder. It is from Yoder's pen that my primary Anabaptist texts of choice issue. Yoder wrote two essays in his later years that explicitly address particularity as a problem in relation to the gospel of Jesus Christ, "'But We Do See Jesus': The Particularity of Incarnation and the Universality of Truth,"[16] and "On Not Being Ashamed of the Gospel: Particularity, Pluralism, and Validation,"[17] from which the above quote is drawn.[18] In both essays, Yoder's strategy is interestingly similar to that of Foucault in that he responds to questions not by answering them in their own terms, but by inquiring into where the questions come from, by showing that the frame of reference in which they are raised is not as monolithically self-evident as we might have assumed.

My claim, in fact, is that Yoder may be read as providing us with at least the beginnings of a genealogy of the problem of particularity. Particularity is a problem for us, as would-be heralds of the gospel, in light of what Yoder often refers to as "the wider world." Yoder sketches a phenomenology of the individual experience of passing from narrow particularity into a wider world, cast in terms that are strikingly similar to the terms that Foucault identifies with the core of the Enlightenment.

> The psychological and sociological momentum which makes the respectively "wider world" more convincing is not derived from rational demonstrations (where would one stand to deliver them?) but from the

social experience of growth and migration from the world of one's past toward a wider, or more accepting, or more complex, or more tolerant, or more decisive, or wealthier world into which one has moved. Narrowness is associated with parental authority; breadth with the teacher who has liberated one therefrom.[19]

The experience of achieving greater maturity, of gaining independence from prior authority figures, of getting a view from what naturally seems a greater height, leads one to shift one's epistemological allegiances to the regime of the wider world. This is not an Origin (*Ursprung*) of the problem of particularity, but a site of its "emergence" (*Entstehung*). The liberation experienced is generally assumed to bear a sort of finality, because it is so often intellectually and emotionally traumatic. According to Yoder, however, it is of great importance that we grasp how "perennial" the form (not the content) of the experience really is. "There is always a wider world claiming that its truths are self-evident. . . . [T]hat was the case in the first century. It is not a new contribution of 'modernity.'"[20] A tendency to push for Truth that coerces belief has its genesis in the shock of having been so parochial. That is, we can trace its genealogy to our abhorrence of prior errors.

> The search for foundations, the urge to find some argument, some mental move, some court of appeal beyond appeal, is thus a learned personal psychic defense against the constantly repeated experience of being overpowered by a wider world. It is psychologically natural, but by the nature of things it is insatiable and logically unrealistic.[21]

To restate Yoder's point, particularity is a problem only in relation to a "wider world." We need not simply assume the Truth of the particular "wider world" that raises the question. Yoder has obviously provided no inductive disproof of a "widest" world, whose perspective would indeed be equivalent to Truth. But what would it be like to have a reason for thinking that *this* is *it*? I suspect we cannot even make sense of the possibility.[22]

Of course, none of this is to say that "the desire for some kind of transtribal validation"[23] is simply a mistake. As Yoder notes, this desire implies respect for interlocutors, inasmuch as we refuse simply to reduce persuasion to force. It also implies that our convictions are genuinely held, not diluted to mere "matters of opinion." Yoder rejects the modern ideal of coercive truth but also the equally modern truth-claim that there is no truth.

> We must abandon the chimerical vision of a set of semantic or definitional moves which would transcend the limits of one's own identity, rationally coercing assent, without taking account of a particular inter-

locutor or a specific dialogical setting. . . . Yet we must not abandon the claim that the validity of what we believe is founded on grounds more solid than whim, flipping a coin, accident, or provincial bias. Instead of seeking to escape particular identity, what we need, then, is a better way to restate the meaning of a truth-claim from within particular identity.[24]

POWER/PERSON

So far, Yoder's resonance with Foucault seems to me significant. Foucault insists that he is never in a position to offer either Truth or solutions to problems in any strong sense. Yet he is equally insistent that genealogy is an ethically significant pursuit. He seeks not to give historical accounts that are True, but to allow people in particular local contexts the freedom to think beyond the categories that have hardened into Truth, to liberate themselves from thought that has become oppressive.

Liberate themselves into what? Foucault seems to assume that only they (the people being liberated) can decide. If Foucault makes a recommendation, and we mistake him for a Theorist, then Foucault believes his recommendation will only become a new form of oppression. Indeed, the ascendance of further oppression is apparently assumed as inevitable.

> Humanity does not gradually progress from combat to combat until it arrives at universal reciprocity, where the rule of law finally replaces warfare; humanity installs each of its violences in a system of rules and thus proceeds from domination to domination.[25]

Herein lies an aspect of Foucault's thought that many find hardest to swallow. If we are doomed to some sort of domination or other, are we not also doomed to apathy? Does not such pessimism lead to quietistic acquiescence to the status quo? Are we not deprived of our ability to distinguish better or worse social arrangements? Foucault responds negatively. In one of his more famous and often-anthologized interviews, he says that

> My point is not that everything is bad, but that everything is dangerous, which is not exactly the same as bad. If everything is dangerous, then we always have something to do. So my position leads not to apathy but to a hyper- and pessimistic activism.[26]

Change *per se* is not the villain in Foucault's view. Criticized rather are Theories that promise radical or global change. "In fact we know from experience," he writes, that the "programs for a new man that the worst political systems have repeated throughout the twentieth century" have "led only to the return of the most dangerous traditions." What Foucault prefers are "specific transformations."[27]

It is worth noting that the general orientation sketched here is unique neither to Foucault nor to thinkers known as postmodern. Returning to the more confessional mode, I have been impressed by the resonance here with elements of what is often called the conservative intellectual tradition (whose luminaries include Edmund Burke, Alexis de Tocqueville, Michael Oakeshott, and Russell Kirk[28]); with the "classical" liberalism of such "Austrian" economists as Ludwig von Mises and Friedrich Hayek;[29] and with the thought of at least some "neoconservatives," including Peter L. Berger[30] and Thomas Sowell.[31] These among others have argued in various ways (which I find compelling) against the notion that human beings can ever be in a position to formulate a definitive blueprint for human society and culture.[32] A consistent theme emerging from the work of all of these thinkers, though emphasized to varying degrees, is deep awareness of the corruption that accompanies power.

What is often portrayed as unique to Foucault's perspective is his conceptualization of power. Foucault sees power not as resource possessed disproportionately by various persons or groupings in society but as an inescapable medium in which we live and interact with each other. This power is deeply intertwined with—and in fact conceptually inseparable from—knowledge. Part of the key to Foucault's "pessimistic activism" is his refusal to conclude from the ubiquity of power relations either to the futility of action, or to the loss of any real significance for the term *knowledge*.

> Perhaps . . . we should abandon a whole tradition that allows us to imagine that knowledge can exist only where the power relations are suspended and that knowledge can develop only outside its injunctions, its demands and its interests. Perhaps we should abandon the notion that . . . the renunciation of power is one of the conditions of knowledge. We should admit that power produces knowledge . . . that power and knowledge directly imply one another; that there is no power relation without the correlative constitution of a field of knowledge, nor any knowledge that does not presuppose and constitute at the same time power relations.[33]

It would take us too far afield to revisit Foucault's conception of power here in detail. What I wish to emphasize again is how interesting it is to compare his perspective with Yoder's.[34] In the case of power, some striking similarities in themes are discernible. For example, Yoder has alluded approvingly to an emphasis in the Reformed tradition on the epistemological dimensions of sin.

> What Protestants call "the noetic effect of sin" poisons not only the ability to will and to do the good, but even the ability to know what it is. What we know does not all become false. Yet what we know naturally is warped, blurred, inadequate. That is one aspect of the need for revelation.[35]

Though the terms are vastly different, the upshot here is arguably not significantly different from Foucault's words above. Perhaps, we could say, we should admit that all of our knowledge is clouded by human fallenness. Perhaps we should give up on the ideal of knowledge not touched by sin.

Yet striking divergences emerge here as well. Central to Yoder's reputation as a "sectarian" theologian is his frequent insistence that Christians are not called to make history come out right but to be faithful.[36] Discipleship involves a renunciation of resistance to the powers of this world that is not simply fatalistic, though it may appear so by the world's standards. Jesus' politics are the politics of the cross. Such a political stance assumes the sort of picture of power painted by Foucault—yet places hope in a radically different sort of power which derives its force from voluntary powerlessness pointing toward the Wholly Other. Yoder further argues that the political vicissitudes of the life of the church place a certain epistemic "spin" on its decisions and confessions: "The community pulls back . . . from any claim to catholic generalizability and infallibility, yet it is believingly, modestly ready to say of consensus reached today, 'It seemed good to the Holy Spirit and to us.'"[37]

The difference between this Spirit-led consensus of the gathered community at a given time and the local and limited projects for liberation envisioned by Foucault is hard to flesh out by any straightforward example. This is precisely because, for both Yoder and Foucault, the discernment must ultimately be local. Yet Foucault is much more unwilling than Yoder to speak in generalities. Yoder after all remains committed to the ability of the gospel to travel between cultures, to remain the same in some important sense while being carried by widely varying discursive formations, as Foucault might say. Consider Yoder's treatment of "pluralism/relativism" as more of a language to speak than a substantive outlook.

> What we need to find is the interworld transformational grammar to help us to discern what will need to happen if the collision of the message of Jesus in our pluralistic/relativist world is to lead to a reconception of

the shape of the world, instead of to rendering Jesus optional or innocuous. To ask, 'Shall we talk in pluralistic/relativist terms?' would be as silly as to ask in Greece, 'Shall we talk Greek?' The question is what we shall say. We shall say, 'Jesus is Messiah and Lord'; but how do you say that in pluralist/relativist language?[38]

The primacy of particularity and the ubiquity of power, for Foucault, mean that the only possible *general* project is the *via negativa* of genealogy. The crucial difference in Yoder, I believe, is the conviction that the gospel is not a theory or a doctrine but a particular *person* who adopts an exemplary (and in fact, theoretically scandalous) stance toward power. It is the *confession* (which is importantly different than a theory or doctrine, I suspect) that "the particularity of the incarnation *is* the universality of the good."[39] Yoder argues that the power of the gospel lies precisely in its being emphatically particular and unashamedly noncoercive. "If we cannot transcend the vulnerability of belief by positing as accessible a nonparticular 'natural,' might we then celebrate confessionally that light and truth have *taken on the vulnerability of the particular?*"[40]

This brings us, of course, into the purview not only of Yoder's essays on particularity, but of the whole argument of his *Politics of Jesus*.[41] My intent is not to review Yoder's arguments in general, but to call attention to the possibility of revelation that he endeavors to articulate—revelation that is historically and culturally particular, but that derives its universality precisely therefrom. Jesus' particularity is exactly what makes it possible for us, who would continue to spread his good news, to

> use any language . . . to enter any world in which people eat bread and pursue debtors, hope for power and execute subversives. The ordinariness of the humanness of Jesus is the warrant for the generalizability of his reconciliation. The nonterritorial particularity of his Jewishness defends us against selling out to any wider world's claim to be really wider, or to be self-validating.[42]

To wax overly dramatic, perhaps, we might think that this move on Yoder's part is exactly contrary to any sort of rejoinder Foucault would expect. I suspect this is overly dramatic because Foucault, like any other hearer of the gospel, is not pinned to any intellectual mat, forced to admit that Yoder's confession is Truth. Foucault might rightly remind us that Yoder's move of emphasizing a person rather than discourse does not itself escape discourse. The dance would then continue.

THREE LINES OF QUESTIONING

So if there is no happy ending, wherein Yoder produces the magic Anabaptist incantation that reverberates in Foucault's soul and forces him to faith, then what may we take from this comparison? Of what significance are my confessions that arise from reading Yoder and Foucault together? At the risk of being rather more linear than a postmodernist should be, allow me to suggest three lines of questioning. These suggestions are as "confessional" as the rest of my reflections; they arise not of themselves from the texts I have been citing, but from my own thoroughly particular reading of them.

First, I suggest that we question our allergic reactions to the so-called pluralist/relativist flavor of putatively postmodern thinkers. Here I believe I am only echoing Yoder: "We may be tactical allies of the pluralist/relativist deconstruction of deceptive orthodox claims to logically coercive certainty, without making of relativism itself a new monism."[43] At least in this sense, I suppose it is apt that my paper is categorized among those "*for*" postmodernity.[44] Just don't ask me to remain the same.

Second, I suggest that we question our current institutional tendencies away from the primacy of the local gathered community. The type of Anabaptism I continue to find worth identifying myself with is the sort that understands its position among other major alternatives on the ecclesiological map. I am still here among Anabaptists, and not in some other fold, partly because we are neither told how we must read Scripture by a denomination or conference nor left alone to puzzle it out as individuals. We struggle prayerfully together in discernment as gathered local communities, where we know and care for one another.

Anabaptist commitment to this approach is undergoing serious test, as there are those in the Anabaptist fold who seek to have congregations removed from their larger denominational conference bodies when congregational discernment is not acceptable (such as when some congregations move to welcome gay or lesbian members). These conference bodies may then make disfellowshipping decisions by vote from a distance, knowing few of the persons whose lives the decision affects. Such disturbing political moves among contemporary Mennonites contribute to my deepening inclination to listen to Foucault.[45]

My final suggestion is that we persistently question any and every alliance, intellectual or political, not primarily in light of some body of doctrine we take to be Anabaptist, but in light of the crucified and resurrected

Lord that the sixteenth-century Anabaptists wished both to know and to follow in life. Do not mistake my suggestion: I do not say make no alliances, for I have no indication that such a course is possible or desirable. But when alliances become allegiances, we are confronted with the old problem of idolatry, and some postmodern prophecy might be called for.

In place of any synthetic conclusion, I cannot do better than to recall Foucault's words, quoted above: "My point is not that everything is *bad*, but that everything is *dangerous*. . . ."[46]

NOTES

1. Friedrich Nietzsche, *Beyond Good and Evil: Prelude to a Philosophy of the Future*, trans. Walter Kaufmann (New York: Vintage, 1966), 89.

2. Friedrich Nietzsche, *The Portable Nietzsche*, trans. and ed. Walter Kaufmann (New York: Viking Penguin, Inc., 1954), 470.

3. I have been pushed in the direction of appreciating inconsistency as a virtue not only by Foucault and Nietzsche, but also by Kierkegaard, and more particularly by Leszek Kolakowski. Cf. Kolakowski, "In Praise of Inconsistency," in *Toward a Marxist Humanism: Essays on the Left Today*, trans. Jane Zielonko Peel (New York: Grove Press, 1968), 211-220.

4. The seminal article for "polygenesis" discussions of Anabaptist origins is James M. Stayer, Werner O. Packull, and Klaus Deppermann, "From Monogenesis to Polygenesis: The Historical Discussion of Anabaptist Origins," *Mennonite Quarterly Review* 49 (April 1975), 83-122. For some particularly interesting examples of subsequent reflection on theological "uses" of Anabaptist history, see J. Denny Weaver, "The Anabaptist Vision: A Historical or a Theological Future?" *Conrad Grebel Review* 13 (Winter 1995), 69-86, and the essays in John D. Roth, ed., *Refocusing a Vision: Shaping Anabaptist Character in the 21st Century* (Goshen, Ind.: Mennonite Historical Society, 1995).

5. Michel Foucault, *The Archaeology of Knowledge*, trans. A. M. Sheridan Smith (New York: Pantheon Books, 1972), 17.

6. I. e., especially the "middle" Foucault, whose "methodology" is most clearly (and deliberately) Nietzschean genealogy. The major books of this period are *Discipline and Punish: The Birth of the Prison*, trans. Alan Sheridan (New York: Pantheon Books, 1977), and *The History of Sexuality, Volume 1: An Introduction*, trans. Robert Hurley (New York: Vintage Books, 1977). While I believe that the theme of particularity is present throughout Foucault's writings, I find that it is most explicit when he is most consciously drawing from Nietzsche.

7. Michel Foucault, *The Foucault Reader*, ed. Paul Rabinow (New York: Pantheon Books, 1984), 32-50.

8. Ibid., 76-100.

9. The secondary literature on Foucault is immense and labyrinthine, and I would not be able to trace the ways in which it has influenced my reading of his work, both

positively and negatively. It might be helpful to some readers, however, to know that I have been influenced most clearly by C. G. Prado, *Beginning With Foucault: An Introduction to Genealogy* (Boulder, Colo.: Westview Press, 1995) and Gary Gutting, ed., *The Cambridge Companion to Foucault* (Cambridge and New York: Cambridge University Press, 1994). I am also deeply indebted to students at Hillsdale College in seminars that I have taught on the sociology of knowledge and on Anabaptist Christianity, where some of the thoughts presented here were first tentatively formulated and criticized.

10. Foucault, *The Foucault Reader*, 50.

11. Ibid., 76. Foucault's reference to the color gray follows Nietzsche's explicit preference for laborious engagement (which he identifies with the color gray) with the actual historical development of morality, over "gazing around haphazardly in the blue ..." Friedrich Nietzsche, *On the Genealogy of Morals*, trans. Walter Kaufmann and R. J. Hollingdale (New York: Vintage Books, 1989), 21.

12. Foucault, *The Foucault Reader*, 77-86.

13. Ibid., 81.

14. Ibid., 79-80.

15. I capitalize the first letter of the word *Truth* to emphasize this Nietzschean question. One might imagine hearing an ominous Wagnerian *Leitmotiv* whenever it is used here. This is not to suggest (as was understood by one person responding to my original presentation) that it is straightforwardly possible to distinguish the sense of Truth being developed here from other senses which are not as problematic. Whereas Nietzsche and Foucault both clearly use the word *truth* in more than one way, and further assume that there *are* truths in some sense(s), I find no clear warrant for concluding that there is any usage in any context which they would not consider susceptible to the question. For a helpful discussion of the multivocity of the word *truth* in Foucault, see Prado, *Beginning With Foucault*, 119-150.

16. John Howard Yoder, *The Priestly Kingdom: Social Ethics as Gospel* (Notre Dame, Ind.: University of Notre Dame Press, 1984), 46-62.

17. John Howard Yoder, "On Not Being Ashamed of the Gospel: Particularity, Pluralism, and Validation," *Faith and Philosophy* 9 (July 1992), 285-300.

18. Yoder, "On Not Being Ashamed of the Gospel," 287 (my emphasis). Particularity is also a central concern in John Howard Yoder, "Theological Revision and the Burden of Particular Identity," in *James M. Gustafson's Theocentric Ethics: Interpretations and Assessments*, ed. Harlan R. Beckley and Charles M. Swezey (Macon, Ga.: Mercer University Press, 1988), 63-94, the content of which overlaps significantly with the other two essays cited.

19. Yoder, "On Not Being Ashamed of the Gospel," 286-287.

20. Ibid., 286.

21. Ibid.

22. To explicitly state what should be understood here: There is clearly no way to show that we will *never* be in a position to have such a reason. My suggestion is only that we cannot *now* make sense of what this would even be like (to say nothing of estimating its likelihood), and that this gives us at least some warrant for supposing that the possi-

bility is extremely unlikely in the future. See MacIntyre's discussion of the force of his arguments in comparison with that of Wittgenstein's "private language argument": Alasdair MacIntyre, *After Virtue: A Study in Moral Theory*, 2d ed. (Notre Dame, Ind.: University of Notre Dame Press, 1984), 101-102.

23. Yoder, "On Not Being Ashamed of the Gospel," 289.
24. Ibid., 290.
25. Foucault, *The Foucault Reader*, 85.
26. Ibid., 343.
27. Ibid., 46-47.
28. Cf. Russell Kirk on the "principle of prudence": "Liberals and radicals, the conservative holds, are imprudent: for they dash at their objectives without giving much heed to the risk of new abuses worse than the evils they hope to sweep away . . . Sudden and slashing reforms are perilous as sudden and slashing surgery. The march of providence is slow; it is the devil who always hurries" (Russell Kirk, ed., *The Portable Conservative Reader* [New York: Penguin,1982], xvii).
29. James Miller notes that Foucault was familiar with the "Austrian School" economists and recommended their writings to his students. Cf. James Miller, *The Passion of Michel Foucault* (New York: Simon & Schuster, 1993), 310. Miller's assumption is apparently that this association casts a negative light on Foucault, an assumption that I do not share.
30. Cf. Peter L. Berger and Richard J. Neuhaus, *Movement and Revolution* (Garden City, N.Y.: Anchor Books, 1970), 20-30.
31. Cf. Thomas Sowell, *A Conflict of Visions* (New York: Morrow, 1987).
32. I would also suggest that there is very significant conceptual overlap here with the interest in anarchism displayed by Jacques Ellul, *Anarchy and Christianity*, trans. Geoffrey W. Bromiley (Grand Rapids, Mich.: Eerdmans, 1991), and Vernard Eller, *Christian Anarchy: Jesus' Primacy Over the Powers* (Grand Rapids, Mich.: Eerdmans, 1987).
33. Foucault, *Discipline and Punish*, 27.
34. In what follows, I am deeply indebted to Eric Ortlund, with whom I engaged in several stimulating discussions of Foucault and Yoder in the course of his preparations of a senior honors thesis at Hillsdale College in the spring of 1998.
35. Yoder, "Theological Revision and the Burden of Particular Identity," 81. The discussion from which this is drawn is in Yoder's contribution to the Gustafson volume mentioned in note 18, but it is explicitly cited by Yoder in "On Not Being Ashamed of the Gospel," 299, n. 18. Yoder recommends a very helpful and incisive discussion of this idea by Merold Westphal, "Taking Paul Seriously: Sin as an Epistemological Category," in *Christian Philosophy*, ed. Thomas Flint (Notre Dame, Ind.: University of Notre Dame Press, 1990), 200-226.
36. Cf. John Howard Yoder, *The Politics of Jesus*, 2d ed. (Grand Rapids, Mich.: Eerdmans, 1994), 237-241. [Equivalent pagination in 1st ed. (Grand Rapids, Mich.: Eerdmans, 1972) is 244-248.]
37. Yoder, *The Priestly Kingdom*, 35.
38. Ibid., 56.

39. Ibid., 62.
40. Ibid., 44 (my emphasis).
41. Op. cit., note above.
42. Yoder, *The Priestly Kingdom*, 62.
43. Ibid., 61. Nietzsche himself is as clear in his rejection of leveling or paralyzing relativism as he is in his embracing of "perspectivism": "There is *only* a perspective seeing, *only* a perspective 'knowing': and the *more* affects we allow to speak about one thing, the *more* eyes, different eyes, we can use to observe one thing, the more complete will our 'concept' of this thing, our 'objectivity,' be. But to eliminate the will altogether, to suspend each and every affect, supposing we were capable of this—what would that mean but to *castrate* the intellect?" (Nietzsche, *On the Genealogy of Morals*, 119 [Nietzsche's emphases]).
44. The paper was originally presented in a session entitled "Anabaptism For Postmodernity," which was balanced by another session, "Anabaptism Against Postmodernity." The irony of the (modern) "either/or" categorization was not lost on the participants in either session.
45. My allusion here is to several disciplinary actions taken by Mennonite conferences in the United States toward congregations that have explicitly chosen to accept, as members, noncelibate homosexual individuals. Unfortunately, because of the volatility of this issue in current Mennonite discussions, I fear my concern might easily be misunderstood. My point here is not at all that these congregations have adopted a correct understanding of homosexuality and the church, while conferences have adopted an incorrect understanding. Rather, my point is that congregations have apparently engaged in prayerful and often painful discernment on the local level, usually over the course of several years, only to have this process summarily negated at the conference level via questionable exercise of organizational power.
46. Foucault, *The Foucault Reader*, 343 (my emphasis).

CHAPTER THREE

"UNIVERSAL TRUTHS":
Should Anabaptist Theologians Seek to Articulate Them?

Thomas Finger

THE POSTMODERN CASE AGAINST UNIVERSAL TRUTHS

Postmodernism is generally skeptical about the possibility of formulating universal truths, especially moral or religious ones. Many postmodernists, that is, challenge the notion that any ethical norm or theological affirmation can be valid for all humankind.

There are at least three reasons for this. First, postmodernism stresses the cultural factors involved in forming concepts and knowledge. Every concept, including biblical ones, originates in particular experiences and concerns of people in specific cultures. To a significant degree, any concept expresses people's particular perspectives on things and their interests in manipulating the world advantageously. Since the perspectives and interests of different cultures are quite diverse, and sometimes quite opposed, postmodernists generally affirm that concepts originating in any one culture (as all concepts do) cannot describe reality adequately for all peoples.

Second, many postmodernists accept philosophical critiques of foundationalism. Foundationalism is the effort to build all valid knowledge on some uninterpreted, indubitable truths, and to link each subsequent affirmation to them through careful logical steps so that the resulting superstructure will be as certain as possible. But current critics argue, essentially, that we have no access to basic truths or facts apart from some interpretive scheme. Everything we know or perceive is conveyed through some framework that gives it a particular meaning and value.[1] And all such frameworks, once again, express the perspectives and interests of some culture. Accordingly, it is claimed, no universal foundations for knowledge exist.

Third, and perhaps most important, many postmodernists criticize universal truth-claims as functioning oppressively. Since general affirmations only express interests and perspectives of particular groups, it is argued that claims that some such affirmations are true for everyone can only be efforts to disguise these interests and impose them on other groups. To say, "the husband is head of the household" is not to enunciate something valid for all times and places, but to impose men's interests on women. Similarly, many postmodernists would regard an affirmation like "Jesus Christ is Lord of the universe" as an effort to impose the interests of individuals, groups, or nations that call themselves Christian on other peoples.

In sum, I have identified three basic postmodern challenges to the notion of universal truth: cultural relativity, antifoundationalism, and oppressive function. In what follows, I will first present an Anabaptist case against universal truths, then an Anabaptist case for universal truths, both organized around these three main themes.

AN ANABAPTIST CASE AGAINST UNIVERSAL TRUTHS

Current discussions about doing theology in Anabaptist perspective suggest that a case against universal theological affirmations could be formed in the following way.

First, in resonance with postmodernism's emphasis on cultural relativity, one could stress that Anabaptists have often existed in distinctive cultural units. Seldom have they sought to blend with majority cultures. As such, Anabaptists, much like postmodernists, are acutely aware of how deeply their perceptions are shaped by their particular circumstances. Accordingly, Anabaptism's most important theological contribution will be to witness to the awareness and lifestyle fostered by its adherents' distinctive experiences, values, and beliefs. Anabaptism provides a critical alternative to the way Christian majorities do theology. Consequently, its theologians should concentrate on making the shape of this alternative clear. They should forego efforts to formulate their beliefs in universal terms that these majorities could accept. For if they do, they will produce just one more variety of majority theology and relegate distinctive Anabaptist themes to minor variations on it.

Second, in resonance with criticisms of philosophical foundationalism, one could note that Anabaptists have seldom done formal, academic theology. They have seldom sought to ground their distinctive witness in, or validate it by, reigning philosophies or sciences. In concert with various "postliberal" and "narrative" theologians, Anabaptists might protest that when theology has sought to root its utterances in universal affirmations, these have turned out to be Western values disguised as absolutes.

This preoccupation, one might continue, has diverted Christian theology from stressing what is really central: the unique communal praxis rooted in Jesus' lifestyle and teaching. It has diverted theology from recognizing that Christian character is formed not by obeying universal ethical principles but by nurture in a particular community with its distinctive ethos and history.[2] Anabaptist theologians, then, should concentrate on elucidating their own communities' values and beliefs and how these are perceived and appropriated, and not emphasize their universal validity.

Third, in line with the postmodernist critique of the oppressive function of universals, Anabaptists could stress that they too have historically been subjugated in the name of beliefs and values purported to be absolute. As a people who have suffered much, they have noticed how fully Jesus identified with the marginalized and downtrodden. This should make Anabaptist theologians especially wary of making alleged universal claims that can downgrade races, classes, genders, nations, and religions. Instead of formulating universals that might be used domineeringly, Anabaptists, taking clues from Jesus, should construct theologies supportive of the aspirations of particular oppressed groups for liberation.

I hope this case against universal affirmations sounds plausible. If so, that may be because it emphasizes many features that many Anabaptists, myself included, think should characterize their theology. In what follows, I propose that all such features can be retained in a theology that aims to make some universal affirmations, and that this attempt can strengthen, and need not weaken, articulation of distinctive Anabaptist themes.

AN ANABAPTIST CASE FOR UNIVERSAL TRUTHS

Cultural relativism

Anabaptist theologians should indeed emphasize distinctive features of their particular tradition. But does it necessarily follow that this distinctiveness will be diluted or falsified if some beliefs are formulated in universal terms?

In the very act of calling one's theology "Anabaptist," one is already moving beyond the particularity of one's sociohistorical location. A great variety of sometimes conflicting beliefs have been called "Anabaptist." Whoever uses this term, then, will already have some notion, if only hazy, as to which beliefs merit the label. In entertaining this notion, one will already have transcended, even if half-consciously, one's particular location in the direction, if not yet of universals, at least of broad historical generalizations.

If we call our theology Anabaptist, we are laying claim to a title applied to numerous groups for over 450 years. If this title is to convey anything significant, we must be able to give some account of what features are central to it. We are claiming continuity with a historic tradition. I find it misleading to use this much debated, praised, and execrated term simply for whatever one may believe today.

Which features, then, might be central to Anabaptism? The issue is too complex to be decided fully here. Nonetheless, I believe several features that have characterized nearly all groups claiming this name can be identified. I also maintain that any such feature should be included in what any theologian means when using "Anabaptist" today. Let me begin with one: I call it *fidelity to origins*.

For over 450 years, almost all groups that have self-consciously accepted the Anabaptist label have retained and cherished memories of their beginnings. They have sought to remain faithful, at least in some ways, to them. Indeed, a major reason for retaining this name is to recall and remain true to these origins.

The origin most commonly referred to, of course, is the Anabaptist movement of the Reformation era. But when we examine this movement, we find it too was seeking to recover and re-actualize an origin it thought had been lost. This was the life of the New Testament church—a communal vitality that pointed to and proclaimed its own decisive origin in the life, death, and resurrection of Jesus. But even these events referred to previous ones: they were seen as fulfillments of God's ancient promises to Israel.

The stories of Israel, Jesus, and the early church, however, were understood not simply as histories of specific peoples but as the means by which God's saving intentions were being actualized for the whole world. The early church, then, set out to proclaim these intentions to all peoples. Early Anabaptists did likewise. Though they gathered in distinctive communities, their purpose was not simply to celebrate their distinctiveness but to respond to all of what God offered to and asked of everyone. Since such possibilities were open to everyone, they undertook missions far more extensive than did other communions of Reformation times.[3] For Anabaptists, distinct and despised though they were, saw themselves participating directly in the climax of God's story as it unfolded across the earth and throughout humankind.

My point is that when we examine the emphasis on fidelity to origins so key to nearly all Anabaptist groups,[4] we find this: the origins at their heart involve vivid awareness of participating in a universal story. That story, of course, was and is actualized through histories of specific peoples. Yet one should not then assume, as many postmodernists tend to, that the particular conceptual forms through which it finds expression are not connected with anything universal. Instead, one is brought face to face with a central biblical paradox: God seeks to reach all nations precisely through the vivid manifestation of the divine intentions through particular peoples.

If Anabaptist theologians, then, seek to articulate the particularity postmodernism prizes, they cannot stop with describing "distinctive" Anabaptist beliefs. They need to acknowledge that many such distinctives are, paradoxically, connected with and express God's universal intentions. Any adequate theology in Anabaptist perspective will be rooted in that universal biblical story to which all Christian theologies in some way appeal.

Emphasizing this story, however, need not blunt Anabaptism's critical, alternative contributions to theology, reducing them to minor variations of a majority approach. On the contrary, its contributions will more likely be minimized if presented simply as products of unique Anabaptist experience. For this will allow them to be benignly dismissed by those majority theologians unsettled by Anabaptist claims. Anabaptists are far more likely to make critical contributions by articulating significant alternative readings of the Christian story. For when a major Anabaptist theme, such as peacemaking, is presented as a central feature of that entire story (rather than, say, simply as one of Jesus' teachings), the overall shape of that story alters in many respects. Such Anabaptist insights can challenge majority theologies at the center, rather than simply suggest minor variations.

Antifoundationalism

Many postmodernists insist that beliefs cannot be based on uninterpreted facts or truths available to everyone: everything is perceived through some interpretive framework which already gives it a specific meaning and value. These frameworks are provided by the diverse communities in which different people participate. But while Anabaptist theologians must surely emphasize the roles played by their distinct communities, must description of these roles preclude all universal affirmations? I will address this issue first, then the more philosophical claims of antifoundationalism.

The communal emphasis

Along with fidelity to origins, among features that characterize nearly all groups claiming to be Anabaptist is the importance of community. Almost all Anabaptists have stressed that one cannot really live the Christian life, and hence understand or theologize about it adequately, except in a corporate context. This communal shaping of all religious knowledge may seem to indicate not only that Anabaptist theologizing cannot be grounded in general truths but further that it cannot go beyond its interpretive communal framework to affirm anything universal.

I have just indicated, however, that Anabaptists have not understood their communal experiences to be the ultimate origins of their beliefs. Instead, these communities endeavor to be faithful to origins that lie beyond themselves and provide the ultimate sources of their life. Such communities are authentic, and their theological expressions adequate, only insofar as they participate in and articulate the universal story that gave them birth.

Phrased in the language of narrative theology, communal reality—especially if it claims a name over 450 years old—consists not merely of current experiences, activities, and structures, but also of traditions that have shaped it. Moreover, though ethical character is formed by communal nurture rather than universal rules, transmission of these traditions is essential to it. This means that the communal shaping of theological beliefs, stressed by postmodernists, includes their shaping by the past. Then if this past originated in and refers to something universal, some of these beliefs will also intend universality.

Accordingly, if we begin with Christian community, and mean by this not simply local communities today, but also those traditions and that sense of community maintained by Anabaptists of the past, we must move beyond particular communities. We must also articulate that universal story in which they play their role.

In passing, however, let me point out that a quite different construal of Anabaptist theologizing might arise if its main starting point were contemporary communal experience alone. In this case, the criteria for affirming something in theology would consist largely of whether or not it seemed relevant to today's communities. In this way, features of Anabaptist and biblical history could be affirmed, denied, or modified according to whether they seemed to enhance contemporary experience. For instance, if Jesus' cross or way of peace no longer seemed relevant, it might be hard to find any other reason for affirming it.

Among Mennonite theologians, perhaps Gordon Kaufman most eloquently prioritizes contemporary experience over historical and biblical tradition. For Kaufman, theological concepts do not originate from revelation or religious traditions. Rather, they are human constructions built up from general cultural experience.[5] "Responsible" theology, accordingly, will speak largely in concepts drawn from its own culture. For instance, cultural sensibilities today indicate that "God" should designate not a personal being but a "serendipitous" evolutionary creativity, a continuous "coming-into-being of increasing complexity, value and meaning."[6]

Employing more postmodernist terminology, Daniel Liechty maintains that "religious knowledge is entirely embedded in the human community from which it originates." Thus one should ask not whether theological claims are true "in some disembodied sense," but consider "how these truth-claims emerged in the life of the community. . . ."[7] Accordingly, theology cannot even say whether God exists (though it also cannot say that God does not).[8] Liechty values past Mennonite communities, for a "Mennonite theology is grounded in a creative tension between historical memory and the ongoing experience of the particular community. . . ."[9] Nevertheless, the only real test of a theological affirmation's validity is whether it expresses what members of a current community are thinking.[10]

Ted Grimsrud perhaps gives current experience greater priority when he insists that "No formulation of theology can help but be a contemporary construct. . . ." This means any effort to re-present traditional beliefs will be "every bit as much a late twentieth-century formulation" as anything from Gordon Kaufman.[11] Consequently, "the central criterion for *our* theology is that it be meaningful for *us*, that it address *our* reality. . . ."[12] Apparently such a theology "can affirm God without positing 'Classical' notions of Transcendence, Eternity. . . ."[13] It will employ Scripture—yet not as an "authority-over" but as a "conversation partner which helps our construction, which emerges through our experience."[14]

These brief remarks are not intended as thorough presentations of or engagements with the important viewpoints of these three authors. I point to them simply as brief indications of how "community," when understood in a postmodern framework, can mean very largely contemporary communities. Furthermore, they illustrate potential results of assuming that "modern experience and life are so utterly different from anything known to—or even imaginable by—the biblical writers."[15] Postmodern notions of community can function quite differently in theology from those in which communities are actually constituted, in part, by past traditions with their universal orientations.

Philosophical considerations

Even if one acknowledges that any Christian theology, including any grounded in distinctive communities, must articulate universal meanings of its universal story, the antifoundationalist challenge must still be addressed: are universal affirmations even possible? Do the cultural origins and perspectival character of all concepts render them non-universalizable?

Since this challenge is philosophical, I address it on these grounds. Essentially, I argue that common postmodern rejections of universal truth are inconsistent. For the notion of universality is in fact presupposed in some basic arguments made against it, and it underlies some of the basic moves made in these arguments. In other words, acceptance of some kind of universal truth, whether one acknowledges it or not, is an indispensable condition of the very possibility of arguing against it. If postmodernist critics were not tacitly presupposing what they claim to deny, they could not make such arguments in the first place.

Such rejections of universal truth are inconsistent in three main ways. First comes the often recognized but rarely emphasized fact that any statement that intends categorically to deny universal truth and/or affirm complete relativism contradicts itself. To say "it is impossible to make statements about reality that are universally true" is to affirm a universal truth: all statements that claim universality are false. This statement, in other words, tries to do what it says cannot be done: to utter a universal truth. One might say it *intends* to be entirely, or universally, true. Yet its particular content, which denies universality, contradicts its basic intention.

A postmodernist might also say, "Whatever any individual or group perceives to be true is so conditioned by their particular experiences, interests, and limitations that it can be valid only for those who share their specific vantage-point." But this statement also intends to state something universally true: that all human perceptions are shaped by factors that keep them from being universally true. Moreover, this statement contradicts itself in that it expresses the perception of some individual or group about reality while it attempts to do something it says such a statement cannot: affirm something universally true.

Something strange is occurring. Such utterances seek to insist that knowledge is inescapably limited to the knower's particular context, yet they can do so only by attempting to stretch beyond that context and affirm something about all knowledge in all contexts whatever. If our knowledge really is wholly limited to our own context, whence comes this ability to look beyond it and compare it not only with some other contexts, but even to intend to compare it with all others? Perhaps we are not only embedded in our cultural contexts but are also in some important way beyond them.

Second, many postmodernists reject universal truth-claims to undermine the oppressive effects such claims can have when wielded by dominant groups, as well as to open up conversations among all kinds of voices. Perhaps no ideal is more lauded among postmodernists than the vision of authentic, uncoerced conversation—and eventually cooperation—among all social, cultural, racial, and gender groups.[16] Much of postmodernism's considerable rhetorical force emerges in protests that modernism has denied this or that group its freedom and/or its voice.

The ideal of open conversation, however, along with corresponding critiques of its absence, implies that some universal rights and values belong to all. It presupposes that every person's voice and experience is valuable and that every person has the right to be respected and heard in free, uncoerced dialogue. The assumption that such rights and dignity belong universally to every person is a necessary, even if unrecognized, condition of the possibility of such conversations—and also of criticisms of the oppressive function that universal affirmations might have in such conversations.

Yet though profound notions of universal equality underlie this valorization of conversation, their exact meaning and significance can emerge only as such interchanges occur. For instance, in such conversations it is not often evident what speaking privileges should be exercised by formerly marginalized voices. Should they speak far more often than traditionally dominant voices? A little more often? Or no more often? Should such conversations include those who resist some notions of equality (for instance, are men allowed to speak who, on principle, deny equal time to women?) Only as such dialogues proceed will the precise nature of the equality that they presuppose become clearer. Nonetheless, if some universal rights and values are not tacitly embraced beforehand—even if mostly as goals to be actualized, as obscure yet powerful hopes for what someday might attain partial realization—such conversations can never begin.

Third, notice another feature of authentic conversation. My views might differ greatly from yours on many subjects. And part of the richness of any interchange between us will emerge from our expressions of this diversity. Yet if we wish truly to communicate, to genuinely interact rather than simply talk at each other, we must both be willing to let our views be revised or critiqued. I must implicitly acknowledge that as you express your beliefs, you might present reasons that accord with truth-criteria that I could accept and obligate me to alter my views. And you must tacitly acknowledge that I might sometime appeal, even if only quite indirectly, to truth-criteria that could cause you to change yours. In fact, if our discussion is to keep going, we must each be searching, even if without recognizing it, for some standards of truth on which we could concur and in light of which we could arrive at compatible conclusions.

Now let this dialogue widen to conversation among many diverse partners—to the kind valorized by many postmodernists. Again, much of its richness will consist in the differences expressed, some of which may seem incompatible. Still, if genuine interaction is to occur, these heterogeneous participants must also be searching, at least implicitly, for broad truth-criteria in terms of which they might come to agreement. Each must be committed to revising views in light of such criteria. Conversation will likely continue only if some such can be found.

Let us suppose this conversation keeps expanding to include more and more kinds of people. As long as they are seeking better understanding, they will keep searching, even if half-consciously, for broader and broader truth-criteria acceptable to all, and they will be committed to altering their perspectives in accordance with these. Ultimately, sincere partners will be willing to accept truths and truth-criteria acceptable to all persons, if such can be found.[17]

My basic point is that for conversations often recommended by postmodernists to succeed, participants, along with their differences and disagreements, must also presuppose that broader and broader criteria for agreement at least might exist. They must be searching for such criteria, even if quite indirectly, and occasionally coming to wider agreements in light of them. In other words, participants must be moving, to some extent, toward universally agreed-on truths. Some movement towards universal truth, then, is a condition of the possibility of postmodern kinds of conversation taking place.

I have outlined three ways in which opponents of universal affirmations themselves often presuppose their reality, even if unknowingly.[18] In none of these, however, are universal truths clear foundations on which assertions or agreements can be built. In this respect, I generally concur with the antifoundationalist perspective of most narrative and postliberal theologians. Most such theologians affirm, as I do, that their main claims are to be understood as universal.[19] Some, however, like Stanley Hauerwas, give little indication, so far as I can see, of how universal statements might be possible and what they might mean. By neglecting this while championing antifoundationalism, it seems to me they leave their own affirmations quite vulnerable to postmodern critiques.[20] It is to help avoid this that I am essaying some positive account of universals.

In my account, universality, rather than providing foundations, is something toward which thought, perhaps often despite itself, aims: a goal it perhaps unknowingly seeks. In theological language, this universal truth is eschatological. It is a reality humans "already" apprehend dimly and on the basis of which they function. Yet complete awareness of universality can only be striven toward, for it has "not yet" fully appeared. The significance of this will emerge as address the third objection to universal truths.

OPPRESSIVE FUNCTION

Universal affirmations have been used to disguise the interests of dominant powers and to oppress Anabaptists and other disadvantaged groups. But Jesus showed special concern for the oppressed. If Anabaptist theologians seek to articulate universal truths, then, will they not be supporting what Jesus opposed?

First, let us consider the affirmation, "Jesus Christ is Lord." Many postmodernists regard this an instrument forged by alleged Christians to impose their interests on others. Of course the affirmation can function this way. But let us ask how this acclamation operates in the universal story at Anabaptism's roots. This narrative climaxes (at least penultimately) in Jesus' life, death, and resurrection. Anabaptism has made this narrative more central for interpreting the faith than have most other communions.

Now what does "Jesus Christ is Lord" mean when the person known through this narrative determines its meaning? This is expressed in Philippians 2, which celebrates Jesus' lordship in exalted terms: "at the name of Jesus every knee shall bend, in heaven and on earth and under the earth, and every tongue confess that 'Jesus Christ is Lord!'" (2:10-11, NRSV). Yet this same person "emptied himself, taking the form of a slave, being born in human likeness. And being found in human form, he humbled himself and became obedient to the point of death—even death on a cross" (7-8).

Here is a strange lordship. It does not dominate its subjects but gives itself totally and utterly for them. It does not manipulate its subjects for its own ends but expends itself to attain their ends. Consequently, true allegiance to this person's lordship can never be associated with allegiance to any unjust or oppressive force. Instead, precisely because it is universal—precisely because if Jesus is Lord, nobody else is—it sharply criticizes other claims to lordship. When rightly apprehended, it frees its adherents from idolatrous lords. I propose that all valid universal theological claims must be understood in light of this servant-lordship at the heart of biblical narrative. Then they will be liberating rather than oppressive.

Second, consider that in today's global village certain destructive forces operate worldwide. Environmental pollution and unrestrained consumer capitalism are examples. On one level, such forces may hurt different people in diverse ways. Unrestrained consumerism, for instance, makes some people poor but others surfeited and depressed. However, since these forces are globally destructive, damaging finally to all, it is quite likely that their deeper dynamisms—e.g., commodification—oppose things central to every human's well-being. It is likely, in other words, that these dynamisms always oppose certain universal human values, and therefore that at least some of their features are always—that is, universally—evil.

Further, since such forces operate globally, they will probably not be countered effectively unless they can be opposed globally. However, people from very different cultures will be unlikely to unite in this way unless they share, at least implicitly, some common convictions about the evil nature of these forces and the human values they oppose. And the more they agree on these things, the more effective will their opposition likely be.[21]

Sadly, however, postmodern emphasis on cultural particularity can tend to undermine today's need for global action. The negative global forces that seek to control us will be only too pleased if each culture and religious communion forgets the universal potential of its convictions and focuses narrowly on its own distinctiveness.[22]

It is true, of course, that universal affirmations often function oppressively today. Unbridled consumerism fabricates bogus universals such as "More possessions always bring greater happiness." But it is equally true that agreement on opposed universal values can do much to counteract them and can be liberating, much as can "Jesus Christ is Lord."

Finally, we should remember that universal truths are "eschatological": they function as overarching, somewhat obscure goals towards which we move rather than crystal-clear epistemological foundations on which we build. Any attempted statement of such truths expresses an intention to articulate something whose full reality lies beyond present grasp. When I affirm, for instance, that "Jesus Christ is Lord," I do not know fully what that means. I will come to understand it more completely only as I follow Jesus. Yet its full content—including, for instance, its significance vis-à-vis the many religions—will only become clear at the eschaton itself.

This means that enunciation of a universal—and no one can avoid enunciating some universals—should be accompanied by a humility that acknowledges, "I do not know all of what this means, but this is the best way I can manage to articulate it now." Expressed in such a manner, universal affirmations need not close off dialogue but can actually invite it. They can be authentic ways of putting one's real self and best thought forward, of saying, "Here is the clearest way I can say what really matters to me," instead of pretending over-politely to have no ultimate convictions.

At the same time, this can be an authentic way of asking, "Now what do you think of it? Let me hear your perspective, and let us explore the implications of all this together." Expressed in such a way, universal affirmations will be far from oppressive. Instead they can lead dialogue partners toward better and broader understanding, often toward practical cooperation, and toward life-giving apprehension of ultimate truth.

Notes

1. See the discussions in William Placher, *Unapologetic Theology* (Louisville: Westminster/John Knox, 1989), 24-38; and Nancey Murphy, *Beyond Liberalism and Fundamentalism* (Valley Forge, Pa.: Trinity, 1996), 90-95.

2. See, e.g., Stanley Hauerwas, *The Peaceable Kingdom* (Notre Dame, Ind. : Notre Dame, 1983).

3. A major thesis of Franklin Littell's classic, *The Origins Of Sectarian Protestantism* (New York: Macmillan, 1964), esp. 109-137.

4. Fidelity to origins differs from the general conservative tendency to value the past in order to preserve what is traditional, for fidelity to origins elicits radical challenges to many traditions. One can seek to retrieve an origin in order to unleash a transforming potential that will overturn stagnating and oppressive traditions that arose after it.

5. Gordon Kaufman, *An Essay On Theological Method* (Chico, Calif.: Scholar's Press, 1975), 1-18.

6. Gordon Kaufman, *In Face Of Mystery* (Cambridge, Mass.: Harvard University Press, 1993), 265, cf. 322-340.

7. Daniel Liechty, "The Seamless Robe of Human Experience: an Essay on (Mennonite) Theological Method," in *Mennonite Theology In Face Of Modernity: Essays In Honor Of Gordon D. Kaufman*, ed. Alain Epp Weaver (North Newton, Kans.: Bethel College), 83, 84. Since all language is a "human artifact," theology is grounded "in human history and human experience" (ibid., 80, 81), and "all values are human creations"; see Daniel Liechty, *Theology In Postliberal Perspective* (Philadelphia: Trinity,

1990), 5.

8. Liechty, *Theology In Postliberal Perspective*, 33.

9. Liechty, "The Seamless Robe of Human Experience," 88.

10. Ibid., 90.

11. Ted Grimsrud, "Mennonite Theology and Historical Consciousness: A Pastoral Perspective," in *Mennonite Theology*, ed. Epp-Weaver, 150.

12. Ibid., 152.

13. Ibid., 151.

14. Ibid., 154. The reality which Jesus and Paul tapped into "is also fully accessible to us when we listen first to God via our own hearts . . ." (ibid., 155). Grimsrud says that he is not necessarily advocating, but simply describing, a "neo-Mennonite" orientation (ibid., 138). Yet because the outlook he sketches is recognizable and important, it seems useful to refer to it by some name; and because he does not differentiate it from his own, it seems appropriate to link it with his. Grimsrud regards this perspective as "legitimate" because it exists in some Mennonite churches (ibid., 138).

15. Ibid., 137.

16. See Placher, *Unapologetic Theology*, 105-122; Richard Bernstein, *Beyond Objectivism and Relativism* (Philadelphia: University of Pennsylvania, 1988), 171-231; Kaufman, *In Face Of Mystery*, 64-69.

17. This general kind of argument can be found in Jurgen Habermas: see Bernstein, *Beyond Objectivism And Relativism*, 182-197, and Stephen White, *The Recent Work Of Jürgen Habermas* (New York: Cambridge, 1988), 22-24, 48-65. See also my "Relativity, Normativity and Imagination: A Dialogue with Gordon Kaufman," in *Mennonite Theology*, ed. Alain Epp Weaver, esp. 212-219.

18. Precisely speaking, I have noted two ways universality is actually presupposed: in attempts to deny it and in ethical values that underlie open conversation. I have sketched a third activity in which at least the possibility of truth must be presupposed: the search for agreements and truth-criteria which keep such conversations alive.

19. See, e.g., Hauerwas, *The Peaceable Kingdom*, 35: "Christian ethics . . . claims truthfulness and therefore a certain universality. . . ." Its "affirmations are true and objective" in that they give us skills "to see and act in the world, not as we want it to be, but as it is. . . ."

20. Placher, however, attempts to provide some definition and defense of universal affirmations in theology *(Unapologetic Theology*, 123-135).

21. In line with Anabaptist tradition, I find that the most effective approach to social issues usually begins at local levels. However, this cannot be done wisely today without awareness of wider, often global, dimensions and interconnections of many local issues. Moreover, effective local action often merges eventually into regional, national, and global activities. In short, I am affirming that at least some significant worldwide action is necessary to combat negative global forces. See my *Self, Earth And Society* (Downers Grove, Ill. : InterVarsity Press, 1997), Chapter 10.

22. The fragmenting tendencies of much postmodernism are sensitively appraised by Michael King in "Angels, Atheists, and Common Ground: Toward a Separatist and Worldly Postmodern Anabaptism," *Conrad Grebel Review* 15 (Fall 1997), 251-268.

PART TWO

ANABAPTIST STORYTELLING AND HISTORICAL MEMORY

FOUR

VALUING THE STORY OF POWER AND TELLING A GRANDER ONE:
Anabaptism and Power Postmodernism in Mutually Enlarging Conversation

Michael A. King

Many stories are told in postmodernist[1] studies; indeed, telling many stories and not one universal narrative is a postmodernist aim. But one metanarrative does underlie many postmodernist stories. That narrative is that *Power is the Grand Story* and all other stories are the little tales, the *petit recits* (as Lyotard might put it)[2] that power tells. I want to suggest that for Anabaptists this story is both fountain of insight and potential idol.

First, more details. According to this tale, to recognize the power of power to shape what we take to be true or real is to recognize we can never gain access to essential principles, unifying structures, master narratives that let us fully grasp what is "really there." Our knowledge is an effect of power and in turn passes power forward to produce new meanings.

Increasingly, Anabaptists too are telling some such story, and there is insight to be gained. For one thing, this story makes sense of our experience as Anabaptists. Beginning in the 1500s with our break not only from the Roman Catholic Church but also the mainstream Reformers, we Anabaptists, the radical reformers, have nurtured a minority perspective. We have opposed that Constantinian conflation of church, culture, and state which came to be called Christendom and helped breed[3] the totalizing Enlightenment philosophies postmodernism is rejecting. If Anabaptist thought has typically not been philosophical, nevertheless bred deep into our bones has been suspicion that Christendom and the Enlightenment are products not of divine but human dynamics—or power.

THE ANABAPTIST TALE OF POWER

Only more recently, however, have we begun to tell our own story as one with power at the center. Let me point to recent examples. Articles in the April 1998 *Mennonite Quarterly Review*[4] tell Anabaptist-Mennonite power tales. In their analysis of "Mennonites and Conflict,"[5] for instance, the concerns of Stephen Ainlay and Fred Kniss intersect with those of postmodernism as they quote Sue Curry Jansen, who says that

> The powerful do not just have the first and last say. They do not just control access to the podium, presidium, or press room. They also determine the rules of evidence, shape the logic of assertion, define the architecture of arguments. The powerful are not just talkers. They are makers and shakers who draw the lines of language and life which others dare not cross.[6]

"Power-knowledge" is the name Jansen gives such power effects. Although Ainlay and Kniss don't highlight this, power-knowledge is a term invented by French poststructuralist Michel Foucault, and as we will later see, identifying this Foucauldian influence is important. But to bracket Foucault for now, there is in Jansen's description an intertwining of coercive power—the power to make others do what you want them to—with the power to define what will or won't be considered valid knowledge or even reality itself. For Ainlay and Kniss the Mennonite story includes both forms of power, as is evident whenever Mennonites in conflict "struggle for this ability to set the boundaries, to draw the lines. . . ."[7]

Responding to their work, David L. Zercher[8] also tells a story of Mennonite power while underscoring aspects of economic power less evident in the Ainlay and Kniss focus on power as ideology. During the 1970s Mennonite writer Ken Reed submitted to Herald Press, denominational publisher of the Mennonite Church, the novel *Amish Soldier*. Herald Press agreed to publish, but then the trouble began. The Amish made clear their opposition to publication of a book they felt gave them a black eye.

Zercher tracks what happened next at several levels. He shows that the initial Herald Press response and a continuing tendency was to portray the issues as other than economic agenda. "Herald Press officials," as Zercher puts it, "defended the novel as an appropriate portrait of the human struggle and the need for God's grace."⁹

Zercher contends, however, that economics were what drove events. First the economic price to be paid if Herald Press published despite Amish opposition led to restructuring and release of the novel as *Mennonite Soldier*. When even this version generated controversy among readers, Herald Press decided it must retreat from its earlier defense of "realistic" fiction. The reason, Zercher contends, "was a determination by Herald Press that, from an economic standpoint, it could only publish what its traditional customer base would tolerate and buy."¹⁰

Herald Press officials are among those "movers and shakers" Jansen describes as drawing "the lines of language and life" which help determine even what we shall consider knowledge. Zercher's sobering finding is that whatever the rhetoric, finances are likely to shape how such power is used.

As one who was for eight years a Herald Press book editor, I affirm Zercher's insight. Indeed I was downsized from Herald Press because publishing decisions to which I contributed generated insufficient revenue. Before I left I participated in decisions according to which Herald Press would not knowingly publish money-losing books. So I contributed to dollar-related drawings of lines around which knowledges Herald Press would validate by publishing and which weaken by rejection. Zercher helps us face how thoroughly publishing economics and theology intertwine. He invites us to evaluate consequences and possible responses. Are there different ways, for example, to structure publishing finances to enable new voices to speak?

As she studies "contest and compromise" in Mennonite weddings,¹¹ Pamela Klassen explores how the story of power unfolds not only through words but also through embodied "ritual and practice." Klassen notes that

> Though Ainlay and Kniss read Foucault as a theorist who understands power in terms of ideas, I interpret him as having a much stronger analysis of the effect of "micropowers" of everyday life on our social bodies: for example, on the ways we relate to authority, family and sexuality.¹²

Through this Foucault-inspired focus on "micropowers" of practice, Klassen highlights the extent to which even such a seemingly benign ritual as a wedding is a "site" in which people conduct "negotiations of power rooted in tradition and change." She notes that the conflict "stirred up" by the three weddings studied "was largely, if not overtly, centered on these women's bodies: how they chose to dress them, carry them and love them."[13] If Zercher asks my publishing self to confront the economic dimensions of the power of publishing, Klassen invites the pastor I also am to examine how power helps construct and is constructed by the rituals of the church I and you help shape.

Gerald Biesecker-Mast brings to his study of "Mennonite Public Discourse and the Conflicts Over Homosexuality"[14] analytic tools indebted to Ernesto Laclau and Chantal Mouffe. "Writing out of the tradition of Marxist political philosophy and following the lead of such revisionists as Althusser, Gramsci and Foucault," he explains,

> Laclau and Mouffe have sought . . . to give more attention to the ways in which human actions are shaped by ideology. In so doing, they have provided scholars with critical tools for describing the social origins and effects of human communication practices.[15]

Using these tools, Biesecker-Mast proposes that one reason such social conflicts as those over homosexuality are so intense is that they form our deepest subjectivities and identities. The conflicts "are not merely about rules and norms but are also battles over the very shape of the social identity."[16] Our deepest sense of who we are, what world we live in, what matters, what's right and wrong, is not so much grounded in objective data to be discovered as in subjectivities and identities shaped in us through interaction and sometimes conflict with each other.

Such insight, Biesecker-Mast concludes, frees combatants in church wars to treat each other as enemies, yes, but enemies to be loved in recognition that whether in war or peace we together make each other who we are. Then we can trust that our "rhetorical struggle carries toward an indefinite future the faith and trust in Christ alone that can provide spiritual unity."[17] As one whose dissertation focus[18] was on the Franconia Mennonite Conference decision to excommunicate Germantown Mennonite Church over homosexuality, I agree that the church needs Biesecker-Mast's hope "in the possibility of miracles that transcend ongoing mutual antagonisms."[19]

A final example of telling the Anabaptist story in terms of power is provided by J. Denny Weaver's analysis[20] of the Anabaptist history of C. Arnold Snyder. Weaver does not claim to offer a thoroughly postmodern assessment of Snyder but does indicate influence by postmodernity, by which he means "a view which recognizes the particular character and social location of every theology rather than assuming there is a universally agreed general or foundational theology. That is, every theology has a genesis in, and reflects, a particular social location."[21]

Weaver then aims to show that Snyder's version[22] of Anabaptism is constructed from a particular location, that of "the so-called 'mainstream' theology generally accepted as orthodox in the western theological tradition."[23] If Snyder had written from Weaver's preferred location, which Weaver describes as "the perspective which makes the story of Jesus Christ genuinely the foundation of truth,"[24] Snyder would have woven historical facts into a different narrative. This preferred story would not have risked accommodating violence as an aspect of Anabaptist history, which by extension may also make it more an option for contemporary Anabaptists.

Weaver's analysis reminds us that "All of us are shaped by our history."[25] It reminds us that whenever we tell the story of whatever we have studied, we are telling not only the explicit story unfolding on the surface of our commentary but also the subtextual tale of our own lives, values, and social locations. As Frederick Buechner similarly reminds us, not only most history but also "most theology . . . is essentially autobiography."[26] And all autobiography is in turn shaped by its social location.

FOUCAULT'S TALE OF POWER

So I do believe that those who tell the Anabaptist story as a tale of power have much to teach. But I also see cause for concern, a conclusion I began to formulate a few years ago when, as a thought experiment, I wrote a paper on "Applying Michel Foucault's Thought to Rhetorical Practice."[27] The rhetoric I had in mind, as the preacher I was and remain, was homiletics. I proposed to examine what happened to preaching if one aimed to make it Foucauldian. I wanted to do this because I was convinced any preacher or thinker in an era as influenced by postmodernism as ours is must understand its attraction and contributions.

And I chose Foucault because he provides a major doorway into postmodernism. Although he died in 1984 and wrote primarily before postmodernism came into full view, his agenda still crucially shapes postmodernist thought and more. To emphasize Foucault's importance, philosopher and Foucault scholar C. G. Prado (1995) quotes James Miller's comment that "At the time of his death . . . Foucault was perhaps the single most famous intellectual in the world," Allan Ryan's similar assertion that "he was the most famous intellectual figure in the world," and Jonathan Arac's judgment that "Foucault's work . . . changed the basis for the work of all scholars."[28] Whether or not such judgments are extravagant, even Mennonites, as shown by references to Foucault scattered through the examples I have cited, are listening to him.

So as one more Mennonite taking Foucault seriously, I asked how he might shape preaching. The exercise taught me much. Foucault teaches me and all of us that when we think we have autonomous, unified selves through which to understand our world and control our destinies, we delude ourselves. I heard in this teaching an echo of Jesus: if we cling to such self-sufficient selves as the West tells us we own, we lose our lives, but if we relinquish the illusion of having knowledge sufficient to master the world, we gain the vastly larger world that appears when our egos stop filtering it.

Foucault helped me grasp the power of what Frederick Buechner says about these matters. Sharing in *The Alphabet of Grace* a stream-of-consciousness account of what throughout one day in his life he learns about God's grace, Buechner describes, for instance, a sleeping self very like the one Foucault envisions: "Beneath the moonlit drifts of sheet, I turn in my sleep and draw up my knees except that there is no *I* at this moment but just my knees which draw up themselves by some complex autonomy of bones, tendons, muscles...."29 By drawing me toward such imagery Foucault showed me how to think and preach a kind of negative theology stressing how much of our Enlightened selves must be scooped out to form the tidal pools in which God's grace can eddy.

Next in my thought experiment I aimed to preach a Foucauldian Bible. Foucault taught me that the Bible is itself an effect of power. I imagined him explaining that it had arisen as Middle East factions and nations rose and ebbed over the centuries. If this tribe had been just a hair more articulate or that one less weakened by plague, alternate voices would have shaped the biblical tale and given us a different book entirely. I saw that as the various councils met to decide which books to canonize, they were swayed by their own variants of ideologies feeding Mennonite conflicts or economic powers shaping Herald Press decisions regarding which books to canonize as appropriately Mennonite.

I take such lessons seriously; there seems little in the biblical record to suggest people then were less likely than now to squabble over where to draw the lines—even before they fully enter consciousness—dividing knowledge from heresy, normalcy from deviance, truth from falsehood. But when I imagined *preaching* this Foucault, there was no "there there." This Foucault "didn't preach." This Foucault taught me how to see effects of power but not how to spy the Holy Spirit who might be working as well amid the murk and the muck.

To show why I worry that any of us who travel too far with Foucault will be left with what will not preach, let me scrutinize just what Foucault has to say about power. Power for Foucault is not primarily material, economic, or coercive. Power does run through and sustain sites of overt coercion but is more than them. This is because power for Foucault creates and supports and makes possible knowledge itself. Our very ability to see this and not that, and to see it *this* way, is an effect of power.

As Foucault puts it, "power is everywhere; not because it embraces everything, but because it comes from everywhere."[30] Power, I am tempted to say in a twisted paraphrase of the apostle Paul, is that in which we live and move and have our being. It undergirds who we are, predetermines how we think, establishes what knowledges can be known, puts its own meanings into otherwise empty words, inaugurates the connection of this to that to create seeming unities which are actually "an unstable assemblage of faults, fissures, and heterogeneous layers."[31]

Although Foucault's handling of power evolved, particularly those power analyses he called "genealogical"[32] have influenced postmodernism. Following Nietzsche, Foucault urges a turn away from that history "in the traditional sense" which thinks it can find objectivity.[33] He calls for a turn toward genealogy, which "seeks to reestablish the various systems of subjection: not the anticipatory power of meaning, but the hazardous play of dominations."[34] Genealogy searches not for what is real/true but rather "disturbs what was previously considered immobile; it fragments what was thought unified; it shows the heterogeneity of what was imagined consistent with itself."[35]

How deluded! Foucault exclaims of those who think they spy the real and true. Far from constructing, brick by brick, an ever more accurate and universal edifice of knowledge, "humanity installs each of its violences in a system of rules and thus proceeds from domination to domination."[36] Foucault is referring here to those rules of language he has previously theorized[37] as enabling "discursive formations," or the patterns of language controlled by power which permit meaning to exist.

Meaning emerges not from the world but is produced by language and the structures of power-knowledge in which it is embedded and which it sustains. Genealogy shows that the history of knowledge is the history of the seizure of discursive formations, and thus of meaning itself, by one domination after another. So power ultimately produces and controls meaning. To interpret, then, is not to uncover the real or true but to unveil "the violent or surreptitious appropriation of a system of rules, which in itself has no essential meaning...."[38] Genealogy sees that the connection of knowledge to truth in any "true" sense is "undone once truth becomes merely an effect—the effect of a falsification we call the opposition of truth and falsehood."[39]

Let me underscore what is at stake here. Foucault is saying that whatever we consider real, true, meaningful is the effect of power. Even the distinction between truth and falsehood is such an effect. If power had driven history in a different direction, we would detect no meaning in defining this as true or that as false.

Maybe with this Foucault in view it is evident why Anabaptists may want to travel only halfway with him. Foucault is telling us names like "God," "Anabaptist," "church," "love," mean something to us, matter to us, because we are located here, not there, because once upon many times power took our story this way, not that. There *is* insight here—but is this the only story we want to tell?

GADAMER'S DIFFERENT TALE

If not, there are more paths taking us beyond Foucault than I can explore, but let me survey two. One path takes us back, back behind Foucault, behind postmodernism, to affirmation of truths and knowledges not constructed by power. I respect those who walk this path; I value, for instance, the stance of Caleb Miller, who, in his own call for Mennonites to "be wary of postmodernism,"[40] affirms that "the true and the real are what they are independently of our cognitive efforts. . . ."[41] Yet even as I suspect Miller has this right, I have less faith that in our *knowing* of the true and real we escape history's effects.

This sends me on the other path, which is to affirm with Foucault and others that power shapes our knowing but then to ask what happens when this same insight is turned on itself. Here the contradictory, paradoxical nature[42] of this approach emerges. What happens to the Grand Story of Power *if it is itself* an effect of power? Does a power analysis of power at least partly devour power? If we ask of Foucault and postmodernists and power-analyzing Mennonites what power has made the tale of power meaningful to them, do we glimpse the possibility that this focus too is arbitrary and could be replaced by another?

These are larger questions than I can fully answer, but they at least fallibly take me where I want to go. They suggest that it is possible to be postmodernist while taking a different path.[43] Here I am thinking of the trail blazed by Hans-Georg Gadamer, my dissertation mentor, whose approach to interpreting texts and even life itself is called "philosophical hermeneutics."

Like Foucault, Gadamer has played his own central role in shaping contemporary thought. As Hugh Silverman notes, "Gadamer's hermeneutics has permeated not only philosophy, literary study, and theology, but also legal studies, sociology, intellectual history, art history, and cultural studies."[44] Like Foucault, Gadamer spies no doorway above history for entering a room full of objective truth.

Then Gadamer turns unlike Foucault. This is evident in their contrasting views of language. Here is Foucault: "We must conceive discourse as a violence we do to things, or, at all events, as a practice we impose on them. . . ."[45] Then Gadamer. Rather than a violence we do to the world, language is what makes the world available to us: "the object of knowledge and statements is always already enclosed in the world horizon of language."[46] Language is not a violence we impose on the world but our doorway into it. Complexities of linguistic theory must be bracketed here, but apparent even in this brief introduction to Gadamer is concern to move beyond alienation between the world and what we can know of it.

Now Gadamer gives us no simplistic "real" world, because what we can know is made available to us by what he calls "effective history."[47] This effective history points toward the crucial role the past plays by "effecting" or shaping the biases I bring to any attempt to understand even before I begin consciously to think. But whereas Foucault speaks of meaning structures which are empty until power fills them, Gadamer talks of meaning that makes itself known to us in the same way as what is beautiful does. When we seek to understand something, "what is meaningful" in it, says Gadamer, "captivates us just as the beautiful captivates us. It has asserted itself and captivated us before we can come to ourselves and be in a position to test the claim to meaning that it makes."[48] "The idea," he explains, "is always that what is evident has not been proved and is not absolutely certain, but it asserts itself by reason of its own merit in the realm of the possible and the probable."[49]

In contrast to Foucault, Gadamer is teaching that effective history has itself been shaped by and in turn passes on to us something not so different from what Miller calls "the true and the real." Gadamer contends that in human communities whose members are open to those truths that present themselves as compellingly as the beautiful does, there can be spied a "sensus communis." By this he means those time-honored wisdoms tested by and lived out in community.[50]

So to follow a Gadamerian path into postmodernism is to agree with Foucault that no objective perspective above history is available. It is also to replace Foucault's belief in the falsity of the distinction between true and false with faith that history passes on truths that matter, that mean.

This will preach. There is a "there" here. Now the Bible, for instance, can be seen as the record of the *sensus communis* of folk who trusted the truths history made evident to them. Referring to the attitude with which we must approach whatever we seek truly to understand, Gadamer makes the memorable comment, surely in awareness of echoing Jesus, that "One must lose oneself to find oneself."[51] From here it seems no great stretch to see Gadamer as teaching a Bible that passes on the lessons of those who have sought to lose themselves, invites us to do likewise, and even points toward the divine power who sets history and its beauties and truths in motion in the first place.

Now, my conviction that Christians and Anabaptists can travel farther into a postmodernism shaped by Gadamer than by Foucault does not mean insights indebted to Foucault are to be dismissed.[52] The harshest criticisms of Gadamer[53] are that he buys his warmer wisdoms at the expense of ignoring the colder realities of power Foucault so emphasizes. My point is not that Anabaptists who want to engage postmodernist trends should stop attending to Foucault but that we should do so critically, aware of where Foucault may take us, and ready to attend to such a different voice as Gadamer's.

Let me briefly sketch what resources Gadamer might offer Anabaptists through one more quick look at examples earlier cited. Take Ainlay and Kniss. Among "interesting questions" they think should be pursued in studying Mennonites and conflict are these:

> Who . . . were the power elite and what systems of power-knowledge dominated Mennonite life during these periods? Who were the "opposition parties?" What determined who won? What interests did the various parties pursue? What were the consequences for the losers?[54]

These are valuable questions; I look forward to hearing answers as Mennonites confront their own embedding in power-knowledge.

Note how thoroughly, however, power-knowledge guides the questioning. In addition I would like to hear Anabaptists asking questions stimulated by Gadamer. Gadamer makes two memorable and pertinent moves. For one, he contends we can only begin to know through the grid of foreknowledges, prejudgments, prejudices, and biases effective history breeds in us. This is why he says that "Prejudices are biases of our openness to the world."[55] For another, he believes we can only grow in understanding and knowledge as we risk our initial prejudice in openness to the truth present as well in the prejudice of another.[56] If one imagines an initial prejudice as a spotlight illumining one small aspect of the world, then many prejudices joined together brighten a larger swath.

Imagine if we asked amid Mennonite conflicts not only power questions but also these: What are the prejudices in play? What truth does each spotlight? How might the holders of these prejudices, remembering that one must lose oneself to find oneself, risk them in quest of insight greater than either alone possesses?

Interestingly, Biesecker-Mast's questions are not far from these. He is asking how Mennonites might bring to bear on conflict "our radical, self-endangering love for the necessary enemy and thus our openness to the possibility of miracles that transcend ongoing communal antagonisms."[57] By reaching this Gadamer-like place on a different path, Biesecker-Mast shows there is more than one way to get here. But is it possible his arrival through Laclau and Mouffe, and behind them, Foucault, is more arbitrary than had he introduced Gadamer? Does he risk imposing on his theorists an outcome their thought does not support? In contrast, does Gadamer from the start teach love of enemies and "self-endangering love?"

Or take Weaver. Plainly he wants nothing to do, finally, with any such Foucauldian notion as that meaning arises from nothing "but the hazardous play of dominations." Rather, he wants to affirm "the perspective which makes the story of Jesus Christ genuinely the foundation of truth." Yet in starting from the Foucault-like conviction that all histories are interested, how does he preserve his history as better than Snyder's? Does he risk dying by the same sword he takes to Snyder's stance?[58]

It seems Weaver must make some choices. If he wants a realm in which one history is foundational, then he needs a philosophy of truth to support it. Foucault and Foucault-like postmodernisms lack that foundation. If he continues to prefer a world in which histories are interested, then Gadamer would permit him to justify his own history as his particular "bias of openness to the world." But Gadamer would also invite Weaver to ponder what Snyder's history has to teach, in faith that as Snyder and others whose emphasis differs from Weaver's joined the quest, the truths of Anabaptist history would ever more radiantly shine.

Finally Herald Press. Zercher's power analysis demonstrates how surely economic pressures form and deform publishing decisions. But Gadamer allows me the opening to testify as well to my conviction that I and others at Herald Press aimed also to open ourselves to books that merited publication because the truth they told deserved, like the beautiful, to shine forth across the church.

Power clouds and even helps produce this and all witnesses. But let the tale of power never become so fully our story that it allows us to tell of nothing else.

NOTES

1. No claim is made here to address all the complex nuances of postmodernism(s). I have done more of that in "Angels, Atheists, and Common Ground: Toward a Separatist and Worldly Postmodern Anabaptism," *Conrad Grebel Review* 15 (Fall 1997), 251-268. But even as I have attempted to respect postmodern complexity there and elsewhere, I have found myself agreeing with the thrust of these questions by J. Lawrence Burkholder: "But what is postmodernity? Does anyone know? Can anyone know?" See "Postmodern Dialectics," *Mennonite Quarterly Review* 72, no. 2 (April 1998), 322. However such questions are finally answered, here I largely bracket them to make relatively general—and hence perhaps more modern than postmodern—statements about how postmodernism intersects with power analysis, especially as inspired by Foucault.

2. Jean-Francois Lyotard, *The Postmodern Condition: A Report on Knowledge*, trans. Geoffrey Bennington and Brian Massumi (Minneapolis: University of Minnesota Press, 1984).

3. As shown by Charles Taylor, *Sources of the Self: The Making of Modern Identity* (Cambridge, Mass.: Harvard University Press, 1989)

4. Vol. 72, no. 2.

5. Stephen Ainlay and Fred Kniss, "Mennonites and Conflict: Re-Examining Mennonite History and Contemporary Life," *Mennonite Quarterly Review* 72, no. 2 (April 1998), 121-140.

6. Sue Curry Jansen, *Censorship: the Knot that Binds Power and Knowledge* (New York: Oxford University Press, 1991), 7; cited in Ainlay and Kniss, 128.

7. Ibid.

8. David L. Zercher, "A Novel Conversion: The Fleeting Life of *Amish Soldier*," *Mennonite Quarterly Review* 72, no. 2 (April 1998), 141-160.

9. Ibid., 156.

10. Ibid., 158.

11. Pamela E. Klassen, "Practicing Conflict: Weddings as Sites of Contest and Compromise," *Mennonite Quarterly Review* 72, no. 2 (April 1998), 225-241.

12. Ibid., 239.

13. Ibid., 238-239.

14. Gerald J. Biesecker-Mast, "Mennonite Public Discourse and the Conflicts over Homosexuality," *Mennonite Quarterly Review* 72, no. 2 (April 1998), 275-300.

15. Ibid., 280.

16. Ibid., 283.

17. Ibid., 299.

18. Michael A. King, "Fractured Dance: Steps and Missteps in Conversation and in Application of Gadamer to a Mennonite Debate on Homosexuality" (Ph.D. diss., Temple University, 1998).

19. Biesecker-Mast, "Mennonite Public Discourse and the Conflicts over Homosexuality," 299.

20. J. Denny Weaver, "Reading Sixteenth-Century Anabaptism Theologically: Implications for Modern Mennonites as a Peace Church," *Conrad Grebel Review* 16 (Winter 1998), 37-51.

21. Ibid., 38.

22. C. Arnold Snyder, *Anabaptist History and Theology: An Introduction* (Kitchener, Ont.: Pandora Press, 1995).

23. Weaver, 44.

24. Ibid., 51.

25. Ibid.

26. Frederick Buechner, *The Alphabet of Grace* (New York: The Seabury Press, Crossroad Books), 7.

27. "Guidelines for the Parrhesiast: Applying Michel Foucault's Thought to Rhetorical Practice" (unpublished paper, Temple University, 1995).

28. C. G. Prado, *Starting with Foucault: An Introduction to Genealogy* (Boulder, Colo.: Westview Press, 1995), 1, citing James Miller, *The Passion of Michel Foucault* (New York: Doubleday, Anchor Books, 1993), 13; Allan Ryan, "Foucault's Life and Hard Times," *New York Review of Books* 40 (1993), 12; Jonathan Arac, ed., *After Foucault* (New Brunswick, N.J.: Harvard University Press, 1991), vii.

29. Ibid., 21.

30. Michel Foucault, *The History of Sexuality, Volume 1: An Introduction*, trans. Robert Hurley (New York: Random House, Vintage Books, 1977), 93.

31. Michel Foucault, "Nietzsche, Genealogy, History," in *Language, Countermemory, Practice: Selected Essays and Interviews*, ed. Donald F. Bouchard (Ithaca, N.Y.: Cornell University Press), 146.

32. Ibid.

33. As Foucault puts it, traditional history "finds its support outside of time and pretends to base its judgments on an apocalyptic objectivity (ibid., 152). This is only possible, however, because of its belief in eternal truth, the immortality of the soul, and the nature of consciousness as always identical to itself" (152).

34. Ibid.,148.

35. Ibid., 147.

36. Ibid., 151.

37. During his "archaeological" period; see Michel Foucault, *The Archaeology of Knowledge, and the Discourse on Language*, trans. A. M. Sheridan Smith (New York: Pantheon Books, 1972); Michel Foucault, *The Order of Things: An Archaeology of the Human Sciences* (New York: Random House, Vintage Books, 1994); Barry Smart, *Michel Foucault* (London: Routledge, 1988), 39.

38. Foucault, "Nietszche, Genealogy, History," 151-152.

39. Michel Foucault, "History of Systems of Thought," in *Language, Counter-*

memory, Practice, ed. Donald F. Bouchard, 203.

40. Caleb Miller, "Why Mennonites Should be Wary of Postmodernism," *Mennonite Quarterly Review* 72 (April 1997), 326.

41. Ibid., 327.

42. See, for instance, Jürgen Habermas, "The Genealogical Writing of History: On Some Aporias in Foucault's Theory of Power," *Canadian Journal of Political and Social Theory* 10 (1986): 1-9. Habermas argues that "The attempt to spare genealogical history a relativistic self-denial with its own means fails" (p. 5) and that Foucault's theory "must, if it is valid, destroy the foundation of validity of the research which it inspires" (p. 3). Thus Foucault's challenge is to allow a discursive space for a Foucault, and this Habermas believes he fails to do. See also similar criticism in Steven Best and Douglas Kellner, *Postmodern Theory: Critical Interrogations* (New York: The Guilford Press, 1991), 171. Likewise, Thomas N. Finger, in "'Universal Truths': Should Anabaptist Theologians Seek to Articulate Them?" chapter three of this volume, sees postmodernism as often caught in self-refutation. The discussion continues, however: see Peter Blum's alternate perspective on Nietzsche and Foucault in "Foucault, Genealogy, Anabaptism: Confessions Of An Errant Postmodernist," chapter two of this volume, which leads him to say that "I take for granted here that neither of them may be dismissed as making simplistically self-refuting claims."

43. I hope I am here taking on some small aspects of J. Lawrence Burkholder's important challenges to Mennonites who value postmodernism. "If Mennonites want to consider postmodernity as a perspective for their self-understanding they had better," he contends, "focus the discussion at the level of philosophical presuppositions." Otherwise, he implies, they risk adopting "the most radical forms of deconstruction," which, he argues, and I am in this paper attempting to show, "arguably lead to intellectual suicide" (Burkholder, "Postmodern Dialectics," 323).

44. Hugh J. Silverman, ed., "Introduction," in *Gadamer and Hermeneutics* (New York: Routledge, 1991), 2-3.

45. Foucault, *The Archaeology of Knowledge, and the Discourse on Language,* 229.

46. Hans-Georg Gadamer, *Truth and Method,* 2d rev. ed., trans. Joel Weinsheimer and Donald G. Marshall (New York: Continuum, 1994), 450.

47. See, for instance, *Truth and Method,* 301-302.

48. Ibid., 490.

49. Ibid., 485.

50. See ibid., 19-29, 485.

51. "Reply to Jacques Derrida," in *Dialogue and Deconstruction: The Gadamer-Derrida Encounter,* ed. Diane P. Michelfelder and Richard E. Palmer (Albany, N.Y.: State University of New York Press, 1989), 57.

52. Nor do I dismiss them in my own scholarship; this is why in "Angels, Atheists, and Common Ground" I draw on Foucault more constructively than critically.

53. To name just a few of the many which could be cited, see, for instance, John D. Caputo, who pertinently says in *Radical Hermeneutics: Repetition, Deconstruction, and the Hermeneutic Project* (Bloomington, Ind.: Indiana University Press, 1987), 171, that Gadamer's "'tradition' is innocent of Nietzsche's suspicious eye, of Foucauldian gene-

alogy. He does not face the question of the ruptures within the tradition, its vulnerability to difference, its capacity to oppress"; Terry Eagleton, *Literary Theory: An Introduction* (Minneapolis: University of Minnesota Press, 1983), 73; Jurgen Habermas, *On the Logic of the Social Sciences*, trans. Shierry Weber Nicholson and Jerry A. Stark (Cambridge, Mass.: The MIT Press, 1988), 170; Robin Schott, "Whose Home Is It Anyway? A Feminist Response to Gadamer's Hermeneutics," in *Gadamer and Hermeneutics*, ed. Hugh J. Silverman, 202-212.

54. "Mennonites and Conflict," 138.

55. Hans-Georg Gadamer, *Philosophical Hermeneutics*, trans. and ed. David E. Linge (Berkeley: University of California Press, 1976), 9.

56. The need for risking is evident when Gadamer notes, in *Truth and Method*, 361, that "anyone who listens is fundamentally open. Without such openness to one another there is no genuinely human bond."

57. Biesecker-Mast, "Mennonite Public Discourse and the Conflicts over Homosexuality," 299.

58. Here Weaver seems vulnerable to the same self-contradiction, noted earlier, that Habermas as well as Best and Kellner think they spy in Foucault's tale of power. Again, however, Blum's alternate perspective (cited above) also deserves consideration in this regard.

CHAPTER FIVE

POSTMODERN PRACTICE AND PARODY:
Dallas Wiebe's *Our Asian Journey*

Paul Tiessen

Listen, you honey-suckers out there, historians would be all right if they'd leave the past alone.[1]

In Dallas Wiebe's major work to date, *Our Asian Journey*, the narrator's encounter with historian C. Henry Smith's Mennonite master narrative, *The Story of the Mennonites*, offers one of American Mennonites' most striking literary introductions to postmodern play. To be sure, this 1997 novel is an aesthetic extension of Wiebe's work: throughout the past four decades his writing has been informed by a postmodern aesthetic.

In this new work, as in his earlier work, Wiebe shows that the postmodern cannot be isolated from moral considerations bearing on our nature and our culture; throughout his career as an American prose stylist he has prophetically engaged the implications for the individual human spirit of a flaccid American society's easily exploited master narratives and mythologies.

But this, his major work, is also explicitly a Mennonite work, and it is in a Mennonite context that he this time reveals his double interest: postmodernism and the moral life. Here he not only presents but also interrogates postmodernism. He interrogates postmodernism's capacity to address issues of narration and power, institution and authority, spirituality and piety, in a specifically Mennonite universe, a society fairly unified by practice and performance, by word, narrative, myth. *Our Asian Journey* is Wiebe's testing ground for a specifically Mennonite postmodern theatrics.

As is typical of his approach throughout his career, Wiebe's performance in *Our Asian Journey* is by turns comedic, parodic, antic. It includes a multivocal mixture of generic ingredients, from an Old Testament-like high seriousness of prayer and sermon to audacious address made directly to the reader (whose relation with the novel is frequently disrupted, as shifts in genre occur from chapter to chapter, and, in the case of chapter two, within a single chapter). At the same time, the novel is filled with serious purpose: moral, political, spiritual, intellectual, cultural. Indeed, Wiebe has claimed that in postmodern humor we may very well expect to find a "moral view" of society, however bleak.[2]

In a discussion in *Mennonite Life* of Armin Wiebe's 1995 novel, *The Second Coming of Yeeat Shpanst*, and with reference specifically to Mennonite writing, Wiebe made these comments about postmodern fiction:

> Most so-called Mennonite fiction, whatever that means, is articulated in traditional forms. Most of it is what is generally called "Realistic," that is, it's the kind of fiction that came as a reaction to Romance in the middle of the nineteenth century and has remained as our dominant kind of fiction. . . . [The postmodern novel] will present difficulties to many readers. To some readers it will seem strange, obtuse, confusing, as will any fiction that is not just a retelling of what the reader already knows. . . . [I]t sets its own terms of narration. It doesn't give you a narration that is simple, familiar, superficial, uplifting and sentimental. That's what you expect in most Realistic fiction. But most writers realize, sooner or later, that the reduction of human behavior to narrative is finally a fraud. The postmodern writers recognized that.[3]

He added, crucially, that "in most postmodern fiction, the dominant tone . . . is irony."[4]

Dallas Wiebe's exploration of postmodernism proposes unfashionable (yet, perhaps, in their running against the grain, madly acceptable) readings of it. As I begin to suggest in my closing paragraph in an earlier essay,[5] in *Our Asian Journey* Wiebe seems to dramatize the possibility of limits to postmodernism. Particularly through his examination of the faith of the main character, the preacher Joseph Toevs, he tests the extent to which a deep humanism and a radical Christian piety might elude the cool and teasing detachments of postmodern address and exceed its presuppositions; or, contrariwise, he may be testing the extent to which such piety stands as postmodernism's finest feature.

Certainly Wiebe wants to insist (in keeping with the postmodern condition) that a stable identity for Joseph Toevs, the protagonist of *Our Asian Journey*, is a fiction. Yet, it is the deeply rooted religious faith of preacher Toevs—tested first by rigors of a fantastical Mennonite pilgrimage from Russia to Central Asia to prepare for the second coming of the Lord in the early 1880s, then by the ridicule of the academic and social establishment in Newton, Kansas, where Toevs arrived in 1884 and lived until 1917—that matter-of-factly takes its place in Wiebe's broader postmodern arrangement of elements and ultimately wins the reader's as well as (it certainly seems) Wiebe's own admiration and empathy.

Through his treatment of Toevs, we come to realize that Wiebe, full of serious mischief in more ways than one, subverts postmodern convention itself, with its irony and parody and pastiche, its insistence on decentered and even contradictory points of view, its resistance to traditional unities and binaries and boundaries, its multiple displacements of reader/text relationship. Indeed, Wiebe's tough and wisecracking narrator comes to realize in the second chapter that even he is subject now and again to the "direction and guidance" of the kind bestowed on Joseph Toevs by a wonderful and gracious God.

STORYTELLERS AND AUTHORITY

It is through the reflections of the narrator in chapter two that Wiebe gives us a mapping—surely to some extent autobiographical—of the historical development of a postmodern Mennonite consciousness stimulated by events in the late 1940s. This narrator, though existing, as Wiebe pointed out in 1990, "in a post-modernist construct,"[6] is at the same time given a strong and specific ethnically Mennonite lineage. He was born in 1930 and "grew up in and around Newton":

> He was a boy poor and of a contrite spirit. He was happy. He was tender and considerate. He loved reading and at the age of twelve read the Bible straight through. He was appalled but got baptized anyway on confession of belief in the First Mennonite Church where Joseph Toevs was elder and minister until 1917. After he graduated from Newton High School, he attended Bethel College in North Newton, Kansas.[7]

When this bookish Mennonite boy became a college undergraduate in the postwar era of the late 1940s, he looked forward to new intellectual horizons. To his astonishment, in this new world he was confronted peremptorily with dogma about what might be acceptable as legitimate Mennonite identity, identity given sheen as Mennonite historical orthodoxy. In time, he felt compelled to lay bare some of the often-unspoken presuppositions which, as he saw, underlay the idea of and insistence on normalcy in the sharply defined Mennonite world. Indeed, later in the 1970s, the narrator sees the inaugural moment of his novel as an act of resistance to forces sustaining convention and genre in his Mennonite context—and apparently immune to some of its contradictions.

Our Asian Journey, then, contains a quite specific project: it becomes a multilayered exploration and interrogation of the alienating effects of strong and generally uncontested social definitions—ultimately, in this novel, class-based definitions—exerted through school and church, textbook and sermon. As the narrator argues, "the way a story is told is not implicit in the materials of the story."[8] How we assemble our pasts helps to determine how we will include or exclude the poor, the contrite, the marginal in our primary stories today and tomorrow.

The narrator insists that we cannot passively accept that "a chronological order is a sufficient order for narrative;"[9] nor can we uncritically let our historians "spin out" what the narrator caustically labels "that great daydream we call 'our past.' Some past.... They never realize that memory ... remembers what it wants to remember."[10] He intimates that what writers conceal in their History might be as significant as what they reveal; Mennonites, like others who may be committed to a particular way of life, are tempted into creating a "daydream," a History, "to reaffirm our bourgeois prejudices that there is plan, there is order, that there is some ultimate reason for everything if we but find it."[11]

It was C. Henry Smith's sweeping and, for so many readers, invigorating 1941 masterpiece, *The Story of the Mennonites*, that so provoked the narrator in 1949. This widely endorsed work—and particularly the seemingly uncritical, institutionalized reception of it—prompted the narrator to follow an intellectual route that would blend with his tendency toward postmodern pyrotechnics. The narrator felt that Smith's grand text was made all the more dangerous by its very grandeur, especially when that text, ostensibly so all-inclusive, led to a diminution of an unprotected quarter in history and society.

As though anticipating Lyotard and many other critical theorists, the narrator saw in Smith's text, and in the unspoken intention of its promoters, a politics of protectionism and exclusion, a determination to make every Mennonite's story fit both descriptively and prescriptively a particular order. Smith's work seemed to imply that there was a consensus about a unified Mennonite identity. For the narrator, any such consensus seemed to represent an unwarranted imposition on individual lives of people, whether in history or in the present. Smith's approach represented, in effect, an exploitation of a realist genre, a form of writing often treated as literal and objective truth. What the narrator perceived as an offense in Smith's history could not have been tempered by Smith's double use of the definite article *the* in his title; signifier and signified here seem bound in space and time absolutely. (Significantly, with the publication of the fifth edition in 1981, revised and enlarged by Cornelius Krahn, Faith and Life Press in Newton reflected the postmodern temper of the times by changing the title to *Smith's Story of the Mennonites*.)

The narrator's attention was caught by "The Great Trek" and "The *Auszugsgemeinde*" sections of Smith's work, where Smith, banker, intellectual, historian, and father of a very liberal, progressive, American way of seeing, deals derisively with Mennonites who had been part of the pilgrimage in the 1880s to Central Asia. The undergraduate narrator, coming to the work like a child filled with curiosity and expectation, picked out in Smith's text what were "callous and sarcastic remarks"[12] about the people who went to Central Asia rather than America, people who, to use Smith's words, expressed the "strange desire to face eastward rather than to follow their brethren to the west."[13]

Although it was, as Smith said, and as the narrator (seeing in it the prospect of a superb story) might have agreed, "the most visionary adventure in all Mennonite history—an exodus to a wild, unknown barren land, in the heart of a Mohammedan population to meet the Lord and inaugurate the millennium,"[14] Smith's approach to it was satiric. Smith spoke of "pious pilgrims" dragging their "weary way" in their "quest for Utopia."[15] He peppered his description with rollicking references to sanity, extremism, millennialism, fanaticism, dreams and visions, ascension and reappearance, celestial travel and foolish belief, simplemindedness and misguidedness, idiosyncracy and blasphemy.[16] In the end, his purpose was plainly didactic, even coercive:

> This episode, one of the strangest in Mennonite annals, deserves this rather detailed treatment here because hereby hangs a moral of interest to Mennonites. Mennonites have been unusually susceptible to unwholesome influences of this sort. A number of times in past Mennonite history undue stress on chiliastic and apocaplyptic views on the part of fanatical leaders, has led to unfortunate results. Even today there is more teaching of this sort in the church, originating largely in certain short cut millennialist Bible schools frequented by Mennonite preachers, than is

wholesome for the church; and which in times of stress might easily lead to tragic results.[17]

Wiebe's narrator saw in Smith's approach a story that did not liberate its primary audience, the Mennonite reader, fully enough, but politically hectored any noncompliant elements in its midst. Smith's language and exhortations caused the narrator considerable anxiety and led him to the conviction that institutional history was too important to be entrusted to such a singular yet standardizing account, especially when it dictated with such precision its own terms of order and of unruliness. For the narrator, Smith's arguments against dangers in aberrant mythmaking and storytelling in the oft-isolated fragments of Mennonite society were themselves ironically manifest in the pressure Smith's text exerted.

In a way, Smith was providing for the narrator arguments parallel to those made by the unnamed leader in the novel who, in effect, blackmailed trusting Mennonites into making the trip to Asia in the first place; see, for example, the debate about history in chapter three.[18] The real Mennonite story, for the narrator, was larger and more flexible, more broadly redemptive, than what Smith (and the dozen eminent men named in his foreword) presented with so much imperious certainty.

Wiebe's narrator, uneasy with the social hierarchy implicit in Smith's approach (some of which was increasingly toned down by Cornelius Krahn in the third and fifth editions), reacts to Smith's attitude with a feeling of great sadness: "He wanted to cry for sorrow of heart,"[19] not least because he personally knew of the depth of human spirit manifest in some who had gone on that trek. As "a young man sensitive to injustice,"[20] he struggled with the terror he felt at the exclusions imposed by history's naturalizing activity. When he heard a college theologian adding to Smith's his own "nasty remark" about the Asian travelers, the narrator decided "then and there to set the record . . . straight"—or rather (and this is such an important point in our reading of Wiebe), the narrator decided "then and there to set the record, by cracky, straight."[21]

The excess of meanings set in motion with the narrator's "by cracky" echoes those prompted by the many other colloquialisms and clichés scattered throughout chapter two, the chapter that offers the novel's most explicit performance of the postmodern (and that, shocking us out of our usual reading habits, gives us a handle on one way of approaching the novel overall). Here we have the narrator undercutting his own text, with his by gosh, by golly, by cracky, and hell's bells[22] (to name a few expressions from decades gone by and taken from a very long list).

On the one hand, then, the narrator's resistance to Smith's single-minded perspective and purpose is a subversive, Bakhtinian resistance and draws on postmodern impatience with the unimpeded grand narrative as a secure text, with beginning, middle, and end all neatly in order, as though it were an adequate means of conveying human experience. But his "by cracky" reminds us that the narrator is ready to slap his own wri(s)ts, too.

The narrator rails against the conventions, the "pack of lies,"[23] of history-making, the "goldarned ideas of the historians,"[24] against clichéd components such as "manifest destiny, *die Untergang des Abendlandes*, the rise and fall of, civil war, *Sturm und Drang*, benevolent dictatorship, the Enlightenment, the Age of Reason, Renaissance, Dark Ages, the frontier, the rise of the middle class."[25] Such antagonism, rather than, say, against a history made up of "steam, bubble gum cards, fried eggs sunny side up, burnt toast, bad luck, *Kindertotenlieder*, the whining of flies,"[26] recalls postmodern theorists' observation that rupture, discontinuity, interruption have displaced those vast unities and fixed formulations of period and century. Gone are what Foucault calls "the solid, homogeneous manifestations of a single mind or of a collective mentality."[27]

As Wiebe's narrator puts it, "Reader, incline your ears; historians are the journalists of necromancy."[28] For all his mugging and clowning, the narrator insists on our recognizing that history is artificially constructed and deliberately perpetuated by particular interests, notably of class. The narrator, in effect exploiting the unspoken tension and dynamic of suppression and control in official dogma and endorsements, participates in the project of detaching history from the ideology of its apparently stable pasts and revealing those pasts to be ideological.[29]

Even old preacher Toevs (who bears a name, Joseph, apparently non-existent among Mennonites in the nineteenth century, and whose middle name is Barnabas), ever modest and self-effacing, claims this: a little too much of what we uncritically call History exerts itself through the authority of institutions where existing forces of class and power typically are extended. Toevs, eighty-three years old and, as it turns out, only days away from death in chapters one and seven of the novel, offers his own analysis of the relationship between class and narration among Mennonites:

> We were held in derision when we came, poor and of a contrite spirit, to America [thirty-seven years ago].... We stood stiffly under their smiles and listened when those "sack cloth and ashes aren't good enough for me" professors at Bethel College devised their contempt for our journey over the whole compass of the earth.[30]

Would a college man be interested in my life? Would an educated man ever care about [my wife] Sarah? Could anyone ever have the learning, patience, understanding, charity to care about our great adventure in Asia? The historians in their arrogance would never care. Already our neighbors make fun of us.[31]

One wealthy Mennonite woman, along with her servants, had abandoned the Russia-to-Asia pilgrimage early and come to Newton. When she sneered at him on his arrival in Newton in 1884, the shocked and relatively unsophisticated and literal-minded Joseph Toevs was abashed. He could only bow his head, hiding his face "from shame and spitting."[32]

Our Asian Journey runs against the view that postmodernism leads to an entirely uncommitted aesthetic. Wiebe achieves this effect by showing that, through deconstructive engagement, there are links between postmodernism and social satire. In its investigation of the distribution of power among social groups or classes, including those in a Mennonite society, Wiebe's novel comes to the verge of introducing us to the field of cultural studies. Indeed, to the extent that it is a project that juxtaposes manifestations of many levels of power, authority, and class, postmodernism calls out to cultural studies and the political activism it brings to settings defined at least in part by socially constructed narrative.

Postmodern performance and perception, put in tandem with the discipline of cultural studies, proposes a kind of agency often feared lost wherever the pastiche of postmodernism, with its comically eclectic assemblages of discourses and genres, yields mainly to what becomes a recollection of the work of the midcentury absurdists. Cultural studies reminds us of the agency in these pluralistically mixed structures, with their apparently competing and contradictory cultural codes. In *Our Asian Journey*, the narrator is arguing for a wrenching of dominant idiom out of its usual resting places, which for him are too definitive and regulating, too reductive and spirit-threatening, and into the egalitarianism of many hands.

SEARCHING FOR A SHORT SKETCH OF MY LIFE

Our Asian Journey is a story enclosing many stories. Even Joseph Toevs, himself a narrator in charge, in varying degrees, of certain chapters in the novel (chapters one, seven, and especially four), thinks he might wade in to tell a story which would address the biases of the official historical record:

> Perhaps I'll write that what a 'honey and locusts shall never pass my lips' historian wrote is not true. Our beliefs were not foolish, our episode was not one of the strangest in Mennonite annals. We were not deceived by

unwholesome influences and what happened to us was not unfortunate results. Is the Bible unwholesome? Is faith unfortunate? . . . Maybe I should write the book and then eat it and make my belly bitter."[33]

This gentle and unassuming Mennonite preacher, looking back on his life, thinks about how he might tell his own wondrous story of his wanderings as a pilgrim to many parts of the earth, including "the brilliant world of Samarkand and Bokhara."[34] But he too (like C. Henry Smith), wants a story that will fix things in their place, once and for all; a story by which he can represent himself exactly. He wants to call it, dutifully, dully, conventionally, "A Short Sketch of My Life as it Reveals the Direction and Guidance of a Wonderful and Gracious God." He is pleased with his bit of progress as a writer: "What I have is a title," he says to himself, believing in the possibility of a unified and unifying narrative vision. "I like my title."[35]

Yet he ponders,

> What will I say? . . . What am I to be, a voice out of a bush? A voice out of a great wind? Should I disturb them [my grandchildren] with mighty and wondrous things and the secrets of the times? How can I be a spring of understanding, a faithful witness? How can I speak of the beginning and the end? . . . I'll write, "You get as old as a cow, but you always learn new things." I'll write, "Chub, chub. A full belly is deaf to learning."[36]

He vaguely seems to realize that he cannot address the incommensurability of things and is given no help by an imagined audience blinkered by narrative conventionalities.

Joseph Toevs has to face the fact that he is at home mainly with the sermons, hymns, and prayer foregrounded repeatedly in *Our Asian Journey*, not with many of the other forms the novel incorporates. For example, when his wife Sarah offers him one of her many teasing riddles, his best response is to become comatose. He "lays his forehead on the table and covers his ears with his hands."[37] In the long chapter four, on his great journey under the Russian and the Asian sky, he begins to dream almost every night. Then he finds it impossible to imagine what he someday might do with the unruly and exotic stories that usurp his placidity, his doggedly conducted pilgrimage among the faithful remnant. Even his dreams begin to invite him into a world for which he has no generic or narrative categories. Late in life, when he wonders how he might pass anything along to his children and grandchildren, he contemplates the many dreams he has had. He thinks about those he has written down in his diary.[38] But he knows there is no audience for dreams: "dreams would be ridiculed."[39]

Wiebe seems to be suggesting that it is the ridiculing of the life of the imagination, of the mind at play, that at least vaguely concerns Joseph Toevs here, as he experiences the tug of convention—the "daydream" of our bourgeois imperatives—against the dream of play and fantasy. By extension, Wiebe seems to be suggesting that more "play" find its way into works such as Smith's. At the same time, Joseph Toevs's uncertainty about his material and his audience symbolizes a dilemma. That is the dilemma facing anyone drawn to the release of energy proposed by the freedoms announced and authorized by postmodernism yet wary of its exotic adventures and seductions.

During Joseph Toevs's desert wanderings, Gerhard Christian Wiebe, an outsider at the edge of the group, offers Toevs an explanation about his wealth of dreams. The explanation seems to expand on Wiebe's contrasting of the daydream of historical and other realist writing with dreams conducted by the mind at play. In this explanation, the white part of the brain becomes linked to convention and genre, the black part to transgression against these:

> The white part is the logical and regulatory part. It has to do with reason. The dark part is the playful and mysterious part. . . . [T]he dark part of the brain, in its playfulness, sets riddles for the light part, hence dreams. The dark part is fun-loving, sardonic, witty, cynical, happy. When the brain becomes tired of regulating the body, when the body is asleep, it plays games with its images. Dreams are the mind playing with itself because of the boredom gathered from the experiences and senses of the body. When the light part of the brain solves the riddles, if it does, the body awakens because new materials, new nourishment, are needed for the riddles.[40]

When the body ages and weakens, dreams and riddles become visions and hallucinations, as the brain searches for more riddles, "a search which is desperate, melancholic, pathetic":[41]

> [T]hat's what happened to John on Patmos. Visions are the brain dancing in the declining body. It is a final celebration, like a Roman Saturnalia, and all rules are suspended, the limits let down for a brief time. . . . That's why people go on pilgrimages. . . . The brain never dies, but the bodies go out into Central Asia. . . . It's really all a search by the brain for its sustenance.[42]

But the earnest Joseph Toevs, Joseph the Dreamer, can take only so much of this. He tells Gerhard that his ideas are interesting but that he had better go out and look after the horses now, or they will never get farther on their journey across the desert. In his deep spiritual agonies, Toevs would not entirely be convinced by the postmodern narrator's approach to the conventional historian in chapter two: "If you want to know the truth about the past you have to read fiction."[43]

A Post-Mennonite Postmodern

Wiebe's work is a revelation of the release of immense creative energy invited by postmodernism, invited by the conversations and recognitions that follow on playfully posing the liberating question "what if?" His writing confirms that opportunities flow from postmodernism to the underdog trapped in the efficiencies of the modernist cul-de-sac and unable to explore and express his or her own particularities. It reveals the ways in which serious literature can provide a testing ground of implications of postmodernism. It reminds us that the condition of being "Mennonite" is not a stable condition; it is a site of contingencies, of ongoing conversation and new commitments, a realization that "Mennonites" have been experimenting with "post-Mennonite" identities.

Wiebe's work reveals as well that Mennonite postmodernisms are written in, informed by, and in conversation with broader postmodernisms. Both Anabaptism and postmodernism (terms that exist in different spheres, at different registers) stand ready to reveal something about the other: their energies, their vulnerabilities, their ongoing metamorphoses, their ever-open invitation to new interpretations. Wiebe's work demonstrates what Foucault found in the study of historical narrative: "attention has been turned . . . away from vast unities like 'periods' or 'centuries' to the phenomena of rupture, of discontinuity."[44]

Respective chapters of *Our Asian Journey*, each falling under a title taken from the name of one of the seven churches addressed in the book of Revelation, are broadly distinctive in generic terms. Chapters one and seven provide first-person reverie, chapter two provides an omniscient yet highly unself-conscious and intrusive narrator, or author-as-narrator. In chapter three the third-person narrator is more detached, but his work is bisected by a kind of dialogic question-and-answer performance which reaches peculiar linguistic formations as it exceeds prophetic enunciation.

Chapter four provides an elegant and restrained, yet moving, 264-page account of the journey in a diary covering the years 1880-85. Chapters five and six are formally written personal letters, one written in 1913, the other (triggering Toevs's reverie of chapters one and seven) in 1921. The multiple genres support multiple voices in the respective chapters. These voices in turn are kept in play in relation to the narrational voice established in the titles of the chapters. And between the lines (as it were) especially in chapters one and seven, a distinctly if moderately felt voice of an implied author provides a kind of interference with Toevs's meditation in those chapters. That an implied author entering from a postmodern zone might play lightheartedly in the intimacies of an old man's thoughts in those two chapters will not surprise the reader who has to deal with the stage presence of an "actual" author in the self-conscious artifice of chapter two.

Through its overall form and structure Wiebe's novel paradoxically reminds us too of the limits of postmodernism as a deconstructive operation. He alerts us to the need to make postmodernism itself aware of degrees of truth, not least the particular truth of individual experience. There are in chapters five and six the sober perspectives of the outsiders, for whom postmodernism and its commodifications are not an option.

And Joseph Toevs (most often painfully unself-conscious throughout) offers a sincere performance of Anabaptist identity which we might very well read as a satire of Wiebe's narrator's postmodern exhibitionism. Of course, as I have suggested, we can read even further, for we are finally invited to acknowledge that Toevs's deeply held religious understanding is so unusual as counter-environment that we grant even it a place in Wiebe's mixture of postmodern ingredients.

Wiebe's playful proposals—his parody doubly transgressive in remaining ever open to parody—suggest two things. First, we must learn to take some of our luxuriously transgressive postmodernisms with our tongue in cheek. Second, we might also want to take some postmodernism very seriously indeed, as an invitation to rereadings and renewals that reject absolutes and reinforce a plurality of ways of telling the "truth" in the real world.

Such a world would be one in which even Joseph Toevs would get to tell others some of the dreams he later recalls, when he thinks of those nights, "asleep in our blankets on the ground, the wind blowing, the jackals crying, standing watch as the great stars turned, I thought I could reach out and touch all heaven. I, Joseph the dreamer, like the Joseph of old, stood in the vast emptiness right beside God."[45]

Notes

1. Dallas Wiebe, *Our Asian Journey* (Waterloo, Ont.: MLR Editions Canada, 1997), 50.
2. Dallas Wiebe, "Review of Armin Wiebe's *The Second Coming of Yeeat Shpanst*," *Mennonite Life* 51, no. 4 (1996), 35.
3. Ibid., 34.
4. Ibid., 35.
5. Paul Tiessen, "Constructing Narrative: An Introduction to Dallas Wiebe and *Our Asian Journey*," in *Migrant Muses: Mennonite/s Writing in the U.S.*, ed. John D. Roth and Ervin Beck (Goshen, Ind.: Mennonite Historical Society, 1998), 126.
6. Dallas Wiebe, "Author's introduction to an excerpt, 'II. Smyrna Friday December 21, 1879 (o.s.) Lysanderhoh,' from *Our Asian Journey*," *The New Quarterly* (special issue, *Mennonite/s Writing in Canada*, ed. Hildi Froese Tiessen) 10, nos. 1-2 (1990): 90.
7. Wiebe, *Our Asian Journey*, 46.
8. Ibid., 47.
9. Ibid., 49.
10. Ibid.
11. Ibid., 51.
12. Ibid., 46.
13. C. Henry Smith, *The Story of the Mennonites* (Berne, Ind.: Mennonite Book Concern, 1945 [1941]), 455. I am grateful to C. Arnold Snyder for his comments concerning C. Henry Smith.
14. Ibid., 456.
15. Ibid.
16. Ibid., 454-62.
17. Ibid., 461-62.
18. Wiebe, *Our Asian Journey*, 68, 73.
19. Ibid., 46.
20. Ibid.
21. Ibid.
22. Ibid., 17, 38, 46, 33.
23. Ibid., 51.
24. Ibid., 49.
25. Ibid., 49-50.
26. Ibid., 50.
27. Michel Foucault, *The Archaeology of Knowledge and The Discourse on Language*, trans. A. M. Sheridan Smith (New York: Pantheon, 1972), 4.
28. Wiebe, *Our Asian Journey*, 50.
29. See Foucault, *The Archaeology of Knowledge and The Discourse on Language*, 5.
30. Wiebe, *Our Asian Journey*, 15.
31. Ibid., 357.
32. Ibid., 345.

33. Ibid., 15.
34. Ibid., 9.
35. Ibid., 13.
36. Ibid., 13, 16.
37. Ibid., 54.
38. Ibid., 13.
39. Ibid., 15.
40. Ibid., 205.
41. Ibid.
42. Ibid., 206.
43. Ibid., 50.
44. Foucault, *The Archaeology of Knowledge and The Discourse on Language*, 4.
45. Wiebe, *Our Asian Journey*, 438.

SIX

CONTEXT, CONFLICT, AND COMMUNITY:
South German Mennonites at the Threshold of Modernity, 1750-1850

John D. Roth

Truly our times resemble the rarest of ages . . . for whoever has lived but today and yesterday in these times has actually lived through years; and stories keep crowding into each other.

Thus an elderly refugee in Goethe's *Hermann und Dorothea*, exiled by the French invasion into Southwest Germany late in the eighteenth century, reflected on his recent past.[1] Between 1792 and 1814 the German territories west of the Rhine River came firmly under French control. The history of that period, from the perspective of the villager and peasant at least, is indeed a history crowded with stories: stories of the blood and bravura of war, of sequestered livestock and robbed granaries, of crop failure and emigration, of social upheaval and political reform. Stories, above all, which conveyed the bewildering reality of change: sudden, compressed, and often violent.

In the relatively short span of two decades, a flurry of French decrees challenged, reformed, or discarded nearly every assumption that had undergirded German feudal society. A French mandate of 1801—the advantages of which, it claimed in the preface, "no reasonable spirit could fail to recognize"—suggested the thoroughness of French intentions. Four centrally administered *Departements* replaced the loose patchwork of fifty-seven smaller German principalities. An independent judicial system in league with a new model of constitutional bureaucracy swept aside the confusing and often arbitrary mosaic of feudal law. Guild regulations and a complex system of restrictive tariffs were abolished. Above all, the principles of citizenship—a society of individuals equal under the law—supplanted the feudal order of estates and subjects.[2]

For the German population living along the Rhine River at the turn of the eighteenth century, social and political assumptions that had structured their lives for centuries were irrevocably transformed, supplanted in a newly constituted world by the "revolutionary-Napoleonic watershed."[3] In the words of historian Helmut Berding, Southwest Germany "had crossed the threshold into the modern world."[4]

To be sure, the Mennonite communities scattered along the western bank of the Rhine represented only a tiny fraction of the German population affected by these reforms. Yet too often the histories of these communities—if they are remembered at all—have been written as if the communities were somehow isolated from world historical events. Certainly biographical sketches, genealogical anecdotes, and celebrative congregational histories have offered fascinating glimpses into the Mennonite world during this period. But rarely have such accounts considered the profound impact of the French Revolution and subsequent reforms imposed by French administrators on Mennonite communities during the first half of the nineteenth century.

Although this essay can do little more than sketch the outlines of that fascinating story, the conflicts that rent the South German Mennonite church after the French occupation point toward themes slated to become central to the broader Mennonite story as it unfolded in Europe and North America during the following century and a half.

At stake in the reforms—both in the church and in the wider society—were fundamental differences in theological worldviews. The sweeping legal, economic, and political reforms of the early nineteenth century were grounded on the basic assumptions of the European Enlightenment: a high value on human reason and individual rights, a commitment to rational and efficient organizational structures, and a deep confidence in the progressive nature of human history. These assumptions, eagerly adopted by some German Mennonites, quickly clashed with a more traditional Mennonite worldview that regarded suffering as an inevitable part of Christian faith and embraced the communitarian ideals of humility, corporate discipline, and the collective wisdom of tradition.

Though readers today may be tempted to dismiss the specific issues that divided the South German Mennonite church as petty or idiosyncratic, the conflict in these Mennonite communities in the first half of the nineteenth century offers a poignant glimpse into the initial encounter of Mennonites with modernity. As such, it offers an instructive backdrop for current conversations about Mennonites and postmodernity.

SOUTHWEST GERMAN MENNONITES IN THE *ANCIEN REGIME*

Virtually all Mennonites living along the upper Rhine during the last half of the eighteenth century were descendants of Swiss Brethren emigrants—religious refugees for the most part. They had been driven out of their native cantons of Zurich and Bern during the various waves of persecution that swept through those regions in the 1640s, the 1660s, and again in the first decade of the 1700s. Along with a host of other religious minorities, these Swiss Brethren—or Mennonites as they are called throughout the rest of this chapter—found a measure of toleration among the feudal princes and lords of Southwest Germany who were seeking farmers to resettle their lands following the devastating depopulation of the Thirty Years' War (1618-1648).

By the middle of the eighteenth century, there were about thirty Mennonite congregations or communities in the Palatinate, which included some 3-4,000 people. No congregation, however, had more than 150 members—and they were widely scattered geographically, some separated from their closest neighbor by as much as five hours of travel. Yet despite geographical distance and the absence of any formal organizational structure, Mennonites in the region maintained a distinctive religious identity.

In part, their identity as a group was imposed on them by a host of idiosyncratic legal restrictions and civil disabilities. Thus most Mennonites in the region were forced to pay an annual "toleration" tax. Their population could not exceed a fixed number. They were not allowed to join guilds or practice any profession apart from those related to agriculture. They could not build distinctive meetinghouses. They were strongly forbidden to engage in any sort of religious proselytizing. Symbolic of their tenuous legal status was the so-called "law of retraction"—imposed by the Palatine Elector on Mennonite landowners in 1726—which gave any person who sold land to a Mennonite the right to buy it back at any time for the original sale price.[5] To be sure, not all of these laws were strictly enforced. But one significant element of Mennonite identity in the eighteenth century was forged in the delicate balance between the paternalistic goodwill of the feudal lord and the various forms of legal, social, and economic restrictions they endured as a tolerated religious minority.

At the same time, the distinctive character of the Mennonite community was reinforced from within by a cluster of theological convictions and practices that clearly separated them from their Catholic, Reformed, and Lutheran neighbors. Mennonites, for example, did not baptize their infants. They refused to swear oaths, carry the sword, or participate in civil governance. At baptism, Mennonites not only promised to follow the commandments of Christ, but they also explicitly vowed to abide by the congregational regulations *(Ordnung)* and to submit to church discipline if they failed to comply. All baptizands promised to marry only in the church, and male members agreed at baptism to accept the call to serve—unpaid and without formal training—in ministerial offices if the lot fell on them.

The style of Mennonite worship further set them apart from their neighbors. Mennonites met for worship in private homes or in meetinghouses built to look like homes. Their hymns, comprised mainly of martyr ballads sung slowly and in unison, came from the *Ausbund*, a Swiss German hymnbook dating back to the sixteenth century. Their ministers—often barely literate farmers—preached without notes, drawing heavily on Scripture passages committed to memory, with a strong emphasis on the suffering Christians could expect to endure at the hands of an unregenerate world. This internal sense of group identity was strengthened even more by a complex network of family ties, shared memories of persecution and suffering, and the energetic efforts of a few itinerant ministers whose informal authority in matters related to church *Ordnung* transcended their particular congregation.

Despite their eccentricities, at the eve of the French Revolution Mennonites had come to enjoy a widespread reputation as hardworking, productive farmers who could be counted on to pay rents and taxes. In the eyes of most contemporary observers, they were models of industry, neatness, and moral rectitude. An official report in 1763, for example, noted that "no more industrious, efficient or peaceful subjects are to be found."[6] Another report to the privy council of the Electoral Palatinate twenty years later—having established that Mennonites do not lie, cheat, steal, quarrel, or beg—concluded that "in short, they are a peaceful, orderly, God-fearing people whose conduct puts many other Christians to shame."[7] Indeed, some Mennonites, such as David Möllinger of Monsheim, were famous throughout the region for their progressive innovations in agricultural reform.[8]

But there were also signs of religious tension and uncertainty in the Mennonite communities during the last half of the eighteenth century. In 1757, for example, Peter Weber, a young, newly ordained minister at Höningen, began holding private meetings for Bible study and devotion which included people from outside the Mennonite church. At these meetings, Weber reportedly was critical of the church's emphasis on tradition and external form. By contrast, he preached "redemption through faith in Christ and His sacrifice, and . . . salvation in that faith alone."9

Though deeply moved by the Anabaptist model of costly discipleship and martyrdom, Weber's hunger for spiritual nourishment led him and his colleagues to look beyond the boundaries of the Mennonite community. His library included the complete works of Pietist leaders like Gerhard Tersteegen and Friedrich Oetinger. Weber avidly read August Herman Franck's *Glaubensweg* and Johann Heinrich Reitz's *Historia der Wiedergeborenen*. He carried on an extensive correspondence with the famous South German Pietiest, novelist, and physician, Heinrich Jung-Stilling, and other prominent urban Mennonite pastors such as Johannes Deknatel in Amsterdam and Lorenz Friedenreich in Neuwied.

Weber was removed from office and only reinstated in 1763 when he—along with a cohort of younger ministers—promised to conduct themselves in "stillness and quiet." But his critique of Mennonite spirituality and his search for sources of renewal beyond the Anabaptist theological tradition point toward tensions latent in the Mennonite community that would find fuller expression in the years after the French Revolution.10

IMPACT OF THE FRENCH REFORMS

In 1792 the Mennonite communities of the Palatinate—along with all of Southwest German society—collided with the modern world in the form of the French Revolution. In October 1792, the revolutionary French army under command of General Custin conquered Speyer, Worms, and Mainz in quick succession, planting liberty trees in villages throughout the Rhineland, while calling on German subjects to join in the revolution. Despite counter-revolutionary efforts by the Austrian and Prussian armies, the French firmly consolidated their military hold on the region by the spring of 1795. Two years later, in a secret article of the Peace of Campo Formio, Austria joined with France and Prussia in conceding French hegemony over the entire west bank of the Rhine River.

Like their neighbors, Mennonites experienced the initial consequences of the French occupation not in the lofty abstractions of revolutionary rhetoric but in the more tangible language of sequestered grain, forced lodging of soldiers, and the raw fear that accompanied each passing wave of troops. Along with their Catholic and Protestant neighbors, Mennonite families either endured the interruptions of warfare, or, like Christian Dettweiler of Kindenheim, they fled "the *Schrecknissen* (horrors) of the French Revolution" to the comparative safety of friends and relatives in Baden or Bavaria.[11]

Adam Krehbiel, an aged Mennonite minister who chose to stay, could only watch in despair as French soldiers turned his meetinghouse at the Weierhof into a temporary barracks and then a granary.[12] A Mennonite farmer from the Spitalhof kept track of the numerous requisitions for wood, hay, and straw demanded by the French. He remembered with special clarity the *Republiksonntag* of 1794, when French Commissars Gibois and Gro planted a liberty tree and held a celebration, "amid gluttony and drunkenness, dancing and music" for their high-ranking officers.[13] Martin Möllinger of Monsheim wrote to Johannes Weber in 1795 that Prussian officers in the Imperial army had plundered his possessions to the tune of 5,000 florins. Three years later Weber recalled his own experiences with the French: "It was a common saying then," he wrote, "that the French never left anything behind except two eyes for crying."[14]

In later years, leaders were quick to blame the general decline in the nineteenth-century Mennonite church on the chaos, upheaval, and antiecclesiastical rhetoric of the French occupation. "Beginning with the French," wrote Hermann Reeder, a minister at the Weierhof, "a relaxed, frivolous spirit spread through the Palatinate . . . which had a destructive influence on the churches."[15] David Kägy of Offstein blamed the influence of French atheism for the collapse of moral standards he observed among Mennonites. "For a while there were no church services held in our whole region," he reflected in 1842, "they were despised . . . and Sunday was not to be recognized at all. For these reasons the sensuous and worldly people among us walked freely down the broad road of lust and temptation."[16]

When a large group of Mennonite ministers gathered at Ibersheim in 1803 and again in 1805 to address matters of common concern, they readily admitted that the church was approaching a crisis. According to minutes from these meetings, members selected by the lot to serve as ministers were routinely refusing to accept their call; it had become commonplace for Mennonites to marry non-Mennonites; baptism was increasingly an empty symbol, formulaic and routine; church discipline was practiced only rarely; and many Mennonites had taken up with "worldly amusements," such as dancing, drinking, and card-playing. Perhaps most painful was the recognition that the principle of pacifism had been endangered by the "voluntary taking up of weapons."[17]

The voluntary nature of the last concern in particular points toward a bewildering ambivalence Mennonites displayed regarding the French military presence. If, for example, Jakob Krehbiel remembered the loss of life and destruction of material possessions wrought by the invading armies, Jakob Ellenberger, an influential Mennonite schoolteacher and preacher from Friedelsheim, could only recall with delight "the drama of the war: the decorated soldiers from different countries on foot and horse, the drum roll, the trumpet blast, the full military music."[18]

In 1804, a Mennonite elder from Neuwied complained that "Mennonite young men want to ride against the *Landesfürsten* with unsheathed swords just like the other citizens' sons"—a lament directed as much against the revolutionary hubris of challenging the Landesfürsten as it was against the "unsheathed sword."[19] In 1805, Heinrich Krehbiel, a Mennonite from the Weierhof, died in Spain while serving with the French army.[20] According to one source, by 1812 nearly every Mennonite family was represented in Napoleon's disastrous campaign into Russia.[21] To be sure, many served as wagoneers rather than infantrymen, but, despite the fact that their religious principles forbade service in the military, "they offered no resistance whatsoever to conscription."[22]

Once French control over the region was ensured, the impact of their presence began to take on deeper, more enduring dimensions. By November 1797 the revolutionary government in Paris—the Directory—had approved a tentative constitution for Southwest Germany and charged the new administrator of the territories, Generalkommisar Rudler, to "prepare the peoples in these regions—stultified by their slavery to the feudal system—for the rights and duties of a republican government."[23] Over the next decade, a white-collar army of French-speaking bureaucrats, recruited on the basis of education and talent, replaced the notables and court society of German dukes and princes. At the same time a new, highly rationalized model of municipal administration replaced the fragmented and idiosyncratic jurisdictions of the ancien regime. Religious institutions—Catholic and Protestant alike—came firmly under the tutelage of the state, a secular government that also guaranteed the freedom of individual religious conscience to everyone, including Mennonites.

The core of these reforms—equality under the law, individual rights, religious liberty, and a secular state made up of citizens equal under the law—was succinctly summarized in 1804 with the introduction of the Code Napoleon, or the French Civil Code. Lucid, simple, unencumbered with confusing casuistry or abstractions, the Civil Code symbolized a modern society premised on principles of reason rather than habits of tradition. Despite complaints about legal fees and *Vielregelei* (red tape), the Civil Code became firmly established in the Rhineland in the first decade of the nineteenth century, penetrating the consciousness of people at all levels of society. "Every illiterate farmer in the Pfalz," wrote folk historian Wilhelm Heinrich Riehl, "became a born professor, a true doctrinaire," brandishing the Code at every breach of trust and arguing vigorously over its principles.[24]

The French occupation of the Rhineland lasted a mere twenty years. But even after allied German armies reconquered the western bank of the Rhine early in 1814, the reforms introduced by the French had already taken deep root. In 1815 attempts by the allied military government to roll back these administrative reforms met with fierce local resistance. Even the conservative Bavarian monarchy, which lay claim to the Palatinate in 1818, left the Civil Code virtually untouched: freedom of religious conscience continued to prevail, and the basic outlines of the French constitution persisted intact through the conservative reaction of the 1820s and 1830s.[25]

On the surface, the initial consequences of these reforms were overwhelmingly positive for Mennonites. For three full centuries, Mennonites had always been wary of civil government, regarding it both as a divinely ordained source of order as well as a potential threat to their very existence. Now suddenly the state turned out to be a friend and protector, a guarantor of civil liberties, religious freedom, and legal equality. No longer merely tolerated at the arbitrary whim of their feudal lords, Mennonites now enjoyed every individual right and liberty afforded by citizenship in a modern state. In the free market of religious opinion that now prevailed, Mennonites could worship as they pleased, build public meetinghouses to rival those of neighbors, and proselytize without fear. They were now free to leave the isolated estates, purchase land without restrictions, pursue university education, and enter any profession or occupation they might choose.

Not surprisingly, many Mennonites in Southwest Germany responded to the new context with an enthusiastic flurry of activities. During the first half of the nineteenth century, Mennonites began to hire seminary-trained ministers from outside the community and pay them for their services. They invested heavily in the construction of new public meetinghouses, replete with bell towers and organs. They published an impressive array of catechisms, hymnbooks, and sermons. They developed a keen interest in education, both primary and secondary. And for the first time in nearly two centuries, they began to organize for missions.

Yet paradoxically, the new age of freedom ushered in by the French political reforms also marked an era of profound uncertainty and division in the South German Mennonite church. By the 1830s a conservative cluster of five congregations, led by Johannes Galle of Monzernheim and David Kägy of Offstein, had formed a *Bund* or conference in opposition to the energetic new projects being initiated by such progressive leaders as Johannes Risser of Friedelsheim and Leonhard Weydman of Monsheim.[26]

As one reconstructs the details of the conflict, particularly through the letters these men exchanged, one cannot help but be struck by the pathos of the division: each of the protagonists in the dispute wrote out of a deep understanding of Scripture; each claimed to be a faithful heir of the Mennonite tradition; each was intent on strengthening the integrity of the church. And even though on the surface the specific issues at stake in the division may strike the modern researcher as petty or small-minded, there was little doubt in the minds of contemporaries that they pointed toward foundational assumptions about faith and its relevance to a rapidly changing culture.

SOUTH GERMAN MENNONITES IN CONFLICT

Leadership

One of the first sources of tension in the Mennonite community in the opening decades of the nineteenth century involved leadership, specifically questions related to the training, calling, and remuneration of ministers. Traditionally Mennonites had selected ministers from within the congregation by means of the lot. Ministers had no special education or training and were to serve for life without pay.

This pattern of leadership reflected, at least in part, the marginal social status of Mennonites in Switzerland and South Germany—given their history of persecution and legal restrictions, they simply did not have access to formal theological training nor did they have resources to fund such training. But Mennonites also harbored a deep suspicion of theological education that went back to the sixteenth century. The basic teachings of Scripture, they thought, were relatively clear and therefore accessible to everyone. Faith was not a matter to be discussed and debated so much as lived. In their experience, the academic training of the university theologians (*Schriftgelehrten*) served mainly to provide sophisticated reasons for avoiding the clear and simple teachings of Christ. Mennonite sermons, by contrast, were not exegetical so much as admonitory, stressing conformity to God's will and the congregational *Ordnung*. Ministerial leadership was thus a calling from God confirmed through the lot, not a position of status or power to be sought after by an individual. That leaders served without pay underscored the spiritual nature of the calling, the congregation-centered approach to hermeneutics, and the freedom of the minister to exercise church discipline impartially.

By the second half of the eighteenth century, however, issues surrounding congregational leadership had become a major problem in Mennonite communities. Increasingly, men were simply refusing to accept ministerial positions when the lot fell to them—and for understandable reasons. Peter Weber, who first sounded the alarm in the late 1750s, once complained in a letter to his brother that most Mennonite ministers in the region were "as suitable to preach as oxen are suited to play the organ." This remark did not endear him to other ministers, though it may well have reflected the sentiments of many.[27]

Ministers meeting at Ibersheim in 1803 lamented the growing shortage of willing leaders and even commissioned Valentin Dahlem to publish a preacher's manual designed to ease the work of the minister by providing written prayers, formularies for church rituals, and aids for catechetical instruction.[28] But the problem persisted, made worse by the fact that many Mennonites, especially young people, found the closely reasoned sermons, rhetorical flourishes, and learned references offered by highly educated ministers in the neighboring Lutheran and Reformed churches more attractive than the offerings of their Mennonite minister-farmers.

Pastoral education was not an entirely alien notion among European Mennonites. For more than a century, Mennonites in Holland and North Germany had favored university-trained men in ministerial offices. In 1811 the Dutch Mennonites even established the first Mennonite seminary.

Thus on the face of it, it was not a rash or reckless decision when in 1820 the Mennonite congregation at Monsheim invited Leonhard Weydmann to serve as their pastor with the understanding that they would pay him for his services. Born in Crefeld to a Reformed father and a Mennonite mother, twenty-seven-year-old Weydmann had studied theology first at

Basel, then at the recently established Mennonite seminary in Amsterdam, and finally, for a short time, at the University of Berlin. He arrived at Monsheim a man well-educated by South German Mennonite standards, having written several essays on mathematics, baptism in the early church, church discipline, and the authority of Scripture.[29] In following decades, the large, influential Mennonite congregations of Ibersheim, Sembach, Friedelsheim, and the Weierhof all hired seminary-trained pastors as well.

To conservatives like Johannes Galle and David Kägy, however, the professionalization of leadership marked a fundamental shift in Mennonite thought and practice, bringing a host of changes which undermined their understanding of the faithful church. They protested vigorously.

A new view of mutual aid

The most immediate consequence of professional leadership had to do with finances. Traditionally, the only "offering" collected in Mennonite congregations was in the form of mutual aid: an informal gathering of money by the deacons for the support of widows, orphans, the infirm, and the poor. But Weydmann—and those who followed him—obviously expected a salary. We do not know many of the details, but, at a minimum, money collected for salaries greatly expanded the traditional Mennonite understanding of mutual aid. At its best, the decision to pay ministers a regular salary acknowledged the need to strengthen congregational life by freeing pastors from the burden of two careers. At its worst, and this was the light in which Galle and Kägy regarded the matter, it redirected congregational wealth away from the needy and turned the office of minister into that of a "hireling," in Kägy's words—a toady responsive primarily to the congregation's wealthiest members.[30]

Hermeneutical divide between pastor and laity

Professional leadership also raised questions about the nature of ministerial authority. From the beginning, conservatives were suspicious of the arrogance that seemed implicit in the educational training of paid ministers. Already in 1819, a year before Weydmann arrived at his pastorate in Monsheim, a controversy had flared concerning an essay he had written on church discipline. Christian Eymann, a layman from Kindenheim, was among those who had expressed misgivings about Weydmann's lax position on church discipline. But it was Weydmann's comments on biblical interpretation that really stoked the fires of Eymann's indignation. The essay itself, unfortunately, is no longer extant. But secondary to Eymann,

Weydmann had insisted that since translators often disagreed among themselves on certain interpretations, "anyone who wants to understand the Bible has to learn the original languages."[31]

This struck Eymann as arrogant and absurd. In the first place, he asked, what made Weydmann so sure—if translators themselves argue about interpretations—that the one *he* reaches is any more correct than theirs? "Can Herr Weidmann [sic] really expect reasonable (if uneducated) people to believe that his interpretation alone should be recognized as the correct one?"[32] In the days of the popes, Eymann continued astutely, the papacy wanted to keep the Bible from the laity so as to make them believe whatever Rome wanted. Now, thank God, things have changed and "there are even Bible Societies of all kinds which spend millions to deliver Bibles into the hands of the most distant heathen."

When Eymann had tried to argue with Weydmann in public, his "rebuttal was regarded as hilarious and hardly worth listening to." Undoubtedly airing the sentiments of others, Eymann concluded his letter saying "Look here, Herr Weydmann, if you imagined that everyone in this region will hear anything said without testing it merely because we are lacking in educated (*studierte*) preachers, then you have deceived yourself."[33]

Eymann's outburst of indignation was only the most pointed of numerous expressions of mistrust among conservative Mennonites over the next two decades directed toward the new cadre of trained ministers whose authority seemed to derive as much from their university credentials as from the hand of God, a virtuous life, or a sense of responsibility to the congregation.

"The Holy Spirit," said John Lapp, a conservative minister from Clarence Center, New York, writing about these developments to his Palatine counterparts, "is not to be had through scholarly studies; the Spirit adheres to a completely different sort of school. . . ."[34] In a response letter, Johannes Galle agreed, juxtaposing the Anabaptist martyrs—who gave up their bodies for the sake of the kingdom, not for money or pride—with ministers who demanded money for their services. In the end, he insisted, "We come to worship God, not the beautiful words of a man who can read Greek."[35]

Changes in church architecture

A third source of tension rising out of the new model of leadership seemed to focus on church architecture, specifically the direct link conservatives saw between the arrival of seminary-trained preachers and the urge to build new churchhouses. Traditionally, of course, Mennonites in the

Palatinate had been compelled by law to meet in homes or in buildings that looked like private residences. Freed by the French reforms from these architectural constraints, however, several congregations began to collect money to build new meetinghouses more commensurate with the training and professionalism of their recently hired ministers. And in the absence of a distinctly Mennonite architectural tradition, the buildings that emerged—much to the dismay of conservatives—looked much like the Lutheran and Reformed churches around them, .

The story of the Weierhof congregation is illustrative. In 1770, after lengthy petitioning to the prince of Nassau-Weilburg, the congregation had built their first meetinghouse, a small, unassuming room that blended anonymously into the façade of hofs and houses. Though the room fell into disrepair during the French occupation, by the 1820s it had been refurbished and restored to use.

In 1835, following the trend of several other congregations, the Weierhof congregation invited its first paid minister, Herman Reeder. Very little is known of Reeder's background.[36] He was educated at a Baptist Seminary in London and directed to the Palatinate by William Heinrich Angas, a Baptist missionary who had visited Palatine Mennonites in the 1820s in the mistaken assumption that the *Täufer* (Baptists) were lost cousins of the English Baptists. Reeder had only recently been ordained as a Mennonite minister in Neuwied.

In 1835 Reeder moved to Kirchheimbolanden with the expressed intention of deepening the spiritual life of the Mennonites there and of cultivating a newly awakened interest in missions. But his first project was the construction of a new churchhouse. Almost immediately after he arrived in the Palatinate, Reeder embarked on a fundraising tour among North German Mennonite churches and the Baptists in England. By 1837 he had collected enough money to finance the construction of a new Mennonite church at the Weierhof.

The new churchhouse was modeled directly after a Baptist church Reeder had seen in Tottenham, England, and built on an elevation that featured an imposing stairway.[37] In 1837, Joseph Galle described the new construction at the Weierhof in concerned tones to his brother Johannes. It was a large building, he wrote, "with 42 steps leading up to it . . . high windows . . . and a chancel or pulpit inside that rises eight feet off the ground." Noting that Monsheim, Sembach, Ibersheim, and the Weierhof all had salaried preachers and all had built new meetinghouses in the recent past, Galle concluded, "It seems that just because they installed a new educated missionary pastor (*Pfarrer*) they must also have a new elegant church." He went on to quote a passage from the prophet Hosea, where Israel "forgot their creator and built a temple."[38]

Galle focused primarily on the sin of pride. But the architectural novelties brought with them other theological consequences which were even more subtle. The belltower on the Ibersheim meetinghouse—a feature borrowed from state churches—clearly suggested that the surrounding village should be publicly summoned to church through the ringing of the bells. Organs called for a skilled, salaried organist and imposed new musical tastes on the congregation. And even if one could justify the raised pulpit (*Kanzel*) for acoustical reasons, its symbolism could not help but underscore the new authority of the professional preacher and highlight the centrality of the sermon in the worship service.

Missions

Simultaneous with the growing tensions related to a professionalized ministry, Mennonites in Southwest Germany engaged in a debate over missions, and the closely related issues of ecumenical involvement and understandings of salvation. Any form of religious proselytizing had been strictly forbidden to Mennonites in the Palatinate before the French occupation. But the Dutch Mennonites had long developed an active interest in overseas missions, and once the French eliminated all restrictions against proselytizing, it might have seemed obvious that Mennonites in Southwest Germany would have eagerly joined in their efforts.

Indeed, initial steps toward mission involvement seemed promising. In January 1824, Leonhard Weydmann had translated and distributed a pamphlet from the Baptist Mission Society in London appealing to Mennonites for support of the foreign mission work already underway among Dutch Mennonite and Baptist missionaries. In the summer of the same year, William Henry Angas—on a tour for the Baptist Mission Society through the Mennonite communities of Prussia, Poland, Bavaria, and Switzerland—arrived in the Palatinate. There he spent four weeks visiting all the local Mennonite congregations in an attempt to promote interest in overseas missions. His efforts were rewarded on July 13 with a gathering of some fifteen Palatine and Hessen Mennonite ministers from eight different congregations who met at the Spitalhof to give Angas an official hearing.

According to the report on the conference, written by Johannes Risser, not everyone present agreed that "foreign help" (referring here to Angas) on spiritual matters was appropriate. Open, however, to new insights into Scripture, they did agree to discuss prayerfully "whether, and by what means, we should initiate in our congregations something to spread and propagate the gospel among the poor heathens."[39] In his sermon, Angas noted that his efforts to promote missions among Mennonites in Holland and Prussia had met with only marginal success. Indeed, some congregations, including several in the Palatinate, had no interest in missions whatsoever and had responded coldly to his encouragement. This attitude could change, Angas argued, only through much prayer and the introduction of better educated leadership.

Following his address, the conference approved Angas's suggestion that he regularly send them translations of the Baptist Mission Society's monthly reports. For their part, church leaders agreed to initiate a mission report one Sunday a month and to hold special prayer for the outpouring of the Holy Spirit on the "poor heathen." Each congregation was also to establish a collection box to be placed next to the alms box at the church door so that "friends of missions" would have the opportunity to make a financial contribution to the mission effort.[40]

Taking the liberty of his role as recorder, Johannes Risser added another six-page defense of the moral integrity of Angas and an appeal for broader support for missions. "How sad," he wrote, "it would be for us if the Lord should return and find us sleeping." Then in an appeal to the conservatives, Risser compared the sacrifice "of our ancestors who were beheaded in the fierce persecution" with the comparatively simple offering of the "widow's mite" in support of the mission program. In his final remarks, Risser announced that the conference would be repeated some time in the near future, and he issued an open invitation "not only to all Mennonite congregations, but to every honest person," even to those in Switzerland and Prussia.[41]

Over the next two decades, progressive congregations in Sembach, Friedelsheim, Monsheim, and the Weierhof aggressively pursued their interest in missions. They held periodic mission rallies, collected funds, circulated translations of the Baptist Missionary Society newsletter, and even supported scholarships (partly funded by Angas) to send promising young Mennonite men to mission schools at Beuggen and Basel.

Conservative leaders, however, resisted all such efforts. In part, their concern was that few of the outside speakers at the mission rallies were Mennonites and therefore did not share any of the distinctively Mennonite theological emphases on nonresistance and separation from the world.

Johannes Galle was also disturbed by the apocalyptical content of the mission society newsletters, especially when they claimed the 1000-year reign of Christ was going to begin in 1836. "When that didn't happen," he grumbled in a letter to a friend, "they published another booklet . . . which was simply full of wise sayings and argued that the 1000-year church was now going to appear in 1839. The book didn't stay in my house more than two days before I sent it back and told them I wouldn't pay a penny for such a book, much less 2 *Reichstaler.*"[42] In another letter, Galle argued on the basis of Colossians 1:5-6 that Christ, through the prophets and apostles, had already completed the work of missions.[43]

But the primary criticism leveled by conservatives against the new mission effort was that they ignored the suffering of Christ which the Christian should expect to endure as a faithful disciple. In numerous letters, Galle and Kägy complained that missionary conferences and literature were part of a larger trend among Protestants to make Christianity palatable to the masses, a trend that simply ignored the traditional *Ordnungen* and congregational discipline that had been central to Mennonite theological self-understanding. By June 1835, in a letter to Johannes Lapp, Galle was nearly ready to concede defeat. Noting that he had already been engaged in an eight-year struggle with the mission society, he bitterly concluded that "they have worked so long by now that any thought of the 'way of the cross' [*Kreuzweg*] has been annihilated among the Mennonites. . . ."[44]

New Publications: Hymnbook, catechism, and plans for reform

Even as the debate over leadership and missions was unfolding, a third line of conflict emerged. This one focused on a cluster of new publications appearing in the 1830s. The new tensions further sharpened the lines of conflict between conservative and progressive Mennonites and pointed toward the emergence of a new Mennonite ethos.

The first of these publications was a private initiative undertaken by Abraham Hunzinger, a thirty-eight-year-old Mennonite from Wimpfen. Hunzinger had enlisted a group of subscribers to finance an analytical study of the German Mennonite church which he titled *The Religious, Ecclesiological and Educational Conditions of the Mennonites or Baptism-Minded.* Published in 1830, the book was a potpourri of history, theology, criticism, and polemic. The first section began in a descriptive mode, listing South German Mennonite and Amish religious doctrines, then slipping into a lengthy harangue against the Mennonite practice of church discipline and their rejection of scientific study.

In the second half of the book Hunzinger offered his solution to church decline. In somewhat pompous tones, he called for dramatic changes in the Mennonite position on nonresistance, endogamous marriage, divorce, and attitudes toward government. The salvation of the Mennonite church, according to Hunzinger, depended on restructuring its polity along the lines of the state churches. Thus he argued in favor of a salaried church council, approved by the political ruler as the church's highest authority; the introduction of church synods; the use of graded Sunday school material for religious instruction through age eighteen; and an endowment raised with the help of the state and the state churches, out of which ministers' salaries might be paid.

Dedicated to the Grand Duke of Baden, Ludwig Wilhelm August, the book clearly appealed to several leading Mennonite preachers. Writing in June 1830, Johannes Risser reported to Johan Jakob Krehbiel that Hunzinger had given him his copy of the book personally along with seven other copies to pass on to other local subscribers. "As is well-known," commented Risser, "[Hunzinger's book] is useful to all of us, especially for preachers and elders [who are] implementing the rebuilding of our congregations, whose decay . . . appears to be imminent." Risser cautioned Krehbiel that the Word of God commands believers to test all things and to "keep only that which is good," but it is evident that he was well-pleased with Hunzinger's effort."[45]

Interestingly enough, Hunzinger's book eventually found its way to America and, in 1862, was reprinted by none other than the American Mennonite reformer John Oberholtzer. Little is known about the reception of Hunzinger's book among the Eastern District Mennonites that emerged out of Oberholtzer's reforming initiatives. However, the highly rationalized approach to church reforms promoted by Hunzinger certainly bear strong resemblances to Oberholtzer's own progressive efforts. [46]

Two years later, in 1832, progressive Mennonites in the Palatinate joined forces to publish a new hymnbook that unleashed fresh controversy. For generations, Mennonite congregations had been using the *Ausbund* as their primary hymnbook, supplemented since the late eighteenth century by a hymnal from the Reformed Church called the *Harfenspiel*. But now that Mennonites were no longer living under the shadow of persecution, progressives increasingly regarded the martyr ballads of the *Ausbund* as anachronistic and tedious.

In February 1827, Johannes Risser, in typically argumentative fashion, wrote a sixteen-page letter to a conservative brother in the church in which he outlined the necessity of a new hymnal. Risser's logic drew on both doctrinal and pragmatic arguments. Appealing to a sense of tradition, Risser argued that any book the church used, "must at least teach our doctrinal differences that exist in baptism and the election of ministers."[47] The other hymnbooks in circulation were in Risser's mind "not quite biblical," for they "contain principally the teachings of virtuous conduct rather than of faith. . . ." Furthermore, Risser continued, besides being too large with 700 hymns, the *Harfenspiel* was "a foreign hymnbook" and therefore not a candidate for reprinting. Without making any mention of the *Ausbund*, Risser proposed that the congregations draw up a new hymnbook of their own, about one-third the size of the *Harfenspiel*. In fact, Leonhard Weydmann, newly hired preacher at Monsheim, had already offered to compile such a book. "We and our churches," concluded Risser, "have an obligation to extend him a helping hand in bringing this pleasant prospect to fruition."[48]

By 1830 Weydmann presented a draft of the book—consisting of 220 of the best "old core songs" (*Kernlieder*) and an appendix of new songs—to a meeting of local ministers. They agreed it would be circulated among the preachers and elders. If it met with their approval, the book should be printed for church use.

Johannes Galle and other conservatives opposed the new songbook from the outset. They claimed it had "eliminated all the good core songs on themes of suffering and the cross." Indeed, in Galle's judgment, the book was so bad that "if someone would hack off the arms and legs or cut away the nose and ears of a person, his body would not be so mutilated as the songbook has been mutilated."[49] In a letter to Johannes Lapp, his conservative counterpart in New York, Galle went on to praise the "right-thinking" (*rechtgesinnte*) Mennonites in America for republishing "the old stories . . . of the *Martyrs' Mirror*," a literary effort that in his mind contrasted sharply with events in South Germany.[50]

Despite loud protests from the conservative minority, the *Christliches Gesangbuch* appeared in 1832. Oddly enough, however, the hymnbook appeared in two versions—alike in all respects except for the title page and foreword. The standard version lacked a foreword and included the subtitle: *Primarily for use among the Baptism-Minded* (*Zunächst für den Gebrauch der Taufgesinnten*). But according to a letter by Johann Weber, progressive Mennonites in Friedelsheim and Sembach had protested against the use of the term *Taufgesinnten*, likely because the old-fashioned name still carried connotations in the popular mind of the discredited *Täuferreich* at Münster. Indeed, Mennonites meeting at Sembach had been so adamant about the matter that, even though many of the books had already been bound, they refused to accept them until a "correction" had been made on the books destined for use in their own congregations.[51] Thus a variant print run of some 200 copies of the new hymnal was arranged in which the words *Taufgesinnten* in the title page were replaced with the phrase *evangelischen Mennoniten-Gemeinen*. Presumably, to their ears, "evangelical Mennonites" sounded more modern, more in line with their *evangelischen*—or Protestant—neighbors.[52]

These setbacks notwithstanding, the 1832 hymnal found ready acceptance in the leading Mennonite congregations in South Germany. Katharina Krehbiel, writing from the Weierhof early in 1833 to her brother Daniel, a recent emigrant to New York, said that the congregation there had started singing through the book, beginning with the "new" songs in the middle, learning all the new melodies as they went. "Every evening people sing. Whole families gather to practice singing new melodies in four parts and some of them have even been sung in church."[53]

The following year, fears among conservatives that advocates for mission conferences and the new songbook were subtly reshaping Mennonite theology were confirmed and deepened when word began to circulate that a group led by Leonhard Weydmann now wanted to revise the standard catechism as well. For at least fifty years Mennonites in the region had been using the thirty-five questions and answers of the *Christliches Gemüthsgespräch* as their basic text for catechechismal instruction. Written in 1702 by the highly respected North German Mennonite preacher and elder Gerrit Roosen, the catechism had found favor among Mennonites in the Palatinate, who frequently reprinted it along with another catechism by Dutch Mennonite Johannes Deknatel, entitled *Anleitung zum christliches Glauben*.[54]

According to Galle, Weydmann and other progressive ministers chafed at certain questions in the Roosen catechism, specifically Article 26 that restricted marriage to other Mennonites, Article 27 against divorce, and Articles 31-33 on church discipline. So Weydmann, openly enlisting the help of local Lutheran clergy, set about to write his own new and improved catechism.

Even before the new catechism—entitled *Christliche Lehre zunächst zum Gebrauch der Taufgesinnten in Deutschland*[55]—appeared in 1836, conservative ministers raised their voices in protest. In a letter to Christian Krehbiel at the Weierhof, one of the proponents of the new catechism, Johannes Galle, contrasted the manner of its presentation with an earlier era:

> Fifty or one hundred years ago when our congregations were scattered from 30-60 hours apart, everyone was informed and worked together

with the Holy Spirit's leading whenever anything important was decided. But this new catechism was prepared in such secrecy and released like a whirlwind on innocent and unsuspecting congregations. Now disunity has arisen because many ministers and deacons—indeed most Mennonite congregations—find it impossible to agree with you in calling light darkness and darkness light, or sweet sour and sour sweet.

"If you want reconciliation," Galle concluded, "then the Weierhofers must first throw away the new catechism; then I will be the first to extend the right hand of fellowship to you."[56]

On February 25, 1835, ministers from six congregations of the conservative union had considered an invitation to meet with Weydmann and others for extended discussion of the new catechism. Rejecting the offer, they dismissed the new book out of hand as an effort to reduce salvation to the Ten Commandments and the Lord's Prayer, something Catholics, Reformed, and Lutheran could also all accept. "Christ called us to the narrow way. . . . Therefore we will stay by those old catechisms [e.g., those by Roosen and Deknatel] that we value most."[57] Eighteen ministers signed the statement.

In April 1835, Kägy organized another gathering of conservative ministers at Sinsheim where he was even more specific in his critique. The new catechism was clearly "not for Mennonites," he argued, since it left out any mention of church discipline or the selection of leaders, marriage, and nonresistance.[58] In a letter the following month he wrote to a brother Galle that "all of our doctrines and church rules (*Ordnungen*) are contained in the thirty-five Questions and Answers and every member and leader can understand them." Weydmann, he claimed to yet another correspondent, "has thrown out the doctrinal basis which separates us from the *Evangelischen Glaubensgenossen* [Protestant denominations]."

In the same letter, Kägy cast the new catechism in the broadest perspective: "because we Mennonites have sat for such a long time in proud peace and have had the gospel without the Passion of Christ we know nothing of the persecution and suffering of our forefathers. Thus many despise the old teaching books which they are now trying to destroy. . . ." Our basis, Kägy continued, "is none other and none newer than the apostle Paul who says in Hebrews 13:5—be happy with what you have."[59] "The Mennonites and the Protestants," lamented Galle, "continue to melt together."[60]

The protestations of the conservatives, however, met with little response. By 1836 the large congregations of Monsheim, Ibersheim, Friedelsheim, Sembach, and the Weierhof all had adopted the new catechism, and the split was sealed.[61]

Conclusion

This summary of the conflicts dividing the Mennonite congregations in Southwest Germany, complicated though it may sound, is actually far too abbreviated. I have not, for example, problematized terms like *modernity*, *progressives*, or *conservatives*. I have not explored here economic aspects of the division or traced the complex role intermarriages and family networks might have played in these tensions. Nor have I given any consideration to the impact of emigration out of Mennonite communities, ties between South German Mennonites and the broader European Mennonite church, the history of the Protestant mission movement, or the possible influence of the ecumenical Protestant Union of 1818 on developments in the South German Mennonite church. Clearly there are many more nuances to the story than I have been able to summarize here.[62]

Despite all these caveats, however, it is clear that something qualitatively new was emerging among Mennonite congregations in Southwest Germany in the early nineteenth century. The legal reforms introduced by the French saved Mennonites from the precarious balance they had long endured as "tolerated" subjects of a feudal prince, always subject to burdensome legal restrictions and always under the shadow of renewed persecution and possible expulsion. The reforms invited—indeed compelled—Mennonites to join with their Catholic and Protestant neighbors in a modern secular society made up of citizens equal under the law. Grounded on the authority of reason, this was a society that celebrated the rights of the individual, separated the church from the state, and honored the individual conscience in matters of religion.

Mennonites in the early nineteenth century, however, were ill-prepared to understand, critique, or creatively engage this new modern context. Progressives like Johannes Risser and Leonhard Weydmann were convinced that the cognitive dissonance between the inherited language of suffering and the reality of religious freedom simply could not be sustained. In a society celebrating individual rights and liberties, notions like endogamous marriage, the use of the lot, and the exercise of church discipline had become eccentric anachronisms. Traditional Mennonite understandings simply did not provide a competitive worldview, especially for young people faced with a new array of choices. In the new world they inhabited, where religion had become a private matter of individual conscience, the

Lutheran language of personal grace was more compelling than the communitarian themes of Mennonite ecclesiology.

In the free marketplace of religious ideas, it simply made sense to organize for missions, to develop budgets and conferences and long-term strategies to win the souls of the lost. In an increasingly bureaucratized culture—organized around principles of efficiency, professional training, and competence—trained and salaried ministers offered clear competitive advantages over the haphazard and quirky system of the lot. In short, a professional pastorate, engagement in world missions, ecumenical contacts, new hymnbooks, and revised catechisms all offered a better "fit" with the emerging public culture.

Johannes Galle and David Kägy, on the other hand, were convinced that costly discipleship—and their understanding of the church as a gathered disciplined community—transcended cultural contexts even as they intuitively sensed that tectonic plates were shifting beneath the Mennonite world. But they were unable to articulate these convictions in a persuasive or sustained manner. In the end, the organizational energies of the progressives—with their resources of education, money, and influence—simply left the supporters of Galle and the Kägy behind.

To be sure, the specific details of this division—the first church split of the "modern" era—were unique to Suthwest Germany. But in many ways, the Mennonite community has been struggling with the issues churned up by the French Revolution ever since. In the following century and a half the same tensions that divided people like Risser and Weydmann from Galle and Kägy were to find an echo in virtually every other Mennonite community in Europe and North America. One need only look at the Oberholtzer division of 1848, the slow split in the Amish church which led to the formation of the Amish Mennonites in the 1860s, the beginnings of the Mennonite Brethren, the Beachy Amish, or even, perhaps, the conflicts looming as General Conference and Old Mennonites pursue integration.

We study these conflicts—modern and postmodern—because they illuminate and contextualize the vexing issues of our own day. We ponder them also because they point us toward timeless questions of continuity and change, of faith and culture, of freedom and order—and ultimately to the mystery of the incarnation itself.

Notes

1. Johann Wolfgang von Goethe, *Hermann und Dorothea* (New York: Macmillan, 1968), 44. Throughout this essay, the term "Sothwest Germany" refers to those lands south of the Mosel River and west of the Rhine known after 1815 as the Bavarian Palatinate.

2. For a translation of this decree, see Herbert Fisher, *Studies in Napoleonic Statesmanship: Germany* (Oxford: Clarendon Press, 1903), 3.

3. Franklin Ford, *Europe, 1780-1830* (London: Longmans, Green and Co., 1970), 1-3, 387, 391; see also F. L. Ford, "The revolutionary-Napoleonic era: How much of a watershed?" *American Historical Review* 69 (1963): 18-29.

4. Helmut Berding and Hans-Peter Ullmann, eds., *Deutschland zwischen Revolution und Restauration* (Düsseldorf: Droste, 1981), 9.

5. "Das Auslösungsrecht gegen die Mennoniten in der Kurpfalz," *Christliche Gemeinde-Kalendar* (1912), 120-134.

6. Quoted in Fritz Hege, "Beruf und Berufung die Mennoniten in der Kurpfalz," *Christliche Gemeinde-Kalendar* (1954), 65.

7. Quoted in "Eine Bekehrungsgeschichte: Aus den Akten des Karlsruhe General-Landesarchiv," *Christliche Gemeinde-Kalendar* (1906), 67.

8. Möllinger was praised throughout the region for introducing crop rotation, new forms of fertilizers, and new breeds of cattle and is still identified in textbooks as the "Father of Palatine Agriculture." For more on Möllinger and other examples of Mennonite agrarian success, see Ernst Correll, *Das schweizerische Täufermennonitum* (Tübingen, 1925), 125ff, as well as the contemporary account of Christian Schwerz, *Beobachten über den Ackerbau der Pfälzer* (Berlin, 1816), 21ff.

9. Quoted in Christian Neff, "Peter Weber, ein mennonitischer Pietist aus dem 18. Jahrhundert," *Christlicher Gemeinde-Kalender* 39(1930), 72.

10. For a fuller account of Weber's story, see John D. Roth, "Pietism and the Anabaptist Soul," in *The Dilemma of Anabaptist Piety: Strengthening or Straining the Bonds of Community?* ed. Stephen L. Longenecker *(Bridgewater, Va.: Bridgewater College Forum for Religious Studies, 1997), 27-33.*

11. Chr. Dettweiler," *Mennonitische Geschichtsblätter* 49 (September, 1902), 77.

12. Gary Waltner, "Aus der Pfalz nach Nordamerika," *Mennonitische Geschichtsblätter* (1976), 15.

13. H. S., "Überlieferungen eines Bauern des Spitalhofes aus der Franzosenzeit," *Christlicher Gemeinde-Kalendar* (1937), 106.

14. Martin Möllinger to Johannes Weber [1795], Hist. Mss. 1-536, Weber Collection, Archives of the Mennonite Church [hereafter cited as AMC]; Johannes Weber to Martin Möllinger, May 17, 1798, Hist. Mss. 1-536, AMC.

15. Hermann Reeder, *Predigten zu Festtagen und bei besonderen Veranlaßungen* (Leipzig: Karl Tauchnitz, 1843), ix.

16. David Kägy to John Lapp, May 22, 1842, 1-536, AMC.

17. Paul Schowalter, "Die Ibersheimer Beschlüße von 1803 und 1805," *Mennonitische Geschichtsblätter* (1963), 38.

18. Jacob Ellenberger, *Ein Lebensbild* (Frankfurt: Deutsches-Reichspost Action-Gesellschaft, 1879), 7.

19. Wilhelm Mannhardt, *Die Wehrfreiheit der Altpreußischen Mennoniten* (Marienburg: Im Selbstverlag der Altpreußischen Mennoniten-gemeinden, 1863), 55.
20. Waltner, "Aus der Pfalz," 16.
21. C. Henry Smith, *The Story of the Mennonites* (Newton, Kans.: Mennonite Publication Office, 1957), 316.
22. Max Springer, *Die Franzosenherrschaft in der Pfalz, 1792-1814: Departement Donnersberg* (Berlin: Deutsch Verlags Anstalt, 1926), 350.
23. Ibid., 146.
24. Wilhelm Heinrich Riehl, *Die Pfälzer: Ein rheinische Volksbild* (Stuttgart, 1846), 261; see also Springer, *Die Franzosenherrschaft in der Pfalz*, 333ff.
25. Cf. Adam Sahrmann, *Pfalz oder Salzburg? Geschichte des territorialen Ausgleichs zwischen Bayern und Österreich von 1813 bis 1819* (München: R. Oldenbourg, 1921).
26. The best overview of this scarcely noted conservative movement can be found in Christian Neff, "David Kaegy von Offstein," *Christlicher Gemeinde-Kalendar* (1925), 39-63.
27. Peter Weber to Johannes Weber, July 9, 1761, 1-536, AMC.
28. *Allgemeines und vollständiges Formularbuch* (Neuwied: Gedruckt bey J. E. Haupt, 1807).
29. Ernst Correll, "Weydmann, Leonhard," *Mennonite Encyclopedia*, 4:938.
30. David Kägy to [?], February 10, 1836, 1-536, AMC. By 1830 there were suggestions afoot among progressives to fund pastoral salaries by establishing endowments, a solution which likely would have removed the minister even further from the congregational orbit.
31. Christian Eymann to Möllinger family and Herr Weidmann, March 25, 1819, Hist. Mss. 1-536, 1/1, AMC.
32. Ibid.
33. Ibid.
34. John Lapp to [Johannes Galle], April 30, 1835, 1-381, 1, AMC.
35. Johannes Galle to John Lapp, January 12, 1836, 1-536, AMC.
36. Cf. Paul Showalter, "Reeder, Hermann," *Mennonite Encyclopedia*, 4:264 and the autobiographical comments scattered through Reeder's published collection of sermons *(Predigten an Festtagen und bei besonderen Veranlaßungen* [Leipzig: Karl Tauchnitz, 1843]).
37. Reeder, *Predigten an Festtagen*, xi.
38. Joseph Galle to John Lapp, March 20, 1838, 1-536, 6/9, AMC.
39. Johannes Risser, Guttbefinden einer kleiner Kirchenversammlung der Mennoniten-Gemeinen. Gehalten auf dem Spitalhof, am 13 Julius 1824 (n.p, 1824).
40. This collection canister can still be seen at the Mennonitische Forschungstelle, Weierhof, Germany. The alms book of the Weierhof congregation shows that donations to mission causes continued regularly after 1824; the congregation even began subscribing to a periodical published by the Basal Mission Society.
41. Risser, *Guttbefinden einer kleiner Kirchenversammlung*, 17-22.
42. Johannes Galle to John Lapp, March 20, 1838, 1-536, 6/9, AMC.
43. "The faith and love that spring from the hope stored up for you in heaven, and which you have already heard about in the word of truth, the gospel that has come to you. All over the world this gospel is producing fruit and growing, just as it has been

doing among you since the day you heard it" (NIV).

44. Quoted in Christian Neff, "Die Männer der alte Richtung," *Mennonitische Blätter* (1907), 96.

45. Johannes Risser to Johan Jakob Krehbiel, October 22, 1830, 1-536, AMC.

46. "Hunzinger, Abraham," *Mennonite Encyclopedia*, 2:845.

47. Johannes Risser to Cousin, February 14, 1827, 1-536, 5/4, AMC.

48. Ibid.

49. Quoted in Neff, "Männer der alten Richtung," 96.

50. Quoted in Ibid., 98.

51. Johannes Weber to [?], October 28, 1832, 1-536, 4/5, AMC.

52. An 1839 re-publication of the hymnal simplified "evangelischen Mennoniten-Gemeinen" to "Mennoniten." Incidentally, it is worth noting that Mennonites in the Sembach and Friedelsheim congregations also began celebrating Reformation Sunday; and in 1850, Leonhard Weydmann, pastor at Monsheim, published a glowing biography of Martin Luther entitled *Luther: A Model Character and Mirror for our Times*.

53. Addendum by Katharina Krehbiel to a letter from Johannes Krehbiel to Daniel Krehbiel, January 6, 1833, 1-536, 7/6, AMC.

54. The most recent publication of the book at the time had been orchestrated (and likely paid for) by David Kägy at Offstein who, in the fall of 1828, ordered 400 copies of the book from the Kranzbuhler printers in Worms (David Kägy to Herrn Kranzbuhler, November 26, 1828, 1-536, AMC). The edition appeared in 1829.

55. The title of this forty-page catechism clearly mirrored that of the recently published songbook. Weydmann apparently was not among those who resisted the use of the term *Taufgesinnten*.

56. Johannes Galle to Christian Krehbiel, December 19, 1835, 1-536, AMC.

57. Quoted in Neff, "Die Männer der alte Richtung," 98.

58. David Kägy to friend [in Bruchhausen], April 18, 1835, 1-536, AMC.

59. David Kägy to "Brother Galle," May 16, 1835, 1-536, AMC.

60. Johannes Galle to John Lapp, March 20, 1838, 1-536, AMC.

61. In 1838, Galle and Kägy responded with a publication of their own. In March of that year, Galle reported to Lapp that Brethren in Switzerland had requested financial assistance to reprint a catechism, the *Christliches Gemuthsgespräch*. In 1829, South German Mennonites had reprinted 500 copies of the booklet and shared several packets gratis with their poorer brethren in Switzerland. It was, Galle claimed, nothing less than the work of the Almighty God, for "just when some wanted to eradicate this catechism, a call from another country ensured its survival" (Johannes Galle to John Lapp, March 20, 1838, 1-536, 6/9, AMC). In 1838 an edition of the *Christliches Gemuthsgesprach* appeared in Basel, undoubtedly with the help of the conservative congregations in South Germany. In the same year an edition of the *Ausbund*, also published in Basel, appeared. It is uncertain, though quite likely, that the South Germans helped to finance that volume as well.

62. I was surprised to discover, for example, that conservative leader David Kägy served in various local political offices, contributed to the construction of the local Protestant church and was a close friend of several Protestant pastors (Cf. Neff, "David Kaegy von Offstein," 45-48).

PART THREE

MARGINAL VOICES AND CHURCH POLITY

SEVEN

WHEN BLOCH POINTED TO THE CAGES OUTSIDE THE CATHEDRAL

Scott Holland

(Muenster, 12 August 1534)
The Anabaptists have the city now:
One night a defrocked priest, one "Bread Bernard,"
Ran naked through the streets crying aloud
That all alone he'd wrestled many nights
With evil spirits (as I well believe)
And God Himself had told him to go forth
Into the public ways to choose the saved.
So out they came, tangled in their sheets
No less than their bad consciences, and said
The day of woe will come on them soon
(Which, no doubt, it will), and beat their heads
On the paving stones, tore their hair,
And showed other ways their perfect faith.
Just after that we brought our armies in.

A certain tailor they have made their king.
He also talks with God, calling himself
The death-angel, and well makes good his boast.
Just bread, says Juvenal, and circuses

Can rule an Empire, but this tailor does
One better: short of bread, thanks to us,
He rules the town with circuses alone.
He parodies the Mass, devises hats,
And with great ceremony disembowels
The luckless wretches he's suspicious of,
He's saved the city from the curse of gold,
I've heard, by taking all of it himself,
And many saintly women came to sing
Hosannas in the highest to his name.
Atop the walls are angels militant
Like none that heaven ever saw.

How strange. . . . [1]

Poet John Burt's narrative description of Münster is enough to make any modern Anabaptist cringe. De-frocked priests running naked through the streets, true believers mocking the Mass, militant prophets bringing in the kingdom with the sword, a tailor king seducing sweet sisters with the word of God and holy kisses.

Little wonder Mennonite historian H. S. Bender, in a skillful rhetorical move called "The Anabaptist Vision,"[2] brought a bishop's soul to discipline the unruly body of Anabaptist historiography and theology. With political and pastoral brilliance, Bender rescued Anabaptism from the trash bin of history as he excommunicated many rebels and redefined normative Anabaptism as an evangelical commitment to Christ through community, discipleship, and nonresistance. Through Bender's historical theology, Anabaptism even won the respect of the reserved suit-and-tie scholars of the American Society of Church History.

Bender's reconfiguration of Anabaptism[3] has been useful for the believers church, giving it a normative narrative and moving it from sect to church status in modern Christendom while retaining some of its original oppositional and countercultural impulses: communal solidarity over the autonomy of the soul, discipleship or ethics over mere orthodoxy, and peace over all holy crusades and politically just wars. For at least some contemporary Anabaptist faith communities, the old era of the bishops has been replaced with the new era of Anabaptist scholars.

Yet Bender's almost exclusive attention to Swiss Anabaptism in the composition of his Vision, and his suspicion of other Free Church radicals who failed to neatly embody the evangelical ideals of community, discipleship, and peace, has cut some of our most interesting ancestors from the family tree: revolutionaries, antinomians, mystics, and radical pietists. So if you would, consider with me the day "When Ernst Bloch pointed to the cages outside the Cathedral."

One afternoon Ernst Bloch and Johannes Baptist Metz were walking the streets of the city of Münster. As their conversation turned to political theology, Bloch pointed to the three iron cages that still hang outside the Saint Lamberti Church. Heretics of the Radical Reformation were executed in those cages. Their bodies and bones remained on public display as a warning to dissenters and witness to the triumph of imperial Christendom. "One must do theology from there," Bloch said to the Baptist.[4]

Although Bloch's declaration was driven by important political concerns, pragmatic considerations would also lead one to conclude that if theology is to continue as a mode of reflection at the beginning of this new millennium, it must be conceived after Christendom in creative spaces outside the Cathedral. Both modern statisticians and postmodern theorists agree: the grand temple of Western Christendom can no longer seduce and satisfy the religious imagination, nor can its old Constantinian heresy provide an interesting or instructive vision of God in the world. God is dead or eclipsed or exiled. Yet as Bloch's prophetic gesture implied, if God is to indeed return, it will be from the cages, from the margins, from life's liminal spaces, from somewhere other, from somewhere *Beyond*.

Literary theorists Gilles Deleuze and Felix Guattari write of the importance of "minor literatures." A minor literature, according to Deleuze, makes intensive and transgressive use of a major language as a witness to the representational incompleteness in all discourse.[5] As such, it points to an Other beyond the metanarrative.

Current, creative scholarship is reminding us of two of Christendom's others: Anabaptists and Jews. Roger Bádham has recently written that

> The Anabaptists became, in their radical otherness, a voluntary Christian counterpart to the Jewish communities in Europe. Like the Jews, they were seen as outside the homogenizing structures of society. Like the Jews, they offered Europe early warning of the pluralism to come and were persecuted for their difference.[6]

Anabaptist and Jewish theological expressions were and are "minor literatures" in the dominant discourse of God-talk. Such literatures can be tempted by tribalistic arrogance or sectarian withdrawal. But they can also be truly public discourses as they work in, through, and even against more dominant expressions of theological writing to render it incomplete, unstable, and unsafe. This imaginative theological composition invites the return of the repressed and exiled; indeed, it invites the return of the Other.

Deleuze and Guattari turn to Kafka as a fine example of the importance of a minor literature. Franz Kafka believed that "writing is a form of prayer." As all faithful Anabaptist preachers and Jewish rabbis know, prayer opens one to an Infinity that reveals every totality to be not only incomplete, but idolatrous.[7] They know that prayer and song in the Jewish and Christian traditions is Doxology against all idolatry and ideology. God is Other beyond Cathedrals, Creeds, and Moral Codes, indeed beyond even the God we name.

BEYOND CATHEDRALS

We with roots in the Radical Reformation have joyfully encountered God in the Cathedral, yet we have also known God in caves, forests, and at the incendiary stake of the executioner. With the postmodern fall of Christendom, how tempting it could be to construct a new Anabaptist Cathedral, supported by the foundational pillars of community, discipleship, and nonresistance—especially nonresistance—the most essential pillar.

How tempting it could be to replace a *Corpus Christianum* with a *Corpus Mennoniticum*. Yet Anabaptism was and is a polyphony, not a harmony. A genuine hermeneutics of peoplehood beyond the Cathedral must engage its many voices, literatures, and narratives, striving not for objectivity but for a spirited intersubjectivity and intertextuality.

There are many wonderful and terrible Anabaptist stories. Here is one not often told. By 1885 a young South German Mennonite named John Horsch had become impassioned by the richness of his Anabaptist heritage after reading Ludwig Keller's book on Hans Denck.[8] Keller celebrated the undogmatic, mystical Anabaptism of Hans Denck and criticized what he considered the overly dogmatic Menno Simons. John Horsch was so inspired by the undogmatic Denck that he planned to encourage European and American Mennonites to adopt Denck's theology as the finest expression of Anabaptism.

In 1887 Horsch emigrated to America with the writings of Denck and Johann Tauler's *German Theology* in his bags. He showed up on the Elkhart doorstep of John Funk, publisher of the Mennonite periodical *Herald of Truth*. He was penniless and looking for work in the American Mennonite publishing community. He found it!

In the next few years he became terribly entangled in the American Fundamentalist-Modernist controversy. Surprisingly, he turned from his beloved Denck and cast his lot with the Fundamentalists, that culture of resentment. Soon, and not surprisingly, he declared that Menno and the Swiss Brethren were the "real Anabaptists." He described the latter as "Anabaptist Fundamentalists."[9]

By 1908 the established Mennonite editor and writer John Horsch carried his message of Anabaptist Fundamentalism to the village of Scottdale, Pennsylvania, the new home of the Mennonite Publishing House and its company church. Along with Daniel Kauffman and others, he helped set the dogmatic tone for a normative Mennonite theology.[10] Now John Horsch had a daughter whom Harold Bender loved and married. H. S. Bender learned much about Anabaptist history from John Horsch. Although Bender certainly moved far beyond the fundamentalism of his father-in-law, he nevertheless clung to Horsch's dogmatic Anabaptist historiography and shunned undogmatic mystics like Denck.[11]

Even now, can't you almost hear the voice of our dear, departed Clarence Bauman as he insisted again and again,

> Hans Denck represents the contemplative genius of the Anabaptist Movement at its highest and best. No understanding of the Anabaptist Vision is complete without coming to terms with the uniqueness of Denck's intellectual spirituality: its inner dynamic, its medieval context, its mystic content, and its Jewish roots.[12]

Unlike the counter-modern projects of Horsch and Bender, postmodern Anabaptism is inviting Denck back to the Lord's Table. Some of us are suggesting that it is even time to invite the Radical Pietists back to the table.

The influence of the great preacher, poet, and historian, Gottfried Arnold, on the development of Pietism can hardly be overemphasized. We have much to learn from him.[13] He spoke of the spiritual life not in terms of duty or even discipleship but as desire: *Die erste Liebe* (The First Love).[14] It was this "love theology" that found its way into themes of much of early Pietist literature, and later into Brethren theology.

Arnold's mystical piety was refreshingly suspicious of both religious community and theological creeds. As a poet and preacher he recognized that the order of community and the language of creeds threatened to collapse *theos* into *logos*. This is always the great temptation of church and creed, to bring Infinity into submission to a historical totality.[15] Arnold also understood very clearly how the formal language of church and creed had been used in the history of the church to punish dissidents and nonconformists who were often true believers. He therefore preached a stubborn but enlightened noncreedalism. His historical work pointed to the absence of disciplinary creeds in the apostolic church and to the terrible violence and persecution that creedal Christianity produced.

This concern is at the center of Arnold's massive work of historical theology, *A Nonpartisan History of Church and Heresy*.[16] Applying the principles of love theology to the entire history of the church, his thesis was that the heretical movements had actually perpetuated the true church, while the orthodox church that disciplined and punished them was in reality the antichurch. He charged that orthodoxy had more to do with the politics of power and position than with the true spiritual church.[17]

Following Arnold's thesis about the manifestation of God in the world, it might be said that the orthodox who control the order of salvation have great political interests in managing a system of church doctrine and discipline wherein all yield submissively to an established theological cycle of sin, repentance, and redemption. Arnold's creative theological criticism demonstrates that in the history of spirituality, *theos*, in moments of *kairos*, refuses the *logos* of orthodoxy. Instead theos enters history and the human soul not through the established formula of sin, repentance, and redemption, but through a heretical revolution of transgression, excess, and gift. Heretics, ecstatics, saints, mystics, pietists, and poets remind us that often God comes first as transgression, then excess, and finally, gift![18]

BEYOND THE CREEDS

We know God through, yet beyond, the Cathedral. Likewise, we know God through, yet beyond, the creeds. One day that great unsystematic theologian Søren Kierkegaard found his melancholic heart strangely cheered while reading about Radical Reformation noncreedalism.[19] He was reading Benjamin Franklin's *Autobiography*, of all things.

Franklin records a conversation he had with the Dunker, Michael Wolfart. Wolfart was talking with Franklin about the problems and possibilities of Brethren pluralism. Franklin suggested that perhaps it would be good for the Dunkers to establish a clear creed and a systematic theology like the rest of Christendom. Franklin writes:

> I told him that I imagined it might be well to publish the articles of their faith and the rules of their discipline. He said that it had been proposed among them, but not agreed to, for this reason: "When we were first drawn together as a society," says he, "it had pleased God to enlighten our minds so far as to see that some doctrines, which we had once esteemed errors, were real truths. From time to time He has been pleased to afford us farther light, and our principles have been improving, and er-

rors diminishing. Now we are not sure that we have arrived at the end of this progression, and at the perfection of spiritual or theological knowledge; and we fear that, if we should print our confession, we should feel ourselves as if bound and confined by it, and perhaps be unwilling to receive farther improvement, and our successors still more so, as conceiving what we their elders and founders had done, to be something sacred, never to be departed from." This modesty in a sect is perhaps a singular instance in the history of mankind, every other sect supposing itself in possession of all truth, and that those who differ are so far in the wrong.[20]

And Kierkegaard laughed, for he also knew that the Jesus story carries us to a God of hope beyond time and narrative closure.[21] Indeed, Kierkegaard understood that this God is beyond even the category of the ethical.[22]

BEYOND THE ETHICAL

Movement beyond the ethical is perhaps the hardest lesson for postmodern Anabaptists. Yes, God is beyond the Cathedral and Creed, but certainly not beyond ethics![23] Many postmodern Anabaptists are as ethically earnest as liberal Unitarians and humanistic Quakers, only worse, gathering in the name of Jesus not for Doxology but for a more splendid orthopraxis!

The great temptation for Anabaptist Fundamentalists like John Horsch was to substitute a doctrine of justification by belief for the gracious mystery of justification by faith. The great temptation for neo-Anabaptists—indeed, even for postmodern Anabaptists—is to substitute an earnest doctrine of justification by ethics for the biblical stories of justification by faith. Ah, but we are saved by grace through faith.

Even as there are many voices in the contemporary church, there are many voices in the Bible. There are even many stories and models of repentance, forgiveness, and redemption. With so many wise and interesting voices from which to learn, why do our ministers, bishops, and theologians find themselves drawn to the harshest words of Scripture? My 102-year-old grandmother used to insist that because Mennonites and Brethren don't believe in war, we must nevertheless find some way to shed blood through our religion. This peace has destroyed many!

Last Lenten season I had the privilege of meeting Father Raymond Brown, whom some call the premier New Testament scholar in North America. He astonished me with words that fell like reckless, irresponsible grace on my well-trained Anabaptist ears. Professor Brown suggested that Jesus teaches us through the parable of the Prodigal Son that there can be forgiveness without repentance. Forgiveness without repentance? Imagine that.

In the gospel story, when the father saw his wayward son from a great distance, for all he knew the young man was returning home for a loan. Or for a larger cut of the family inheritance. But the father did not weigh the prodigal's intentions. Instead the old man ran out to greet him and fell on his neck with kisses.

Brown was careful to state that this is just one narrative. There are also hard words in the Bible. Yet shouldn't we, as members of the peace church tradition, be most attracted to stories of tender mercies and extravagant love?

The stern language of discipleship and ethics rarely saves anyone. Ah, but the elegance of holy kisses has called many sinners home. This I know. This is not mere liberal tolerance; this is reckless grace. In our Anabaptist zeal to keep salvation ethical, may we also keep it graceful; may we also keep it artful.

BEYOND THE GOD WE NAME

God is beyond the category of the ethical, God is beyond the Cathedral, God is beyond the creed. Indeed God is beyond the God we name. Jews and Anabaptists writing minor literatures can easily join the prayer of that great heretic, Meister Eckhart, "Oh God, Beyond the God I name!"[24]

The rabbis teach us that Genesis is not the beginning of religion and morality; Genesis, in the words of Aviva Zornberg, is *The Beginning of Desire*.[25] Emmanuel Levinas, standing between Judaism and postmodernism, insisted that "The relationship with the Infinite is not a knowledge but a Desire."[26]

A deeper understanding of imagination, mystery, and grace has returned Desire to postmodern Anabaptist theology. This postmodern theological writing is not driven by mere duty or discipleship but is itself a light in the head and a fire in the belly. It is passion. With the return of Desire to theology there is less austerity, humility, morality, and self-rejection—and more play, poetry, story, irony, mystery, grace, carnal vitality, and creative power in the blessed work of theological composition. With the return of Desire we may again know *jouissance*, the pleasure of the text, for with the return of Desire, God has returned, and with the return of God, you see, we have the return of the strong author.[27]

Long before the postmodern death of metaphysics, the seer, sage, and preacher Ralph Waldo Emerson declared that a philosopher or moral theorist must work by art, not metaphysics. Unhappy with both moral philosophers and philosophical theologians, Emerson wrote, "I think that philosophy . . . will one day be taught by poets."[28]

Last month I was reading Emerson on a commuter flight from Pittsburgh to Manchester College in Indiana. My eyes fell on a passage that gave me such intense pleasure that I almost stood up and read it aloud to the other passengers. Being a very reasonable and respectable Anabaptist preacher, I of course did not. But I will conclude this essay with it.

Emerson of course not only influenced the great poet of radical democracy, Walt Whitman, he also greatly influenced that counter-modern divine, Friedich Nietzsche, and his longing for a strong soul.[29] This passage is from his inspired essay, "The Poet:"[30]

> The poets are thus liberating gods. The ancient British bards had for the title of their order, "Those who are free throughout the world." They are free, and they make us free. An imaginative book renders us much more service at first, by stimulating us through its tropes, than afterward, when we arrive at the precise sense of the author. I think nothing is of any value in books, excepting the transcendental and extraordinary. If a man is inflamed and carried away by his thought, to that degree that he forgets the authors and the public, and heeds only this one dream, which holds him like an insanity, let me read his paper, and you may have all the arguments and histories and criticism. All the value which attaches to Pythagoras, Paracelsus, Cornelius Agrippa, Cardan, Kepler, Swedenborg, Schelling, Oken, or any other who introduces questionable facts into his cosmogony, as angels, devils, magic, astrology, palmistry, mesmerism, and so on, is the certificate we have of departure from routine, and that here is a new witness. That also is the best success in conversation, the magic of liberty, which puts the world, like a ball, in our hands. How cheap even the liberty then seems; how mean to study, when an emotion communicates to the intellect the power to sap and upheave nature: how great the perspective! Nations, times, systems, enter and disappear, like threads in a tapestry of large figures and many colors; dream delivers us to dream, and, while the drunkenness lasts, we will sell our bed, our philosophy, our religion, in our opulence.

I could write more about the God beyond the Cathedral, beyond creeds, beyond ethics and beyond the God we name. However, I must conclude with a line from the poet W. S. Merwin: "If you find you no longer believe, enlarge your temple."[31]

NOTES

1. From the narrative poem of John Burt, "Viglius Zuichemus," *Salmagundi* 111 (Summer 1996), 166-169.

2. See J. M. Stayer, W. O. Packull, and K. Deppermann, "From Monogenesis to Polygenesis: The Historical Discussion of Anabaptist Origins," *Mennonite Quarterly Review* 49 (April 1975): 83-121. For an analysis and criticism of "normative Anabaptism," see Rodney Sawatsky, "The Quest for a Mennonite Hermenuetic," *Conrad Grebel Review* 11 (Winter 1993), 1-21. Mennonite historian Arnold Snyder has recently published an introduction to Anabaptist history and theology, which, unlike many earlier works in the field, struggles seriously with the reality of polygenesis, yet in an imaginative search for a "theological core," demonstrates significant areas of consensus in the midst of conflict (C. Arnold Snyder, *An Introduction to Anabaptist History and Theology* [Kitchener, Ont.: Pandora Press, 1995]).

3. H. S. Bender, "The Anabaptist Vision," *Mennonite Quarterly Review* 16 (April 1944), 67-88. This version of Bender's classic reconfiguration of Anabaptism was reprinted with minor revisions from *Church History* (March 1944), 3-24.

4. I learned about this exchange between Bloch and Metz from Jürgen Manemann during a personal conversation with him in the summer of 1997 at Columbia University, where we were both doing research under an ARIL Coolidge Fellowship. Manemann is a member of Metz's circle of political theologians on the Roman Catholic faculty at Münster.

5. Gilles Deleuze and Félix Guattari, *Kafka: Toward a Minor Literature* (Minneapolis: University of Minnesota Press, 1986). Christian theologian Charles Winquist has recently noted the usefulness of thinking of theology in terms of Deleuze's notion of a minor literature in his *Desiring Theology* (Chicago: University of Chicago Press, 1995).

6. Roger Badham and Ola Sigurdson, "The Decentered Post-Constantinian Church: An Exchange," *Cross Currents* (Summer 1997), 155. I have corresponded with Badham about this matter. Further, I have been in touch with the Postmodern Jewish Philosophy Network and their electronic journal *Textual Reasoning* in exploration of Badham's interesting links between Jews and Anabaptists after Christendom. Two important collections of postmodern Jewish essays have recently been published: Steven Kepnes, ed., *Interpreting Judaism in a Postmodern Age* (New York: New York University Press, 1996); Steven Kepnes, Peter Ochs, and Robert Gibbs, eds., *Reasoning After Revelation: Dialogues in Postmodern Jewish Philosophy* (Boulder, Colo.: Westview Press, 1998).

7. This essay emphasizes the many possibilities for the postmodern "return of God." Some years ago, I participated in a memorable conversation with Wayne Booth (at a narrative conference in a Utah ski lodge) in which he offered some interesting reflections on the possibility of "deconstruction as a religion revival." Booth grew up in the Mormon Church and thus is no stranger to the many uses of minor religious literatures within the dominant narratives of Christendom. He has recently published a paper on the constructive use of deconstruction: "Deconstruction as a Religious Revival," in *Christianity and Culture in the Cross Fire*, ed. Hokema and Fong (Grand Rap-

ids: Eerdmans, 1997), 131-152. My other work tracing "the postmodern return of God" appears in *Mennonite Quarterly Review* (April 1997) and *Cross Currents* (Fall 1997).

8. Ludwig Keller, *Die Reformation und die älteren Reformparteien* (Leipzig: S. Hirzel, 1885).

9. The best narrative account of the evolution of John Horsch's theology from "undogmatic to dogmatic Anabaptism" is found in the first chapter of Abraham Friesen's new book, *Erasmus, the Anabaptists and the Great Commission* (Grand Rapids: Eerdmans, 1998), 6-19.

10. See John Horsch, *Modern Religious Liberalism* (Reprint; New York: Garland, 1988; original pub. 1921) and *The Mennonite Church and Modernism* (Scottdale, Pa.: Mennonite Publishing House, 1924).

11. Note the new Bender biography by Albert N. Keim, *Harold S. Bender 1897-1962* (Scottdale, Pa.: Herald Press, 1998).

12. Clarence Bauman, ed. and trans., *The Spiritual Legacy of Hans Denck: Interpretation and Translation of Key Texts* (Leiden: E. J. Brill, 1991). Daniel Liechty has recently edited, translated, and introduced a collection of Anabaptist writings on spirituality. Note especially his translations of South German and Austrian Anabaptists in *Early Anabaptist Spirituality: Selected Writings* (New York: Paulist Press, 1994). My evolving work suggests these mystics had a more independent "Christomorphic" spirituality in contrast to the more communal "Christocentrism" of the Swiss evangelicals.

13. Gottfried Arnold's life, theology, and connections to medieval mysticism and spirituality are treated in Peter Erb's *Pietists, Protestants and Mysticism: The Use of Medieval Spiritual Texts in the Work of Gottfried Arnold* (1666-1714) (Metuchen, N.J.: The Scarecrow Press, 1989). Also see Peter Erb, ed., *Pietists: Selected Writings (Classics of Western Spirituality)* (New York: Paulist Press, 1983).

14. Arnold published *Die Erste Liebe* as a book in Frankfurt in 1696. He speaks of the Christian life in the language of "a first love" (Rev. 2:4). His links to the great love mystics are evident in this work, and this "love Pietism" was warmly received by the early Brethren.

15. Postmodern theology and philosophy share some of the concerns of the premodern mystics and Pietists about the problems of "naming God" in language and "thinking God" through creed and church. Note also David Tracy's concerns about the captivity of *theos* and *logos*, which is the grand temptation of the discipline of theology, in "The Hidden God," *Cross Currents* 46 (Spring 1996), 5-16; and "The Return of God," in *Naming the Present* (Maryknoll, N.Y.:: Orbis Books, 1994), 36-46.

16. Gottfried Arnold, *Unparteyische Kirchen und Ketzer Historie*, 3 vols. (Frankfurt am Main: Thomas Fritsch, 1699-1700).

17. Donald P. Durnbaugh's new narrative history of the Brethren, *Fruit of the Vine* (Philadelphia: Brethren Encyclopedia, 1996), captures how redemptively oppositional and subversive Arnold was in his historiography, which championed many heretics as true believers and condemned many orthodox as the antichurch.

18. A creative study showing connections between postmodern categories such as

deconstruction, transgression, excess, gift and the experiences, expressions and discourses of saints, mystics, and heretics is Edith Wyschogrod's *Saints and Postmodernism* (Chicago: University of Chicago Press, 1990). Also, for a fine postmodern interpretation of the great mystics and their writing, see Don Cupitt, *Mysticism After Modernity* (Malden, Mass.: Blackwell Publishers, 1998).

19. Vernard M. Eller, "Kierkegaard knew the Brethren—sort of," *Brethren Life and Thought* 8 (Winter 1963), 57-60.

20. Benjamin Franklin, *Autobiography* (New York: Henry Holt and Co., 1912), 128-29.

21. This is to remind the reader of the irony, play, and pleasure in Kierkegaard's texts. Consider his statement on holy laughter: "Something wonderful has happened to me. I was caught up into the seventh heaven. There sat all the gods in assembly. By special grace I was granted the privilege of making a wish. 'Wilt thou,' said Mercury, 'have youth or beauty or power or a long life or the most beautiful maiden or any of the other glories we have in the chest? Choose, but only one thing.' For a moment I was at a loss. Then I addressed myself to the gods as follows: 'Most honorable contemporaries, I choose this one thing, that I may always have the laugh on my side.' Not one of the gods said a word; on the contrary, they all began to laugh. From that I concluded that my wish was granted, and found that the gods knew how to express themselves with taste; for it would hardly have been suitable for them to have answered gravely: 'Thy wish is granted.'" See Roger Poole and Henrik Strangerup, eds., *The Laughter is on my Side: An Imaginative Introduction to Kierkegaard* (Princeton: Princeton University Press, 1989), 241.

22. For the purpose of clarification I must stress that I am not suggesting that Kierkegaard's program would move us to a place "without ethics." I am, rather, calling attention to the Dane's understanding of a God "beyond" the category of the ethical. A fine experiment in postmodern ethics with the work of Kierkegaard in view is John D. Caputo's *Against Ethics* (Bloomington: Indiana University Press, 1993).

23. What might this movement "beyond the category of the ethical" look like? In a forthcoming essay I argue that the final years of Dietrich Bonhoeffer demonstrate a movement beyond ethics on behalf of the Other. "First We Take Manhattan, Then We Take Berlin," *Cross Currents*, 1999-2000.

24. Matthew Fox, *Breakthrough: Meister Eckhart's Spirituality in New Translation* (New York: Image Books of Doubleday and Co., 1980). Also see Reimer Schurmann, *Meister Eckhart: Mystic and Philosopher* (Bloomington: Indiana University Press, 1978).

25. Avivah Gottlieb Zornberg, *Genesis: The Beginning of Desire* (Jerusalem: The Jewish Publication Society, 1995).

26. Emmanuel Levinas, *Totality and Infinity*, trans. Alphonso Lingis (Pittsburgh: Duquesue University Press, 1969).

27. I develop this more fully in my "Theology is a Kind of Writing: The Emergence of Theopoetics," *Cross Currents* 47 (Fall 1997), 317-331.

28. Emerson is quoted here by John Dewey in his University of Chicago lecture, "Emerson—The Philosopher of Democracy," May 25, 1903. See Dewey, *Characters*

and Events (New York: Holt, Rinehart and Winston, 1929), 70. In the constructive development of my own Theopoetics I am grateful for my conversations with poets Julia Kasdorf and Jeff Gundy and for their literate approach to Anabaptist history, thought, and life.

29. See George J. Stack, *Nietzsche and Emerson: An Elective Emerson* (Athens, Ohio: Ohio University Press, 1992). Among the many contemporary Nietzsche commentaries, the most engaging work I have read is Lesley Chamberlain's *Nietzsche in Turin: An Intimate Biography* (New York: Picador of St. Martin's Press, 1996).

30. Alfred Kazin, introduction to *The Essays of Ralph Waldo Emerson*, by Ralph Waldo Emerson (Cambridge, Mass.: The Belkuap Press of Harvard University Press, 1987), 236-237.

31. W. S. Merwin, *Second Four Books of Poems* (Port Townsend, Wash.: Copper Canyon, 1993). From the poem, "A Scale in May," p. 112. A special thanks to Jeff Gundy, who first recited this great Merwin poetic fragment to me.

EIGHT

MENNONITE LITERATURE AND POSTMODERNISM: Writing the "In-between" Space*

Hildi Froese Tiessen

> *But still the crossroads does have a certain dangerous potency; dangerous because a man might perish there wrestling with multi-headed spirits, but also he might be lucky and return to his people with the boon of prophetic vision.*[1]

It seems to me it is best to temper a project like the one I embark on here with self-reflexive humor. One cultural studies theorist has offered this observation on what we seem to be involved in when we speak of postmodernism:

> When it becomes possible for people to describe as "postmodern" the decor of a room, the design of a building, . . . the collective chagrin and morbid projections of a post-war generation of Baby Boomers confronting disillusioned middle age, the "predicament" of reflexivity, a group of rhetorical tropes, . . . a process of cultural, political or existential fragmentation and/or crisis, the "de-centering" of the subject, an "incredulity toward meta-narratives," the replacement of unitary power axes by a pluralism of power/discourse formations, the "implosion of meaning," the collapse of cultural hierarchies, . . . the decline of the university, . . . broad societal and economic shifts into a 'media', 'consumer' or 'multinational' phase, a sense . . . of "placelessness" or the abandonment of placelessness . . . or (even) a generalized substitution of spatial for tem-

poral co-ordinates—when it becomes possible to describe all those things as "postmodern" (or more simply, . . . as "post" or "very post") then it's clear we are in the presence of a buzzword.²

WHERE TO BEGIN?

Clearly, my first challenge is to focus on something. To establish a context for that focusing, I will offer a general observation from Andreas Huyssen: "No matter how troubling it may be, the landscape of the postmodern surrounds us. It simultaneously delimits and opens our horizons. It's our problem and our hope."³ To begin to focus on the literary, we could add to these words a remark by literary critic Robert Wilson, who has observed that "post-modernism bears in itself a nebulous frontier, an unmapped zone of bogs and tangled bush, between its uses as a period, and as an analytic-descriptive, term."⁴ With these words, Wilson actually begins to bring order to the plethora of perspectives the discourse of postmodernism offers the literary scholar. Wilson speaks of two "archives" of postmodernism that "overlap and coincide" but nevertheless demonstrate two principle ways in which the postmodern finds expression in the literary world. And it is the world of literature that interests me here, and some of the various ways the literary and the postmodern have engaged each other, and how we might look at that engagement relative to the work of some writers who continue to write out of their Mennonite experience.

Postmodernism interests the literary scholar, first of all, as a historical condition that draws our attention, as cultural theorist Stuart Hall puts it, to "some of the deeply contradictory tendencies in modern culture."⁵ As *a historical condition or period*, postmodernism challenges notions of stability, coherence, unity; it throws into question any certainties; it demands to see all sides, to defer judgment, to make all that once went without saying subject to interrogation. Such challenges cannot help but affect the ways we write and read literary texts or see history, narrative, trope, convention. As a *literary style* the postmodern prefers discontinuity and multiplicity over order and unity; it favors the playful, the ironic, the derivative, the subversive, the self-reflexive. The character of a literary work we speak of as postmodern tends to be provisional, decentered, fragmented, eclectic; it tends to focus on the local and the particular. It blurs boundaries, breaks rules, mixes codes, subverts convention.

Where the period and the style we have come to speak of as postmodern perhaps converge most notably in the literary world, as elsewhere, is in challenging all "givens," the givens by which we live and the givens by which we express that living. That is, postmodernism challenges the legitimizing master narratives of history—what Linda Hutcheon, citing Lyotard, refers to as "the received wisdom or the grand narrative systems that once made sense of things for us."[6] In the arts, postmodernism challenges the presumed imperatives of style we refer to as convention.

The postmodern impulses to question, to problematize the givens, to challenge their authority, is evident in the work of a number of writers writing among Mennonites today. "I don't pretend to have answers," Rudy Wiebe's good friend, postmodernist Robert Kroetsch, has remarked with some degree of earnestness, "I am much more interested in the questions we ask ourselves than in the answers we hide behind."[7] Mennonite writers like Rudy Wiebe and Di Brandt, for example, would tend to agree with him.

In this paper, I hope to demonstrate that one way postmodernism has informed the literature we refer to as " Mennonite" is in offering, in the model of the dismantling of the master narrative, a means by which Mennonites can productively interrogate their culture. A useful strategy for this interrogation is a rhetorical device Linda Hutcheon has named "postmodern irony." By means of postmodern irony a number of Mennonite writers have challenged the givens of Mennonite culture without being utterly dismissive of that culture. They have rather, in fact, begun to demonstrate a way for Mennonites to move beyond the monolithic and dualistic categories in terms of which they have tended to function. They have created the possibility for members of the Mennonite community to begin, in the words of cultural studies theorist Iain Chambers, to "break with the silent authority of certain inheritances," to rework the past "from another vantage point,"[8] and to create new anti-monolithic models of discourse by means of which to engage the postmodern world and to initiate continuing transformations within it.

I am interested in how contemporary critical thinking can inform our understanding of the place of literature in Mennonite culture and thought. Like many Canadianists (who live with an awareness of Canada's marginal position internationally and her marked discontinuities domestically), I have taken a particular interest, in recent years, in the critical language of postcolonialism. My interest in postmodernism lies in areas where the concerns of these two contemporary critical discourses overlap: in their foregrounding of the marginal, the particular, the local over any version of a totalizing center, for example; in their often productive challenging of the "givens" by which we have tended to live. Both postcolonialism and postmodernism, as Linda Hutcheon has remarked, have been "embroiled in debates and dialogues with the past."[9]

It is this sort of dialogue, or this type of confrontation, with inherited narratives—what poet Di Brandt calls "the official story"[10] and perceives as a religiously infused discourse, with its own imperialist centralism—that finds expression in some of the work of Mennonites writing today. "I doubt the *official* given history," Rudy Wiebe remarked in an interview conducted by Shirley Neuman in 1980. "You know there is another side to the story and maybe that's the more interesting side. Maybe even truer?"[11] Di Brandt is more strident, less tentative than Wiebe, when she speaks of "taking off the clothes of the official story, layer by layer, stripping away the codes we have lived by to get to the stories underneath of our real, aching bodies in the world."[12]

CHALLENGING THE OFFICIAL STORY, PRODUCTIVELY

At this point postmodernism, like any -ism, is not, of course, the answer. But its disruptive presence, which is certainly both theoretical, irreverent, and sometimes simply modish, has produced a space in the West in which to explicitly evaluate the adequacy of our accounts. . . . Put in other terms, the world we inherit and inhabit can still be transformed.[13]

Of course, the challenging of "the official story" or, to employ the language Rudy Wiebe uses in his first novel, *Peace Shall Destroy Many*, the questioning of "the ways of the fathers," began in Mennonite literature some decades ago. When Wiebe's novel first appeared in 1962, many Mennonites did not take easily to the fact that it challenged the idealized projects of community leadership, and, by implication, questioned the fixed set of protocols by which at least some Mennonites had come to live.[14] Joseph Dueck is the character most relentless in his refusal to accept the givens by which the patriarch in the novel, Deacon Block, maintains control of everything that happens in this isolated sectarian community. Dueck has no recourse but to leave after laying open to question the community's metanarrative and its tyrannies.

I do not mean to suggest that *Peace Shall Destroy Many* is a postmodern work, either in sensibility or style. In fact, Wiebe's modernist temperament is revealed when in the end he resolves the contradictions at the core of the novel by ridding the community of the forces that once denied or concealed all disorder, fragmentation, and contradiction. But Wiebe's work is prophetic. Over the past twenty years or so, while voices of creative writers among Mennonites have grown in number and intensity, questions such as Wiebe raised, about what lies at the heart of Mennonite culture as lived in communities scattered throughout North America, persist.

However, unlike Wiebe's own Joseph Dueck, those who insist on asking the questions now do not go away anymore. That is, even the voices of those who in effect spiritually leave the community of Mennonites—which nevertheless seems to remain a kind of monolithic force shaping the way many of these writers encounter and interpret the world—continue to speak and to be heard, both in the community and out. The questions that impel such Mennonites to give expression to their experience of the religious and cultural communities in which they grew up readily find a place in the postmodern world, which is particularly hospitable to discontinuities of experience and identity. In fact, one of the most compelling questions for Mennonite writers, if one is to judge from a fairly comprehensive survey of the work they have produced over the past two decades or so, concerns the apparent contradictions that have become so palpable in the Mennonite ethos itself, where the codes that once gave shape and coherence and meaning to the members of a community seem to function, if at all, only in fragmented ways.

A question implicit in many of the stories and poems produced by writers who have been nurtured in Mennonite communities in Canada, especially in the second half of this century, is what to make of a world that once seemed to so many to be whole. That is the world Di Brandt, mixing irony and nostalgia, calls "not the worldly world out there full of complacency and sin but the Mennonite world the real world of flower gardens & apple trees & green villages with names like Blumenort & Rosengart & Schoenwiese both gentle & proud"[15]—a world which, on closer examination, appears to have had little real coherence at all.

Like pretty well everyone in my generation, I was trained in literature to read texts as a New Critic. We began with the assumption that every work of art was a coherent whole, and our analysis followed. Every literary trope and stylistic flourish was made to offer its unique and necessary contribution to the whole. Whatever did not fit we skillfully ignored. If we literary critics were to explore self-consciously our migration from the New Criticism to our eventual embrace of other ways of receiving texts, if we were to document our abandonment of the ruse of unity and order and coherence, and our discovery of how to engage the silence, the fragment, and the gap, we might provide, in that documentation, an analogue for how many Mennonite writers have come to see the Mennonite world.

And we might, in the best of circumstances, begin to feel comfortable "trusting," in the words of Robert Kroetsch, "to fragments of story, letting them speak their incompleteness."[16] What else is the New Critic's coherent text than a paradigm for the master narrative that validates certain modes of being even as it silences or consigns to the margins whatever does not seem to fit the substance and momentum of the complete One?

POSTMODERN IRONY:
A DISCOURSE OF COMPLICITY AND CRITIQUE

Postmodern theory with its crazy affinities for contradictions and split identities and discontinuous narratives . . . gave permission for my own crazy, contradictory story.[17]

Mennonites are "trying always to keep the story the same," Di Brandt observed at a literary conference in Ottawa in spring 1998. Brandt speaks of "having to recognize" in herself "the 'rebel traitor thief,' willing to sell out, blow up, throw away the family stories and the official narratives of the culture, for art."[18] She regards her writing as a transgressive act, "transgressive and dangerous."[19] This is writing, she observes, that "breaks apart the official story, the inherited Mennonite narrative,"[20] that challenges what Hutcheon refers to as the "total explanatory system"[21] of a culture. Some of Brandt's work can indeed be seen as transgressive. Some registers a lament for undelivered promises and lost souls, sorrow for a fractured world. Thus her work reflects the split between an idealized world sustained by codes and conventions and "real," lived experience—a split, in the words of critic Coral Ann Howells, that tends to reveal "the incompleteness or falsity of tradition."[22]

> *at Basil's*
> Menno's sons meet every Wednesday
> evening at Basil's for beer they
> pretend they've gone worldly eat
> chicken fingers with honey dip
> burn each other's cigarettes but
> the room is made of mirrors & if
> you look past their jokes & their
> bland faces you can see the backs
> of their heads through the smoke
> beginning to crack open & Menno's
> guts spilling out Jake wears his
> baseball cap everywhere even to bed

> so he won't have to think about the
> split in his skull getting wider each
> year his mother worries about him
> Pete figured out long ago how to
> make the room dance he doesn't mind
> the numbness in his chest after the
> third or so it reminds him strangely
> of home though he will cry someday
> Pete will for another chance & where
> will Menno's promises be then & where
> was God when all these young men
> felt their souls crumble to dust &
> where is he now when all i can see
> in the mirror is the vines & tendrils
> of something wild growing in their
> brains & where's my long lost brother
> Mike who might have inherited the
> earth with me Menno where's Mike[23]

This poem, which reveals something of the poignant sense of loss Brandt's transgressive voice occasionally allows, can be found soon after an unnamed poem, a fragment of which follows here, also from Brandt's second collection, *Agnes in the sky*:

> the man in the pulpit quotes Jesus
> & Shakespeare to prove the world
> is still round a perfect circle in
> God's eye despite acid rain & the
> hole above Antarctica ripping the sky
> apart. . . .[24]

Brandt's work, as this short excerpt of an untitled poem suggests, challenges defining narratives that are not restricted to the narratives of the Mennonites. Brandt, richly informed by and involved with other Canadian literary feminists, refers, in her allusion to Shakespeare, for example, to the Great Tradition that has for centuries defined the nature of English (and, of course, Canadian) literary history. With Robert Kroetsch, Brandt would agree that "one of the tasks of writers [is] to say, once we adopt a certain story which we all tell and retell, what is being left out, what is being concealed, what is being hidden, what is being ignored?"[25]

Like Di Brandt, Rudy Wiebe expresses in his work a distrust of grand narrative systems. But Wiebe tends to direct his skepticism at the dominant, eastern Canadian and Eurocentric interpretations of the history of the Canadian West more often than at any Mennonite narratives. (When Wiebe has challenged the latter, as in *Peace Shall Destroy Many* in 1962 and *My Lovely Enemy* in 1983, community response to his work has tended to be swift and negative and fairly fierce.) Like Brandt, Wiebe is tenacious about exploring what the master narratives of our culture have left out. Like her, he is committed to telling the minority story, from the minority perspective. One of his most recent projects was writing the script for a four-hour, two-part adaptation for television of his award-winning 1973 novel, *The Temptations of Big Bear*. The film was shown on the national network CBC in early winter 1999.

Wiebe has taken great delight in the fact that the native characters in the film of his novel spoke English, the language English-Canadian television audiences of course most readily understand. Their English colonizers spoke in a language Wiebe constructed for them. Wiebe calls it jabberwocky. Its roots are distinctly Low German, he explains with a sly grin. He wanted consistency in the language he developed for the British invaders and, after all, Low German, Wiebe's mother tongue, occurs in the same family of languages as Old English. So Queen Victoria was referred to on national television as "de Fruh" and Russian Mennonites in Canada were presumably able to pick up other echoes and nuances in Wiebe's distinctly postmodern exercise. As for the rest of the country, translations of what the British were saying were provided by subtitle. One assumes the Canadian audience at large got the postcolonial message of the film. Meanwhile, Mennonites had the added opportunity to ponder several layers of irony.

The playfulness of Wiebe's approach in his film script was, of course, evident in the text of *Big Bear* itself, where the English invaders' attempts to impose their inflexible way of seeing the world was shown, over and over again, to amount to utter foolishness. Wiebe has commented on his own method of dismantling the ways of the English in their colonization of the Canadian West, and the subsequent historical rendering of that colonization in the neatly ordered, Eurocentric histories that emerged—full of absences and elisions—out of eastern Canada. In an interview, he said that "once you have taken this angle, this attitude of telling the minority story, then you drop in the majority documents and see how stupid they sound or what kinds of ironic changes you can ring on them. It's amazing how ironic it sometimes becomes."[26]

Rudy Wiebe has discovered in irony what Linda Hutcheon calls "a popular strategy for working in existing discourses and contesting them at the same time."[27] Hutcheon, who, as I have observed, has written a great deal on the subject of postmodern irony, speaks of it as one of the "major strategic rhetorical practices of postmodern art."[28] It allows writers, she notes, "to address a dominant culture from within its own structures of understanding, while still contesting and resisting those structures."[29]

Rudy Wiebe's use, on the page immediately inside the front cover of *Playing Dead*,[30] of a map of the Canadian North with south at the top of the page is a perfect example of the strategy Hutcheon has in mind here: the inversion "at once inscribes and subverts the conventions and ideologies"[31] of the dominant order. We all recognize the map and have no reason to doubt its dimensions, but the fact that it is upside-down (from our conventional perspective) objectifies it and causes us to raise questions about why it has always seemed "natural" to us for it to be the other way around. With south to the north, the upside-down map both acknowledges and contests the force of the dominant culture. The map is not wrong; it is problematized, shown to be subject to interrogation.

Wiebe manipulates the language of the dominant order in such a way as to make it, in effect, the base of the very disruption he undertakes. Similarly, in some of Di Brandt's most transgressive poetry she too throws into question the fairly evangelical discourse that shaped her religious sensibility. The trope of Jesus as lover sits at the base of her "missionary position" poems in her first collection, *questions i asked my mother*.

> *missionary position* (1)
> let me tell you what it's like
> having God for a father & jesus
> for a lover on this old mother
> earth you who no longer know
> the old story the part about the
> Virgin being of course a myth
> made up by Catholics for an easy
> way out its not that easy i can
> tell you right off. . . .[32]

The series of six poems, of which this is the beginning of the first, ends with one in which the speaker takes a dozen lovers—for God "made twelve a / good number for mates." This last poem in the series is followed by a page that has on it only three words: "just kidding ma."[33]

Brandt's work depends on irony, on the often playful treatment of a contradiction, a doubleness; on a "parodic recall" or "critical revisiting"[34] of some element of past experience. Her treatment of an evangelical Mennonite camp experience in a short prose piece ironically entitled "how i got saved" works in the same way.

> the Talk with the counselor this caught me by complete surprise i was sitting at the blue picnic table under the trees one afternoon with my counsellor Miss Krahn i had just finished reciting the entire lot of verses from Abraham & Isaac to *In the beginning was the Word* feeling relieved . & not a little proud when she asked me quite suddenly was i a Christian yes i answered quickly startled at the question & when did you become one she asked   i don't know i said i can't remember   but you're sure you're saved she said doubtfully pencil poised above my card   God they're keeping a file on us i thought & i don't have a date   from that day for many years i worried about the problem of my conversion which came to a head every summer at Bible camp some years i felt miserable & dark despair about my inevitable damnation other years i cited some uplifting religious experience or another & thus located my salvation temporarily on the calendar i'm wondering now if it was a cumulative file & whether they did graphs on the fluctuation of our spirits from one year to the next every summer i wanted desperately to say no i'm not saved to see what they'd do to me how they'd snare me 'n make me a Christian but i never quite trusted them to meet the demand of the moment they would see me slipping into hell i thought & they wouldn't be strong enough to pull me out so i let it pass[35]

The kind of dismantling Brandt undertakes, to objectify an aspect of what for years went without saying in her own Mennonite culture, occurs as a more humorous—but no less probing—episode in a recently published short story by Rosemary Nixon, entitled "Mennonite Your Way." This story, by one of the few Swiss-Mennonites among the many Mennonite writers in Canada, provides a commentary on how conservative Mennonite women have been encouraged to see themselves.

> For years [grandmother] Beulah [Gingrich] has had their name in the Mennonite Your Way travel directory. The Floyd Gingriches. They've entertained guests from all over the States, from Niagara Falls, Ontario; Attica, Saskatchewan; Antwerp, Belguim; Iceland. When Winnie and Roy reached high school, sixteen years ago, Floyd encouraged her to enter the directory.
> It's a way to serve, he said. Floyd's name. Her work. Floyd believes only women who work endlessly in the service of the Lord keep out of

trouble. After sixteen years, here they are, at last on the other side, Mennoniting *their* way across the country.

Beulah and Floyd, Swiss Mennonites from Pennsylvania on their way through Saskatchewan, stumble on Queenie McClancy, a rough-and-tumble, worldly woman familiar to Nixon's readers for her outrageous ways. Queenie wears shorts, cooks out of tins and boxes, and casually uses the Lord's name in vain. Over the course of an afternoon she comes to represent a kind of freedom to Beulah, who begins to re-think the nature of her own existence as a woman.

> [Beulah] stares at Queenie's knees, and Queenie stares back at Beulah's covering. Up to now she has seen herself always as a representative of something—a Mennonite, a Christian, a mother, a grandmother. At Queenie's table Beulah fantasizes her history, her tie to Mennonite blood, Anabaptist blood.
>
> [Queenie talks, while they sit around her kitchen table, and Beulah muses.]
>
> Those treasured childhood stories of people fried in frying pans for their faith, drowned in Swiss lakes, burned in fires. Generations of women sacrificing, of women serving. This woman Queenie is snatching from Beulah her picture of the world. Beulah knows what good women, Christian women, don't do. They don't wear jewelry. They don't dress immodestly. They don't cut their hair.
>
> [Queenie keeps talking, and grandmother Beulah begins to fantasize.]
>
> She feels noise rise in her chest and coughs to quell it. Lift up your heart. Lift up your voice. Rejoice. How can she claim such freedom? She longs for adventure. For a drugstore romance. For another planet. She looks down at herself, doubtful, betrayed into this future, while Floyd slurps his tea. Her body's a disguise. Has been so since the birth of her first child thirty-five years ago. Beulah imagines herself her own woman. Hitched to nothing. Donning shorts to dig in her Pennsylvania garden. Serving canned soup. Making lewd remarks. Making advances. Floyd resisting.
> "It's not natural," he says, snapping his false teeth. "You're fifty-seven. Act like a natural woman."[36]

Postmodern irony functions similarly in these pieces by Brandt and Nixon, to reveal the contrary—ultimately irreconcilable—elements in each case.[37] Postmodern irony, Hutcheon remarks, "allows a text to work in the constraints of the dominant while placing those constraints *as con-*

straints in the foreground and thus undermining their power."[38] The tension in these stories remains unresolved for the reader, especially for the "insider"—the member of the community in which these sorts of episodes occur, the person who understands the irony, the one who "gets it." The postmodern irony of these stories is not utterly dismissive of the thing mimicked or displaced. Nor does it result in any glib resolution. In the best of circumstances, it "opens up new space, literally between opposing meanings, where new things can happen,"[39] or, to borrow words from Iain Chambers, it "reveals an opening, not a conclusion: it always marks the moment of departure, never a homecoming."[40]

NEGOTIATING THAT SPACE

The Mennonite writers who employ postmodern irony use it as a means by which to negotiate a space that lies somewhere between what we might call an idealized world of tradition and the postmodern world of contingency and fragmentation in which all of us find ourselves. Postmodern irony lends a kind of authenticity to both those places but ultimately authorizes neither. Neither pole of the tension is finally satisfying; each is problematic. And there is no resolution. "Trust me," David Waltner-Toews has observed, "the truth lies /somewhere in between."[41] Postmodern irony begins to name, to give form to, that in-between space. By its mode of operation it rejects the simple structure of closed dualistic systems and allows for both ambiguity and new possibility. It helps us, in the words of Chambers, "as we attempt to transform our histories, languages and recollections from a point of arrival into a point of departure."[42]

The person who negotiates the undefined territory of the postmodern is, as Stuart Hall has suggested, a kind of nomad, traveling "in a world in which the authority of previous guides has apparently crumbled."[43] The question that remains is how to occupy, name, negotiate the middle space that has come to represent the complexity and contingency—and the opportunity—of our lived experience. Through the use of postmodern irony, a number of Mennonite writers have discovered a way to gather up traces of Mennonite culture in order to arrange them in new patterns that enable us to see in and among them things we have not seen before. These writers pick over and put together fragments of memory and lived experience and, in the process, create stories that confer sense and elaborate what Chambers calls "a poetics of the possible."[44]

In the best of their work some contemporary Mennonite writers break up what Chambers refers to as a "particular language of tradition and truth" and invoke "a different vision of meaning, another language in which the repressed and displaced reappear and begin to speak." By their action, they produce "another sense of the past, and with it the future."[45] In the re-inscribing of voices, stories, and events, they give expression to the hopes and disappointments, passions and fears of our lived experience. They provide windows through which we can see a new realm of the possible. The postmodern condition and the postmodern gesture, then, serve, in some Mennonite literature at least, to create "a space of transformation" in a cultural landscape that might otherwise seem to offer merely "the scene of a cheerless destiny."[46]

NOTES

*Research for this article was supported in part by the Social Sciences and Humanities Research Council of Canada.

1. Chinua Achebe, "Named for Victoria, Queen of England," *The Post-Colonial Studies Reader*, ed. Bill Ashcroft, Gareth Griffiths, and Helen Tiffin (New York: Routledge, 1995), 191.

2. Dick Hebdige, "Postmodernism and 'the other side,'" *Stuart Hall: Critical Dialogues in Cultural Studies*, ed. David Morley and Kuan-Hsing Chen (New York: Routledge, 1996), 174-75.

3. Andreas Huyssen, *After the Great Divide: Modernism, Mass Culture, Postmodernism* (Bloomington: Indiana University Press, 1986), 221.

4. Robert Rawdon Wilson, "SLIP PAGE: Angela Carter, In/Out/In the Post-Modern nexus," *Past the Last Post: Theorizing Post-Colonialism and Post-Modernism*, ed. Ian Adam and Helen Tiffin (Calgary: University of Calgary Press, 1990), 111.

5. Stuart Hall, in Lawrence Grossberg, "On postmodernism and articulation: An Interview with Stuart Hall," in *Stuart Hall*, 131.

6. Linda Hutcheon, *The Canadian Postmodern: A Study of Contemporary English-Canadian Fiction* (Toronto: Oxford University Press, 1988), 15.

7. Robert Kroetsch, *A Likely Story: The Writing Life* (Red Deer, Alberta: Red Deer College Press, 1995), 131.

8. Iain Chambers, "Waiting on the End of the World?" in *Stuart Hall*, 206.

9. Linda Hutcheon, "'Circling the Downspout of Empire,'" *Past the Last Post*, 169. Hutcheon remarks that, unlike the postmodern, which tends to be politically ambivalent, the postcolonial possesses "a strong political motivation that is intrinsic to its oppositionality" (168).

10. Di Brandt, *Dancing Naked: Narrative Strategies for Writing Across Centuries* (Stratford, Ont.: The Mercury Press, 1996), 36.

11. Rudy Wiebe, in Shirley Neuman, "Unearthing Language: An Interview with Rudy Wiebe and Robert Kroetsch," in *A Voice in the Land: Essays By and About Rudy Wiebe*, ed. W. J. Keith (Edmonton: NeWest Press, 1981), 230.

12. Brandt, *Dancing Naked*, 36.
13. Chambers, "Waiting on the end of the world?" 206.
14. See Rudy Wiebe, "The Skull in the Swamp," *Journal of Mennonite Studies* 5 (1987): 8-20.
15. Di Brandt, "how i got saved," *Why I Am a Mennonite: Essays on Mennonite Identity*, ed. Harry Loewen (Scottdale, Pa.: Herald Press, 1988), 27.
16. Robert Kroetsch, *The Lovely Treachery of Words: Essays Selected and New* (Toronto: Oxford University Press, 1989), 24.
17. Brandt, *Dancing Naked*, 35.
18. Ibid., 10.
19. Di Brandt, "'that questioning self,'" *Sounding Differences: Conversations with Seventeen Canadian Women Writers*, ed. Janice Williamson (Toronto: University of Toronto Press, 1993), 46.
20. Brandt, *Dancing Naked*, 36.
21. Linda Hutcheon, *Splitting Images: Contemporary Canadian Ironies* (Toronto: Oxford University Press, 1991), 2.
22. Coral Ann Howells, quoted in Hutcheon, *Splitting Images*, 97.
23. Di Brandt, *Agnes in the sky* (Winnipeg: Turnstone Press, 1990), 11.
24. Ibid., 5.
25. Robert Kroetsch, "Closing Panel," *Acts of Concealment: Mennonite/s Writing in Canada*, ed. Hildi Froese Tiessen and Peter Hinchcliffe (Waterloo: University of Waterloo Press, 1992), 225.
26. Rudy Wiebe, in Shirley Neuman, "Unearthing Language," 230.
27. Hutcheon, "Circling the Downspout of Empire," 170-71.
28. Hutcheon, *Splitting Images*, 39.
29. Ibid., 31.
30. Rudy Wiebe, *Playing Dead: A contemplation concerning the Arctic* (Edmonton: NeWest Press, 1989).
31. Linda Hutcheon, *The Politics of Postmodernism* (New York: Routledge, 1989), 11.
32. Di Brandt, *questions i asked my mother* (Winnipeg: Turnstone Press, 1987), 28.
33. Ibid., 34.
34. See Hutcheon, *The Canadian Postmodern*, 10.
35. Brandt, "how i got saved," 30.
36. Rosemary Nixon, "Mennonite Your Way," *Conrad Grebel Review* 15 (1997), 141-42.
37. Hutcheon's "post-modern" irony is another variant of the several kinds of irony that have acquired currency throughout the ages. Postmodern irony, as Hutcheon describes it, is not to be confused with the sort of irony that drew praise from the New Critics: a rhetorical device that synthesizes and reconciles opposites into a whole, and hence serves to resolve dissonance in a work. Hutcheon's irony offers not resolution, but a kind of ongoing creative tension. It serves to probe and problematize rather than to resolve the issue at hand.
38. Hutcheon, "Circling the Downspout of Empire," 177.

39. Hutcheon, *Splitting Images*, 17.

40. Iain Chambers, *Migrancy, Culture, Identity* (London: Routledge, 1994), 122.

41. David Waltner-Toews, "Forty Lies (and Some Truth) for My Fortieth Birthday," *The Impossible Uprooting* (Toronto: McClelland & Stewart, 1995), 128.

42. Chambers, *Migrancy*, 7.

43. Iain Chambers, *Border Dialogues: Journeys in postmodernity* (London: Routledge, 1990), 81.

44. Ibid., 111. Chambers's chapter entitled "Voices, traces, horizons" is an evocative exploration of the condition of "homelessness" in a postmodern world; he attempts to articulate something of "the vital network of voices, traces and horizons in and through which we grasp and construct our historical, that is, complex and lived, sense of the world we inhabit."

45. Ibid., 111.

46. Ibid., 112.

NINE

(IN)VISIBLE CITIES, (F)ACTS OF POWER, (HMM)ILITY, FATHERS AND (M)OTHERS: Anabaptism, Postmodernity, and Mennonite Writing

Jeff Gundy

(IN)VISIBLE CITIES

To be a Mennonite writer in a postmodern time might mean, among other things, encountering powerful, formative *texts* as much at odds as these two:

> Although the definitive history of Anabaptism has not yet been written, we know enough today to draw a clear line of demarcation between original evangelical and constructive Anabaptism on the one hand, which was born in the bosom of Zwinglianism in Zurich, Switzerland, in 1525, and established in the Low Countries in 1533, and the various mystical, spiritualistic, revolutionary, or even antinomian related and unrelated groups on the other hand, which came and went like the flowers of the field in those days of the great renovation.[1]

> [S]tructure—or rather the structurality of structure—although it has always been involved, has always been neutralized or reduced, and this by a process of giving it a center or referring it to a point of presence, a fixed origin. The function of this center was . . . above all to make sure that the

organizing principle of the structure would limit what we might call the *freeplay* of the structure.²

It does not take great interpretive skills to see the tension between these two statements. Harold Bender proposes to define an origin, establish a point of historical and theological presence, draw a clear line between "evangelical and constructive Anabaptism" and various aberrations from it. This is precisely what Derrida skeptically says Western metaphysicians, theologians, scholars, and politicians have always sought to do: to create a center that will not only organize the structure of society or a subset like the Mennonite church, but also limit the "freeplay" in that structure and function as a means of control and a way of defining boundaries. Derrida does not deny the power of such claims about origins, but does insist that all "origins" are human constructions rather than objective Truth. For him, everything is difference; there is no first principle, no origin, no Unmoved Mover.

I do not mean to argue that Derrida is entirely right in this matter or Bender entirely mistaken in his efforts. The literature on both subjects is far too voluminous and complex for my amateur status as postmodern critic and Anabaptist historian. But the contrast between their ways of thinking about history and meaning provides a starting point for exploring what Mennonite creative writers have been doing, consciously or not. They have been complicating and resisting the idea that there is one identifiable True Center of Anabaptist history and experience. And they have been problematizing the corollary idea that the Anabaptist community rightly belongs to those who wish to establish a fixed set of standards from which others— including our own "mystics, spiritualists, revolutionaries, and antinomians"—can and should be excluded.

Since Rudy Wiebe's *Peace Shall Destroy Many* arrived some thirty-five years ago, a whole series of startling new imaginative texts under some aspect of the term *Mennonite* have emerged in North America. Whether we like it or not, today all sorts of novelists, poets, dramatists, and others claim some kind of allegiance or connection, current or nostalgic, to Anabaptism. They also claim the kind of imaginative freedom that historically many Anabaptists have distrusted, if not banned outright. These texts generally deal with lived experience and often with the relation of such experience to the abstract creeds, dogmas, and disciplines of various Mennonite communities. They do not seek to replace history and theology but to supplement them. They aim to provide other sorts of news and information, to bring a wider range of voices into our hearing.

Postmodernism tells us that Harold Bender's Anabaptist Vision, whatever else we might say about it, is a linguistic construct. Its relation to historical events and verifiable reality is by definition problematic and imperfect. I hasten to add that this recognition applies to every text we produce. If anything, accepting this premise makes our work both more imperative and more problematic because we are (or should be) always aware that we will never get anything quite right, that if our work is remembered at all it will quite surely be critiqued and corrected by others whose work will itself be in turn forgotten or abused. We are constantly driven to generate meaning which is inevitably and constantly incomplete and imperfect. To be aware of that incompletion yet press on anyway I take to be one crucial element of the postmodern condition.

Consider Edgar Allen Poe's famous story, "The Purloined Letter." What does this story "mean?" To trace just one series of fairly recent interpretations, Marie Bonaparte reads the story as a Freudian sexual allegory, with the letter as clitoris—hidden as it is in "plain sight" in the letter-box just above the womb-symbol of the fireplace. Jacques Lacan's post-Freudian psychoanalytic reading finds the story structured around a series of "triads"—groups of three people around the letter, functioning as open "signifiers" whose meaning is never revealed.[3] Jacques Derrida argues that Bonaparte and Lacan both miss the essential mystery and open-endedness of the story, that in fact it embodies "an endless drifting-off-course" and a nearly infinite nesting of stories and texts one within the other.[4]

Who is "right?" Each reading offers certain insights, surely—and surely none exhausts the story or closes off further readings. In the appropriate context we might make finer distinctions among them, compare them to others, judge this one more persuasive, that one more relevant. In that process we would continue to generate new understandings—by synthesizing, comparing and critiquing, by bringing our own critical and theoretical categories to bear, by returning to the original text with fresh or more informed perspectives.

As we work at any such process, our readings may strike others as profound or ridiculous, important or trivial, and their distribution will be subject to such responses and other factors of the literary economy. But the process remains one of constant and open-ended negotiation. Surely interpretation, literary, biblical, and otherwise, has always proceeded in this fashion. Postmodernism has only made us more aware of the process.

I do not take this endless deferral of "final" meaning, to echo Derrida, to imply a mindless relativism in which, because no reading is absolute, all readings are reduced to hapless undecideability. But I will resist the temptation to take up the complicated argument about how meaning is negotiated here. I am more interested in the production of texts than in their interpretation. My concern is to argue that the deferral of absolute certainty—the refusal to claim that as limited human beings we have access to Truth, capital T—opens a valuable and important space for discourse that has often been unavailable to Mennonites. Such discourse may seem frighteningly anarchic, even subversive, but I believe the multiple voices and visions we are beginning to hear and see have a great deal to tell us.

This poem by Di Brandt speaks in one of those long-silenced voices.

nonresistance, or love Mennonite style
(for L. & the others)

turn the other cheek when your brother
hits you and your best friend tells fibs
about you & the teacher punishes you
unfairly if someone steals your shirt
give him your coat to boot this will
heap coals of fire on his head & let him
know how greatly superior you are
while he & his cronies dicker & bargain
their way to hell you can hold your
head up that is down humbly knowing
you're bound for the better place where
it gets tricky is when your grandfather
tickles you too hard or your cousins
want to play doctor & your uncle kisses
you too long on the lips & part of you
wants it & the other part knows it's
wrong & you want to run away but you
can't because he's a man like your father
& the secret place inside you feels itchy
& hot & you wonder if this is what hell
feels like & you remember the look on
your mother's face when she makes
herself obey your dad & meanwhile her
body is shouting *No! No!* & he doesn't
even notice & you wish you could stop

being angry all the time but you can't
because God is watching & he sees
everything there isn't any place to let
it out & you understand about love the
lavish sacrifice in it how it will stretch
your woman's belly & heap fire on your
head you understand how love is like
a knife & a daughter is not a son & the
only way you will be saved is by
submitting quietly in your grandfather's
house your flesh smouldering in the
darkened room as you love your enemy
deeply unwillingly & full of shame.[5]

As I read Bender and Derrida together, let me investigate this poem using Michel Foucault's comments on the operation of post-Enlightenment social power. Foucault finds a visual image for such power in Jeremy Bentham's plan for a circular prison in which all the inmates could be observed while unable to see their observer, which he called the "panopticon."

> Hence the major effect of the Panopticon: to induce in the inmate a state of conscious and permanent visibility that assures the automatic functioning of power. So to arrange things that the surveillance is permanent in its effects even if it is discontinuous in its action; that the perfection of power should tend to render its actual exercise unnecessary . . . in short, the inmates themselves should be caught up in a power situation of which they are themselves the bearers.[6]

In Brandt's poem something very like the system Foucault describes is clearly in operation. The subtly but radically pernicious understanding of "nonresistance" the "you" of this poem has internalized traps her into radical subordination to men aligned with the terrifying image of an eternally watchful masculine God that rules her claustrophobic world. As Foucault suggests, this "you" disciplines herself; the system of power has convinced her she has no option except utter submission.

This poem and others like it have helped me understand the dark ways terms like *humility* and *nonresistance* can function, especially when used as code words for submission to patriarchal oppression. Di Brandt unpacks the hidden senses of these terms by using elements of her personal experience, the testimony of others, and her intuitive sense of one facet of Mennonite reality to create a text that demands our attention—if not as the "whole truth," as *a* truth among the others, one seldom found in official denominational pronouncements.

Some readers may resist this poem, argue that it overdramatizes and exaggerates for effect, that most Mennonites are not so oppressed. Others may react with satisfaction—"Yes, they're all that way." Both these reactions seem to me partly valid, but *partly* is the crucial word. It is too simple and easy either to accept or to reject this poem, and other such texts, wholesale. We must learn, I think, to complicate our understandings, to open ourselves to such testimonies and take them for what they are: necessary supplements that are each incomplete but which, cumulatively, can bring us closer to knowing the world as it truly is.

One of my favorite postmodern texts is a strange, short book by Italo Calvino titled *Invisible Cities*.[7] In that book the explorer Marco Polo describes to Kublai Khan the exotic cities he has encountered in his travels—though it is not clear whether these cities "really" exist or whether Polo is making them up to please his host and friend. And of course the cities are "really" made up by Calvino, the author. Yet in their weird specificity and quirky detail they seem *almost* the sort of places that might actually exist. They invite all sorts of intriguing speculation about the nature of life, language, and reality.

We might think of poems like Di Brandt's as making visible the invisible cities among us—those exterior and interior places of incredible variety and intensity that our fellow human beings, Mennonite and otherwise, inhabit. In reading such work I find myself drawn into lives and images that have forever changed my sense of the "real world," whether the poems and stories are "really true" or not.

I think we need such work to be as various and even contradictory as possible. Let me dwell for a moment on the question of apparent contradictions. I confess that my own "Mennonite" book, *A Community of Memory*,[8] is partly a response to texts like Di Brandt's. My own experience of family and of Mennonite community was much less brutal and repressive than the one she describes, and my book clearly reflects that. I have been pleased and gratified by the book's reception. More than once, however, I have heard it said that my book is somehow a "correction" of the "angry" poets, that because I do not seem resentful about my childhood they should not complain about theirs, that because I wrote a book that flirts with nostalgia and dallies with sentimentality I must think all Mennonites are really pretty good.

As you know if you have read the book—and if you haven't, I of course think you should—I *do* think some Mennonites are pretty good. I am not taking back anything I wrote there. But I have no desire that it become some sort of definitive image of "the Mennonites." My book, Di Brandt's books, and all other poems and stories by Mennonites and others we come to know must each be seen as at most a summing-up of one person's vision at a specific moment, what my old teacher John Oyer used to call one "point in space and time." My new work may have a quite different tone, as indeed it is much too simple and unfair to take any one of Di Brandt's poems as summing up her whole worldview. As writers continue to do that work with honesty and passion and integrity, it will be as varied in tone and substance as Mennonites are, as life itself is.

F(ACTS) OF POWER

If poems are necessary supplements, they are also unavoidably acts of power. The Palestinian-born critic Edward Said has written well on the "worldliness" of texts; he argues that they are "always enmeshed in circumstance, time, place, and society," that they have their "meaning *in the world.*"[9] Said draws support from Nietzsche and Foucault for his analysis of texts as "fundamentally facts of power." One difficulty of the kind of supplementarity and interplay among texts I am promoting here is, of course, that such interplay is never just play. If Di Brandt is allowed to complicate the Mennonite master narrative with a story of nonresistance gone terribly wrong, how can that narrative be used, as Harold Bender hoped to use history, as a tool for evangelism and institutional progress? What other and even more disconcerting voices might demand to be heard? What might happen to the church as institution if they are "allowed" to speak?

Imaginative writing has often been perceived as a threat to the elites that govern self-defined communities, though that threat is usually described as a threat to the community itself. Its stories may well question, if not undermine, the primary narrative. I have heard it said openly that control of "the" Mennonite narrative belongs with historians and theologians. They can be trusted to get the story right, at least mostly, due to their commitments to reason and certain kinds of evidence and their working in a community of mutual critique and evaluation. Poets and creative writers, this line of thinking goes, lack such self-governing mechanisms and are susceptible to willfulness, whim, individualism, and pride.

Let me quickly stress that the Mennonite church needs its historians and theologians. We have produced some extraordinary ones. But their very fidelity to fact and reason also creates limits. A historian cannot (or at least should not) write lengthy narratives based on hunch and intuition and pass them off as objective history. A theologian cannot, or should not, argue a theological vision just because she is in love with the language she finds when she muses on it. Poets and novelists, however, can and must work beyond fact and reason. This is not a task to undertake lightly; neither is it a task that we can abandon because it makes others nervous.

I might propose that we are stuck with the poets whether we want them or not. Something has happened akin to the process Jonathan Schell describes in Poland during the rise of Solidarity. At the key moment, Schell writes, the opposition ceased trying to seize political power from the state and simply began to take action

> "as if" Poland were already a free country. And once those in opposition began to act that way something unexpected happened. As soon as they started to act "as if," the "as if" started to melt away. . . . There a small realm of liberty was created. . . . merely by fearlessly carrying on the business of daily life it grew powerful.[10]

It seems to me the recent outpouring of Mennonite writing similarly began when enough Mennonite writers simply began to act as if they were free to write what they chose or felt compelled to write, regardless of the consequences, and to find places to publish that work, especially outside strictly Mennonite circles. Strangely, it seems that only after their work became public "outside" Mennonite communities could it filter back in to be paid serious attention in the church.

Shifts of power and authority follow, of course. For women like Di Brandt, Jean Janzen, and Julia Kasdorf to have become almost household names among Mennonites would have been unthinkable even a generation ago, unless they were missionary martyrs. (I suspect that some days Di and Julia, at least, may think that phrase uncomfortably relevant.) But it is clear that their poems have done cultural work among Mennonites that was not being done otherwise—and, incidentally, quite different work for each of them.

Both the production of imaginative writing by Mennonites and its reception or rejection in Mennonite communities are bound to be entangled in power relations. We have little choice but to continue what is surely an eternal negotiation about the master narrative by which we will live, how we will tell our story to our children and our friends, our enemies and our new recruits. What this story will be, and who will decide how it will be told, are questions of power. Allowing a few people to decide what this story will be and how it will be told concentrates that power in ways I think not truly Anabaptist and makes it all but inevitable that the story will be incomplete. Encouraging many voices to speak in conversation, even those that frighten or dismay us, is vital if we are to tell the whole, rich, troubling, inspiring reality of our history and experience. In a recent essay Julia Kasdorf also suggests as much.

> This is the work we all have been given to do. To live our lives and know ourselves, so that we may be present to others in the world, we must constantly construct ourselves in conversation with others. We cannot see ourselves as given or already "consummated," for then we would be static, "finalized," in Bakhtin's word. We would be dead."[11]

What does it mean, in Kasdorf's phrase, to "be present to others in the world?" What is "the world," anyway? Everything outside our home church? Our local conference? Are some Mennonites of "the world" and others not? What about the Quakers and the Brethren? What about James Dobson and Pat Robertson? As she asks elsewhere in the same essay, "[would] Mennonites regard their community as the self or the other?"[12]

I was quite young in the days of the Vietnam War when I began to sense (dimly) that neither "the church" nor "the world" were single, unitary entities. The world outside the church had many sides, and I found myself quite drawn to some that distrusted "the Establishment" at least as much as my home church distrusted the world. The counterculture of the sixties valorized sincerity over smooth surfaces, pacifism over violent nationalism, simple living over mindless consumption, emotional honesty over hypocritical platitudes. Of course this counterculture also valorized electric guitars, "free love," casual drug use, and bell bottoms—but still its critique of American popular and civic culture overlapped in significant ways with what I learned in church. I can still remember my mother having to admit that she could not argue with the sentiments of the Beatles song "Can't Buy Me Love," though she did not have much use for the music.

On a different level, I suggest that in some ways Mennonite communities *are* "the world" Mennonite writers must be "in" but not entirely "of" if they are to write. The people I live among now, most of them educated, sophisticated, and broad-minded, have been exceedingly supportive of my writing. Yet it is still something that sets me a little apart. This is not a complaint. I want to be that way, for reasons hard to explain, as I like sitting up in the balcony where it is usually less crowded and, if I get into the front row, I can sing as loud as I like without worrying that the person in front of me will hear my shaky notes and wish I would tone it down.

Throughout this chapter I have repeatedly used the first person plural. Yet I know how problematic such usage is. In the Mennonite world I often find myself stirring restlessly at the ways this "we" is used. The question of who "we" are, who speaks for "us," and the extent to which "we" identify with or dissociate ourselves from such communal pronouncements is a complicated and important one.

As it matters among Mennonites, it also matters in wider spheres, where similar claims of definition are often made. Consider the use of "we" in this passage from an essay on the recent novel and film *Damage*, in which a man's affair with his son's fiancé leads to the son's death:

> According to a psychoanalytic cultural theory outlined by MacCannell that posits a universe beyond Oedipus, in place of the oedipal, patriarchal father, we now have the brother. . . . By forbidding oedipal desire and demanding narcissistic *jouissance* . . . the new regime promotes an infatuation with death in actual or symbolic forms that engenders what might be called Lacanian tragedy.[13]

Essays like this one tempt me to respond, as the old Lone Ranger joke has it, with "What you mean 'we,' kemosabe?" I am, indeed, enough a part of this literary-critical world to know some of the terms, to have even seen the movie, but mostly my life, it seems to me, has very little to do with such arrangements. Yet it is all too easy to reject such analyses without paying careful attention to them. The glib dismissiveness with which some respond to anything under the sign of postmodernism can cover a rather desperate fear that seeks to avoid the new and threatening simply by mocking it.

What is said under the sign of postmodernism surely needs response and critique at many levels. But I think we need engaged and informed critique, not mere fearful rejection. And there may be surprises along the way, for postmodernism offers a great many possibilities. At a conference a few years ago, I attended a reading by postmodern novelist Kathy Acker. She described her work as "post-secular" and "post-cynical," then read a passage describing the relationships of women in an Egyptian brothel, including extremely specific descriptions of various sexual activities.

The next day I bought one of her books—strictly as a souvenir, of course—worked up the nerve to ask her to sign it, and got into a brief but intriguing conversation. As a small-town Mennonite academic and boringly monogamous heterosexual, I did not expect to find a whole lot in common with a crew-cut, tattooed, and multiply pierced West Coast bodybuilder whose work deals, among other things, with the possibilities of pornography and free sex for social change and liberation. Yet when I told her a little about my work on *Community of Memory*, she responded with what seemed genuine enthusiasm, especially about the importance of personal community and writing that grows out of such community in vital ways. There are many ways of finding connection, though I have not yet worked up the nerve to include extended descriptions of sex here or in my next book.

(Hmm)ility

The claim implied in using the communal "we" connects directly to questions of arrogance and humility. I have probably written too much about that last term already, much of it in an essay that some of my friends assure me will never be forgiven.[14] In that essay I was groping toward what I would now describe as a *voluntary* humility, a yieldedness that can only be realized from a position of a certain security—a surrendering of power only possible if one has some power to give up. I still argue that some people—especially white guys with official positions and/or tenure, like me—need to keep learning and practicing that kind of humility. But I wish I had more clearly distinguished such a stance from what my friends have made me realize has too often been a phony rhetoric of humility, a tool of the powerful for enforcing submission, a "yieldedness" that means mere silencing and oppression, especially for women and minorities.

In a recent essay Elaine Swartzentruber describes something much like the humility I had in mind.

> This Embodied Body of Christ is marked with a humble awareness of the limits of bodiness that neither eschews the real effects of criss-crossing lines of power, love, desire, etc., nor tries to dissolve the productivity of those lines into some claimed "transcendental authority." This marking would not allow any among us to claim a transcendent authority for decisions we make, for lines we draw, for people we include or exclude from our fellowship, for the lines we will not cross.[15]

Such a vision of humility, I suggest, implies that Mennonite writers might willingly accept a role as "minor" authors who might aspire to produce a minor but genuine literature. Gilles Deleuze and Félix Guattari, writing especially about Franz Kafka and his status as a German-speaking Jew in Prague, argue that such a position has its advantages. Against the dream of instituting an "official language," even in a local way (surely a dream we institutional Mennonites should recognize), Deleuze and Guattari suggest that Kafka takes an opposite approach.

> There is nothing that is major or revolutionary except the minor. To hate all languages of masters. . . . To make use of the polylingualism of one's own language, to make a minor or intensive use of it, to oppose the oppressed quality of this language to its oppressive quality. . . . How many styles or genres or literary movements, even very small ones, have only one single dream: to assume a major function in language, to offer themselves as a sort of state language, an official language. . . . Create the opposite dream: know how to create a becoming-minor.[16]

The dream I have is of a community of many voices, all free and none in control, all listening to many voices: of the Spirit and Scripture, of their personal and shared traditions, of each other. Deleuze and Guattari elsewhere suggest that a good metaphor for postmodern society is the rhizome, the sort of branching, organic, decentered network formed by the clumps of foxtail that keep invading my garden. The modesty and interconnectedness of this image are appealing: "A rhizome has no beginning or end; it is always in the middle, between things, interbeing. . . ."[17]

In *Thus Spoke Zarathustra*, Nietzsche tells a suggestive story about the writer's role in postmodern community. "Of three metamorphoses of the spirit I tell you," Nietzsche writes, "how the spirit becomes a camel; and the camel, a lion; and the lion, finally, a child." The camel is the "strong reverent spirit that would bear much." "What is most difficult, O heroes, asks the spirit . . . that I may take it on myself and exult in my strength? Is it not humbling oneself to wound one's haughtiness? Letting one's folly shine to mock one's wisdom?"[18] The humble, obedient camel must give way to the rebellious lion, however, who contends with the "great dragon" of received authority.

Though the lion cannot himself create new values, he resists the closed institutional system of the dragon, demanding the freedom of "a sacred 'No' even to duty," and thus prepares the way for the child:

> The child is innocence and forgetting, a new beginning, a game, a self-propelled wheel, a first movement, a sacred "Yes." For the game of creation, my brothers, a sacred "Yes" is needed: the spirit now wills his own will, and he who had been lost to the world now conquers his own world.[19]

What is this sacred Yes the child utters? Jane Hirschfield says it is "the beginning of genuinely original creation, the moment in which the writer can turn at last toward the work without preconception, without any motive beyond knowing the taste of what is."[20] In such a metamorphosis the "camel" and the "lion" do not vanish; their commitments to reverently "bearing much" and to necessary rebellion remain somehow in the reborn child's new beginning.

To claim the freedom and innocence of the child over the burdens and responsibilities of the "adult" is no small thing, however. What might it mean to become as children again, to take a new chance at the game of creation? Hirschfield also writes suggestively on the artist's role in culture in crossing liminal boundaries.

> As a person who carries the liminal for his culture, [the artist's] role is to be undefended, to take what is given.... What is put into the care of such a person will be well tended. Such a person can be trusted to tell the stories she is given to tell, and to tell them with the compassion that comes when the self's deepest interest is not in the self, but in turning outward and into awareness.[21]

This unselfish, outward turn of the self is not easily accomplished, nor always easy to trust, I recognize. I would not claim to have achieved it myself; yet somehow I think I know it when I encounter it. It is there, I believe, in much recent writing by Mennonites; here is just one example, from the vision that comes to Joseph Toevs near the end of Dallas Wiebe's *Our Asian Journey*:

> It is difficult to know what to write in my memoir when my time is at hand and death will soon come like a thief in the night. I could write that you can't go out and meet God by walking back and forth on the same field. I could write that you can't own a farm and be a pilgrim. I could write that if you see tongues of flame on your farm your crops are on fire. ... When you're running from the antichrist you don't stop at a hotel. When the antichrist is on his way you don't sit on a rocker and wait for him. When you walk with the Lord your feet have to touch ground. When you've been to Samarkand, Aberdeen isn't much.... In America, the woman clothed with the sun is hooked to an electric wire. I could write that you won't suffer and be purified if your plagues are land, stock, machinery, money, clothes, your wife and the neighbors' dogs. I could write all that but I won't.[22]

Wiebe's narrator makes a good postmodern move at the end, claiming to cancel his own prophetic utterance while leaving it stubbornly present, ringing in our ears. In this complication, I think, is the voice of Nietzsche's child-artist, who on the one hand demands our attention and on the other claims to know nothing for sure, who insists on both the right to testify and the freedom to make things up, who like Whitman accepts his and her own internal contradictions and the multitudes inside every human being. To accept such mystery and turmoil means abandoning the dream of a neat and tidy and singular way to follow. But the dream of such simplicity, we should know by now, is only a human dream, and a dangerous one. As Auden wrote in his "Epitaph on a Tyrant," "Perfection, of a kind, is what he was after, / And the poetry he invented was easy to understand."[23]

FATHERS AND (M)OTHERS

You may have noticed how many of the quotes in this essay concern fathers. In a workshop recently, Hildi Froese Tiessen presented a quick anthology of contemporary Mennonite writers. I found myself thinking that the tone, though not the form, of much of the work she read seemed closely related to the author's relationship to his or her parents, especially the father. For those of us with churchly backgrounds, of course, family and religious issues are inevitably and almost inextricably intertwined.

My book of poems, *Flatlands*, ends with a poem called "Seams" and with these lines, which have always seemed strange even to me, but which I believe have something to do with these issues.

> See the red-tailed hawk
> that just found dinner in the pond. See
> the hill's curve, like a fine rump,
> too big and dark for you to hold. Feel
> the seam of earth and sky, how every moment
> you are on the border. This won't last.
> The giants will return, and pity us,
> and say we can go with them if we find
> our mothers, if we ask them first. And if
> we find them, they will say we can.[24]

In her remarkable book *Black Sun: Depression and Melancholia,* Julia Kristeva writes of the powerful human yearning for reunion with some un-nameable, archaic, perhaps forever unavailable Other. She suggests that much of both art and religion are driven by this desire, which can yield both the greatest ecstasy and the blackest despair. The intensity and depth of our need make faith the terrible necessity that it is, because our quest for this Other is indeed beyond all certainty, its only reality the kind of interior experience that much of the Anabaptist tradition—and, surely, much of human history—teach us to regard with suspicion.[25] Oscar Wilde writes unsettlingly, "Men die for what they *want* to be true, for what some terror in their hearts tell them is not true."[26] Faith, he suggests, is the yearning for reunion with what terror tells us may not be there at all. Among its other, concrete meanings the Church is avatar of this yearning, our collective gathering of it.

I do not know why I believe we have to go back and find our mothers and our fathers. But I believe we do. We have to ask their permission to set off with the giants—whoever *they* are—but whether they say yes or no, we need to set off on the journey. On the way there will be time for hearing the stories of the giants and asking them to listen to ours, and talking with each other until, perhaps, we reach a place where we know as we are known. The stories will nourish and sustain us on the way, but they will not be easily told nor understood. They will include a dream of "evangelical and constructive Anabaptism" in which we might all live joyfully, purely, and peacefully together, and a nightmare of "nonresistance" as unredeemed misery in which the powerful abuse and terrify the meek. They will contain mystery, pain, darkness, and suffering that seems utterly undeserved and meaningless. They will also speak of love and beauty and meaningful sacrifice, and of a world so lovely and full that it seems incredible we should be born into it.

We can talk at length about how this telling might take place, as I have been doing here, but more important is the telling itself. There are many cities and more to be built, visible and invisible, beautiful and ugly, old and new, with streets of mud and of gold. Let us build them and walk their streets, alone and together. Let us speak and listen, learn and teach, worship and cry out, and in so doing perhaps discover something of what it means to be people of God—together.

NOTES

1. Harold S. Bender, *The Anabaptist Vision* (Scottdale, Pa.: Herald Press, 1944), 11.

2. Jacques Derrida, "Structure, Sign, and Play in the Discourse of the Human Sciences," in *The Critical Tradition: Classical Texts and Contemporary Trends*, ed. David S. Richter (New York: Bedford/St. Martins, 1989), 960.

3. Jacques Lacan, "Seminar on 'The Purloined Letter'," *The Purloined Poe: Lacan, Derrida, and Psychoanalytic Reading*, ed. John P. Muller and William J. Richardson (Baltimore: Johns Hopkins University Press, 1988), 32.

4. Jacques Derrida, "'The Purloined Letter,' *The Purveyor of Truth*," *The Critical Tradition: Classical Texts and Contemporary Trends*, ed. David H. Richter (New York: Bedford/St. Martins, 1989), 971.

5. Di Brandt, *Agnes in the Sky* (Winnipeg: Turnstone, 1990), 38-39.

6. Michel Foucault, "Panopticism," *Ways of Reading*, ed. David Bartholomae and Anthony Petrosky (Boston: Bedford/St. Martin's, 1996), 183.

7. Italo Calvino, *Invisible Cities*, trans. William Weaver (New York: Harcourt Brace Jovanovich, 1972).

8. Jeff Gundy, *A Community of Memory: My Days with George and Clara* (Urbana: University of Illinois Press, 1996).

9. Edward Said, "The Text, the World, the Critic," *The Critical Tradition: Classical Texts and Contemporary Trends*, ed. David S. Richter (New York: Bedford/St. Martins, 1989), 1024, 1030.

10. Jonathan Schell, "Reflections: A Better Today," *The New Yorker* 61 (Feb. 3, 1986), 61.

11. Julia Kasdorf, "Bakhtin, Boundaries and Bodies," *Mennonite Quarterly Review* 71, no. 2 (1997), 178.

12. Ibid., 173.

13. James M. Mellard, "Josephine Hart's *Damage*, Lacanian Tragedy, and the Ethics of *Jouissance*," *PMLA* 113, no. 3 (May 1998): 396.

14. Jeff Gundy, "Humility in Mennonite Literature," *Mennonite Quarterly Review* 63, no. 1 (1989), 5-21.

15. Elaine K. Swartzentruber, "Marking and Remarking the Body of Christ: Toward a Postmodern Mennonite Ecclesiology," *Mennonite Quarterly Review* 71, no. 2 (1997), 264.

16. Gilles Deleuze and Félix Guattari, "What Is a Minor Literature?" *Falling Into Theory: Conflicting Views on Reading Literature*, ed. David H. Richter (Boston: Bedford, 1994), 171.

17. Gilles Deleuze and Félix Guattari, *A Thousand Plateaus* (Minneapolis: University of Minnesota Press, 1993), 25.

18. Friedrich Nietzsche, *The Portable Nietzsche*, ed. and trans. Walter Kauffman, (New York: Penguin, 1954), 137, 138.

19. Ibid., 139.

20. Jane Hirschfield, *Nine Gates: Entering the Mind of Poetry* (New York: HarperCollins, 1997), 41.

21. Ibid., 223.

22. Dallas Wiebe, *Our Asian Journey* (Waterloo, Ont.: MLR Editions Canada, 1997), 443-44.

23. W. H. Auden, *Selected Poetry of W. H. Auden* (New York: Vintage, 1971), 51.

24. Jeff Gundy, *Flatlands: Poems* (Cleveland, Ohio: Cleveland State University Poetry Center, 1995), 77.

25. Julia Kristeva, *Black Sun: Depression and Melancholia*, trans. Leon S. Roudiez, (New York: Columbia University Press, 1989).

26. Oscar Wilde, "The Portrait of Mr. W. H.," quoted in Ellis Hanson, *Decadence and Catholicism* (Cambridge, Mass.: Harvard University Press, 1997), 234. I heard this first from Scott Holland.

PART FOUR

PRACTICAL DISCIPLESHIP AND LITURGICAL RENEWAL

TEN

RECOVERING THE ANABAPTIST BODY
(To Separate It for the World)

Gerald Biesecker-Mast

THE EARTHLY CITY AND THE CITY OF GOD

As Jesus makes clear in his high priestly prayer, he has sent his disciples into a world to which they do not belong to witness to a knowledge of which the world is not aware. "I have given them your word, and the world has hated them because they do not belong to the world, just as I do not belong to the world," Jesus prays to God before his death, according to the gospel of John. "As you, Father, are in me and I am in you, may they also be in us, so that the world may believe that you have sent me."[1]

With these words, Jesus in John's Gospel articulates a precarious church-based identity rooted in the otherness in relation to the world of the community of believers—even as they are to make that identity available to the world. No wonder Jesus pleads for his disciples' protection. On the one hand, to make their home and mission among those who consider them strangers leaves them vulnerable to the temptation of isolation or the danger of persecution. On the other hand, to be charged with making the unknown known in such a context is a delicate matter that risks compromising the strangeness of God with the familiarity of the world.

The struggle to negotiate this narrow and rocky path of the pilgrim church, caught between citizenship in the city of God and mission to the people of the world, has preoccupied Christian writers and thinkers throughout church history. Paul, for example, seeks to ground this negotiation in a vision of the church as a universalizable spiritual body that exceeds the ethnic specificity of the Jewish people and gathers into itself people of many cultures and nations. Concerned with the purity of this body, he urges nonconformity to the world and the covering of women's heads in worship.[2] Committed to missionary outreach, he abandons many Jewish purity codes and embraces the gifts of Gentile outsiders. Thus, Paul's writings can be read as an ongoing struggle to define a Christian specificity that was at the same time neither Jew nor Greek, male nor female, slave nor free.[3]

Augustine also devotes much attention to the tension between the otherness of the church and its mission in the world. Flirting with a Platonic dualism that he nevertheless resists in its full implication, Augustine seeks to resolve the contradictory identity of the church by linking its distinctiveness with its holy aspirations more than with its visible deeds. Writing against Donatists and Pelagians, he insists that the church could not be without spot or wrinkle until the eschaton and that in the meantime, wheat and tares must grow up together in the congregation of God.[4]

In his magnificent book *The City of God*, however, Augustine spins a vision for a pilgrim people of God shaped by their primary love for the ruler of the heavenly city and their temporary home in the earthly city.[5] As Dominique Colas has pointed out, Augustine's appropriation of Platonic dualism consolidates the utopian identity of Christianity into a dualistic logic that endangers the vitality of civil society by encouraging intrinsic doubt or suspicion by Christians toward temporal earthly political regimes in anticipation of that better city where the supreme good has been achieved.[6]

Even though Augustine makes it abundantly clear that the city of God would only come through the grace and mercy of God, not through human effort and violence, and that pilgrim Christians should in the meantime seek the well-being of the earthly city, Colas argues that this Augustinian eschatology nonetheless includes seeds of fanaticism. These might grow into projects unwilling or unable to make the ontological and eschatological distinctions that divide the temporal from the heavenly and the present from the future. They might thus be incapable of preserving space for a civil order constructed around necessities of the imperfect present.[7]

Not surprisingly, for Colas a primary example of Christian fanaticism is the Anabaptist movement of the sixteenth century, which, in its zeal to destroy paintings and sculptures, exemplifies the fanatical desire to replace mediating images and representations with the real thing and in so doing to overcome the temporal with the eternal. The picture of Anabaptism Colas paints is a violent one: smashing images, destroying churches, taking over cities, and executing opponents.[8] It is obvious that Colas has less interest in the complicated reality of the Anabaptist movement as revealed in the sources than in using the grisly excesses of the movement to make his theoretical point, which is a good one: the legacy of dualism in Western political thought both energizes and subverts the societies it has founded by providing an enduring utopian impulse that has inspired both constructive activism and destructive paranoia.

This point rings true despite the narrow range of violent representative anecdotes chosen by Colas to illustrate Anabaptist fanaticism. Anabaptists of all kinds did seek to live under the reign of God literally and in their present. Anabaptists everywhere assumed that Jesus' way was to be followed without reservation or delay. However, not all Anabaptists sought to enforce the reign of God with the sword, which is a crucial difference.

ERASMIAN NEO-PLATONISM AND ANABAPTIST NAIVETE

Abraham Friesen offers a compelling account of the Anabaptist debt to Erasmus which confirms Colas's overall argument, if from a sympathetic rather than hostile perspective. According to Friesen, the Anabaptists are unique in appropriating Erasmian humanism as an actual rule of life, not merely an ideal. Erasmus, committed to moral reform through renewed access to Jesus' teachings, restates more clearly than his contemporaries a radical Christocentrism that emphasizes pacifism, avoiding oaths, Christian brotherhood, centrality of baptism, and instruction of adult believers.

However, Erasmus can stress these teachings without leaving the Catholic Church because he assumes a neo-Platonic framework in which the church in reality can only approximate these ideals. The Swiss Brethren and other Anabaptist groups who read Erasmus's annotations and paraphrases of the New Testament, unburdened with the neo-Platonic distinction between inaccessible ideal forms and their available dim shadows, assume that the teachings of Christ as illuminated by Erasmus should simply be put into place without delay or apology. "Through Luther's reformation and Zwingli's legacy, the Anabaptists developed an interpretive model different from that of Erasmus," Friesen explains. "That model rejected the latter's Platonic interpretive scheme but not the ideals Erasmus had sought to establish as the ideal forms of Christianity."[9]

What should be clear by now is that the same absence of a theoretical dualism makes possible both the violent iconoclasm of the Münster Anabaptists and the pacifist biblicism of the Swiss Brethren. Both share in common an erasure of the epistemological and eschatological distinction between, for example, the ideal forms, which for neo-Platonists constituted the coming city of God and their shadowy reflections in the earthly church of Christ. In so doing, the Anabaptists gain the confidence to assert their capacity to live according to the rule of Christ immediately.

At the same time, the Anabaptists lose a conventional theological tool for negotiating the precarious tension between inhabiting the world and identifying with Jesus. Whereas Erasmus can lament the distance between his world and that of Christ without assuming that his world is irretrievably lost, the Anabaptists have to assume that this distance requires crossing without delay. Their contemporaries in the Reformation movements can assume with Augustine that wheat and tares should be left to grow up together in the church. But the Anabaptists can only accept a visible church, without spot or wrinkle. Lutheran reformers can postulate that faith alone brings salvation and that therefore moral actions are of secondary importance to correct belief. Yet the Anabaptists can only insist that moral fruits are necessary evidences of spiritual commitments.[10]

The Anabaptists refuse to acknowledge the neo-Platonic Erasmian distinction between the ideal of Christ and the necessary imperfection of Christ's church as well as the Lutheran distinction between the inner, spiritual kingdom and the outer, material one. This leaves them with a far simpler and more dangerous distinction: "believing and unbelieving, darkness and light, the world and those who are come out of the world, God's temple and idols, Christ and Belial."[11]

As is clear from the complex and troubled history of Anabaptist communities and movements, concrete and literal separation from the world is a goal that not only divides the church from the world but also the church from itself. The difficult work of disentanglement from worldly iniquity outside the church becomes a struggle to ascertain the dregs of worldliness that reside in the church. Soon arguments about what is worldly and what is not lead to division after division. In describing the experience of Dutch Anabaptists, Sjouke Voolstra captures this tendency well, though he perhaps overstates the generalization. "The pursuit of holiness is always at odds with the pursuit of unity, whether of church and society or of the church itself," he writes.[12]

Indeed, recognition of this struggle between holiness and unity has led a number of scholars to call for reading Mennonite history as a history of conflict.[13] Unfortunately, the most common forms of such analysis have tended to assume that conflict must always be a sign of disunity and thus be inherently negative.[14] But if conflict has often originated from and reinforced division, there is also reason to believe conflict can emerge from and even strengthen a community that emphasizes unity over autonomy. In traditional Mennonite communities, for example, conflict may be constituted less by competing demands for individual rights and privileges and more by divergent convictions based in common study of Scripture and commitment to Christ.

When conflict arises from such divergent understandings of a common pursuit of holiness, then it may be that conflict is best described not as the opposite of unity, but rather as either an exploited or lost opportunity for reconciliation. As John Howard Yoder has written, "the functional meaning of church unity is not that people agree, and therefore work together but that where they disagree they recognize the need to talk together with a view toward reconciliation."[15]

The inability to recognize the difference between unity and agreement has led to numerous unfortunate consequences, including fear of conflict, calls for charismatic leadership, and the privileging of individual spirituality over collective worship. Most troublesome, though, in my view, is the tendency to reduce the gospel to a short list of essentials about which there is widespread agreement, then to relativize the remaining "secondary" issues. In this way the most controversial, and thus most vital aspects of the gospel, including the call to visible countercultural witness, are rendered benign.[16] For example, as Voolstra notes, in Dutch Mennonite history Mennonites sought common ground with other Christians, whether the Collegiants, the Calvinists, or other Mennonite groups. In so doing they began to identify with a "subjective, affective, internalized, reasonable, and moral religion" rather than with an outward church visibly separate from the world and "without spot or wrinkle."[17]

Emphasis on lived faith need not inevitably lead to conflict, however. In the early magisterial Reformation, obsession with doctrinal correctness at the expense of a lived gospel was what led to "incessant quarreling." Meanwhile, the emphasis among Erasmian humanists on a "regenerate life" led to more peaceful coexistence, according to Abraham Friesen.[18]

Among Anabaptist-Mennonites, the temptation has always been to inch toward the Lutheran emphasis on the invisible church and, as a result, to tolerate social immorality while obsessing about doctrinal correctness. Granted, such movement toward belief-focused rather than a practice-focused Christianity is made for understandable reasons. People grow weary of conflict and countercultural living. The witness of the church seems to depend on making the gospel more "user friendly." And many have bad memories of an imposed uniformity as a strategy of nonconformity. Yet for those committed to a concrete Christian witness in the manner of the early Anabaptists—indeed, of the early Christians—this movement can only be viewed as a subversion of vigorous Christian discipleship.

One response among those who fear the assimilation of Anabaptist-Mennonite churches into the cultural and ecclesiological mainstream has been to assume that since traditional Mennonite cultural distinctives are dying an inevitable death, we had better find a distinctive theological ground on which to build the church. This is a proposal I fully support.[19] Yet while I affirm this effort to find a distinctive Mennonite theology, to work at the task that was only begun by Anabaptist forbears, I also believe theology by itself is not sufficient to sustain visible countercultural communities of witness to Christ's inbreaking reign. We must find a way to live our theology, not merely affirm it. We must learn to become motivated at our very core of being to follow Christ and not merely assent to his views. To do this we must teach a gospel of action and discipleship, of lived faith, and of moral fruits.

The following discussion of such a practice of discipleship is deeply informed by three kinds of sources. First, I draw on old Anabaptist texts which demand a visible and defenseless discipleship in Christ.

Second, I am indebted to the creative theological and historical work of Mennonite writers like Lois Barrett, Harold Bender, J. Lawrence Burkholder, Tom Finger, Guy Hershberger, Beulah Stauffer Hostetler, C. Norman Kraus, Donald Kraybill, Theron Schlabach, J. Denny Weaver, and John Howard Yoder and many others who have sought to reconstruct a distinctive Anabaptist-Christian witness for the contemporary context.

Finally, I engage the discipline of rhetoric, which has struggled against Plato to enflesh the texts of human communication rather than render them as benign, dim reflections of more fundamental yet relatively inaccessible realities.[20]

The one thing all these sources share in common is the effort to constitute the word as deed and the deed as word while refusing to get rid of the distinction between the two. Put simply, all these sources can inspire us to name the words we speak as actual deeds or fruits of discipleship while at the same time reading the deeds we do as literal words or witnesses of faith. It is my contention that this insistence on the twofold Christian witness of word and deed, without making either one the slave of the other, can reinvigorate the visible, alternative embodiment of the way of Christ in the believers churches of the twenty-first century.

The central theological distinction in this performative ecclesiology will not be the Platonic priority of forms over their shadows, nor the Augustinian differentiation between the earthly and the heavenly, nor yet the Lutheran division of the visible and the invisible. Rather, at the core is the gospel separation of the cross from the sword. It is this separation, I believe, that can invigorate a compelling public witness, preserve the church's visibility, and absorb apocalyptic conflicts. By way of concrete example, I want to suggest how such an approach deals with two intractable problems for Anabaptist ecclesiology: the relation of the church to the world that 1) inhabits it and 2) that it inhabits.

Visibility and Separation

The baptismal texts of Paul in Romans 6 put to rest any idea of God's grace as excuse for moral relativism. They provide a theological basis for believers churches to seek to become communities of regeneration, hope, and healing. "How can we who died to sin go on living in it?" Paul asks.

> Do you not know that all of us who have been baptized into Christ Jesus were baptized into his death? Therefore, we have been buried with him by baptism into death, so that, just as Christ was raised from the dead by the glory of the Father, so we too might walk in newness of life.[21]

Throughout the rest of the chapter and for several chapters after, Paul repeats and extends this argument, insisting that the grace of God frees the body from sin's dominion and opens an alternative moral regime—obedience to righteousness rather than slavery to sin.[22] This alternative regime depends on the word of faith, not the letter of the law (10:5-10) and welcomes into membership those formally excluded (11:13-24).

However, the primary fruit of such faith is holiness, nonconformity, intellectual renewal, and the capacity for discernment (12:1-2). Furthermore, these fruits are manifested not in a single individual but are dispersed throughout the body of Christ as a variety of functions or "gifts" in the church (12:3-7). Finally, the specific polity that pervades all of these functions is genuine love, which Paul describes as rejoicing in hope, patient in suffering, perseverant in prayer, generous in giving, hospitable to strangers, and nonresistant to enemies (12:8-21).

Here in a nutshell are the main features of the visible, witnessing church that Anabaptists like Michael Sattler, Menno Simons, and Anna

Jansz sought to recover. In this approach, we find no effort to hedge the limits of an imperfect status quo against the potential of a more perfect future. We discover no posing of inner assent against outer corruption. Instead, the most significant qualifier of the new community, its holiness and its fruits, is nonviolent and suffering love. This love, far from constituting benign tolerance, is practiced in the context of a fruitful community of nonconformist disciples who engage in collective discernment and mutual aid. As Paul writes elsewhere, such discernment may involve the restoration of brothers and sisters who are "detected in a transgression."[23]

In the Anabaptist tradition, such restoration has historically included an interpretation of Matthew 18 to include disfellowshipping those who refuse the counsel of the believing community. However, among leaders such as Michael Sattler and Menno Simons, there was a clear acknowledgment of the enormous burden such "restoration" entails. Consequently, there were repeated calls to undertake such an effort with the spirit of love, meekness, and understanding.

Michael Sattler, for example, in his letter to the church at Horb, admonishes his people "not to forget love, without which it is not possible that you be a Christian congregation."[24] After summarizing Paul's eloquent text on love in 1 Corinthians 13, Sattler writes,

> But if you love the neighbor, you will not scold or ban zealously, will not seek your own, will not remember evil, will not be ambitious or puffed up, but kind, generous in all gifts, humble and sympathetic with the weak and imperfect.[25]

This is a clear example of the Anabaptist alternative to dualisms of present and future, outer and inner, shadow and form, which legitimated a morally compromised, invisible church. This alternative calls for a church without spot or wrinkle but insists that love is the way to tend to such a community.

I cannot be emphatic enough about the dangerous terrain on which this approach places the church. The work of reconciliation is distinguished from the sin of judging during such a restoration process only by the presence of nonresistant and suffering love. When the ban is used in a power struggle or to negotiate political space in the church or to keep the most people happy, then the witness of biblical church discipline and separation is tarnished.

Then the church becomes compromised in one of two ways. Either it succumbs to a conventional kind of political correctness or replaces biblical discipline with liberal autonomy. Menno speaks to this question in his earlier writings on church discipline, before he was persuaded to accept what I believe to be a less biblical view that it was appropriate to excommunicate without warning and that restoration must be predicated not merely on repentance but on signs of transformation. According to Menno, the ban must be used only in the context of patience, forbearance, and intent to heal: "For we do not want to expel any, but rather to receive; not to amputate, but rather to heal; not to discard, but rather to win back; not to grieve, but rather to comfort; not to condemn, but rather to save."[26] Only in such a context can the ban be an "act of love," even though some will see it as an "act of hatred."[27] In his second work on excommunication, Menno is quite clear about the high stakes difference between the holy and sinful use of the ban:

> For if it (excommunication) be done without the Word and Spirit, without love and brotherly diligence, but through bitterness, anger, or a false report, not conformable to the Word, or for reasons not deserving the ban, then it is not a work of God, no medicine to the soul, nor fruit of pure love; but a Satanic contention, a corruption and a pestilence to the soul, and evident fruit of the flesh; in short, a curse and an abomination, and stench before God.[28]

It is notable that the Jakob Ammann party, in their letter of confession in 1700 three years after the Amish schism, acknowledge with grief that their exercise of the harsh ban against the Swiss ministers was sinful, even though their intentions were for the well-being of the church. "We confess that the ban also applies to us, and for this reason we do not stand apart from the church without guilt, and we desire to be reconciled with God and man as much as possible."[29] This letter seems to indicate that Amman and his fellow ministers had finally realized they had crossed the line from a process of reconciliation into the sin of judging as a result of actions not qualified by patient and suffering love.[30]

My larger point here, though, is that the danger of this terrain must not prevent us from seeking to be the church without spot or wrinkle that Anabaptists like Sattler and Menno sought to restore. It is at this crucial point that we are pressed as members of Christ to exhibit the strange and scandalous otherness of the love of Christ. We are required by love to discipline one another, and we are required by love to do so nonresistantly without arbitrary exercise of power. Further, we must proceed under the assumption that the process of reconciliation might reveal that we have not acted in love, despite our best intentions, as Jacob Ammann apparently discovered. This is a hard teaching that we have not yet learned well.

No less difficult than the church's relation to worldliness in the church is the church's relation to the worldliness outside the church. I take as a point of departure the Schleitheim articulation of this relationship as glossed by John Howard Yoder, which is really also a careful reading of Romans 13.[31] The antagonism between the church and the world is unmistakable—believing versus unbelieving, light versus darkness, Christ versus Belial, etc. In the world, structures of governance are in place that frequently usurp God's authority and thus cannot be trusted. Yet these structures are nevertheless ordered—put in place and given limited authority—by God. They are therefore not to be violently overthrown.

So the sword is ordered by God but outside the perfection of Christ. It is not for us to take up on behalf of the church's protection our visions of a better world or even of the kingdom of God. In other words, the otherness of the church is preserved not only by its separation from the world, but also and perhaps more importantly, by its refusal to protect this separation by means of the sword.

In John Howard Yoder's *The Christian Witness to the State*, this approach is developed more fully in one of the most eloquent arguments on behalf of an anti-Platonic political theology I have seen. As Yoder describes it, "the present historical period is characterized by the coexistence of two ages or eons," with the "essential difference between the two eons" not being "temporal, since they coexist" but rather a "matter of direction."[32] In this model, "the old has already begun to be superseded by the new, and the focus of that victory is the body of Christ, first the man Christ Jesus, then derivatively the fellowship of obedient believers."[33]

Thus Yoder can say that "the church is not fundamentally a source of moral stimulus to encourage the development of a better society—though a faithful church should also have this effect—it is for the sake of the church's own work that society continues to function."[34] Yoder attacks all efforts to bless the status quo by monumentalizing through ontology either the eschatological divide between the city of God and the earthly city or the epistemological gap between the church and the world. Yoder's way of putting it is that "the difference between Christian ethics for Christians and a Christian ethic for the state is therefore due to duality not of realms or levels but of responses."[35]

The political and psychological effects of accepting Yoder's position are profound. We are human subjects not yet fully constituted or shaped by the call of Christ and the church. Yet we are constituted to a significant extent as subjects of the nation-state and its ideological and economic projects. Thus we find that the demand to be subject to Christ and to serve God alone splits our consciousness and unravels our identity.

We find, for example, that our membership in the global church undermines our allegiance to national interests. We find that the injunction to mutual aid and sharing in the local brother-sisterhood of believers challenges our autonomy as the consumer-subjects of a global capitalist economy. And so we discover in our everyday lives that to become slaves to Christ is indeed an act of liberation that is a life work, dependent on God's grace and inconceivable outside of the church.

Because we cannot engage in this struggle alone, we would do well to heed the words of Anna Jansz, written to her son Isaac in 1539 before she was executed in Rotterdam: "But where you hear of a poor, simple, cast-off flock, which is despised and rejected by the world, join them; for where you hear of the cross, there is Christ; from there do not depart."[36] At this place of the cross we have come full circle from discipline as a struggle against the world which still inhabits the church to discipline as a blessing for the believing community that still inhabits the world.

In both of these aspects, the church's aspiration to be a church without spot or wrinkle constitutes at some moments a concrete instantiation of such a church and at other moments a failure yet to be such a church. The process of disentanglement from the world is a difficult practice made possible only by the grace of God, which as we have seen, is both a helping hand and a safety net. It is in light of such grace that we are both empowered toward transformation and saved from our fall, both regenerated and justified.[37]

In our efforts to embody both aspects of this grace as Christ's body, we cannot establish an a priori formula for determining when we have exercised adequate forbearance and patience and now have reached the time for transforming discipline and separation. What we do discover is that in the process of struggling as a church to be both long-suffering and agents of transformation, we are plunged into both failure and success. We on the one hand fail again and again despite our best intentions, and on the other hand God's transcendent spirit intervenes again and again to exceed miraculously our worst failures.

We discover, for example, that just as we keep confronting the sinfulness of the world in the church and are then required to struggle with it, so also do we keep confronting the godliness of the world outside the church and are then blessed by recognizing it. Scott Holland's work has taught us to look for traces of God in public spaces and worldly places, to discover the reign of God not only in the safety of the sanctuary but in the solidarity with the stranger.[38] Our early Anabaptist forbears did not know what to make of halfway Anabaptists who refused believers baptism and thus remained outside the "true church" but at the same time risked their lives to protect the true believers.[39] The mutually exclusive responses to this question played a significant role in the Amish schism and exhibited that unresolvable tension between God's extravagant grace and God's empowering grace, between the beauty of God's creation and the holiness of God's people that should not be rendered benign by safe theological formulas or the collapse of one aspect into the other.

Thus the concrete separation of church and world espoused in Schleitheim and indeed in the New Testament begins with the assumption that matters are yet muddled and the church must struggle in the present to make visible the reign of God that is on the way, although not yet entirely realized. This is quite different from various ontological dualisms, which claim that the reign of God already exists perfectly in an invisible or future dimension no matter how compromised matters are in the visible present.

LANGUAGE AND THE BODY

To recover the full measure of possibility offered by replacing ontological dualism with concrete separation qualified only by suffering love, we need to take brief note now of two developments associated with the postmodern turn. The first is the dispersion of power from sovereign centers. The second is the expansion of the importance of symbolic action.

Perhaps Foucault more than anyone has called our attention to the declining significance of the state as the central origin of social subjection. According to Foucault, instead of thinking about power as primarily emanating from such central locations as the formal institutions of governance, we should think instead of power as exercised from innumerable spaces in contemporary societies where seemingly benign control is exercised over social behavior and identity. This includes, for example, clinics, hospitals, prisons, educational institutions, research centers, and the host of corporate and public bureaucracies, not to mention the mass media.[40] Such a view demands that we think through our relation to worldliness not only by our troubled relationship to the state, but also, and perhaps more importantly, through our often unexamined relationship to the institutions, economies, practices, and public and private spaces of our everyday lives.

One specific location of power that has become more visible today is the power of language to shape us and the world as we experience and understand it. It was to such terrain of discursive practices that Foucault gave much attention. Judith Butler, for example, has shown how the theoretical work of Foucault, Althusser, and Austin sheds light on the vulnerability of the human body to the linguistic actions that also sustain it. According to Butler, "Language sustains the body not by bringing it into being or feeding it in a literal way; rather, it is by being interpellated in the terms of language that a certain social existence of the body first becomes possible."[41] Butler calls attention to the power of naming to bring our bodies a certain level of self-consciousness that includes most notably a fear of death and anxiety about survival.[42]

Consequently, the experience of being named, which always begins with the voice of the other, makes us quite vulnerable to the social-linguistic practices that address us and call us into social being. This is why hate speech, for example, carries the capacity to do great harm, although Butler notes that the powerful responses to hate speech prove that such dehumanizing naming practices are not totalizing and that it is possible to resist them effectively.

If we accept the proposition that we humans are linguistic creatures whose very sense of self is produced through social texts, then we must acknowledge that an enormous amount of power is carried by those institutions, social networks, and symbolic practices in which we live, move, and have our being. We must furthermore acknowledge that our struggles with the principalities and powers from which we seek to extract ourselves to be subject to Christ are not merely governmental bodies in, say, Washington, D.C., or Ottawa, though we certainly must struggle with them. Neither is our battle only with the corporate and financial institutions that control the world's money supply, although we certainly must struggle with them as well.

Rather, and perhaps even more importantly, our struggle also includes critical resistance to media texts. We need to resist the media texts siphoned into our living rooms and our office computers to name us as carnal consumers. We must challenge the ideological practices of schooling that seek to address our young people as patriotic Americans who should aspire to be all they can be, whether in the army or in the marketplace. We should work toward economic subversion of a market system that names us first of all as property owners whose worth is judged by the size of our bank accounts or investment portfolios.

Furthermore, if we then recognize our vulnerability to the social power of the institutional and textual networks in which we live our daily lives, we must also ask where the resources for faithfulness lie for those of us who seek to follow Christ in deed as well as word. Having understood that the power of address is a social practice, not something the individual can simply dredge up from within an isolated self, we will begin to recognize in a new way the truth of Paul's statement that we are either slaves to Christ or slaves to sin. We will grasp that freedom cannot be achieved through individual autonomy.

For Christians, as Yoder and Hauerwas have argued, the primary resource for social and political resistance in obedience to Christ will be the church. At the same time, we must acknowledge with Scott Holland the many good voices that address us from surprising and strange locations, as the voice of God cannot be confined to the sanctuary.[43] Indeed, one task of the church is perhaps to open the ears of God's people to the voice of the Other that these days is mostly colonized and made safe for consumption by captains of Western cultural industries.

For the church to maintain or perhaps recover its capacity effectively to name its members as disciples of Christ, no longer enslaved to sin, and charged with the mission of bringing God's witness of peace to the world, the church must first of all recover the body of Christ as its concrete form of existence. By this I mean that Christians will first of all be addressed in their churches as members of Christ's body whose daily actions and habits either strengthen or weaken that ecclesial body. For such a collective consciousness to gain authority and power, the people of God will need to be trained in the school of Christian performance skills. In other words, they will need to become aware of the symbolic and social meaning of everyday acts that were once considered meaningless habits of personal preference but now are understood to signify the location of loyalty and the vitality of witness.

Unfortunately, the greatest resources in the Anabaptist-Mennonite tradition are often neglected because of problematic forms cultural distinctiveness has taken throughout our history. However, the church is not merely an excuse for individual autonomy—an endorser of the cultural status quo. Rather, the church is to be an alternative moral regime concretely separated from worldliness. Thus we need to give more attention to precisely those symbolic and cultural practices Mennonites have been sloughing off in recent decades. This includes such important symbolic actions as avoiding fads and fashions, refusing to participate in nationalistic rituals, and living without the daily influx of mass-mediated texts.

Just one controversial example illustrates the point. The woman's head covering was a symbolic expression of headship for (Old) Mennonites and still is for Old Order and conservative Mennonites today. But is the stylistic and symbolic ethos of consumer choice and thus liberal autonomy the best alternative fashion statement for Mennonites who seek to give expression to the biblical notion of mutuality in marriage and family relationships? What would it mean for men and women to give expression in their clothing choices, living arrangements, and household economies to mutual fidelity under the headship of Christ alone rather than to the consuming myth of individual autonomy under the rule of the market? What would it mean for both men and women to recover the visible body of Christ, if not through covering women's heads, then through other countercultural coverings and congregations of believers' bodies?

WORDS AND DEEDS

In the remainder of this chapter I advocate a discipleship of performance that makes our bodies members of Christ's body, vulnerable in our corporate and bodily witness to the world created and loved by God, a world from which we are also called to separate to make God's love known in word and deed. I use the term *performance* to describe our discipleship because I think it can help us better grasp the bodily, material character of our witness and perhaps extend into the worship of our everyday lives a stronger sense of the roles we play in the drama of God's redemption story.[44]

Such a performative discipleship is characterized by consciousness of audience, attending to the response of the Other to the acts of the disciple, without simply acceding to conventional wisdom or the status quo. Similar to what Jeffrey Nealon has called an "alterity politics" (over against identity politics), this performative discipleship is focused less on abstract ideals that are unachievable and more on the concrete actions that are called forth by the neighbor.[45]

As Nealon writes, "it is not a necessary failure or the resentment of a broken promise that drives alterity politics; rather, it is the positive promise and concretization of different actions, practices, and organizations that orient and give force to an alterity politics of response."[46] This commitment to concrete, material, bodily solidarity with the Other—with that which is on the Way—prevents an Anabaptist discipleship of performance from becoming a merely respectable adaptation of the gospel to mainstream values and comforts.[47] Indeed, for Anabaptists, such a solidarity with the Other has most often been expressed in terms of conscientious objection to any program, institution, law, or practice that conscripts self or neighbor into a politics of the uniform, a rendering of the Other as the same, whether by baptizing the child or by killing the enemy.[48]

The broad outline of an Anabaptist discipleship of performance is sketched already in the *Martyrs Mirror*, also entitled *The Bloody Theatre*. In van Braght's introduction, he contrasts the drama of Anabaptist martyrdom both with the "fashionable comedies and fanciful dramas" of Grecian theatres and with the dangerous exigencies of his own time and place, the seventeenth-century Dutch Golden Age.[49] "What difference is there between us and them?" he asks. "Certainly only this," he answers, "that they all persevered unto the end nay, unto a cruel death, without departing to the right or to the left; which we have not yet done."[50] In this struggle to persevere to the end without turning to the right or left, a motif repeated again and again throughout the Anabaptist letters published in this book, the dangers faced by the martyrs are portrayed as less seductive than those of his own more comfortable context:

> These times are certainly more dangerous; for then Satan came openly, through his servants, even at noon-day, as a roaring lion, so that he could be known, and it now and then was possible to hide from him; besides, his chief design then was to destroy the body: but now he comes as in the night, or in the twilight, in a strange but yet pleasing form, and, in a two-fold way, lies in wait to destroy the soul; partly to trample under foot, and annihilate entirely, if this were possible, the only saving Christian faith; partly to destroy the true separated Christian life which is the outgrowth of faith.[51]

An Anabaptist discipleship of performance inspired by the alterity politics of the *Martyrs Mirror* is less a liberal celebration of multiculturalism and more a radical struggle against the demonic—those forces and powers that blaspheme God and "regard human blood and swine's blood about alike."[52] Of particular interest to me in this description of the strategies used by the chief antagonist of Christians, who find themselves in a scene of seduction rather than terror, is the twofold attack "Satan" is said to make on "the saving Christian faith" and "the true separated Christian life." It is to this twofold attack on faith and life that an Anabaptist discipleship of performance has a twofold response: the truth performed in word and deed.

The first aspect of this twofold response will be the *performance of words as deeds*. By this I mean that Anabaptist Christian verbal or textual witness will seek in its symbolic action not to reflect, however imperfectly, some deeper or wider or future ideal or universal that is on the other side of an epistemological or eschatological divide. Sought instead will be means to give concrete witness to the incarnation of God in Jesus Christ.

Anna Jansz witnessed eloquently to this difficult and narrow Way "of the prophets, apostles, and martyrs," of the "dead under the altar," of those who "follow the Lamb wherever he goeth."[53] In describing this very particular Way, Anna compellingly cites the imagery from 2 Esdras 7:6-8 of a city "full of all good things" whose "entrance thereof is narrow, and set in a dangerous place to fall, like as if there were a fire on the right hand, and on the left a deep water: and only one path between them both, even between the fire and the water. . . ."[54] Such a specific and perilous witness will be both dialogical and transformative, both nonviolent and intrusive, as C. Norman Kraus has recently argued. That is, it will seek to intervene defenselessly in the culturally and historically bounded contexts of contemporary Christian mission to "introduce the kingdom of God as a real human possibility."[55]

In understanding the word as gospel deed more than theological reflection, we will also give more attention to the rhetorical and poetic movement of texts as spoken or written practices with the capacity to wound and heal, to discourage and motivate, to antagonize and inspire. Having forgotten Platonic dualism, we will be free to welcome the poets that Plato banished from his perfect society in *The Republic*. We will welcome the poets because, as Scott Holland has written, "poetry is connected to the concrete, contingent, complicated realm of embodied passion and as such threatens the rule of reason."[56] A visible church that is a defenseless embodiment of suffering love must seek to dethrone from its pedestal the rule of Reason, while engaging in their full variety the concrete experiences of Christ's vulnerable members.

The literature of the visible church will thus include texts that describe the beauty and terror of the world as well as the hope and failure of the church. This literature will include doctrines and poems, liturgies and novels, systematic theologies and creative nonfictions, sermons and histories, prayers and arguments, catechisms and children's stories, biblical exegesis and scientific hypotheses. Such literature is a gift of faith that can sustain and nourish the life and witness of the body of Christ and its members by providing scripts for its performance.

The second aspect of the twofold discipleship of performance I am suggesting is the *performance of deeds as words*. By this I mean that Anabaptist Christians will seek in their daily lives and actions not to act with pragmatic utility according to the requirements of the "real" world as it is widely understood. They will aim, rather, to perform in their public and private practices the script of God's redemption drama as it is constituted by the Scriptures. By such actions the members of Christ's body attest to the alternative reality of God's reign. They highlight their status as a "peculiar people" who, as Rodney Clapp has argued, will engage in a liturgical politics that puts on parade the church's allegiance to a transforming God.[57]

The performance of deeds as words will involve demonstrations and protests; daily acts of kindness and weekly gifts of money; refusals of military service and boycotts of corporations; car-driving habits and car-avoiding habits; caring for children and for our elders; potlucks and small group activities; organization creating and organization challenging. To do these things well we will need to affirm the work of CEOs and housewives, construction workers and office secretaries, performers of the fine arts and cultural workers in the popular media. In short we will need to consult the widest range of organizing and directing skills available in the church to help it tap into the full wealth of possibility for human engagement and service in the name of Christ.

Both of these aspects of our resistance to the work of "Satan"—the word as deed and the deed as word—will be brought together in the church's regular gathering for liturgical and spiritual renewal in worship of the risen Lord whose reign has come and is being established. For such worship gatherings to be revitalized, we will likewise need to gather the gifts and functions of all the believers and members of Christ who can together proclaim, enact—indeed, perform—the glorious drama of the gospel's unfolding, regenerative power. In this gathered and dispersed body of Christ, separate from yet fully engaged in the world, we can find the hope of our salvation and the world's.

Notes

1. John 17:14, 21b (NRSV).

2. Dale Martin, *The Corinthian Body* (New Haven: Yale University Press, 1995), 229-249.

3. Daniel Boyarin, *A Radical Jew* (Berkeley: University of California Press, 1994), 180-227.

4. Jaroslav Pelikan, *The Christian Tradition, Volume 1: The Emergence of the Catholic Tradition* (Chicago: The University of Illinois Press), 308.

5. According to Augustine, "two cities have been formed by two loves: the earthly by the love of self, even to the contempt of God; the heavenly by the love of God, even to the contempt of self." Furthermore, he writes, "In the one, the princes and the nations it subdues are ruled by the love of ruling; in the other, the princes and the subjects

serve one another in love, the latter obeying while the former take thought for all" (book 14:28), St. Augustine, *The City of God* (New York: The Modern Library, 1950), 477.

6. Dominique Colas, *Civil Society and Fanaticism* (Stanford: Stanford University Press, 1997), 55.

7. Ibid., 42-154.

8. Ibid., 99-138.

9. Abraham Friesen, *Erasmus, the Anabaptists, and the Great Commission* (Grand Rapids, Mich.: Eerdmans, 1998), 37.

10. Abraham Friesen, "Menno Simons and the Beginnings of Dutch Anabaptism," *Mennonite Quarterly Review* 62, no. 3 (July 1998), 355-362.

11. See article IV of the Schleitheim *Brotherly Union*, John Howard Yoder, trans. and ed., *The Legacy of Michael Sattler* (Scottdale, Pa.: Herald Press, 1973), 38.

12. Sjouke Voolstra, "'The colony of heaven': The Anabaptist aspiration to be a church without spot or wrinkle in the sixteenth and seventeenth centuries," in *From Martyr to Muppy*, ed. Alastair Hamilton, Sjouke Voolstra, and Piet Visser (Amsterdam: Amsterdam University Press, 1994), 21.

13. Stephen Ainlay and Fred Kniss, "Mennonites and Conflict: Re-Examining Mennonite History and Contemporary Life," *Mennonite Quarterly Review* 72, no. 2 (April 1998), 121-139; Fred Kniss, *Disquiet in the Land* (New Brunswick: Rutgers University Press, 1997), 1-18; and John D. Roth, "Community as Conversation: A New Model of Anabaptist Hermeneutics," *Essays in Anabaptist Theology* (Elkhart, Ind.: Institute of Mennonite Studies, 1994), 35-47.

14. Kniss introduces his recent book by contrasting the sentiments of the hymn, "Blest Be the Tie That Binds," with the conflicts he will describe in his book which he says show that "'the fellowship of kindred minds' may be anything but a 'peaceable kingdom'" (Kniss, *Disquiet*, 1-2).

15. John Howard Yoder, *The Royal Priesthood* (Grand Rapids, Mich.: Eerdmans, 1994), 292.

16. J. Denny Weaver, "Which Way for Mennonite Theology?" *Gospel Herald* (January 23, 1996), 1-4.

17. Voolstra, "The Colony of Heaven," 15-29.

18. Friesen, "Menno Simons," 361.

19. J. Denny Weaver, "Is the Anabaptist Vision Still Relevant?" *Pennsylvania Mennonite Heritage* 14, no. 1 (January 1991), 2-12.

20. A partial list of such texts would include John H. Yoder, trans., *The Legacy of Michael Sattler*; Leonard Verduin, trans., *The Complete Writings of Menno Simons* (Scottdale, Pa.: Herald Press, 1956); Cornelius Dyck, William Keeney, and Alvin J. Beachy, eds. and trans., *The Writings of Dirk Philips* (Scottdale, Pa.: Herald Press, 1992); Lois Barrett, *Building the House Church* (Scottdale, Pa.: Herald Press, 1986); Harold Bender, *The Anabaptist Vision* (Scottdale, Pa.: Herald Press, 1944); J. Lawrence Burkholder, *The Problem of Social Responsibility From the Perspective of the Mennonite Church* (Elkhart, Ind.: Institute of Mennonite Studies, 1989); Thomas Finger, *Systematic Theology: An Eschatological Approach*, vols. 1 and 2 (Scottdale, Pa.: Herald

Press, 1985-89); Guy Hershberger, *War, Peace, and Nonresistance* (Scottdale, Pa.: Herald Press, 1946); Donald B. Kraybill, *The Upside-Down Kingdom* (Scottdale, Pa.: Herald Press, 1978); Theron Schlabach, *Gospel Versus Gospel* (Scottdale, Pa.: Herald Press, 1980); J. Denny Weaver, *Becoming Anabaptist* (Scottdale, Pa.: Herald Press, 1987); John Howard Yoder, *The Politics of Jesus* (Grand Rapids, Mich.: Eerdmans, 1972); Rosamond Kent Sprague, ed., *The Older Sophists* (Columbia, S.C.: University of South Carolina Press, 1990); Aristotle, *On Rhetoric*, trans. George Kennedy (New York: Oxford University Press, 1991); John Poulakos, *Sophistical Rhetoric in Ancient Greece* (Columbia, S.C.: University of South Carolina Press, 1995); Brian Vickers, *In Defence of Rhetoric* (Oxford: Clarendon Press, 1988).

21. Romans 6:2b-4 (NRSV).

22. My reading here closely follows that of Tom Finger in his *Systematic Theology, Volume II*, 119-120.

23. Galatians 6:1 (NRSV).

24. Yoder, *Legacy*, 59.

25. Ibid.

26. Verduin, *The Complete Writings of Menno Simons*, 413.

27. Ibid.

28. Ibid., 469.

29. John D. Roth, trans., *Letters of the Amish Division: A Sourcebook* (Goshen, Ind.: Mennonite Historical Society, 1993), 109.

30. Ibid., 110.

31. John Howard Yoder, "'Anabaptists and the Sword' Revisited: Systematic Historiography and Undogmatic Nonresistants," *Zeitschrift für Kirchengeschichte* 85 (1974), 135.

32. John Howard Yoder, *The Christian Witness to the State* (Newton, Kans.: Faith and Life Press, 1964), 9.

33. Ibid.

34. Ibid., 13.

35. Ibid., 32.

36. Thieleman J. van Braght, *The Bloody Theater or Martyrs Mirror* (Scottdale, Pa.: Herald Press, 1985), 454.

37. Alvin Beachy, *The Concept of Grace in the Radical Reformation* (Nieuwkoop: B. De Graaf, 1977), 174-175.

38. Scott Holland, "So Many Good Voices in My Head," *Cross Currents* 49, no. 1 (1999), 72-83.

39. Roth, *Letters*, 11.

40. Michel Foucault, *Power/Knowledge: Selected Interviews and Other Writings 1972-1977* (New York: Pantheon Books, 1980), 104-108.

41. Judith Butler, *Excitable Speech: A Politics of the Performative* (New York: Routledge, 1997), 5.

42. Ibid.

43. Stanley Hauerwas, *The Peaceable Kingdom* (Notre Dame: University of Notre Dame Press, 1983), 96-115, and Holland, "So Many," 76-79.

44. Rodney Clapp, *A Peculiar People: The Church as Culture in a Post-Christian Society* (Downers Grove, Ill.: InterVarsity Press, 1996), 137-139.

45. Jeffrey T. Nealon, *Alterity Politics: Ethics and Performative Subjectivity* (Durham, N.C.: Duke University Press, 1998), 1-15.

46. Nealon, *Alterity Politics*, 15.

47. Elsewhere I have offered a more detailed description of a concrete discipleship that challenges such binaries as spirit versus flesh, mind versus body, universal versus particular, male versus female, and ethics versus desire (Gerald J. Biesecker-Mast, "Spiritual Knowledge, Carnal Obedience, and Anabaptist Discipleship," *Mennonite Quarterly Review* 71, no. 2 [1997], 201-226).

48. Gerald J. Biesecker-Mast, "Jihad, McWorld, and Anabaptist Transcendence," *Mennonite Life* 52, no. 3 (September 1997), 4-15.

49. van Braght, *Martyrs Mirror*, 6-11.

50. Ibid., 8.

51. Ibid.

52. Verduin, *The Complete Writings of Menno Simons*, 198.

53. van Braght, *Martyrs Mirror*, 453. For a recent biography of Anna Jansz, see C. Arnold Snyder and Linda A. Hecht, eds., *Profiles of Anabaptist Women* (Waterloo, Ont.: 1996), 336-351.

54. Ibid.

55. C. Norman Kraus, *An Intrusive Gospel?* (Downers Grove, Ill.: InterVarsity Press, 1998), 42.

56. Scott Holland, "Theology is a Kind of Writing: The Emergence of Theopoetics," *Mennonite Quarterly Review* 71, no. 2 (1997), 233.

57. Clapp, *A Peculiar People*, 114-125.

ELEVEN

LEITOURGIA BEYOND ALTAR AND SACRIFICE:
How Then Shall We Worship/Serve God?

John Richard Burkholder

INTRODUCTION

I begin with a recent pre-modern experience, one of the few times in my life I have come close to a gut-level realization of what it might have felt like to become an Anabaptist in the sixteenth century. In April 1998 my wife Sue and I underwent a cross-cultural baptism in the south of Spain: full immersion into pre-Reformation medieval Catholicism.

We were encountering *Semana Santa* (Holy Week) in the holy cities of Toledo, Granada, Cordoba, and Seville. Night after night I marveled at the seemingly endless parades of *pasos,* elaborately decorated religious floats depicting larger-than-life scenes from the passion of Jesus along with baroque representations of the Virgin. Representing countless hours of loving labor and precious materials, the parades moved slowly through crowded narrow streets. Melancholy music from uniformed bands orchestrated the well-dressed *hombres* and giggling teenagers alongside somber matrons in black and lace. Now and again we caught glimpses of the laboring-class boys and men shrouded beneath the heavy pasos, sweating and groaning to the doleful strains of the horns. And all of it was being extensively covered by local and even national Spanish television crews.

I was aware of contradictory motives and emotions, both in the crowds and in myself. I discerned both humility and pride, attitudes of penitence decked out in the regalia of grandeur. From my readings on *Semana Santa* I knew that leading citizens and high officials had donned the penitential hoods and were walking silently for hours on end, in a public display of submission to the church (but only once a year!).

Inwardly I tried to hang on to my postmodern cool: accepting, tolerant, nonjudgmental. But other emotions wanted to take over. Yes, I knew I was a tourist, a nonparticipant observer, but nevertheless my deep Anabaptist convictions were challenged. From my angle, the whole bloody portrayal was just one more example of perpetual sacrifice in the name of Jesus. I was sad, dismayed, even angry. This was abhorrent misplaced devotion, more pagan than Christian—it was a display of human religiosity, certainly not the gospel of Jesus! How did Jesus get so distorted? Could this sorry masquerade be the culmination of centuries of Christendom?

Of course, such troubling spectacles are not limited to the Roman Catholic world by any means. In July 1998 the headlines and TV images from Northern Ireland also focused on preparations for elaborate religious processions. The Protestant Orange Order insisted on marching through culturally Catholic neighborhoods. In the sound bite interviews, they argued with genuine pathos for their right to celebrate their unique ideological mix of religious, cultural, and political notions. I recalled some lines from Conor Cruise O'Brien: "An icon of the Bible, in its aspect of 'The Secret of England's Greatness,' is hauled in annual Orange processions along with King Billy and Queen Victoria as a sort of tribal talisman and charismatic source of power."[1]

And I remember well, from my first trip to Ireland over two decades ago, a revealing conversation outside the church pastored by the notorious Ian Paisley. Sue and I were greeted by a stereotypical sweet old lady. After we explained that we were visitors from the United States, not from Canada as she first surmised, she exclaimed brightly, "And I'm from Carrickfergus, where King Billy saved us from the Pope"—as if it had been a religious epiphany that happened last week, rather than three centuries ago.[2] Here was an unsolicited example of that casual blending of political pride and religious symbolism which continues to undergird strife and bloodshed.

While I was preparing the first draft of this essay in July 1998, the Sunday paper published a few lines from the Church of England's Archbishop of York. Worried about public adulation of the late Princess Diana as the new museum dedicated to her memory was opened, he was quoted as saying, "We should be careful that she is not worshipped. That worship should be directed to the God who created her."³

He got it right. But in a secular postmodern world virtually emptied of valid religious symbols, what else can one expect? In a realm where vestiges of medieval practices are documented by postmodern high-tech media and criticized by enlightenment rationalists, how is it possible to identify authentic religion? Or is that question itself out of order? Who knows what it really means to worship God?

PROVOCATION FROM A "POST-CONCERN" PRIEST

But it was not such random observations on religion in our tangled postmodern times that launched this essay. The original stimulus came from a provocative conversation with an old friend named Amos Orley Swartzentruber, now living in active retirement in Florida. Orley, then a Mennonite missionary in Paris, was a founding member of the 1950s Concern Group whose members sought Anabaptist renewal. After a doctoral program in Old Testament, he has spent the last several decades as an Episcopal priest.

But he continues to pay attention to goings-on in the Mennonite world and does not hesitate to make sweeping comparative judgments, both between past and present and between church traditions. He argues that modern Mennonites are doomed to extinction because their church life no longer has a central focus. Lacking the high-church anchoring in liturgy, the Apostles' Creed, and the enduring symbols of altar and sacrament, what is it that orients and motivates Mennonites? With the irretrievable loss of the traditional rural community and its sustaining cohesion, Mennonites have only sermons, four-part singing, and service projects. What constitutes a stable focus for Mennonite faith and worship? Will we make it through the twenty-first century?

These priestly proddings exposed my simmering suspicions about a time of troubles in Mennonite church life. I had to accept his criticism to the extent it paralleled my own laments regarding the thinness of much we call worship. But I reacted against his assumption that a sacramental orientation was preferable. For, as my introduction here illustrates, I had come to distrust much of traditional ecclesiastical practice. I was disgusted with the distorted symbols of blood sacrifice and suffering that dominated medieval theology and its residue in modernity, as evidenced in Spain and Ireland, and many other places. This is what sacramental theology and worship has wrought, I concluded.

For some time I had been absorbing an alternative reading of theology from a neo-Anabaptist perspective, particularly the critiques of conventional thought on atonement from such as C. Norman Kraus, Harry Huebner, J. Denny Weaver, and John H. Yoder. Along with these longtime companions, I was engaging compatible postmodern theological perspectives from such writers as Stanley Hauerwas,[4] James McClendon,[5] and John Milbank.[6] My latest learnings were enhanced by the fascinating theories of René Girard[7] and his disciples. In readings among Girardians such as James Alison,[8] Gil Bailie,[9] Dominique Barbe,[10] and James G. Williams,[11] I had been finding new sources of support for my suspicions regarding theology and church practice shaped by traditional ideas of atonement and sacrifice.

Now I was being told that my treasured neo-Anabaptist orientation was inadequate. It was too narrowly ethical, too esthetically shallow, and too psychologically moralistic. And I had to admit to myself that perhaps this "post-Concern" priest was on to something! The ideal of a community of countercultural disciples needs much more than well-argued academic theology to sustain and nurture it through this new century.

Convinced that worship life is indeed a crucial element in the needed renewal, but likewise still convinced of the wrongheadedness of those traditions grounded in altar and sacrifice, I began to look again at the roots of authentic worship in the biblical account. And I chose to read the Bible with the help of a Girardian lens, with its categorical juxtaposition of human religion over against the unique revelation of the end of sacrifice in Jesus.

The remainder of this chapter is the report of a work in progress. It might be viewed as complementary to Stanley Hauerwas's effort at teaching Christian ethics by way of the liturgy. Demonstrating his Anabaptist accent on a countercultural faith community ("resident aliens"), Hauerwas distinguishes his approach from mainstream generic Christian ethics, saying that

> Troeltsch and Niebuhr underwrote the assumption that Christian ethics should be an ethics for anyone, since such an ethic was a necessary correlative to the presumption that Christianity is a civilizational religion. In contrast, I argue that the very fact that Christians must be gathered to worship suggests that the audience for Christian ethics must be those who have been shaped by the worship of God.[12]

Alongside that approach, I want to show how selected learnings from the Bible, contemporary literature, and theological scholarship, with some marginal attention to the pervasive postmodern context, can provide resources for understanding, criticizing, and reshaping our churchly practices, in particular those words and actions we call "worship." The reader should be aware that I am not concerned here with the much-discussed "worship wars." I am not treating the form or content of Sunday morning events; I do not pretend to any competence in liturgics or esthetics as such. Those are important topics for some other occasion; my aim here is to reposition a theology of worship.

My central concern is theological. I want to begin to uncover and explore the fundamental meanings of certain biblical affirmations and their implications for the relation between the subjective needs of worshippers and the objective fact of God, that God whom Christian believers know through the story of the Bible and the person of Jesus Christ. For further emphasis, I employ Girardian insights to explore an alternate way to move beyond the pervasive traditional logic of altar and sacrifice.

Reasonable Service or Spiritual Worship?

As a textual foundation, I posit one of the few New Testament passages that attempts to prescribe the logic of proper Christian worship; it is also the only text that speaks of a *living* sacrifice.

> I appeal to you therefore, brothers and sisters, by the mercies of God, to present your bodies as a living sacrifice, holy and acceptable to God, which is your spiritual worship. Do not be conformed to this world, but be transformed by the renewing of your minds, so that you may discern what is the will of God—what is good and acceptable and perfect. (Rom. 12:1-2, NRSV)

This is an appeal—an appropriately postmodern term. It is not a demand or a rationally founded argument, but a pleading, a claim, grounded only in the narrative account of what God in his mercy has done, with the implicit recognition that some will respond and others ignore.

The claim comes just after a doxology, a lyric paean of praise expressing Paul's awesome awareness that the task he has attempted—to explain the revelation of God in Christ—simply cannot be encompassed in ordinary words.

> O the depth of the riches and wisdom and knowledge of God! How unsearchable are his judgments and how inscrutable his ways! . . . For from him and through him and to him are all things. To him be the glory forever. Amen. (Rom. 11:33,36, NRSV)

Most commentaries on Romans make much of the turning point in the book at chapter 12, from theological argument to practical exhortation. But perhaps the key to a (postmodern?) understanding of the whole epistle may well be this outburst of pure praise. Theology and ethics revolve around this axis—the performative language of worship "lost in wonder, love and praise."

With that high note still ringing, Paul issues his call to a living sacrifice. Having already in the epistle made clear that the cross of Jesus means the end of sacrifice in the old system, the metaphorical language here calls for an expression of devotion to God that does not involve death or victims. Called for instead is ethical commitment to live according to God's will. To do that, says Paul, is the essence of true worship—a practice not merely ceremonial but logical, reasonable, appropriate (the Greek adjective is *logikos*). The classic King James speaks of a living sacrifice "which is your reasonable service." So is it reasonable service or spiritual worship? Or both? Do they really say the same thing?

It is instructive to outline the logic of worship language in the Bible. In the history of the covenant people, formed through the deliverance of Exodus, the Hebrew words used for "service of God" and "worship of God" are almost interchangeable. Corresponding to that usage, the New Testament words *latreia, leitourgia,* and cognates are variously translated as "service," "work," "ministry," and "worship."

As a generic concept, worship has to do with establishing a relationship between humans and some form of divinity, however what is reverenced may be conceived. Anthropological studies of worship revolve around experiences of fear and awe and propitiatory activities. The literature usually makes much of the striking similarity of religious activity in widely divergent cultures, times, and places.

The biblical account also speaks of sacred seasons, sacred places, consecrated persons and practices. But in biblical teaching, there is no strict division between daily work and the adoration of God; everything that believers do ought to be an act of worship. The service that the chosen people owes to God is not limited to ceremony and ritual but encompasses every domain of life.

The biblical drama reaches its points of crisis when the people assume they can contain God, use God, tie God down. Of course, in so doing, they are actually serving themselves. Self-worship is akin to serving idols. Thus the ongoing mission of the Hebrew prophets is to call back to the service of the one true God, the Living One who cannot be bought or manipulated.

Yahweh is not truly served by the building of sacrificial altars or splendid temples. Again and again the lesson is repeated: "I desire mercy and not sacrifice" (Hos. 6:6, NIV); "What does the Lord require but to do justice, and to love kindness, and to walk humbly with your God" (Mic. 6:8, NRSV). Expressions of piety cannot hide disobedience.

Although Scripture does not simply substitute an ethical code for a system of religious practices, the expected response to the presence of the Almighty One encompasses both faithful service and profound reverence. Without the dimension of authentic transcendence, religious practices carried out solely for their pragmatic moral value can only lead to legalism and self-righteousness. Biblical worship evokes the presence of One who wills to be sole Lord of life, because this One has already offered grace and mercy in the revelation of divine purpose.[13]

We have already noted the scope of leitourgia as embracing worship, work, and service. In the course of tracking the biblical usage of "liturgical" language, I discovered an intriguing interplay of cultic and moral connotations, as the root words in context are open to both emphases. It is surprising how often some modern translations speak of "worship" in places where the classic King James Version uses the language of "service" to God.

As an example of this tendency, in Exodus 10 the NRSV at five or six places (3, 8, 11, 24, 26) speaks of worshiping God. Meanwhile, KJV speaks of *serving*. Or in the oft-repeated text from Deuteronomy:

> So now, O Israel, what does the LORD [Yahweh] your God require of you? Only to fear the LORD your God, to walk in all his ways, to love him, to serve the LORD your God with all your heart and with all your soul.... (Deut 10:12, NRSV)

But verse 20 is rendered "You shall fear the LORD your God; him alone you shall serve [KJV] /worship [NRSV]." One can locate a number of similar switches among translations and versions.

Thus the issue evoked by the heading of this subsection: reasonable service or spiritual worship? Viewing the apparent direction of translating choices, one might pose this question: Do we see a spiritualizing trend? Is the moral being narrowed to the cultic? With this kind of twist, some readers may still be tempted to believe that God is pleased with them if they multiply outward acts of religious observance. Keeping visible the intrinsic connection of worship, work, praise, and service is essential for faithfulness to the biblical way—the obedience of a living sacrifice.

Excursus:
Worship—Modern, Premodern, or Postmodern?

For those who may ask if worship is even thinkable for the postmodern mentality, there may be a parallel, or a parable, in noting how C. S. Lewis viewed modernism nearly a half-century ago. In his 1954 inaugural lecture at Cambridge University, Lewis spoke of modernism as the greatest break in the history of the West—more decisive than the shift from Antiquity to the Dark Ages, or from the Middle Ages to the Renaissance. The "unchristening of Europe"—the lapse from a Christian ethos to a post-Christian reality—was a more traumatic cultural change than the "christening" at the time of Constantine. Lewis's reasoning was that

> Christians and pagans had much more in common with each other than either has with a post-Christian. The gap between those who worship different gods is not so wide as that between those who worship and those who do not.

Lewis went on to warn against equating post-Christian with pagan.

> A post-Christian man is not a Pagan; you might as well think that a married woman recovers her virginity by divorce. The post-Christian is separated from the Christian past and therefore doubly from the Pagan past."[14]

In other words, there is no turning back. Postmoderns cannot go home again, as Umberto Eco has observed. Yet neither can we cut ourselves off from the past. The postmodern mood is, among many other things, a phenomenon of lost innocence and self-conscious irony.[15]

Postmodernism, with its secular awareness of what biblical theology labels as the Fall, may well be a useful stance for deconstructing and then reconstructing biblical worship. Thus I propose that we accept this contemporary gift of an open space for recovering the true worship of biblical people. If the given cultural ethos is pluralist, secularized, fragmented, then there is no need to establish and defend philosophical foundations for such practices. In postmodernity, what difference does it make to anyone how Christian believers behave? Who cares?

As those who call ourselves Christians, we do care enough about faithfulness in worship to want to make sense out of it all. So for a handle on a larger understanding of all that worship may entail, I suggest learning from the ambitious project of René Girard, who challenges us (in the title of his major work) to rediscover things hidden since the foundation of the world.[16]

UNVEILING THE VIOLENT SACRED

In a series of world-acclaimed studies, René Girard has claimed to expose and analyze the central role of violence in religion and of religion in culture. Girard has explored and developed his distinctive and provocative views through a comprehensive and complex series of investigations over more than three decades, using varied classical, literary, and anthropological sources.[17]

His exhaustive study of numerous ancient myths and primal religions uncovers the phenomenon of the scapegoat as a universal mechanism of social control. At a time of crisis, with the threat of uncontrolled violence and chaos, the whole society gangs up to do away with a randomly chosen victim—a scapegoat is sacrificed. Collective guilt is discharged on the victim; the community is "purified;" the societal threat collapses; and order is restored. From this "founding murder" a religious myth arises to justify the whole event: the deliberate killing of an innocent victim is eventually called a divine necessity. By thus obscuring the origins of human sacrifice, religion functions as "organized violence in the service of social tranquility." Warriors are turned into worshippers in this original culture-preserving mechanism. These themes are demonstrated again and again in Girard's work, from the recital of primordial myths to the sacrificial cults of most religious systems.

Girardian insights can show up in the most unexpected places. A few years ago, while escaping more serious responsibilities, I was surprised to hear a Girardian aphorism in a Hollywood B-movie thriller. Just to be sure, I checked out the video, and there it was: "The cornerstone of civilization is human sacrifice." Actor Nick Nolte was portraying Maxwell Hoover, a tough police detective in 1950s Los Angeles. After an intense interview with a high-ranking military officer who had been subjecting enlisted men, without their knowledge, to dangerous atomic radiation experiments, Hoover/Nolte reflected on the officer's philosophical defense: "a hundred die so that a thousand may live." To his police colleagues, he reported it cynically and succinctly as "The cornerstone of civilization is human sacrifice."[18]

The thesis is stated more academically by the late missionary priest and theologian Dominique Barbe.

> All societies are basically erected on the mangled bodies of human victims. *This is the case even materially,* as archeology knows so well. Excavation of the walls and main gates of ancient cities has often unearthed the mortal remains, the skeletons, of human beings long ago sacrificed in a

ritual of consecration of these cities. <u>This is the conception with which the Bible will make a break.</u>[19]

That biblical break is the stunning and perhaps most controversial novelty of Girard's work. Most fruitfully for our purposes, he has discovered that the counterforce to these pervasive mythological concealments is found in the prophetic advance of the Hebrew Bible. The First Testament posits an exodus out of that ancient common religiosity that had obscured the evil of violence by covering it with sacred myth and ritual. Alone among the world's religions, the Bible begins (despite frequent lapses) to engage and challenge that sacred violence by daring to tell the story *from the standpoint of the victim*. Following the growing critique of sacrifice expressed by the Hebrew prophets (Hos. 6; Amos 5; Isaiah 1; Micah 6; see also Psalm 40), the New Testament reveals a God who actually takes the place of the sacrificial victim.

Girard of course has to wrestle with the ambiguities and even contradictions in the Hebrew Bible's views of responsibility for the death of the victim, as in the Servant Song of Isaiah 53. Is the guilt placed on the human community or on God as perpetrator? But Girard states that the Gospels are unequivocal, replacing the violent God of the past with a nonviolent God who demands nonviolence rather than sacrifice. "The Christ of the Gospels dies against sacrifice, and through his death, he reveals its nature and origin by making sacrifice unworkable, at least in the long run, and bringing sacrificial culture to an end."[20]

For those with eyes to see, the cross exposes the falsity of all myths of human sacrifice and scapegoating, whether embedded in the Bible or in human religions. The rationale for sacred violence is destroyed. The gospel of Jesus stands over against the endless cycle of violence that began with "an eye for an eye." The cross represents the final sacrifice that ends all human sacrifice, as the one true and living God takes the place of the victim.[21]

In light of cross and resurrection, the only sacrifice appropriate for Christian believers is the voluntary, living sacrifice of the will as set forth in Romans 12. For those who have eyes to see that which has been hidden from the foundation of the world (to echo Girard's provocative title), sacred violence is exposed and defeated once for all, although its horrible shadow still haunts the hurting world that has not yet grasped the revelation. Empowered by the resurrection, a new worshiping community begins to walk the nonviolent way of the cross.[22]

BEYOND SACRIFICE

Girard's sweeping world-historical schema has of course not escaped criticism. His tendency toward categorical pronouncements leaves him vulnerable to challenge and revision. But the overall achievement has been compared to the nineteenth-century intellectual giants—Hegel, Marx, Nietzsche, Freud—who continue to cast their shadows, even as they have been subject to necessary correction.

Our particular focus here on the meaning of biblical sacrificial language is enriched by the work of James G. Williams, who has explored the role of sacrifice in the Hebrew Bible in the light of Girard's theory of religion and culture. In his comparative study of both sacrificial and nonsacrificial readings of Scripture, Williams argues that

> while a sacrificial reading of the Bible is possible, a nonsacrificial approach is better able to account for the Bible's distinctiveness. This distinctiveness stems from the biblical witness to the revelation of the God of victims and includes a polemic against sacrifice and violence, especially as that polemic is found in the prophets.[23]

As Anabaptist-Mennonites who want to be biblically faithful people, we cannot simply discard the language of sacrifice, but its inadequacies must be exposed and its influence diminished. A sectarian minority is in a privileged position to recognize and counter the long Constantinian tradition of sacrificial motifs in support of religious establishment and political empire, with their consequent rationalization of bloodshed. Surely we can agree that the sacrificial metaphor is dangerous and harmful when it becomes the rationale for violence, as in such places as Northern Ireland where brutal killing for a purely political cause is falsely garbed with the religious trappings of sacrifice and martyrdom.

How then can a Girardian perspective advance an effort at re-thinking a theology of worship? Simply put, there continues to be a great deal of confused, contradictory, and just plain wrong use of sacrificial metaphors in both theology and the worship life of the churches. The ambivalence and dissonance appear at both popular and more sophisticated levels.[24]

Can we find the appropriate way to get beyond sacrifice? Of course, presumably most of those who consider themselves postmodern have long ago relegated any serious consideration of sacrifice to the dustbin of history. Or at least they think superficially that they have done so. They identify with the way Stanley Hauerwas begins his sermon subtitled "The End of Sacrifice": "We think that the whole point of our lives is to create a world that makes sacrifice irrational."[25] But Hauerwas's aim is to expose the fact that the world around us, supposedly secular and postmodern, may think it has done away with the ancient idea of religious sacrifice—whereas in fact the symbols and surrogates are everywhere. He observes that "We pile murder on murder in our desperate attempt to create a history, a space, free of murder." Hauerwas's sermon comes to a climax with the gospel affirmation that all "murderous sacrifice is ended by this one mighty sacrifice of God through which we—that is, the church—have been made part of God's sacrifice, God's life, for the world."[26] God. Sacrifice. Life. World. We are brought back to the heart of the Romans 12 proclamation: a voluntary living sacrifice as the manifestation of true worship.

A Detour "On the Way" into the Blue Mountains

While preparing this chapter, I was re-reading what is perhaps the first postmodern Mennonite novel, Rudy Wiebe's *The Blue Mountains of China*.[27] Although that choice of reading was not prompted by this investigation, just a few pages from the end of that powerful epic I stumbled across a few paragraphs, almost overlooked in the complexity of the narrative, that offered another stunning insight into the rhetoric of sacrifice.

The setting is a roadside ditch near Calgary, where the young Mennonite wanderer John Reimer has paused from his solitary cross-bearing pilgrimage across the prairies. He is engaged in earnest conversation with an ad hoc bunch of curious visitors who unknowingly bring together remnants of family stories from earlier chapters of the novel. Reimer has just been delivering the only sermon in the book, an impromptu exposition of Jesus' revolutionary new "Sermon on the Mount" society. The core of the argument is obviously borrowed from John Howard Yoder, as Wiebe has freely acknowledged. "[T]his is a Jesus society and you repent, not by feeling bad, but by *thinking different.*"[28]

Among the diverse party of listeners is the worldly-wise Elizabeth Driediger, a forty-eight-year-old university language teacher long distant from her Mennonite roots. A few pages earlier (in chapter thirteen), she had been abruptly faced with her tradition as she spontaneously befriended the elderly Jakob Friesen from Russia, on his way to visit relatives in Canada. Their conversation had only started to scratch the surface as they began to share fragments of their very different stories of suffering, flight, and loss of faith that many Mennonites experienced in the "communist utopia" of the Soviet Union.

Reimer's exhortation ends abruptly when a police officer commands,

> There has to be a better society possible in the world than that. There's too bloody much sacrifice in the world already, so many dunderheads all over the place serving others, carving their bloody way up in the World Sacrifice Association. God. We need a world where everybody can live for himself, just be himself.

And John Reimer retorts, "You want everybody except you dead?"[29]

I read this as a classic but unknowing Girardian exchange, analogous to the aphorism from *Mulholland Falls* above.[30] It points to the tension between the horror of compulsory blood sacrifice, imposed by so many traditional religious and political systems, and the open possibility of voluntary self-sacrifice, which, of course, is not without its mixed motives and outcomes.

Although there is no setting of formal worship as such in Wiebe's sprawling novel, there are acts of sacrifice—both brutal killing for abstract political purposes and striking instances of concrete and costly self-giving. Mother Frieda Friesen's poignant lifelong quiet commitment to family obligations stands alongside the amazing self-chosen return of David Epp to certain suffering and death in his Russian village. Epp, the knowing innocent, acts in vain hope that he might save others from their certain fate. Acting alone, he embodies the classic scapegoat role, but his voluntary sacrifice transcends that anthropological stereotype and becomes a source of inspiration for later generations.[31]

The other "living sacrifice" in Wiebe's narrative is the cross-bearing John Reimer. After giving most of his young adult life to conventional church-related service projects in Algeria and Paraguay, Reimer comes home and realizes he has to "think different." So he starts his trek across Canada, bearing a wooden cross in Canada's centennial year. This is possibly the most untypical Mennonite action in the whole narrative. Carrying a symbolic cross does no earthly good. It is not an act of service. Reimer is not even handing out tracts to explain his mission. Although his beliefs and motives seem confused, he is "on the way" (the title of that climactic chapter). I believe we need to view Reimer's pilgrimage as a quintessential act of praise, somehow linked to Paul's lyric at the end of Romans 11.

HOW THEN SHALL WE WORSHIP?

The *Letter to the Hebrews* posed a problem for René Girard in the 1970s, because he had been reading it as simply a restatement of Old Testament sacrificial theology, making God responsible for the death of the victim.³² But through further study and dialogue with such colleagues as Raymund Schwager, Girard has recognized the tension between the given historical narrative of the biblical sacrificial system and the revealing of the new way of nonviolent and nonsacrificial relationships, culminating in Jesus' self-offering as the final sacrifice. Girard "thus affirms a positive, derived sense of 'sacrificial' as the willingness to give of oneself to others and to commit oneself to God . . . out of love and faithfulness to the other."³³

With this awareness in mind we turn to several texts from Hebrews, the New Testament writing which gives most attention to the sacrificial motif. First we note the writer's bold way of placing a quotation from Psalm 40 (an anti-sacrificial text) in the mouth of Jesus.

> Consequently, when Christ came into the world, he said, *"Sacrifices and offerings you have not wanted, but a body you have prepared for me; in burnt offerings and sin offerings you have taken no pleasure. Then I said, 'See, God, I have come to do your will, O God' (in the scroll of the book it is written of me)."* [from Psalm 40 . . .] When he said above, "You have neither wanted nor taken pleasure in sacrifices and offerings and burnt offerings and sin offerings" (these are offered according to the law), then he added, "See, I have come to do your will." He abolishes the first to establish the second. And it is by God's will that we have been sanctified through the offering of the body of Jesus Christ once for all. (Heb. 10: 5-10, NRSV, emph. added)

At stake here is how we understand the will of God in relation to the cross of Christ. Does God directly intend that Jesus the Son be offered as ultimate sacrifice, or does God transforms the evil of the cross into the means that enables believers to do the will of God (i.e., sanctification)? However that theological judgment is made, the whole biblical sacrificial system is brought to an end in the death of Jesus Christ. Further, the end of that sacrifice—end in the sense of its goal—is the doing of God's will. Jesus' self-giving transforms the idea of sacrifice from victimization to a pattern for obedient living. Again the cultic is overshadowed by the moral, as we move from the bloody altar to the self-offering of discipleship.³⁴

Another example of the peculiar logic of sacrifice in Hebrews is quoted at length by John Milbank in his densely argued reconstrual of atonement theology. Hebrews chapter 13 climaxes a series of admonitions about mutual love and hospitality with an odd illustration regarding animal bodies buried outside the camp:

> Jesus also suffered outside the city gate. . . . Let us then go to him outside the camp and bear the abuse he endured. For here we have no lasting city,

but we are looking for the city that is to come. Through him, then, let us continually offer a sacrifice of praise to God, that is, the fruit of lips that confess his name. Do not neglect to do good and to share what you have, for such sacrifices are pleasing to God. (Hebrews 13:12-16, NRSV)

The intriguing logic of this passage links the "sacrifice of praise" with "doing good," that is, obedience in sharing and serving. Milbank comments, "Christ has abolished the sacrifices of the earthly city. . . ; but instead he has inaugurated a new kind of efficacious sacrifice of praise, self-sharing and probable attendant suffering which unites us with him in the heavenly city."[35] Both the Romans and Hebrews texts announce the end (as finality) of sacrifice as practiced at the altar to realize the end (as goal) of sacrifice as service, worship, and praise—leitourgia. The authentic worship of the church is a living sacrifice of praise and obedience.

To be sure, most Anabaptists are probably more comfortable encouraging each other to do good and to be obedient rather than simply to offer praise to God. For praise seems so impractical, so non-utilitarian. We do not quite know what to make of the John Reimer approach, his solitary walk westward with no obvious purpose, no goal: "I had to . . . forget about doing something, even about doing what I thought good. . . . I am not going anywhere."[36]

Toward a Conclusion

One might well ask if this essay is going anywhere! Let me recap the journey. When my ongoing study of contemporary Christian ethicists and the Girardian literature was interrupted by critical questions from a post-Anabaptist priest, I agreed immediately that we urgently need more appropriate resources to sustain a life of discipleship in Christian community.

Over against my disgust with the distortions of so much that is supposed to represent worship in our postmodern (as well as modern and premodern!) cultural context, I was attracted to the Romans 12 text with its startling interplay of the language of sacrifice, service, and worship. After reporting findings from a hasty review of biblical words associated with worship, I employed Girardian cultural analysis. My aim there was to underscore the tyranny of misused sacrificial language that continues to claim innocent victims. I illustrated the difficulties with sacrificial themes through examples from film and literature. All of this comes together in my appropriation of biblical texts that locate the specifics of cultic practices in the more inclusive framework of leitourgia understood as the full and comprehensive service of God.

But more is needed than recovering the power of disciplined living as the token of proper worship or the rejection of sacrificial victims. If, as has been observed, an integral part of the "work" (i.e, liturgy) of Christian worship is praise, more attention must be given to modalities of praise that harmonize rather than clash with these other dimensions.

Especially as Anabaptist-Mennonites with our ethical and pragmatic orientation, we need to ponder what Leander Keck has written.

> Authentic praise of God acknowledges what is true about God; it responds to qualities that are "there" and not simply "there for me." . . . In other words, God is to be praised because God is God, because of what God is and does, quite apart from what God is and does for me.[37]

We can do no better than to return to that important axis of praise that links the first and second parts of the Epistle to the Romans. "O the depth of the riches and wisdom and knowledge of God! How unsearchable are his judgments and how inscrutable his ways!" (Rom. 11:33, NRSV) These words evoke the necessary sense of reverence, of mystery, of transcendent glory that characterize authentic worship. For the necessary balance, however, that dimension must be placed alongside the admonitions of the writer to the Hebrews: "Let us continually offer a sacrifice of praise to God. . . . Do not neglect to do good and to share what you have, for such sacrifices are pleasing to God." (Heb. 13:15-16, NRSV)

"For from him and through him and to him are all things. To him be the glory forever. Amen." (Rom. 11:36, NRSV)[38]

Notes

1. Conor Cruise O'Brien, *States of Ireland*, (New York: Pantheon), 287.

2. Personal conversation, July 1978.

3. David Hope, Archbishop of York, as quoted in clipping from July 5, 1998, *South Bend Tribune*.

4. Stanley Hauerwas, *In Good Company: The Church as Polis* (Notre Dame, Ind.: University of Notre Dame, 1995); *Wilderness Wanderings: Probing Twentieth-Century Theology and Philosophy* (Boulder, Colo.: Westview Press, 1997).

5. James Wm. McClendon Jr., *Doctrine: Systematic Theology, Volume II* (Nashville: Abingdon, 1994).

6. John Milbank, *Theology and Social Theory: Beyond Secular Reason* (Oxford, UK: Blackwell, 1993); *The Word Made Strange: Theology, Language, Culture* (Oxford, UK: Blackwell, 1997).

7. René Girard, *Things Hidden Since the Foundation of the World,* in collaboration with Jean-Michel Oughourlian and Guy Lefort, trans. Stephen Bann and Michael Metteer (Stanford, Calif.: Stanford University Press, 1987); *The Girard Reader,* ed.

James G. Williams (New York: Crossroad Publishing, 1996); *Violence Renounced: René Girard, Biblical Studies, and Peacemaking*, ed. Willard M. Swartley (Telford, Pa.: Pandora Press U.S., 2000).

8. James Alison, *Knowing Jesus* (Springfield, Ill.: Templegate Publishers, 1994); *Raising Abel: The Recovery of the Theological Imagination* (New York: Crossroad Publishing, 1996).

9. Gil Bailie, *Violence Unveiled: Humanity at the Crossroads* (New York: Crossroad Publishing, 1995).

10. Dominique Barbe, *A Theology of Conflict and other writings on Nonviolence* (Maryknoll, N.Y.: Orbis Books, 1989).

11. James G. Williams, *The Bible, Violence, and the Sacred: Liberation from the Myth of Sanctioned Violence* (Valley Forge, Pa.: Trinity Press International, 1994); "'Steadfast Love and Not Sacrifice': A Nonsacrificial Reading of the Hebrew Scriptures," in *Curing Violence*, ed. Mark I. Wallace and Theophus H. Smith (Sonoma, Calif.: Polebridge Press, 1994).

12. Stanley Hauerwas, "The Liturgical Shape of the Christian Life: Teaching Christian Ethics as Worship," *In Good Company*, 157-158.

13. These perspectives on biblical worship are summarized from R. Martin-Achard, "Worship," in *A Companion to the Bible*, ed. J. J. Von Allmen (New York: Oxford, 1958), 471-474, and J. S. McEwen, "Worship," in *A Theological Wordbook of the Bible*, ed. Alan Richardson (London: SCM Press, 1950), 287-290.

14. Lewis is quoted in Kenneth A. Myers, *All God's Children and Blue Suede Shoes: Christians and Popular Culture* (Westchester, Ill.: Crossway Books, 1989), 110-111. The original lecture is referenced as *"De Descriptione Temporum" They Asked for a Paper: Papers and Addresses*, (London: Geoffrey Bles, 1962).

15. Umberto Eco, *Postscript to the Name of the Rose* (San Diego: Harcourt Brace Jovanovich, 1984), 67ff.

16. See note 7.

17. In addition to the works cited in note 7, Girard's writings dealing with religion include *Violence and the Sacred* (Baltimore: Johns Hopkins, 1977); *The Scapegoat* (Baltimore: Johns Hopkins University Press, 1986); and *Job: The Victim of His People* (Stanford: Stanford University Press, 1987). Numerous other writings and a sampling of titles from Girardian scholars, both affirming and critical, are found in the bibliography of *The Girard Reader* as well as in notes and bibliography of *Violence Renounced* (see note 7).

18. *Mulholland Falls* (MGM/UA Home Video, 1996; the script is credited to Peter Dexter).

19. Barbe, *A Theology of Conflict*, 24; italics in original, underlining added. Barbe makes striking and original use of Girard to frame his nonviolent reading of the Bible.

20. Girard, *The Girard Reader*, 18. Girard's arguments are not beyond criticism; see *Violence Renounced* for critical as well as affirming responses.

21. To my friend, Victor Stoltzfus, I owe the insight that God's action in Jesus, taking the place of the victim, is made even more revolutionary and reconciling by the fact that Jesus at the same time *forgives* the perpetrators. See the powerful treatment of

this theme in Miroslav Volf, *Exclusion and Embrace: A Theological Exploration of Identity, Otherness, and Reconciliation* (Nashville: Abingdon Press, 1996), 119-125. Christian theology has always taught that a central meaning and benefit of the death of Jesus is the forgiveness of sins. But forgiveness does not get much attention from Girard; the word is not found in the indices of his major writings. (Girardians such as Alison and Bailie do correctly deal with this important theme.)

22. In James G. Williams's 1996 conversation with René Girard, printed as the "Epilogue" to *The Girard Reader*, Girard affirms his belief in the resurrection as "objective event," disagreeing with Bultmann's concession to the worldview of modern technology (Girard, *The Girard Reader*, 280). That same fascinating conversation also offers Girard's candid account of his Christian conversion (283-288), as well as an "unknowing" tribute to Anabaptists, when he speaks of those in Christian history who have grasped the nonsacrificial reading: "All those who have tried to follow the way of Christ and the Kingdom of God, living as nonviolently as possible, have understood, though not necessarily intellectually" (273).

23. Williams, "Steadfast Love and Not Sacrifice," 70.

24. I wonder, for example, how we as Anabaptist-Mennonites engage the fulsome language of a hymn such as "In Thy Holy Place We Bow," number 2 in *Hymnal: A Worship Book*. In spite of its worthy lineage from Mennonite writer S. F. Coffman and composer J. D. Brunk, all that imagery of holy place, temple, fire, and sacrifice seems to evoke rather questionable themes for Anabaptists!

Anabaptist theologians necessarily continue to work with sacrificial themes. C. Norman Kraus and J. Denny Weaver are quite cautious with the concept in their treatment of atonement theories, whereas Jim McClendon suggests that the church must return to the metaphor in its eucharistic practice (McClendon, *Doctrine*, 235).

25. Hauerwas, "Standing on the Shoulders of Murderers: The End of Sacrifice," *In Good Company*, 165.

26. Ibid., 167. It's interesting that Hauerwas makes his case without reference to Girard!

27. Rudy Wiebe, *The Blue Mountains of China* (Grand Rapids, Mich.: Eerdmans, 1970). I chose to classify Wiebe's novel as "postmodern" because of the abruptly juxtaposed dislocations in time and space and narrator as well as the apparent lack of a unified authorial vision. But literature scholar Ervin Beck regards it as "modern" fiction because, "although the story is fragmented and told from different points of view, the book nevertheless assumes that there is a unity, a purpose behind it all that the reader needs to seek out" (personal correspondence, October, 1998). In relation to Wiebe's work, see also Hildi Froese Thiessen, "Mennonite Literature and Postmodernism: Writing the 'In-between' Space," ch. 8 in this volume.

28. Wiebe, *Blue Mountains*, 216; italics in original.

29. Ibid., 216.

30. See the quotation at note 18.

31. Ervin Beck writes that the figure of David Epp combines the themes of "service, worship, sacrifice and community . . . Epp collaborates with his community in the great escape and gives himself as a sacrifice for all in the context of the communion

service" (personal correspondence, October 1998).

32. Girard, *Things Hidden*, 227ff.

33. James Williams, editorial note in *The Girard Reader*, 70.

34. I am indebted to the late Marlin E. Miller for much of this commentary on sacrifice in Hebrews, from his unpublished paper "Girardian Perspectives and Christian Atonement" (1994), which is now reproduced under the same title in posthumously refined form in *Violence Renounced*, ch. 1.

35. John Milbank, *The Word Made Strange*, 151.

36. Rudy Wiebe, *Blue Mountains*, 225.

37. From a quotation referenced simply as *Christian Century*, December 16, 1992.

38. The author thanks readers of earlier drafts who asked appropriate questions and gave valuable suggestions: Ervin Beck, John J. Fisher, Sally Weaver Glick, John D. Rempel, Christy Risser, and Victor Stoltzfus. Of course, any errors or deficiencies remain the author's own.

TWELVE

THE LORD IS STILL MY SHEPHERD WHEN I SING:
Experiencing God in Postmodern Anabaptist Worship

Marlene Kropf

INTRODUCTION

In his book, *Hymns to an Unknown God,* postmodern author Sam Keen confesses:

> I can't go back to traditional religion. Neither can I live within the smog-bound horizon of the secular-progressive faith. So I search for a way to unite the demands of the head and the heart. Without falling into mindless faith or surrendering to authority, I want to find a way to lean on the everlasting arms.
>
> The truth of the spirit, as I know it, is better conveyed in song and poetry than by propositions. The best of the Christian tradition, which continues to nourish me, is expressed in the music it inspired. Often, my mind is uncomforted by any set of beliefs that can stand the test of doubt, but when I listen to Bach's "Sheep May Safely Graze," my soul lies down beside still waters and a mysterious Lord is still my shepherd.
>
> The journey we are undertaking must contain a melodic element. We need to heed the advice of Socrates' daemon who advised that the practice of philosophy without musical accompaniment is hazardous to

the soul. *There is something essentially musical about the Western spiritual path* [italics mine].¹

Many contemporary Anabaptists find themselves dwelling in the same philosophical neighborhood as Sam Keen. Raised in traditional religious environments shaped both by premodern and modern assumptions,² they discover in adulthood that the faith handed down no longer suffices. When such people become seekers after God, how do they find God? How do they experience God? The conviction of this chapter, like that of Sam Keen, is that many postmodern Mennonites³ need music to encounter the divine. To put it plainly, Mennonites taste God and touch God when we sing. Singing is our sacrament, and we would be bereft without it.

WHAT DOES IT MEAN TO BE POSTMODERN?

Sally Morgenthaler, well-known writer and consultant on worship, describes postmodernism, the biggest philosophical shift in over 200 years, as "a reaction against the long, dry reign of rationalism." She goes on to cite its defining characteristics:

> As a postmodern, you're right-brained as well as left. You're pro-mystery and anti-humanist. You consider yourself spiritual, but not necessarily religious. You believe there are other ways of knowing besides reason (e.g., intuition and emotions) and that truth goes way beyond what we can discern or verbalize.... You agree with 63 percent of other Americans who believe, "Nothing can be known for certain except those things one experiences in one's own life."⁴

In describing the implications of this philosophical stance for worship, Morgenthaler quotes a twenty-seven-year-old pastor from Seattle, Washington, whose growing congregation works consciously to reach postmoderns.

> Worship for postmoderns needs to address the whole person, not just the intellect. The mind must be engaged and taught, not with steps or formulas, but with grand narratives. The heart must be moved to value and live the gospel in all of life. And all five senses must be engaged to experience God.⁵

As a way of engaging the senses, music has always played a significant role in worship, both in the Hebrew culture that preceded Christianity and in the Christian church. Because the early Anabaptists and Mennonites have tended to neglect the arts and sensory experience in worship, except for music, this particular element of worship has become a privileged, if lonely, place of divine encounter for many. To understand the crucial role of music in Mennonite worship and particularly its potential for enriching the postmodern experience of God is the focus of this chapter.

WHAT HAPPENS WHEN MENNONITES SING?

Between 1994 and 1996, I joined Ken Nafziger, Professor of Music at Eastern Mennonite University (Harrisonburg, Va.), in a research project to discover what happens to Mennonites when we sing.[6] We conducted in-depth interviews with nearly 100 Mennonites diverse in background and age. Though some of those interviewed were professional musicians, most were ordinary singers who could be found in any Mennonite congregation on a given Sunday morning. We asked such questions as—

- What happens between you and God when you sing?
- What happens between you and others when you sing?
- What active responses have hymns inspired in you?
- What is the earliest hymn you remember? Why?
- Is your singing prayer? Who is the God you sing to?
- Are you transported when you sing? Where do you go?
- When do you need to sing? Why?
- Are there holy places . . . holy times . . . visions . . . when you sing?

Though people sometimes struggled to answer these questions (it was something like asking fish to examine the water in which they swim), one question called forth quick and instinctive responses. We asked, "What would you do if someone decided that from here on out there would be no more singing in worship?"

We heard responses like these:
- "Do you mean, What would I do besides leave?"
- "I'd find another church."
- "I get so weary of words. The reason I go to church is to sing."
- "My prayer book would have been taken from me."
- "I'd dry up. It would feel like something is being squeezed out of me. Even as you ask the question, it's like someone putting a vice on me and draining everything out of me. I'm even getting short of breath now. I wouldn't last long."

One person confessed that she is a Mennonite because of the singing. She said,

> I went to another church for awhile that wasn't Mennonite. I really liked their theology better, but frankly, I just couldn't stay there because there

was no music. It was pathetic. I even tried leading singing there, but the sound didn't come back to me and I didn't know how to get it. It seemed hopeless, so I came back to the Mennonite Church.

Some interviewees were asked, "If you had to choose between singing and preaching in worship, which would be the last to go?" They all had the same answer, though many hesitated before responding. Typically they said something like, "Well, I know I *should* say that preaching would be the last to go. The truth is, music is more important to me than preaching."

Even theologians and preachers gave that answer. A prominent Mennonite theologian-preacher said, "How do I get in touch with spiritual things in worship? Because I'm so cerebral, I'd think it would be hearing or preaching a sermon. But the most powerful thing is music."

What quickly became apparent is that in the absence of a weekly eucharistic tradition, singing functions for Mennonites as sacraments do in liturgical churches. It is the moment we encounter God most directly. However, when Mennonites were asked to tell what happens when they sing, they talked first about what happens on the horizontal level—the human connections that occur when we sing.

That connection begins on a physical level and later extends to heart and soul. One person said,

> When we sing, we all use our bodies, we all lift our lungs, we breathe in and out together, we keep the pitch together. What I am doing with my body connects me with other bodies—even bodies of the past. We sustain the spirits of the past through this physical act.
>
> I like this with feeling very much—the sense of history when we sing. I feel the cloud of witnesses very strongly—mother and father, uncles and aunts. I love it when we sing real old texts because the old voices are present.

In another person's imagination, singing together requires the cooperative spirit of dancing.

> On Sunday morning there was the beginning folk dance. We would sing until everyone got into their places—gathering songs, the gospel songs. There were always three songs at the beginning and usually one before the sermon. When we sang, there was a certain exhilaration. Singing gave us a way to get beyond some of our problems, past the legalism that divided our congregation.

To sense the spirit of harmony in the midst of singing expands the experience. One person said, "I know that everybody is with a hymn, with the music, because the women are listening to the men. We are listening to each other, and that makes me *shiver* when that happens."

Making sound together emphasizes interdependence, mutuality, interconnectedness, loss of detachment from the group—what Anabaptists called *Gelassenheit*, the willingness to surrender one's own self and strength to God and others. When one person explained, "By losing myself [in singing], I gain more for myself," he was describing the paradox of letting go of self and receiving the gift of community.

In the memories of those interviewed, an important element of the horizontal connection was that *anyone* could participate in singing. One person said, "I never had the feeling that I had to be very good to participate. It was just something everybody did—and lustily!"

Those interviewed were keenly aware of the gifts of emotional and spiritual support they received in the midst of singing. A woman reflected on what happened in worship during the weeks her father awaited death.

> Our family was preparing ourselves and Dad was preparing himself for death, and yet he was still here. In worship an interactive kind of thing went on that was important to me. The congregation had no idea what I was hearing in those songs—sometimes I was singing and sometimes not singing but entering into another dimension of life and death. The songs we sang were crucial in helping me move through that process.

Another person reflected, "Singing undresses us. When we sing, we bring our bodies into the room, and our souls are undressed. I have this image of all these souls speaking to each other, then *real* things starting to happen."

Singing together is an act of relationship—between women and men, old and young, leader and people. But the deep bonds formed by song have even more significance. What Mennonites told us is that the body of Christ is created as we sing together. Some called what happens "magic"—the amazing harmony and unity that come to be because of a song. One person concluded simply, "I can love my church better when I sing with my church."

Although it was relatively easy for Mennonites to talk about what happens on a human or horizontal level when they sing (and understandable, given Mennonite emphasis on viewing the horizontal relationship with sisters and brothers as an integral part of one's relationship with Christ[7]), it was far more difficult for many of those interviewed to speak about what happens between them and God. Often they stumbled for words, searching for ways to express the inexpressible. Yet what was abundantly clear is that meeting God is the heart of the matter. On their way to talking about how singing connects them with God, those interviewed often reflected first on the powerful emotions created by song.

By culture Mennonites are a reserved, unexpressive people. We are reluctant to reveal deep feelings. We would rather show our love for others by building barns or feeding the hungry. Yet our faith is profoundly important to us. When we sing, we discover deep wells of desire for God's presence and love. One person we interviewed observed,

> We Mennonites are considerably more comfortable expressing our piety when we sing than in any other form. We are not nearly as free when we pray out loud in a group, and we certainly are not willing to be as pious in our language in a discussion or a sermon. Though we sing, "Open the wells of grace and salvation," we don't talk that way. But we are willing to sing using that kind of language.

Another person described Mennonite life as having "a very flat emotional landscape" and remembered the powerful emotions generated by certain songs—"My Jesus as thou wilt," "The ninety and nine," and "Just as I am." Another observed, "Songs give me permission to be fervent." A pastor said, "Music helps me keep the boat upright, keeps me from capsizing. Sometimes I say that if I hadn't had the enjoyment of music, I probably would have had to see a psychiatrist once a month over the years I've been in ministry." Though not all emotions can be construed as responses to God, Mennonites tend to label emotions hymns produce as communication coming from God or a response to God. Perhaps what happens is that these emotions open up an otherwise closed channel of awareness—and in the context of hymn singing, that openness is directed to God.

When reflecting more directly on the vertical connection—that is, the way hymns open a pathway to God, those interviewed talked about the capacity of both texts and tunes to mediate an encounter with God. Especially conscious of the power of poetic texts, people easily recited memorable lines. One person told us the first hymn she remembers singing was an old gospel song, "The love of God is greater far." She recalled,

> My father loved that song, and I loved the imagery in it—an ocean of ink, skies of parchment, every stalk on earth a quill, every man a scribe, draining the ocean dry to write the love of God. I just had a lot of fun sitting in church pondering that image.

Often the images of a text provoked continuous and ongoing reflection. One person quoted the line, "Here in this world, dying and living / we are each other's bread and wine" from the hymn, "What Is this Place,"[8] and said this image would sustain for weeks, months, and years to come—indeed for a lifetime.

The biblical image of God as sheltering rock in the refrain of "A Wonderful Savior Is Jesus, My Lord" appealed to several people. One said,

> I think the poetry is just wonderful—"He hideth my soul in the cleft of the rock, where rivers of pleasure I see." I spent time at Joshua Tree National Monument, a desert place in California. When you've been out in the sun, the cleft of a rock is the most wonderful place—it's just a-h-h, you find this little place in the rock where you can get away from the sun, and it's cool and you can get into the rock and cuddle up and get relief from the sun.

Many of those interviewed were aware that sacred biblical texts—certain psalms, a gospel story, or Scripture texts in classic works such as the *Messiah*, for example—have become a treasured part of their experience through song. One person remembered how a gospel story lived in a song.

> My favorite song leader was a short, curly-haired man whose rapport with the congregation was magical. Though he could lead any hymn with conviction and energy, he was especially gifted at directing the more dramatic hymns. I can still see him lead the swelling and falling lines of the hymn, "Master, the tempest is raging." At the beginning of the refrain, the whole congregation would soften to a pianissimo, "The winds and the waves shall obey my will; peace be still," then rise to the great crescendo, "No water can swallow the ship where lies the Master of ocean and earth and skies," and fall away again to the quiet confidence of "Peace, peace be still." There was no question but that the song took us out on the lake with Jesus. Even more, we sang all our own storms in that hymn and reaffirmed our trust in the Prince of peace.

That familiarity with biblical and poetic texts in song also forms the theology of singers should not be surprising. Both theology in the abstract as well as functional theology—the beliefs that shape people's everyday experience of God—are often derived from the songs they sing. An explicit connection between theology and song came in the following story:

> The depth of meaning of 1 Corinthians 15:22–"For as in Adam all die, even so in Christ shall all be made alive," is nowhere more fully expressed for me than in the melody, harmonies, and chord progressions of Handel's short chorus in the Messiah, "Since by man came death." The idea of Christ being the everlasting source of life for all humanity is surely one of the most profound theological ideas in Scripture. Yet the words alone

can be barren. And in the hours of grief, they may not really comfort us. While it is true that the 1 Corinthians text holds a truth for our heads, it may not get to our hearts or to our bones or breath or blood. To me there is no question but that music becomes the carrier of deeper truth or expanded truth.

> In the midst of the chorus, an exquisite musical phrase is repeated,
> For as in Adam all die,
> for as in Adam all die. . . .

When I come to the end of that haunting line, I wait suspended in my mortality where I remember all my griefs: the big ones and little ones, enormous tragedies like the Holocaust and a tornado that destroyed a church on Palm Sunday. I remember personal griefs: two grandmothers who died before I knew them, babies born too soon to live, a dear friend's mental illness, relationships broken, hope vanished. And as the song opens a place for me to name my griefs, a space is created to hear and receive the valiant assertion of the gospel, "Even so in Christ shall all be made alive."

I believe in the resurrection as much because of Handel's music as because of Paul's theological assertions.

Beyond creating understanding and belief, singing is a gateway to prayer for Mennonites. Other traditions have their own prompt for prayer: icons or incense or stained glass windows or silence or the Eucharist or the words of a prayer book. For Mennonites the prompt for prayer is singing. Mennonites pray *best* when they sing.

When interviewees were asked, "Are you praying when you sing?" many if not all agreed that they were. A child responded simply, "I try to mean the words I sing—I just kind of sing it to God." Another person said,

> Learning to pray by myself as a youngster was something that was not natural. I'm not sure we really teach children to pray. But I just sort of stumbled on to hymns as a way to pray. I remember going through the hymn book when I was quite young and coming to "The Old Rugged Cross." I remember crying and crying. Somehow it touched me as I sang and prayed alone. It's not a song I would choose now, but at the moment, it gave me a way to pray.

Another person said, "A song is often a prayer that can't be prayed or that needs to be prayed when I can't pray. For me it is the prayer that doesn't end, so in some ways when I do music, I feel like I am obeying the Scripture to pray without ceasing."

A musician responded, "I guess you know prayer is one of those words that has baggage for me. But if I would describe prayer as a sort of two-way communication, it definitely feels like when I'm singing I'm plugged in, and it's going both ways."

What was clear is that in singing hymns, people meet the many faces of God: tender and compassionate, yearning, suffering, merciful, loving, holy, majestic, powerful. Some even found congruence between the "sound" of a particular hymn and a particular dimension of God's character. One man commented that in the old German hymn, "Gott Ist die Liebe," he senses God's love in the "incredible gentle and playful sound that the music communicates."

For some, encounter with God through song has a mystical quality:

> In my memory, the hymn we often sang first on Sunday morning was a nineteenth-century text and tune by Robert Lowry, "O Worship the Lord in the Beauty of Holiness." The first chord on the word "O" was always held for a dramatic moment before we moved on to sing the rest of the hymn. Women's voices, clear and soaring, sang a duet in the middle of each stanza; then the hearty male voices joined them in the vigorous refrain, "Oh, glory hallelujah. . . ." When the song was finished and the last notes hung in the air, the presence of God was palpable—holiness was everywhere, mingling with the sunlight that danced above us.

Beyond an immediate encounter with God, hymns also provided strength, courage, and healing for people. A seminary dean reflected on the great solace and encouragement he found in particular texts and music as he battled spinal meningitis. Through two surgeries and many months of recuperation, he became more deeply aware of the power of song to mediate God's restoring strength.

> Providentially, in the weeks immediately preceding my illness, I had been listening to Mendelssohn's *Elijah* and practicing the choruses in preparation for the annual Bach Festival. This music and the texts coursed through my mind during those agonizing hours of pain, uncertainty, and fear. "He shall give his angels charge over thee, that they shall protect thee in all the ways thou goest."
>
> In the lonely hours of sleeplessness: "He watching over Israel slumbers not nor sleeps." What if I am left an invalid or my family must go on without me? "Cast thy burden on the Lord and he shall sustain thee." How long can this ordeal last? "O rest in the Lord." Do I have the strength to see it through? "Lift thine eyes, O lift thine eyes to the mountains, whence cometh help. Thy help cometh from the Lord, the maker of heaven and earth." What a lesson in preparation for the inevitable crises of life!

"When my life is almost gone.... take my hand, precious Lord, lead me home."⁹

For one woman interviewed, an old gospel hymn became a testimony of healing after the trauma of sexual abuse was confronted in her family. She told of choosing to sing "It Is Well with My Soul" at her wedding. Though she had needed to stay away from her family for at least two difficult, fragile years, they were able to be reunited at her wedding. Even though not all the healing was complete, it was "a mountainous sort of accomplishment" to be able to sing these lines:

> My sin [meaning her family's sin]—not in part, but the whole,
> is nailed to the cross, and I bear it no more,
> praise the Lord, praise the Lord, O my soul!

Beyond the personal arena to the political, singing has motivated people and provided a sense of direction. One woman described singing as both a political act in the midst of present realities and an expression of hope in God's ultimate vision of a reign of justice and peace:

> Music-making is so many things: it's the eschatological thing—joining the heavenly choir, joining that eternal praise. In the face of a world that's willing to blow itself up, what is a faithful response? Well, to sing and dance! Singing hymns is a political kind of act because it says who is in control. And I'm not!

What the research interviews provide is a rough map or a kind of diagnostic grid for understanding the content and consequences of the spiritual encounters that occur in the midst of singing. One way of summarizing that map or grid is to say that as we sing, Mennonites are formed in faith in three fundamental ways.

1. Our vision of God is formed. In singing we encounter a revelation of the word of God—the living word of the risen Christ as well as the written word of Scripture.

2. We are formed into Christian community. In singing we discover ourselves bound in love to one another and to the body of Christ in many times and places.

3. Our life is formed as people of the Spirit in the world. In singing we are transformed as we find comfort, healing, and new life, which empower us to love and serve Christ in the world.

With abundant power to transform both inner and outer reality, singing is indeed a wondrous gift to worshipers—whether that is the worldwide church at worship, the local church family gathered on Sunday, or the person who worships in solitude. Music brings comfort, healing, peace, joy, and delight; it also probes, convicts, and propels us to action. What happens when Mennonites sing is far more complex than anyone would ever dream—our music is intertwined with the very fiber of our faith and, in the image of poet George Herbert, it is "thy silk twist let down from heav'n to me . . . [to] both conduct and teach me, how by it to climbe to Thee."

Toward a Spirituality of Song in the Postmodern Church

At the end of the twentieth century, the Western world finds itself in the midst of a spiritual revolution. In her book, *A History of God*, British scholar Karen Armstrong observes that the twentieth century is the only age in history that has not regarded some form of faith as natural and normative.[10] Yet in ways no one could have predicted, the most secular people in the history of the world have become eager to engage the world of the spirit. Eugene Peterson, pastor-turned-professor, looks at this development with a somewhat skeptical eye.

> Overnight spirituality has become a passion for millions of North Americans. It should come as no surprise [though] that a people so badly trained in intimacy and transcendence might not do too well in their quest. Most anything at hand that gives a feeling of closeness—whether genitals or cocaine—will do for intimacy. And most anything exotic that induces a sense of mystery—from mantras to river rafting—will do for transcendence.[11]

Nor has this quest for spiritual reality bypassed the church. A renewed interest in spiritual retreats and in many kinds of prayer experiences as well as divergent new paths in worship from the charismatic to Taizè-style sung services give evidence of a spiritual awakening.

Though the traditional modes of Anabaptist spiritual formation—preaching, teaching, modeling—are extremely valuable, and in fact were largely sufficient in a time when communal bonds were strong, they no longer suffice in a world of powerful, competing external influences which have deformed the faith and commitments of many. During an era when people seek direct experience of the spiritual world, some have left their congregations in search of spiritual vitality elsewhere. Others have simply drifted away and succumbed to the lure of materialism and secularism.

Although churches offer a variety of responses to this dilemma, one thing is clear—vital worship that speaks to and calls forth responses from both mind and heart is essential. Whether that style of worship leans toward the charismatic or the liturgical or some other flavor does not seem to be nearly as significant as whether it re-unites the separated head and heart. What the research interviews amply show is that singing is the one sure way such integration happens for Mennonites. If faith is to grow and thrive in our congregations, postmodern Mennonites need to sing.[12]

Why does music in particular open the doorway to the divine? In his book *Faithquakes*, seminary professor Leonard Sweet asserts, "Music is the means to God for much of postmodern culture." He explains how people in the industrial era lost their voices to machines—and ultimately their souls. Sweet suggests that group singing and interactive musical experience are the chief community-building forces of the postmodern era. With power to move people beyond themselves, Sweet concludes that music is a key for recovering the soul.

> Music is an absolute imperative if postmoderns are to move outside of themselves, connect with others, and build community. One can motivate and move individuals to an experience of God without music—perhaps. But to have a community experience of God's presence, to bring a community of faith to a "catalytic moment," music is a must.[13]

Such a high view of the power of music to form and shape the people of God is not new, of course. From ancient times, music and spiritual experience have been intimately connected. A familiar portion of Paul's letter to the Christians at Colossae, for example, encourages believers to sing.

> Let the word of Christ dwell in you richly;
> teach and admonish one another in all wisdom;
> and with gratitude in your hearts,
> sing psalms, hymns, and spiritual songs to God. (Col. 3:16, NRSV)

Theophan, an Orthodox Christian of the eighth century, not only encourages Christians to sing but suggests that the act of singing is directly linked with the Holy Spirit's action in the believer. "Desire to be filled with the Spirit, and sing with that aim in mind. *Singing will set alight the Spirit*" [emph. added].[14]

On their way to persecution and death, early Anabaptists sang hymns glorifying God and fortifying themselves for the trials they were about to endure. From *Martyrs Mirror* comes one such story where, in 1546, four Anabaptists were condemned to death and delivered to the executioner.

> When they were being led out to the slaughter, they boldly and joyfully sang. The brethren then knelt down and fervently prayed, offering up

this burnt offering as their final farewell to the world. . . . They then blessed each other and exhorted one another to steadfastness, to be strong and of good cheer, saying, "Today we shall be together in the kingdom of the heavenly Father."[15]

Thomas Troeger, Iliff School of Theology preaching professor, says "Singing, not just listening to the music of others, but setting our own throat, mouth, ears and head vibrating with the sound of God's praise, is one of the most ancient and constant ways that the Spirit has been evoked."[16]

Though the church indeed has a precious heritage of song and spirituality, we find ourselves asking: Will the church's music still bring people into the presence of God in the postmodern church? As traditional patterns of life give way to the rich but confusing pluralism of North American life at the end of the twentieth century, will the songs we sing still have the power demonstrated by the interviews?

The following story suggests that music has not lost its power to mediate God's presence. A woman whose education was steeped in rationalism found her life falling apart. As an agnostic and existentialist, she had no faith to provide a buffer or sense of meaning in the trauma of personal failure and family loss she endured. She explains

> On a rainy November morning, I went to the piano to practice a soprano aria from Handel's *Messiah* for an audition. After fifteen minutes of two-octave scales that were smooth as running water, I started singing, *"Come unto Him, all ye that labor; Come unto Him, ye that are heavy laden, and he will give you rest."* Carried by the ravishing melody, the words began to enter my very being like warm oil, bringing an invitation to rest. The habitual bodily anxiety began to melt away. A promise of rest seemed to float on the breath. The try-hard muscles of my upper back smoothed a little, softening the hero shoulders, easing the long-term, low-grade tension in the gut. It was as though a love I had never known was pouring forth from in me. Only months later did I recognize this moment as the beginning of my conversion. It was a bodily experience of incarnation, a gut knowledge of the surpassing love of Christ.
>
> Six months later I walked into an unfamiliar church known to have an altar call. Responding to the invitation to "Come unto Him," I went forward. Had that invitation come through a sermon or the written word, it would have been killed off by the dragons who guarded the door of my rational world view. But something about a song is nearly irresistible in that it reaches both the mind and the heart, the former with meaning, the latter with beauty. It has taken me a long time to realize that of the two, the heart is the larger source of intelligence for me.[17]

Eventually this convert to Christian faith found her way to a seminary to study. While there she found her faith in a living Christ deeply challenged by historical-critical studies: Was there indeed a resurrection? Is Christ God? An intense struggle became unbearable at a Christmas Eve Eucharist and haunted her until New Year's Eve when she went to bed "with a despair darker than any in memory." Then

> Before dawn on the first day of the new year, the despair returned. But in the middle of the dark, I noticed a melody. A song was playing inside my head. After having breakfast and cleaning the kitchen, the song was still there. I recognized the title—it was "Love divine, all loves excelling," not Hyfrodol, but Beecher, the tune we sang back in Tennessee. I took the hymnal to my prayer place in the back room and sat down to read the words:
>> Love divine, all loves excelling, Joy of heaven to earth come down,
>> Fix in us thy humble dwelling, All thy faithful mercies crown!
>> Jesus, thou art all compassion, Pure unbounded love thou art;
>> Visit us with thy salvation, Enter every trembling heart.
>
> Like lectio lasers, certain phrases cut through the bars of skepticism—"*Breathe thy loving Spirit into every troubled breast, Let us all in thee inherit, Let us find thy promised rest.*" Those words in that long-forgotten melody addressed the greater intelligence of my heart with a knowledge deeper than logic; the hymn gave me the words my heart longed to pray—Jesus, you who are pure unbounded lover, enter this trembling heart. This time it was I who invited Him to "Come." The rational dragons surrendered their totalitarian hold to the astonishing power of a majestic old hymn. I knew with my muscles and bones that the hymn was a prayer formed in me by the Holy Spirit. It was a final surrender into mystery for the sake of a lover I could not live without.[18]

In this story of God's love being poured out in a needy human heart, it is the postmodern inclination to trust the power of a personal experience that opened a doorway to the sacred and brought freedom and release. Yet the obvious limitation of personal experience is its subjectivity (because every human life is unique, personal experience is limited by the particulars of any given history). Even with these limitations, however, the desire of postmoderns for personal experience clearly represents an open door for the church to introduce people to the reality of God.

If these interview responses are valid, then the experience of singing together in worship can and does satisfy the deep need for a personal encounter with the sacred—a meeting that engages the whole person: body, heart, and mind. Not all will be comfortable using the term *sacrament* for what happens when we sing. The historic aversion to the term among Mennonites (because of its close connection with the authoritarian state church that persecuted early Anabaptists) may make it unusable for some.[19]

Without the traditional language of sacramental theology, however, it has been difficult for Mennonites to validate the very real spiritual significance of this important act of worship. With our strong preference for ethics and a gritty determination to live our faith in ordinary, daily ways, the church has been malnourished or underdeveloped when it comes to mystical communion or beauty that calls forth adoration and praise.[20] It may be that Mennonite detachment from the sacramental tradition has caused us to overlook what is the most obvious and powerful locus of God's presence in Mennonite worship: *hymn singing*.

By whatever name we call it, if we choose to recognize its power and then make ample place for Spirit-inspired singing as an essential ingredient in Mennonite worship,[21] we will provide a sturdy foundation for the faith of the next generation. Then our children will know what one person, who represented many, told us.

> When I remember my childhood whole—and not just its parts, it seems to have been filled with song. Though more sophisticated folk might look askance at some of our musical choices and expressions, it was the act of singing which drew my congregation together and formed us as God's people. We sang our prayers of confession and praise; we sang our longing for healing and transformation; we sang our joy as members of God's family; and while we stood around fresh graves in the church cemetery, we sang our hope in the resurrection. Without our music, our faith would have been barren. We would have been condemned to a prosaic, rational religion without passion or joy. Instead, our music gave us a faith with flesh and blood and breath and ushered us into realms of glory and grace. I can't imagine a more wondrous gift.

If we keep on singing, we will know that the Lord is still our Shepherd because our songs will set the truth quivering in our bodies, minds, and souls. Singing brings us into the presence of the Shepherd who leads into green pastures and beside still waters to the eternal feast of God's presence.

NOTES

1. Sam Keen, *Hymns to an Unknown God: Awakening the Spirit in Everyday Life* (New York: Bantam Books, 1994), 5-6.

2. Recently someone gave me shorthand definitions for *premodern, modern,* and *postmodern*: A premodern person believes the text is sacred; a modern person wants to

know the meaning of the text; and a postmodern person says, "Who needs a text?"

3. Because the research on which this paper is based was conducted among (Old) Mennonites and General Conference Mennonites, Mennonite experience, not the entire range of contemporary Anabaptist groups, is the context for the thesis of this essay.

4. Sally Morgenthaler, "Out of the Box: Authentic Worship in a Postmodern Culture," *Worship Leader* (May-June, 1998), 24.

5. Ibid., 25.

6. These research interviews became a significant part of my Doctor of Ministry project, "Singing as Sacrament: An Exploration of the Role of Hymn Singing in Mennonite Spiritual Formation," May 1997. Interviewees included both (Old) Mennonites and General Conference Mennonites as well as recent and longtime church members across North America who ranged in age from pre-teens to the mid-eighties.

7. In *The Theology of Anabaptism* (Scottdale, Pa.: Herald Press, 1973), Robert Friedmann summarizes in the chapter on "Ecclesiology" that "the vertical relationship 'God to man' and the horizontal relationship 'brother to brother' are inseparable" (121).

8. "What is this place" is the first hymn in *Hymnal: A Worship Book* (Scottdale, Pa.: Mennonite Publishing House, 1992).

9. George R. Brunk III, "When My Life Is Almost Gone," *Crossroads* (Spring, 1996), 30.

10. Karen Armstrong, *A History of God: The 4000-Year Quest of Judaism, Christianity, and Islam* (New York: Alfred A. Knopf, 1993), xix.

11. Eugene Peterson, "Spirit Quest," *Christianity Today* (November 8, 1993), 28.

12. We may also need to renew our understanding of ritual and symbol, but that is a topic for another essay.

13. Leonard Sweet, *Faithquakes* (Nashville, Tenn.: Abingdon Press, 1994), 63-64.

14. Theophan in *The Art of Prayer: An Orthodox Anthology*, quoted in Gabe Huck, ed., *A Sourcebook About Liturgy* (Chicago: Liturgy Training Publications, 1994), 36.

15. Thielman J. Van Braght, *Martyrs Mirror* (Scottdale, Pa.: Herald Press, 1950), 475.

16. Thomas H. Troeger, "The Hidden Stream That Feeds: Hymns as a Resource for the Preacher's Imagination," *The Hymn* 43 (July 1992), 12.

17. Kay Collette, "Spirit's Songs," *Presence: An International Journal of Spiritual Direction* 1 (May 1995), 65.

18. Ibid., 66.

19. Augustine, however, in the fifth century included singing on his sacraments list.

20. It may also be true that our inattention to sacraments has weakened our ethical commitments. A commitment to justice and an openness to mystery can, in fact, enhance one another.

21. Spirit-inspired singing may differ in style from one congregation to another. Those interviewed included persons from congregations with a variety of musical preferences—some traditional, some charismatic, some contemporary. People's reflections about what happens when they sing did not seem to differ according to the style of music their congregation preferred.

PART FIVE

RELIGIOUS PARTICULARITY AND SOCIAL IDENTITY

THIRTEEN

NICAEA, WOMANIST THEOLOGY, AND ANABAPTIST PARTICULARITY

J. Denny Weaver

INTRODUCTION

As has been pointed out more than once, postmodernity has multiple definitions and meanings. One frequently cited dimension of postmodernity is that it makes us aware of the particularity of traditions. Stated another way, postmodernity has meant abandoning the idea that there is a universally recognizable answer or answers to theological and ethical questions that confront us. For some, that recognition has been liberating. For others it has proved bothersome or even threatening.

I am one for whom postmodernism has been liberating. Not liberating in the sense that postmodernity opens the door to believe new and/or foolish things because there are no longer limits or norms. Rather, liberation from the fear that a truth professed from within a small tradition, precisely because it comes from a small tradition, is thereby specifically and innately less credible than a truth proclaimed in a supposedly wider or broader or more general tradition. We are now free to develop a theology that specifically reflects our professed Anabaptist commitment to Jesus, whose story is intrinsically nonviolent. We are free to express that commitment to Jesus in a church that is a witness to rather than a supporter of the social order.

In addition, developing that theology reveals that the supposed wider or broader or more universal church is also particular and has its own specific context. Thus the particular tradition of Christendom is also called on to justify itself as well with reference to the nonviolent story of Jesus, rather than simply claiming authority as the general, universally recognized answer. To anticipate a point we will return to later, acknowledging these particularities is not an assertion that we just need to become comfortable with pluralism. Such acknowledgment does mean that divergence from Christendom's formulations does not automatically signify error. More importantly, the implications of such particularity include making the Christendom tradition subject to correction or adjustment on the basis of analysis from the particular space of the Anabaptist tradition.

Anabaptists developed as several small groups that rejected the identification of church with society or church with social order, or what in modern terminology would be called a "Christian society." The sixteenth-century opponents of Anabaptists, whether Roman Catholic or several versions of Protestant, were a continuation of the millennium-long legacy of identifying church with the social and civil order in a supposedly Christian society. The theology identified as classic orthodoxy emerged out of the early stages of the church that came to be identified with the social order. The way I want to pose the question about absolutes or universals is to ask, "Is theology that emerged from the church that identified with the social order for everyone, or does it reflect a particular tradition(s) and is therefore a worthy conversation partner but not a universal or normative theology?" This chapter explains why I think the latter choice is the correct one.

Despite vigorous discussions about postmodernity among Anabaptist academics from many disciplines, I still have a sense that we have not yet seriously engaged this fact: the theological tradition of classic orthodoxy, and specifically Nicene-Chalcedonian Christology and Anselmian atonement, is a particular tradition that reflects a particular understanding of the relationship of the church to the social order. We have not yet taken seriously that stances inside and outside the power structure of society may significantly affect what one sees theologically. In other words, we have not yet come to terms with the fact that theology produced by and for people in authority (whether a dominant class, a government, or a hierarchy) may differ significantly from theology produced by and for people who are outside of and/or oppressed by the people in authority.

My first section explains briefly how I see Anabaptists denying the particularity of the classic tradition. Then there is my two-part response. The first part is a direct reply to current arguments. The second part introduces womanist conversations concerning the same type of issues. Then in conclusion I suggest what all this implies for Anabaptist discussions about particularity and universality.

DENYING PARTICULARITY

Several observations suggest to me that we are still struggling to understand whether theology identified as classic orthodoxy is a universal, normative tradition or is rendered particular by a specific context. First, there continue to be persistent efforts by Anabaptist theologians to find common ground with the Constantinian church, both historically and with today's heirs to the established church. Such efforts often include the search for some place one step back that enables us to find some wider or broader or more general perspective from which to observe that Anabaptist and/or Mennonite and/or free church theology or eccelesiology is not as different from Christendom's theology and ecclesiology as previously thought.

This step back enables us, it is argued, to see that contrary to our earlier sense of distance and separation from the Constantinian church, we can now see after all that we are both engaged in some common task. Such tasks may include these: First, building institutions or structures. Second, trying to live on the land unselfishly and responsibly.[1] Third, searching for a common theology by adding our distinct emphases to a foundation established by Christendom or by constructing a theological edifice on a super grid that uses big blocks of Christendom theology alongside Anabaptist theological building blocks.[2] Fourth, Anabaptist history can be reinterpreted to make the point that Anabaptists had a lot more in common with magisterial reformers than previously thought—Anabaptists had many sword-bearers, as they did, and Anabaptists and magisterial reformers all confessed the same creeds.[3] I suggest that this perceived need by Mennonites to find common ground between Constantinian and Anabaptist traditions seems to presuppose some sense of generalness or normativeness or universality in the Constantinian church that Anabaptists need to vouchsafe credibility or truthfulness.

A second basic observation is this: In response to John H. Yoder's beginning historical "relativizing"[4] of Nicene-Chalcedonian Christology in his *Preface to Theology*[5] or to my own more recent work which has pushed farther the argument that Nicaea-Chalcedon-Anselm reflect the Constantinian church, there are now several published efforts to defend Nicaea. This is done by distancing it from Constantine and from the hierarchical church that produced it. This perceived need to defend Nicaea (and Chalcedon and Anselm) seems to presuppose a generalness or normativeness or universality of Nicaea that demands our affirmation of it. It appears to assume that Anabaptist particularity should defer to Christendom's perceived universality.

Such efforts to locate Anabaptist theology in a wider or broader or more general truth harbor an apparent reluctance to acknowledge the particularity of the established church and its thought. Stated differently, I suggest we have given insufficient attention to the potential theological significance of Anabaptist ecclesiology that refuses to fuse the church with the social order, or to the potential difference between a social location that identifies with the dominant social order and one that does not. In contrast to efforts to find common ground with Constantinian theology, this paper argues that Anabaptists and the established church tradition, or social locations inside and outside the prevailing social order, constitute different, particular viewpoints. They may then produce two distinct theologies and approaches to ethics.

Again to anticipate some responses as well as eventual conclusions, it is important to say this: claiming an Anabaptist particularity as the basis for a theology based on a believers church rendition of the story of Jesus is not to claim that Anabaptists can or should "go it alone." The goal is not to argue that Anabaptism should unfold with no regard for the tradition of orthodoxy or developments in the history of doctrine. An Anabaptist or believers church understanding of Jesus did not spring up in autochthonous, isolated fashion in the sixteenth century. Rather, the believers church perspective is part of the common heritage of all Christians, beginning with some of the early church fathers that defended pacifism, as well as some of the suspects in the early church (such as Donatists), parts of the monastic tradition, and so on.

In fact, with extensive qualifications and additions, the Apostles' Creed can be shown to stand in this tradition, although the addendums I would add qualify it in such a way that it can no longer stand alone as a point of agreement among all Christians. Of course Anabaptists, both historical and modern, are part of the large collection of folks identified by the name Christian. Thus a particular Anabaptist theology must interrogate and enter conversation with any and all parts of the Christian tradition. In that conversation, however, the crucial question is whether we allow Christendom to define the issues and the basis of dialogue. Do we assume a foundational, universal quality for the orthodox positions, which places them above critique and makes Anabaptist respectability depend on showing how we fit into them? Or can Anabaptists enter the conversation with a sense that we can correct as well as be corrected, that Anabaptist particularity can instruct Christendom particularity as well as the reverse?

A Defense of Christendom

In a recently published essay, "Constantine and the 'Fall' of the Church,"[6] Daniel H. Williams defends Nicaea against free church critique. He makes arguments used by several recent Anabaptist theologians. To summarize, Williams rejects the free church idea of a "fall" of the church, which would imply that the apostolic period of the church "can be appropriated in a pure, unmediated way."[7] As a test of the fall thesis, Williams's essay asks whether there was a loss of theological identity with the changes in the church after Constantine, as the fall idea would suggest. Williams argues that doctrinal formulation was not yet entirely dependent on imperial politics in the fourth century. For example, while Athanasius or Ambrose "were only too willing to receive promotion of their ecclesiastical platform by orthodox emperors," they also "rejected the notion that the affairs of doctrine and Church should be legislated single-handedly by imperial policy."[8]

Thus the relationship between church and state in the fourth century was one of interdependence. Each entity was defined by the other without collapsing into the kind of unity discerned and proscribed by the fall thesis. Conciliar and local church creeds acted on each other in the same way.[9] Further, the acceptance of Nicaea (or Constantinople) was a "much more fragmented and gradual affair than the 'fall' paradigm allows." Although Nicaea functioned as a "theological hermeneutic for defining orthodoxy and heresy" in the fourth and fifth centuries, it had "by no means usurped the traditional language with which the congregation worshiped or baptized its members."[10]

Such arguments serve to preserve the Nicene-Constantinopolitan theology from undue influence by imperial politics. Thus Williams says that we should not "reduce the development of the early Church's doctrine to an epiphenomenon of fourth-century ecclesiastical politics."[11] Williams concludes that, whereas there were important changes in the status of the church in and after the fourth century, "the essential formulation and construction of the Christian identity was something that the fourth century *received* and then expanded on through its biblical exegesis and liturgical life as reflected in the creedal traditions."[12]

Williams postulates that the continuity between the post-apostolic period and the Christianity of the fourth and fifth centuries is

> more complicated and durable than free church typologies of ecclesiastical history have been willing to allow. That there were linguistic or conceptual innovations to the original kerygma of Jesus was a necessary outcome . . . of redefining the parameters of orthodoxy in their age.

But these redefinitions and refinements took place "in the shadow of the worshiping experience of the churches"; thus,

> these formal and local expressions of theological faithfulness were understood in a dynamic relationship of complimentarity which was not circumvented by the political and social benefits provided by Constantine and his successors for the Church.[13]

PRELIMINARY RESPONSES

As the first part of my argument about the particularity of traditional orthodoxy, I want to outline a brief reply to points raised by Williams.

1. Finding early versions of what came to be Nicene formulas,[14] and the fact that Nicaea was not accepted as normative orthodoxy until at least late in the fourth century, do not necessarily rescue Nicene theology from the impact of the church in which it became the accepted and prevailing view. The changes by which the early church became identified with the social order began already in the second century, if not earlier, and were gradual and evolutionary. Theology likewise evolved gradually. Finding these several and early versions—so that Williams can say that the fourth-century church "received" rather than developed it—combined with the protracted process of its acceptance merely demonstrates the evolutionary character of changes in both church and church theology.

2. Describing a change in the orientation of the church from the apostolic or early church era to the nascent imperial church in the fourth century need not assume, imply, nor require the idea of a pristine early church that serves as a perfect model. There was no such thing. I agree with Williams's point that free church theologians ought not assume that there was a pristine period from which there could be a subsequent fall. Paul's letters give ample evidence of the divisions and problems in the imperfect church of the New Testament. And the book of Revelation, which has a clear ecclesiology of a church distinct from the social order, thereby also reveals the temptation of the church to cease its opposition and to take the easier path of accommodation. One can speak about a reorientation of the church

from first to fourth or fifth century without assuming there was a pristine early church.

This reorientation can be described as an evolutionary shift from an initial orientation of a church that intended to be shaped by the story of Jesus (although this was never perfectly achieved)—and thus assumed that it posed a contrast to the social order—to a later condition of a church that came to accommodate and identify with the social order. Describing this reorientation as an evolutionary shift does not require that the change involved a specific, willful intent to abandon an ethic oriented around Jesus.[15]

Observing that change from orientation one to orientation two does not require either that the ideal of the first stage was perfectly attained (it never was) or that the orientation of the second stage was an intentional disregard for Jesus (it was not). When an athlete switches from baseball to football, observing that he changed sports requires neither that he had attained perfection in the first sport nor that practicing the second sport is necessarily a *willful* disregard or disrespect of the first. Certainly, observing the change in orientation of the church from apostolic to imperial does not imply or require the idea of a pristine early church. But without calling it an *intentional* abandonment of the teachings of Jesus, one can still observe this: by the fourth century, the church was well along an evolutionary path from a church that distinguished itself from the social order to the church that accommodated itself to the social order.

That accommodation included but was not limited to several stances. One was acceptance of imperial or other political support when those authorities supported the doctrines or policies of the church's hierarchy. Another was accommodation of the sword in what had once been a pacifist church. One can observe this transition, ask questions about faithfulness, and inquire how doctrines that emerged from the church of the second stage might reflect that context without requiring or assuming either a pristine first stage or a *willful* intent to abandon Jesus in the second.

3. The important point of the shift symbolized by Constantine is the evolution from church that was distinct from the social order to the church that accommodated the social order. That accommodation was never a total fusion. Even in later epochs when the church was most dominant, political authorities still resisted policies of popes and bishops. As already noted, Williams described the situation in the fourth century as one of "interdependence" between church and state. That description, however, leaves fully in place the point that the changes concerned the church's

coming to accommodate, support, and express itself through the institutions of the social order. Williams is merely describing the complex character of that evolution.

Whether these changes in the early church constitute a "fall" is a theological more than a historical question. That there were changes seems not to be in dispute. What is disputed is the extent to which the changes constitute gain or loss, or whether the changes impacted the fundamental character of the church. To argue that the changes were good or did not affect the fundamental character of the church implies that identifying with the social order and accommodating the sword are issues unrelated to the character of the church and not included in what it means to follow Jesus. In contrast, at least until recently, Anabaptists have considered the church identifying with the social order and accommodating the sword to be issues that change fundamentally the character of the church and discipleship of Jesus.

4. Regardless of the complexity of the evolutionary changes, the direction of change seems clear. It is possible to ask whether the Nicene-Constantinopolitan Christology that was eventually accepted as the universal tradition reflects more the church at the head of the evolutionary path or the becoming-imperial church that accepted it.

In making that evaluation, one might consider Williams's own comments about the willingness of pro-Nicene churchmen to appeal to imperial power when it supported them. Or Rosemary Jermann's frank statement that "we find nothing in the creed" regarding the "active involvement in attempts to better society" that appeared in the preaching of the Cappadocians who were champions of Nicene theology. Thus Jermann suggests, we should find such contributions to the creed "in the context of that community's commitment to the apostolic faith."[16]

Or one can review R. C. P. Hanson's description of the churchly politics of Basil of Caesarea, one of the three Cappadocians. Although Basil lived in ascetic style, he was from a wealthy, land-owning family. As bishop, he cooperated with imperial politics when it suited, and he functioned as a manipulative and authoritarian politician."[17] Also by this time, use of the sword was coming to be accepted for Christians. I have argued that the abstract formulas of Nicaea (and latter Chalcedon) allow one to affirm the truth of Jesus without being challenged on the issue of the sword.[18]

In contrast, defining Jesus in terms of the gospel's narrative of Jesus does challenge the use of the sword. It appears that regardless of how complex the evolutionary process, the formulas that emerge as the universally accepted norms reflect this church approaching the social order on the terms of the social order, including the sword, rather than a church oriented (however imperfectly) by the narrative of Jesus. As the following section (as well as note 64) argues, believers church folks are not the only ones to make that observation.

The efforts to distance Nicaea from its imperial, hierarchical church context by locating its origin earlier and its acceptance later all deal with the very particular way that Nicaea developed within and was eventually accepted as universal norm by a particular church. Pushing the acceptance of Nicaea farther along in history seems to me to lessen rather than strengthen the authority it might have for free church adherents.

Finally, on the question of whether Nicaea reflects the context of the becoming-imperial church rather than the first-century church, I pose another question. Is there any other development of ideology where historians would argue that the development was not impacted by or reflective of its social location? Take, for example, the development of Adam Smith's capitalism in eighteenth-century England. Or the origin of Marxism in the conditions of nineteenth-century England. Or the emergence of liberation theology in twentieth-century Latin and South America.

Does this argument concerning the particularity of Nicaea mean that it is not important to affirm that Jesus is of God? Certainly not. It is crucial to affirm Jesus' identity with both God and humankind. The argument about particularity is really about whether Nicaea is the only way to talk about the relationship of Jesus to God. Or whether one must use or can only use the philosophical assumptions and categories of Nicaea to expound and preserve the New Testament's view that Jesus is of God. It is even probably the case that if one assumes the philosophical backdrop of Nicaea, and if one asks the question posed by Nicaea in terms of that philosophy, then Nicaea may well be the correct and best answer. But this particularity of the Nicene formula also suggests why it cannot float above particularity as a universal statement.[19]

WOMANIST RESPONSES

Anabaptists are not the only folks who have engaged in some conversation with and about the legacy of Constantinian theology. As black women, womanist theologians emphasize their particular social location as people who have confronted the threefold experience of racism, sexism, and classism. Although Anabaptist theology has had almost no interaction with womanist theology, I think it is instructive to introduce elements of the womanist discussion about theological implications of their particularity and its relationship to classic theology inherited from Europe.

Anabaptists originated as a bundle of traditions outside of the established church, sometimes by expulsion and other times by their own choice. Early in the tradition, significant suffering and persecution marked that location outside of the established church. The black church in North America also came into existence outside of the dominant churchly tradition, sometimes by choice and other times against its will. Significant oppression has marked that social location outside the dominant churchly tradition. It casts light on our discussions to see what womanists, in a social location outside the dominant tradition, say in conversation with the dominant theological tradition.[20]

The following introduces womanist theology, but it is not a comprehensive analysis of all womanist writing, nor an outline of their entire, wide-ranging agenda. I am choosing to highlight comments from womanist discussions about particularity and its implications for the presumed universality of the classic, European theological tradition.

Central to the womanist agenda is the racism of both American society and the predominantly white feminist movement, the sexism of the black church, and poverty, which is only worsened by sexism and racism. Although womanists write for black women and the black church, they hope white audiences sometimes listen in. As Kelly Brown Douglas says, "dialogue with black women's history is also imperative for students who are not black and female. It gives them a chance to discover their relationship to black women's history."[21] All womanists speak out of the context of at least the threefold experience of racism, sexism, and poverty. I want to show in an introductory way how that agenda shapes their approach to theology and ethics and discussions of particularity and universality.

In her *Black Womanist Ethics*,[22] Katie Cannon speaks knowingly of the difference between ethics for the dominant class and ethics for the dominated class. Her reflections on the relationship of faith and ethics began as a young child when she heard the central affirmations of Christianity taught by her grandmother, such as "God's universal parenthood which engendered a social, intellectual and cultural ethos, embracing the equal humanity of all people." She wondered how to relate that doctrine to the oppression and exploitation of black people.

> How could Christians who were white, flatly and openly, refuse to treat as fellow human beings Christians who had African ancestry?. . . Was there any way to reconcile the inherent contradictions in Christianity as

practiced by whites with the radical indictments of and challenges for social amelioration and economic development in the Black religious heritage?[23]

Cannon came to realize that the dominant and the dominated had different ethical systems. The dominant system was "predicated on the existence of freedom" and stressed such virtues as "self-reliance, frugality and industry." Practicing these qualities enabled one to develop positive self-image and to move upward in society. But when this same society withheld economic and political power from blacks because of their supposed inferiority, the values of self-reliance, frugality, and industry were ineffectual for African Americans.[24] The dominant system assumed that the moral agent possessed "self-determining power," but withheld that freedom from blacks. Language about accepting suffering and making sacrifices for a principle sound very different when one is in a position to choose to suffer as opposed to "the masses of Black people," for whom "suffering is the normal state of affairs."

Thus in the black community, the values that define desirable character "must always take into account the circumstances, the paradoxes and the dilemmas that constrict Blacks to the lowest range of self-determination."[25] In contrast to the dominant ethic, "Black faith and liberation ethics" discuss "defying oppressive rules or standards of 'law and order' which unjustly degrade Blacks in the society," purge blacks of self-hate, and promote their "human validity." Such ethical values from the black community "are not identical with the body of obligations and duties that Anglo-Protestant American society requires of its members."[26] *Black Womanist Ethics* draws on the particular experiences of African American women to develop a liberation ethic that empowers African Americans and confronts the racist, male-dominated, and classist elements of North American society.

Another example of a specific difference between dominant and dominated perspectives appears in the discussion of theodicy. Cannon uses analysis of the sermon, "The Wounds of Jesus" from a Zora Neal Hurston novel, to show that African Americans perceived the problem of theodicy differently than has the dominant theological tradition. According to the assumptions of the dominant theology, an omnipotent God could choose to prevent evil. Thus to ask how evil can exist when there is an omnipotent God calls into question the existence of God.

Womanists such as Cannon observe that slaves and other oppressed African Americans posed the question of theodicy very differently. Slaves never doubted that God existed. The particular sermon of Cannon's analysis emphasizes a story of redemption for African Americans that began with Jesus' wounds suffered for them on Calvary. Evil and suffering did not originate with God but with people in the garden and continues in the white folks who maintained the evil of institutions such as slavery. Drawing on those insights, Cannon says that a womanist approach does not ask whether God exists and how to justify God's goodness in the face of evil. "Rather womanist protagonists contend that God's sustaining presence is known in the resistance to evil."[27]

Biblical scholar Renita J. Weems's description of a womanist approach to the Bible makes quite clear that the social location of the interpreter is an important dimension of the interpretation. To control what they knew, slaves were forbidden to read, and slave owners communicated the Bible orally to present what they considered a fit interpretation for slaves. What slave masters had failed to recognize, however, was that once the slaves had heard the biblical material, they could interpret it as they saw fit.[28] And slaves, including specifically African American women, interpreted in terms of their experiences of oppression. The experience of oppression taught African American women that interpretation was "not just a matter of whose reading is 'accurate,' but whose reading is legitimated and enforced by the dominant culture." Further, experience of oppression then forces "the marginalized reader to retain the right . . . to resist those things in the culture and the Bible that one finds obnoxious and antagonistic to one's innate sense of identity and to one's basic instincts for survival."[29]

Thus when considering the matter of the Bible as an authoritative text, it is not really the "texts per se that function authoritatively." Rather, "it is reading strategies, and more precisely, *particular* readings that turn out, in fact, to be authoritative."[30] Historical-critical methodology could then protect the autonomy of the text from doctrinal readings apart from any historical setting in the nineteenth century. But such readings can also serve negatively when those in power use it to undermine marginal communities by "insisting that their questions and experiences are superfluous to Scripture and their interpretations illegitimate, because of their failure to remain objective."[31]

Weems thus asserts that how one reads and interprets the Bible depends in a significant way on the interpretive community with which one identifies. The multiple layers of oppression in the experiences of African American women thus lead them "to be sensitive to oppression wherever it exists, whether in society or in narrative plots."[32] For one example of womanist interpretation, Weems comments on the letter of Philemon and the return of Onesimus, the slave. A liberationist emphasizes that "however ineradicable" slavery was in Rome, and "however pastoral and tactful the tone of the letter," in fact Onesimus had run away "in all likelihood because he did not want to remain a slave," and his return to Philemon was involuntary.[33]

Weems uses the exodus as another example of womanist interpretation. Since exodus stood at the heart of Israel's efforts to be the people of God that confronted "elitist, despotic, totalitarian, oppressive values and policies" in neighboring societies, exodus (and the biblical books that contained it) became the source for the slaves' dreams about

> a new way of being in the world. . . . A reading of slave narratives will show that for African American slave women and men Christian hope was anchored in the story of a God who heard the outcries of the enslaved and in turn delivered them from the bondage inflicted by their taskmasters.[34]

As a third example, Weems notes the story of Hagar, which Delores S. Williams develops at some length. Williams critiques modern feminists for assuming that the experience of white women is normative for all women. Examples include the racist attitudes of such nineteenth-century feminists as Susan B. Anthony and Elizabeth Cady Stanton, who helped to prevent African Americans from gaining the vote in the aftermath of the Civil War.[35] Williams's *Sisters in the Wilderness*[36] draws on a great deal of historical material in developing a womanist perspective on the experience of black women.

Williams holds up Hagar, servant of Abraham's wife Sarah, as the biblical figure with whom black women identified. As understood by black women, Hagar's story is the story of the slave woman, the woman whose destiny is and has been "shaped by the problems and desires of her owners."[37] For Sarah, motherhood is a privilege that will grant her status in the world. For Hagar, motherhood is a coerced experience, forced on her by Sarah, her mistress. As a slave, Hagar is forced to submit to the advances of Abraham. She functions as Sarah's surrogate. In other words, Hagar is exploited by a woman as well as by a man.

After the birth of Ishmael, Hagar takes her son and escapes into the wilderness, making herself "the first female in the Bible to liberate herself from oppressive power structures."[38] In the wilderness, Hagar and Ishmael are facing death when God comes to them. On one occasion, as a matter of survival, God tells Hagar to return with Ishmael to the tent of Abraham and Sarah, to the place of bondage. The second time God provides Hagar with new vision so she can use her own resources to survive.[39]

This story of Hagar becomes the paradigm of the female-centered tradition of African American biblical appropriation. Williams calls this the "survival/quality-of-life tradition of African-American biblical appropriation."[40] It embodies the elements of the lives of many African American women: pregnancy and motherhood as a coerced experience, struggle for survival with only God as a support, various kinds of surrogacy, and economic realities related to homelessness.[41]

This story of Hagar sets up Williams's womanist critique of early black theology for its inattention to the status of black women, and her critique of absence of race consciousness in much of feminist theology. It also sets up Williams's fundamental critique of traditional, satisfaction, and substitutionary atonement theology in which Jesus functions as "the ultimate surrogate figure."[42] Given the exploited experience of black woman as surrogates, womanist theologians are understandably hesitant to endorse any understanding of Jesus' work that models surrogacy.

This clear sense that the dominant theological perspective cannot speak for black women leads Williams to conclude with a strong call for a theology that speaks for African American Christians and specifically for African American women who are Christians. African American Christians need doctrine in their churches. But they need *doctrine that emerges from African American people's experience with God*, not doctrine "inherited" from oppressive Eurocentric forms of Christianity, not female-exclusive doctrine formulated centuries ago by male potentates. The unromanticized, egalitarian African heritage and the slaves' experience with God articulated in their narratives, tales, and songs are what begin to provide materials for the construction of African American Christian doctrines of resistance. God's continuing work in the African American community's ever-present struggle for economic justice, for physical and emotional survival, and for positive quality of life provides "the stuff" of black Christians' doctrines of resistance.[43]

The writers in Cheryl Sanders's *Living the Intersection* all confront the absence of the concerns of black women in the Afrocentricism made prominent by Molefi Kete Asante.[44] Again one notes the importance of the particular perspective of African American women. Although Afrocentricism has challenged white supremacy and the exclusion of Africans from the story of civilization, these womanist writers point out that the stories and the concerns of black women have been excluded from Afrocentricism.

Jacqueline Grant's *White Women's Christ and Black Women's Jesus*[45] pursues the difference between white and black perspectives in an analysis of feminist Christology. Like other womanists, Grant points out ways both nineteenth- and twentieth-century feminist thought has neglected or mistreated the experience of black women. In an essay concerned with revisioning the idea of servanthood, Grant asks,

> Which women's experience is the source of theology? Further, one could ask, how do these experiences impact the direction taken in one's theological perspective? Is it the experience of the daughters of slaveholders or the experience of the daughters of slaves? These two experiences are irreconcilable as they stand.[46]

Like other womanists, Grant asserts that

> Black women must do theology out of their tri-dimensional experience of racism, sexism, classism. To ignore any aspect of this experience is to deny the holistic and integrated reality of Black womanhood. When Black women say that God is on the side of the oppressed, we mean that God is in solidarity with the struggles of those on the underside of humanity.[47]

These sketches from womanist theologians illustrate their sense of the difference that perspectives of race and gender make but without yet raising specifically the postmodern discussion about universality and particularity. Some womanists have also entered that discussion. Their sense of the particularity of an African American woman's experience brings into clear relief the extent to which the traditional or classic theology inherited from European Christendom is white-oriented, patriarchal, and male-dominated. It is thus not at all surprising to read that womanists dispute the existence of a general or universal perspective and assert the particularity of all theology.

In her essay "Hitting a Straight Lick with a Crooked Stick," Katie Cannon notes the "precarious predicament" in which being a black womanist ethicist places her.

> On the one hand, my task as a *Christian social ethicist* is to transcend my blackness and femaleness and draft a blueprint of liberation ethics that somehow speaks to, or responds to, the universality of the human condition. On the other hand, my task as a *womanist liberation ethicist* is to debunk, unmask, and disentangle the historically conditioned value

judgments and power relations that undergird the particularities of race, sex, and class oppression.⁴⁸

Cannon goes on to explain that claimed neutral methods of reasoning actually "contain deeply hidden biases" that hinder the interests of black women. "Universality does not include the Black female experience."⁴⁹ "Lives of Black women cannot be fully comprehended using analytical categories derived from White/male experience. Oftentimes such concepts covertly sustain a hierarchy of White supremacy, patriarchy, and exploitative power."⁵⁰ The liberation ethicist thus works "in opposition to the academic establishment" as well as building on it.⁵¹ Since "theoethical structures are not universal, color-blind, apolitical, or otherwise neutral . . . the womanist ethicist tries to comprehend how Black women create their own lives, influence others, and understand themselves as a force in their own right."

Put differently, a true liberation ethic for African Americans must deal with the particularities of the black experience, including specifically the experience of black women. In so doing it also challenges the claims to universality of the dominant tradition. Focusing on the particular question of women and of black women will "reveal the subtle and deep effects of male bias on recording religious history" and the presumption that "only men's activities have theological value." Further, a black liberation ethic will accurately acknowledge the contributions of black women to the black church and "recognize and condemn the extent to which sex differences prevail in the institutional church, in our theological writings, and in the Black church's practices."⁵² Truth comes through the particular rather than a search for or a claim to the universal.

I suggest that Cannon's focus on the particularity of a black liberationist ethic challenges us to examine seriously the implications of efforts by Anabaptists to validate Anabaptist theology and ethics in some more general or universal Christendom theology. Such moves may in fact involve the abandonment of particular Anabaptist emphases on nonviolence (as well as questions that concern race and gender) in exchange for the particularity of Christendom's orthodoxy.

As her way of asserting the particularity of womanist theology, Emilie Townes pointedly calls womanist writing "biased." It very specifically reflects the particularity of the threefold experience of black women. Thus while feminist thought has begun to address its "legacy of ignoring race and class issues" and black theology to correct its disregard for "gender and class," womanist theology continues its "critical perspective" on these modes of theological discourse. Womanists apply that same critical perspective to "Eurocentric discourse." "Much of what womanist thought seeks to debunk is the notion of universals and absolutes." In contrast to claims to universality, "womanist thought is intentionally and unapologetically biased." Townes calls this a bias "for a diverse and faithful community of witnesses." These witnesses work for "love and justice in the midst of oppression and fallenness." This bias thus shows that "all forms of theological discourse are open for reconsideration and critique," including womanist discourse.[53]

In other words, stated in terminology used earlier in this essay, the particularity of the womanist critique makes plain the particularity of inherited Eurocentric theology of Christendom. Then to assert the universality of that classic theology is to deny the validity of the womanist experience and perspective. The womanist critique is firmly rooted in the "African American church and its people" that it also challenges along with traditional theological discourse.[54]

Townes's book *In a Blaze of Glory* pursues this challenge as a call for justice based on the particularity of black women and the triple oppression of racism, sexism, and poverty as well as heterosexism.[55] "Womanist spirituality is embodied, personal, communal." She writes, Townes says, from the perspective of "what my life in the Black Church in the U.S. has taught me about faith—my faith. Unlike the modernist search for universal truths, I reflect from the particularity of my own faith journey." After noting the several congregations and family members who comprise that particularity, Townes concludes, "This particularity, this conscious touchstone, may well manifest dimensions of universality, but it does not exhaust it."[56]

We do not need to assess the details of Townes's critique of both male and white dominance as distinguishable but overlapping evils[57] to say this: the critique reveals the particularities of both whiteness and maleness of American society and the maleness of the African American church. The particularity of the critique is necessary because the hegemony of an imbalance of power makes the inequality appear "normal and right." Hegemony also "works to keep the dominant group in power by promoting its own worldview as neutral, universal, and moral. This works to ensure that those who do not have power see the world the way those who do have power see it."[58] Although male hegemony was the particular focus of these comments, they apply equally well to the hegemony of whiteness as neutral, as universal, and as moral. It is against these claimed neutral hegemonies that womanists are developing the concerns articulated within a theology of resistance.

I note two specific womanist comments about classic, European Christology. Kelly Brown Douglas's *The Black Christ*[59] develops a womanist perspective on Christology in conversation with the African American tradition. Douglas notes that a theology that focused on belief in the incarnation, with little attention to what Jesus did on earth, enabled slave owners to be Christian and also justify slavery. "What Jesus did on earth has little if anything to do with what it means for him to be Christ. His ministry to the poor and oppressed is virtually inconsequential to this interpretation of Christianity."[60] There were two key implications. First, little was required for salvation. One had merely to accept the belief that God had become human in Jesus. Thus "white people could be slaveholders *and* Christian without guilt or fear about the state of their souls," and blacks could be Christians without challenge to their status as slaves. Second, slavery actually served a good purpose since it "provided the opportunity for Africans to attain this salvific knowledge" about the incarnation.[61]

Douglas describes her own womanist pilgrimage with classic Nicene-Chalcedonian Christology. Womanist understandings emerge, she says, from the black tradition in which men and women "confessed Jesus as Christ because of what he did during his time as well as in their own lives. They did not make this confession because of his metaphysical make-up." Those in the slave community "were most likely unaware of the Nicene-Chalcedonian tradition," as are many African American Christians today. Douglas herself did grow up in the Episcopalian tradition and could recite the Nicene creed. She accepted it as part of the wider Christian tradition. Nevertheless, she says, the creed did not explain for her how Jesus was the Christ. "Reflective of my upbringing in the wider Black religious community, I believed that Jesus was Christ because of what he did for others, particularly the poor and oppressed." The Nicene-Chalcedonian formula is not integral to that confession, Douglas notes, and many black Christians "tend not to consider it relevant to their own beliefs about Jesus."[62]

Along with the fact that Nicene-Chalcedonian tradition does not seem relevant for many black Christians, Douglas addresses several aspects of the Nicene-Chalcedonian formulation that appear inconsistent with her reading of Jesus as presented in the Gospels. For one, by focusing on incarnation, "it diminishes the significance of Jesus' actions on earth. His ministry is virtually ignored." Further, the confession "moves directly from the act of incarnation to the crucifixion and resurrection," which implies that "what took place between Jesus' birth and resurrection—the bulk of the Gospels' reports of Jesus—is unrelated to what it means for Jesus to be the Christ." Finally, emphasizing the uniqueness of Jesus' metaphysical nature

> makes what it means to be Christ inaccessible to ordinary Christians. There becomes little reason to strive to be an example of Christ in the world, because to be Christ requires a divine incarnation, which happened only in Jesus. . . . He is seen as someone to be worshipped, believed in, but not followed or imitated.

Douglas concludes that "A womanist understanding of the Black Christ avoids these shortcomings." Nonetheless, this womanist understanding does not remove Nicene-Chalcedonian speculation from the picture. Rather,

> This formulation is seen as a part of a continuing tradition in which those who confess Jesus as Christ attempt to discern the meaning of that confession. It does not, however, have any normative significance as womanist theologians attempt to articulate Christ's meaning for the Black community.[63]

That is, womanist particularity points to the particularity of Nicaea-Chalcedon. Rather than allowing Nicaea-Chalcedon to float in an authoritative and normative status that transcends particularity, this womanist critique has made it one conversation partner among several.

Although Delores Williams's *Sisters in the Wilderness* deals primarily with atonement doctrine, she also notes the implications of a womanist critique of Nicene-Chalcedonian Christology. She expresses the concern that the discussion of Christology be more than an abstract issue debated by the academicians. Williams's comments echo Douglas's critique that the abstract categories of Nicaea and Chalcedon lend themselves to claiming Jesus while justifying oppressive acts in the name of Christ.

> Black women's question about Jesus Christ is not about the relation of his humanity to his divinity or about the relation of the historical Jesus to the Christ of faith. Black women's stories . . . [and] an Afro-centric biblical tradition . . . attest to black women's belief in Jesus/Christ/God involved in their daily affairs and supporting them. Jesus is their mother, their father, their sister and their brother. Jesus is whoever Jesus has to be to function in a supportive way in the struggle. Whether we talk about Jesus in relation to atonement theory or Christology, we womanists must be guided more by black Christian women's voices, faith and experiences than by anything that was decided centuries ago at Chalcedon.[64]

DISCUSSION

Claims by Anabaptists to absolutes and universals, or to assert the universality or generalness of a piece (such as Nicaea) of some version of a supposedly wider European theology, sound very much like reasserting the dominant theology critiqued by womanists. Asserting a universal and then attempting to show womanists how our reinterpretation of some segment of traditional European theology such as Nicaea can encompass their concerns risks dismissing the experience of black women at the hands of those whose theology we mean to rescue. Explaining to womanists that they can or should retain the traditional Christological formulations because Anabaptists have redefined them to include womanist concerns may be a higher level parallel of male Anabaptist theologians telling women to retain *man* as the generic term for all human beings because in our new theology the men have redefined man to include women. As more than one womanist implies or states, claiming to have a universal truth is a way to assert the neutrality of one's own theological bias while denying the validity of another's particular truth.

Suppose we do then bring traditional European theology (such as Nicaea-Chalcedon) down off the authoritarian pedestal of generalness and universality. Suppose we acknowledge that we cannot articulate universally recognizable absolutes and truth-claims. Does this then leave us swimming in the sea of relativity some observers so fear of postmodernity?

I think not. What we can do in the face of the pluralism of the particular truths that characterize postmodernity is to make confessional claims about a particular story that we believe has universal significance. And that particular story is the one about Jesus. This is not a redefined old universal under another name. It is not a new way to assert a universal. It is a claim about a particular event, the event of Jesus of Nazareth, when there is no external place far enough back or wide enough or high enough or general enough to adjudicate our claims objectively vis-à-vis someone else's claims about the universal significance of the Jesus event or of some other particular tradition or event. Thus the question is not whether there are universals, but rather, "How do we live in this pluralistic realm when there is no universally recognized truth-claim?"

My argument here is not original. I suggest that we return to John H. Yoder's "But We Do See Jesus."[65] In this now nearly two-decades-old essay, whose first version was the keynote address for the 1980 Bluffton College Believers Church Conference on Christology, Yoder wrote that relative relativism/pluralism is the nature of the world, but that in that pluralism, our mission is to "proclaim a Lord and invite to repentance."[66] In the heart of the essay, Yoder used five christological texts to show how New Testament writers took the story of Jesus into some new and different cosmic vision. He then employed the language and imagery of that vision to say that Jesus is both above the cosmos in charge of it and beneath it suffering in human form. For Yoder, Jesus' death and resurrection achieved a cosmic victory in which all—both New Testament writers and readers—share.[67]

But what is bothersome in the pluralistic world is that that victory, or the truth of that victory, is not fully evident. As Yoder said, "We still do not *see* that the world has been set straight. We still have no *proof* that right is right."[68] And in that case, the most profound demonstration that Jesus truly is the Lord when there is no proof, Yoder concluded, is that we would want to follow him when we do not have to. "We don't have to, as they [the disciples] didn't then."[69]

In that context, the pluralism that today we call postmodernity is an ally. We can be tactical allies with those who deconstruct "deceptive orthodox claims to logically coercive certainty" or with those who use "liberation language to dismantle the alliance of church with privilege."[70]

Yoder's more recent essay, "See How They Go with Their Face to the Sun,"[71] puts this witness to a pluralistic world in a biblical, Jewish, and early church context. The key motif for the essay comes from Jeremiah 29:7, in which the exiles are told to "seek the welfare of the city where I have sent you into exile, and pray to the Lord on its behalf, for in its welfare you will find your welfare."

In Babylon, the exiles lived without trying to take charge of the social order. Canonization was an aspect of maintaining Jewish identity in the diaspora. Stories of Joseph, Daniel and his three friends, and Esther show the risk of faithfulness to their people and to the will of God "when civil disobedience could have cost them their lives."[72] But as exiles, the Israelites also learned and worked with and became at home in the language and the culture and the skills of the host society. Even as exiles they contributed to the welfare of the host society.

It is widely recognized that for most of their early centuries Christians were pacifist. But for Yoder, this pacifism was not the result of suddenly finding a new orientation in Jesus. Rather, "the ethos of the early Christians was a direct prolongation and fulfillment of the ethos of Jewry."[73]

Jesus' impact in the first century added more and deeper authentically Jewish reasons—and reinforced and further validated the already expressed

Jewish reasons—for the already well-established ethos of not being in charge and not considering any local state structure to be the primary bearer of the movement of history. The second generation of witnesses after Jesus, the apostles, added another layer of further reasons. These were still utterly Jewish in form and substance, having to do with the Messiahship of Jesus, his lordship, and the presence of the Spirit.[74] So Yoder concluded, "Until the messianity of Jesus was replaced by that of Constantine, it was the only ethos that made sense."[75]

At no point in this trajectory from Babylon to Constantine[76] was loyalty to the culture of the people of God dependent on whether or not it made sense to the Babylonians. There was thus "no problem of shared meanings" with the hosts, since the Jews were at home in the host culture. But the Jews nonetheless maintained a "loyalty to their own culture . . . [that] was not dependent on whether the Babylonians accepted it, yet much of it was not only transparent but even attractive to Gentiles."[77] In fact, they could make it "a virtue and a cultural advantage of their being resident aliens" that they did not expend time and energy fighting over "civil sovereignty." And "since God is sovereign over history, there is no need for them to seize (or subvert) political sovereignty in order for God's will to be done."[78] Being freed of the need to control civil sovereignty also "enhanced their cultural creativity over against" the polytheistic religions of their neighbors.[79]

Thus the Jews in Babylon did not "try to bridge the distance between their language world and that of their hosts by a foundationalist mental or linguistic move, trying to rise to a higher level or dig to a deeper one" to find some common ground between Jews and Babylonians. They did not seek a common language that "would convince the Babylonians of moral monotheism without making them Jews, and to which the Jews could yield without sacrificing their local color."[80]

In other words, there were no redefinitions that both sides could accept on their own terms or steps back to discover in some wider perspective that Jews and Babylonians were after all engaged in some common task such as institution building. Yoder says, "They did not look for or seek to construct common ground. Jews knew that there was no larger world than the one their Lord had made and their prophets knew the most about." And when "Hellenism penetrated their world, they did not hesitate to affirm that whatever truth there was in Plato or Aristotle was derived from Moses,"[81] rather than discovering that Plato/Aristotle and Moses shared some heretofore unrecognized common ground.

It is this stance and status that Jesus, as a Jew, filled out, that was continued in the church as God's people by the generation of the apostles and that was eventually abandoned in the epoch of Constantine. And when the church assumed the role of managing the social order, it was a return to the policy of David, the rise of whose dynasty was "a disappointment not only to Samuel but to God."[82] In contrast, for the exiles the nonnegotiable aspect of their witness was that "there is no other God," which meant the "rejection not only of pagan cult but also of every way of putting their own YHWH/Lord in the same frame of reference with pagan deities." For Jews and others, this anti-idolatry message "was good news. It can free its hearers from slavery to the powers that crush their lives."[83]

THE LAST WORD (FOR NOW)

As a last word, but also as one of the most important aspects of this paper, I want to recall Kelly Brown Douglas's remark about the value of persons who are not black and not female interacting with womanist theology. I hope that discussion of the particularity of womanist theology has made us more aware of the great extent to which Anabaptist theology and our discussions about how potentially to graft it into Constantinian theology have been virtually void of the concerns expressed by womanists about race, gender, and class. It is not that our theology has been explicitly racist and sexist and classist—it has not. But by its silence on these issues, and by our carrying on our theologizing in terms of the traditional agenda, we demonstrate how our theology, alongside traditional European theology, can accommodate and thus dismiss these problems.

We will begin to overcome these omissions when we begin to discuss how concerns raised by African American particularity are addressed and dealt with in our theology. And I suggest that dealing with that particularity will make it more, not less, difficult for Anabaptist theology to accommodate the Constantinian theology. Dealing with that particularity will make it more evident that the agenda really does include accommodation of the sword, assumptions of white superiority, and female subordination.

The challenge of postmodernity is not whether we can figure out how to assert an absolute or a universal in the face of postmodern pluralism. I suggest that the postmodern question that confronts us is whether the particularity we identify with is Anabaptist or from the established church legacy. The challenge is whether we can find the courage to develop a theology out of Anabaptist particularity or choose to find ways and reasons to work out of Constantinian particularity.

The answers do not depend on defining an absolute or determining some place farther back from which to discover that the two are really the same. What matters is our identification with the particular story of Jesus—his life, death, and resurrection—as the most complete revelation of the people of God in the world. It is that story, in the context of the entire biblical story of God's people as resident aliens, in which our particular stories find meaning and/or prophetic critique and/or correction.

The story of God's people as resident aliens is challenged by Constantine's legacy. I suggest that our future as a peace church will be materially influenced by whether we specifically affirm Anabaptist particularity or seek ways to build bridges and find common ground with the Constantinian legacy. In a quest for the right answer, womanists may be unexpected colleagues.

NOTES

1. Gerald Schlabach, "Deuteronomic or Constantinian: What is Constantinianism the Most Basic Problem for Christian Social Ethics?" in *The Wisdom of the Cross: Essays In Honor of John Howard Yoder*, ed. Stanley Hauerwas, Chris Huebner, Harry Huebner, and Mark Nation (Grand Rapids, Mich.: Eerdmans, 1999), 449-71.

2. Thomas N. Finger, *Christian Theology: An Eschatological Approach*, vols. 1, 2 (Scottdale, Pa.: Herald Press, 1985-89); A. James Reimer, "Trinitarian Orthodoxy, Constantinianism, and Theology from a Radical Protestant Perspective," in *Faith to Creed: Ecumenical Perspectives on the Affirmation of the Apostolic Faith in the Fourth Century*, ed. S. Mark Heim (Grand Rapids, Mich.: Eerdmans, 1991), 131-40.

3. C. Arnold Snyder, "Beyond Polygenesis: Recovering the Unity and Diversity of Anabaptist Theology," in *Essays in Anabaptist Theology*, ed. H. Wayne Pipkin, Text Reader Series, no. 5 (Elkhart, Ind.: Institute of Mennonite Studies, 1994), 1-34; C. Arnold Snyder, *Anabaptist History and Theology: An Introduction* (Kitchener, Ont.: Pandora Press, 1995), 83-100.

There is a touch of irony in the fact that Harold Bender's "Anabaptist Vision" is cited both to emphasize distinctions from and agreements with magisterial Protestants. For "Anabaptist Vision," see Harold S. Bender, "The Anabaptist Vision," *Church History* 13, no. 1 (March 1944), 3-24. First presented in December 1943 as Bender's presidential address to the American Society of Church History, this essay came to define Anabaptism for the next generation of scholarship and was a powerful symbol of Mennonite identity from the 1950s until well into the 1970s.

It remains an influential Mennonite statement even in the late 1990s. A chapter of Albert N. Keim, *Harold S. Bender 1897-1962* (Scottdale, Pa.: Herald Press, 1998) analyzes the context in which "Anabaptist Vision" was originally written. Bender seemed to emphasize that although Anabaptists shared an orthodox theological core with magisterial Protestants, Anabaptists nonetheless had an ecclesiology and an ethic that clearly distinguished them. And in the years after it appeared, "Anabaptist Vision" became the mantra and the symbol of a distinct Mennonite church separated from the world.

In contrast, in spite of recent rejection of much of Bender's historical analysis, a number of modern scholars still want to quote a part of Bender's "Vision" but turned on its head. It has become useful to say that although Bender argued that Anabaptists had a distinct ecclesiology and ethic, we should follow his lead in affirming an Anabaptist commonality with the theology of the magisterial reformers. Such perceived need to find that, contrary to earlier assumptions, Anabaptists had much in common with the magisterial reformation seems to presuppose the existence of a wider or more general tradition with which Anabaptists need to be identified.

4. "Relativizing" is John H. Yoder's own term for his historical presentation of Nicene and Chalcedonian theology. See John H. Yoder, "That Household We Are" (unpublished paper, 1980). This paper was Yoder's keynote address at the Believers Church Conference on Christology, Bluffton, October, 1980, which asked whether there was or could be a specifically believers church approach to Christology. In a comment added to the paper after the conference, Yoder noted four recent developments which had made the question posed by the conference important. One was the "narrative and relativizing approach" he had "taken to the development of early Christian dogma, with special reference to the development of the christological creedal statements," in his *Preface to Theology* (see note 5).

5. John H. Yoder, *Preface to Theology: Christology and Theological Method* (Elkhart, Ind.: Goshen Biblical Seminary; distributed by Co-op Bookstore, 1981), 120-58.

6. Daniel H. Williams, "Constantine, Nicaea and the 'Fall' of the Church," in *Christian Origins: Theology, Rhetoric and Community*, ed. Lewis Ayres and Gareth Jones (London and New York: Routledge, 1998), 117-36.

7. Ibid., 122.

8. Ibid., 130.

9. Ibid.

10. Ibid., 125.

11. Ibid., 131.

12. Ibid. (emphasis Williams's).

13. Ibid.

14. The point about finding creedal terms, as well as mixed atonement metaphors, before Nicaea is also made by Thomas Finger, "Christus Victor and the Creeds: Some Historical Considerations," *The Mennonite Quarterly Review* 72, no. 1 (January 1998), 31-51.

15. Thus Williams is correct to protest as a "fantastic generalization" my now ten-year-old remark that in the post-Constantinian church, "Christians came to believe that it was more important for them to preserve the empire than to live the teachings of Jesus" (J. Denny Weaver, "Christology in Historical Perspective," in *Jesus Christ and the Mission of the Church: Contemporary Anabaptist Perspectives*, ed. Erland Waltner [Newton, Kans.: Faith and Life Press, 1990], 96). A better statement would be that there was a gradual change in how the church understood what it meant to live the teachings of Jesus. A part of the change was arriving at the idea that the important

part of following Jesus was to imitate his attitude of love; it then followed that that love could be expressed through the institutions of the social order, such as the army, which supported the political authorities who supported the church. Another part of that change was deciding that the hard sayings of Jesus were councils rather than teachings applicable to all Christians. The fact that individual writers reflect different dimensions of these developments over a period of time does not change the fact that there was an overall evolution in process.

16. Rosemary Jermann, "The Fourth-Century Cappadocian Witness," in *Faith to Creed: Ecumenical Perspectives on the Affirmation of the Apostolic Faith in the Fourth Century*, ed. S. Mark Heim (Grand Rapids, Mich.: Eerdmans, 1991), 88.

17. R. P. C. Hanson, *The Search for the Christian Doctrine of God: The Arian Controversy 318-381* (Edinburgh: T. & T. Clark, 1988), 679-86.

18. J. Nelson Kraybill recounts the story of the execution of Inca monarch Atahualpa while European conquerors recited their creed. Priests could chant the creed, Kraybill wrote, "because the creed had gutted the Gospel of its very core, removing any reference to the way Jesus actually lived." As a specific example of a creed that does not mention the way Jesus lived, Kraybill cites the Apostles' Creed, from which "the life, teaching and example of our Lord" are "missing" (Kraybill, "The Incarnation as Peacemaking Strategy," *Mission Focus* 4 [1996], 47-49, quotes 49).

19. J. Nelson Kraybill notes that "there is no need to jettison" a historic creed such as that of Nicaea. But he describes it as "technical and preoccupied with metaphysical problems such as defining what part of Jesus was man and what part was God. That issue was not the passionate concern of New Testament writers, and surely is not what grips the imagination of a broken world today" (Kraybill, "Incarnation as Peacemaking," 50).

20. It would be equally useful for Anabaptists to observe black theology's dialogue with the dominant tradition. See J. Denny Weaver, "Theology in the Mirror of the Martyred and Oppressed: Reflections on the Intersections of Yoder and Cone," in *The Wisdom of the Cross: Essays in Honor of John Howard Yoder*, ed. Stanley Hauerwas, Chris Huebner, Harry Huebner, and Mark Nation (Grand Rapids, Mich.: Eerdmans, 1999), 409-29; J. Denny Weaver, "Confessing Jesus Christ from the "Margins," *Direction* 27, no. 1 (1998), 28-40.

21. Kelly Brown Douglas, "Teaching Womanist Theology," in *Living the Intersection: Womanism and Afrocentrism in Theology*, ed. Cheryl J. Sanders (Minneapolis: Fortress Press, 1995), 150. Garth Kasimu Baker-Fletcher similarly notes that his theology "is written in a Black voice to Black folks, but ought to be seen also as part of the transgressive naughtiness that challenges all persons to partake of its particularity as a way of looking at their own cultural, religious, and racial particularities" (Baker-Fletcher, *Xodus: An African American Male Journey* [Minneapolis: Fortress Press, 1996], xiv).

22. Katie G. Cannon, *Black Womanist Ethics* (Atlanta, Ga.: Scholars Press, 1988).

23. Cannon, *Black Womanist Ethics*, 1. See also Cannon, "Moral Wisdom in the Black Women's Literary Tradition," in *Katie's Canon: Womanism and the Black Soul of the Community* (New York: Continuum, 1995), 57.

24. Cannon, *Black Womanist Ethics*, 2. See also Cannon, "Moral Wisdom," 58.
25. Cannon, *Black Womanist Ethics*, 3. See also Cannon, "Moral Wisdom," 58-59.
26. Cannon, *Black Womanist Ethics*, 3. See also Cannon, "Moral Wisdom," 59.
27. Katie Geneva Cannon, "'The Wounds of Jesus': Justification of Goodness in the Face of Manifold Evil," in *Katie's Canon*, 101-12, quote, 111. A similar perspective developed from other African American sources is in Clarice J. Martin, "Biblical Theodicy and Black Women's Spiritual Autobiography: 'The Miry Bog, the Desolate Pit, a New Song in My Mouth,'" in *A Troubling in My Soul: Womanist Perspectives on Evil and Suffering*, ed. Emilie M. Townes, Bishop Henry McNeal Turner series, vol. 8 (Maryknoll, N.Y.: Orbis, 1993), 13-36.
28. Renita J. Weems, "Reading *Her Way* Through the Struggle: African American Women and the Bible," in *Stony the Road We Trod: African American Biblical Interpretations*, ed. Cain Hope Felder (Minneapolis: Fortress Press, 1991), 60-61.
29. Ibid., 63.
30. Ibid., 64 (emphasis is Weems's).
31. Ibid., 66.
32. Ibid., 69.
33. Ibid., 74.
34. Weems, "Reading *Her Way*," 75. Vincent Wimbush noted that in the nineteenth century, African Americans began to use this reading of the exodus to counter the claims of white Americans that the Promised Land was a paradigm of the European possession of the American promised land. "African Americans pointed out that their own experience in the New World was an antitype of the ancient Hebrews' experience with respect to Palestine" (Wimbush, "The Bible and African Americans: An Outline of an Interpretative History," in *Stony the Road We Trod*, ed. Cain Hope Felder, 91).
35. Delores S. Williams, "The Color of Feminism: Or Speaking the Black Woman's Tongue," *The Journal of Religious Thought* 43, no. 1 (Spring-Summer 1986): 42-58.
36. Delores S. Williams, *Sisters in the Wilderness: The Challenge of Womanist God-Talk* (Maryknoll, N.Y.: Orbis Books, 1993).
37. Ibid., 15.
38. Ibid., 19.
39. Ibid., 5.
40. Ibid., 6.
41. Ibid., summarized in ch. 1, developed more fully in chs. 2-5.
42. Ibid., 162.
43. Ibid., 217-18.
44. Cheryl J. Sanders, ed., *Living the Intersection: Womanism and Afrocentrism in Theology* (Minneapolis: Fortress Press, 1995).
45. Jacquelyn Grant, *White Women's Christ and Black Women's Jesus: Feminist Christology and Womanist Response*, American Academy of Religion academy series, no. 64 (Atlanta: Scholars Press, 1989).
46. Jacquelyn Grant, "The Sin of Servanthood: And the Deliverance of Discipleship," in *A Troubling in My Soul*, ed. Townes, 208-09.

47. Grant, *White . . . Black*, 209.

48. Katie Geneva Cannon, "Hitting a Straight Lick with a Crooked Stick: The Womanist Dilemma in the Development of a Black Liberation Ethic," in *Katie's Canon*, 122.

49. Ibid., 123.

50. Ibid., 124.

51. Ibid.

52. Ibid., 127-28.

53. Emilie M. Townes, "Introduction: On Creating Ruminations on the Spirit," in Townes, *A Troubling in My Soul*, 2.

54. Ibid.

55. A number of womanist writers have spoken out to oppose discrimination against gays and lesbians and include heterosexism as another kind of oppression that they oppose.

56. Emilie M. Townes, *In a Blaze of Glory: Womanist Spirituality as Social Witness* (Nashville: Abingdon, 1995), 13.

57. Ibid., 68-88.

58. Ibid., 72.

59. Kelly Brown Douglas, *The Black Christ*, The Bishop Henry McNeal Turner studies in North American Black religion, no. 9 (Maryknoll, N.Y.: Orbis, 1994).

60. Ibid., 13.

61. Ibid., 13-14 (emphasis Douglas's).

62. Ibid., 111-12.

63. Ibid., 112-13.

64. Williams, *Sisters*, 203. These comments on Nicaea-Chalcedon by Kelly Brown Douglas and Delores S. Williams have their counterparts in James Cone's black theology. For example:

> What are we to make of a tradition that investigated the meaning of Jesus' relation to God and the divine and human natures in his person, but failed to relate these christological issues to the liberation of the slave and the poor in the society? . . .
>
> Few, if any, of the early Church Fathers grounded their christological arguments in the concrete history of Jesus of Nazareth. Consequently, little is said about the significance of his ministry to the poor as a definition of his person. The Nicene Fathers showed little interest in the christological significance of Jesus' deeds for the humiliated, because most of the discussion took place in the social context of the Church's position as the favored religion of the Roman State. It therefore became easy to define Jesus as the divinizer (the modern counterpart is "spiritualizer") of humanity. When this happens, Christology is removed from history, and salvation becomes only peripherally related to this world. . . .
>
> Since the Church and its bishops (during the age of Constantine and thereafter) were not slaves, it did not occur to them that God's revelation in Jesus Christ is identical with the presence of his Spirit in the slave community in struggle for the liberation of humanity. They viewed God in static terms and thus tended to

overlook the political thrust of the gospel. This procedure was consistent with the God of Plotinus but not with the God of Moses and Amos. (James H. Cone, *God of the Oppressed*, rev. ed. [Maryknoll, N.Y.: Orbis, 1997], 104, 107, 181)

65. John Howard Yoder, "'But We Do See Jesus': The Particularity of Incarnation and the Universality of Truth," in *The Priestly Kingdom: Social Ethics as Gospel* (Notre Dame, Ind.: University of Notre Dame, 1984), 46-62.

66. Ibid., 59.

67. Ibid., 53.

68. Ibid., 61 (emphasis Yoder's).

69. Ibid., 62.

70. Ibid., 61.

71. John Howard Yoder, "'See How They Go with Their Face to the Sun'," in *For the Nations: Essays Public and Evangelical* (Grand Rapids, Mich., and Cambridge, U.K.: Eerdmans, 1997), 51-78.

72. Ibid., 57.

73. Ibid., 68.

74. Ibid., 69.

75. Ibid., 70.

76. In an unpublished essay available from his webpage that summarized points from both "But We Do See Jesus" and "See How They Go," Yoder wrote, "Relative relativism/pluralism (as I said already in 'But We See Jesus') is a product of monotheistic and messianic relativizing of Caesar and of the ethnos. For other people, for Constantinians, to relativize or to admit diversity may be a dilution of one's control claims, and thereby by implication a dilution of one's truth-claims, or a loss of character but not for us" (John Howard Yoder, "Absolute Philosophical Relativism is an Oxymoron" [unpublished, John Howard Yoder webpage, 1993, Http://www.nd.edu/-theo/jhy/writings/method/relativism.htm]).

77. John Howard Yoder, "See How They Go," 72.

78. Ibid., 67.

79. Ibid., 71.

80. Ibid., 73.

81. Ibid.

82. Ibid., 60; see also 65.

83. Ibid., 76-77.

FOURTEEN

ANABAPTIST AUTONOMY, EVANGELICAL ENGULFMENT, AND MENNONITE *MESTIZAJE*: Three Postmodern Options

Douglas Jacobsen

Before launching into the main body of this essay, it is necessary for me to set this piece in two different frames of reference. The first is quite personal and relates to my own "Mennonite" identity. The second is more abstract in nature, focusing on what I understand to be the theological core of Mennonite identity.

A Personal Frame of Reference

I begin with a confession: In a certain sense and to some degree I am a Mennonite. This essay reflects my struggle to understand what that means. In the typical picture of being Mennonite, one cannot, of course, be a Mennonite "in a certain sense" or "to some degree." One either is or is not a Mennonite. But that is not true for me nor, I am quite certain, for a good number of other "Mennonites."

When I say I am a Mennonite in a certain sense and to some degree, I mean that although I do not belong to a Mennonite church, my Christian faith has been deeply molded by Mennonite experiences, ideals, ideas, and associations. This process began while I was an undergraduate trying to think my way toward a pacifist response to the Vietnam War and to war in general.[1] It continued after college when for a short time I attended and taught a Sunday school class at a Mennonite congregation in Bucks County, Pennsylvania, where a friend of mine was pastor. (I think I actually may have been more Mennonite than the minister of this church, who was at the time completing an M.Div. at Westminster Theological Seminary, known for its strongly Reformed theological orientation). My warm feelings for Mennonites were later an important part of my decision to accept a teaching post at Messiah College (founded by and still connected with the Brethren in Christ, a member denomination of the Mennonite Central Committee).

Currently my closest neighbors are all Mennonites turned Brethren in Christ (one Yoder, one Steiner, and two Martins). In good Mennonite fashion we share a driveway and own several pieces of yard equipment in common. My oldest daughter has served as a teacher in Zambia with Mennonite Central Committee. I continue to participate in a good number of Mennonite gatherings, and my name is on the list of Anabaptist-Mennonite scholars put together by the Toronto Mennonite Theology Center. Finally, at one recent academic gathering of scholars and religious leaders in Chicago I was introduced (by one who knows me well) with just one religious adjective: "Douglas Jacobsen, Mennonite." In short, I can call myself a Mennonite of some kind and other people seem to recognize some validity to the claim.

But there is countervailing evidence you also need to know—parts of my personal profile that look non-Mennonite. For example, I was nurtured into Christian faith in the context of the Evangelical Free Church, a rather exemplary "evangelical" denomination, and I am currently a member of the United Church of Christ, typically described as the most liberal denomination in America. I was raised in and around New York City, not on a farm in Pennsylvania, Ohio, or Kansas. My father was a Marine who served in the Pacific theater during World War II. In terms of ethnic heritage, I am of Norwegian descent, not Swiss, German, Dutch, or Russian.

I graduated from Wheaton College (Ill.), and I co-chair the Evangelical Theology Group of the American Academy of Religion—two involvements that give me good evangelical but not necessarily Mennonite credentials. I hang out with Pentecostals and am currently completing a book on the history of Pentecostal theology. I feel more at home in African American worship than perhaps any other churchly setting. Like many persons of my generation, I almost became a Catholic after reading Thomas Merton; I still find the Catholic vision of faith attractive. I am also a committed ecumenist, holding in high regard the work of the National and World Councils of Churches. All in all, these parts of who I am do not look very Mennonite, at least not at first glance.

Overall, I rank "Mennonitism" as one of the most significant influences in my Christian faith and life. But having said that, I must add that probably no Christian dimension of who I am (even the Mennonite one) can claim a controlling market share of my religious soul. Obviously I have a somewhat difficult time describing my particular Christian identity with any simple single-word label. The more pertinent question, however, is whether or not the polyglot Christian profile I have just described can legitimately be called "Mennonite."

In this chapter I argue that this question ought to be answered in the affirmative. In the postmodern world in which we now live, the multi-breed form of Christian faith I have just described is becoming, and will become, more and more the norm. Persons in the traditional Mennonite circles of church and family are discovering every day that they are also attracted to ideas and ideals from outside that world. At the same time, more and more people from outside the old Mennonite social networks are becoming attracted to various Mennonite beliefs and practices. These folks do not necessarily feel any great inclination formally to become Mennonites, but they know they are Mennonite in some way nonetheless.

THE THEOLOGICAL CORE OF MENNONITE IDENTITY

What exactly does it mean to be Mennonite? I see being Mennonite as a certain way of being Christian—a certain way of understanding the gospel and responding to it. Being a Mennonite Christian is one way among several ways of being Christian. It is one species of Christian faith among others like, for example, Catholic monastic faith, or feminist Protestant faith, or Pentecostal "Jesus only" faith, or Missouri Synod Lutheran faith.

If it is relatively easy to distinguish between these different kinds of Christian faith, it is much less easy to know comparatively and qualitatively how to evaluate these differences. To ask that kind of comparative-quality question may, in fact, be to traffic in near meaninglessness. It seems akin to asking which is the better language: English, Chinese, or Zulu? How would one even begin to answer that question?

Perhaps the best we can do now is be clear about what we ourselves mean when we use certain adjectives to describe our faith, then to seek to demonstrate the validity of our understanding of the gospel by the way we live. The purpose is not somehow to prove our own religion to be better than another's, but to try to be faithful disciples of Jesus with eyes open to how we and others actually practice our faith (knowing all the while that our own individual visions of faith are both flawed and insightful in numerous ways).

At the heart of the Mennonite species of faith, as I see it, is an understanding of the gospel as an intimately connected double act of reconciliation: reconciliation of humans with God and reconciliation of people, estranged from each other by sin and wounds of sin, with each other. Neither aspect of this double reconciliation takes precedence; rather, each enables and requires the other. I see this vision of Christian faith as "simply what the gospel is all about." I *feel* it as the core of the gospel. I am convinced this is the bedrock foundation of the gospel.

As soon as I say that, however, I have to add that I may be wrong. I know others feel strongly that the core of the gospel needs to be expressed in different terms (for example, in terms of justice, or holiness, or mystical union with God). I can understand some of those different visions of Christian faith and can respect them. What is more, I have learned much from them. But, try as I might, I simply cannot make myself believe that any other vision of Christian faith articulates the core of the gospel as well as the Mennonite vision of Christian faith outlined above. It is because I feel this way that I want to be able to call myself a Mennonite in a certain sense and to some degree. But not just my theological identity is at stake here. I think the core reconciliatory vision of Mennonite Christianity ought to move Mennonites who locate themselves more fully "in" the movement to develop a more expansive understanding of Mennonite identity.

Having made that appeal, however, I immediately admit that not all "Mennonites" (understood either in terms of "birthright" membership in the movement or in terms of current institutional affiliation with a Mennonite church/congregation) would necessarily agree with my vision of what it means to understand the gospel in a Mennonite way. There are, in fact, numerous ways to parse Mennonite faith. Because this is the case, the proposal put forth here needs to be situated somewhere on the larger map of Mennonite theological options.

SITUATING MY ARGUMENT

Mennonites in North America have always had a number of identity options. There have been Old Order and more progressive options. There have been Swiss and Dutch/Russian options. There have been Pennsylvania options and Canadian, Midwestern, and California alternatives. I think as well of Gordon Kauffman's humanistic (a-theistic?) Mennonitism and of James Reimer's catholic/orthodox Mennonitism. I would add the Wesleyan/Pietistic Mennonitism of the Brethren in Christ to the mix. The list could be extended.

Of late, however, the simplifying mechanisms of North American culture and scholarship have tended to focus attention more and more on only two options. These two will serve as my points of reference in this chapter. They are the *evangelical* Mennonite option and the *Anabaptist* Mennonite option. There are undoubtedly numerous reasons for the contemporary prominence of these two options (and some are discussed below). My problem, however, is that neither option seems especially well-fitted to preserve and articulate the reconciliatory themes that I see as central to Mennonite theology. Both seem too prone to separate people from each other—too ready to draw clear and distinct boundaries around the community of faith in distinction to everyone else.

This essay accordingly explores a different vision of what it might mean to be a Mennonite Christian and especially to be a reconciliatory Mennonite in a pluralistic, ecumenical, postmodern world. I will call this model "Mennonite *mestizaje*." *Mestizaje* is a Spanish word describing the mixing of people groups. The term *mestizo* is used to refer to a person with "mixed" racial heritage. My focus will be on what Mennonite identity can and should mean given the mixed/mestizaje character of Christian faith in contemporary postmodern America. America's mixed/mestizaje Christian faith is evident in the general religious culture of the nation, it is reflected in almost all of the nation's varied ecclesial communions, and it is present in the individual lives of most American Christians (especially those under the age of, say, thirty-five).

My suggestion is that many older Mennonite theological categories are not fully adequate to grasp this mestizaje reality. In particular, new understandings of church community and Christian ethics will need to be developed in the emerging mestizo vision of Mennonitism. Mestizo Mennonites may well find the Hispanic theological images of the church as people on pilgrimage (*romeria*) or as an extended family more helpful than images of church as separate exemplary community or as fervent evangelistic organization.

Regarding ethics, practices of compassion and forgiveness might actually prove more fruitful starting points for mestizo Mennonites than either head-on crusades for justice and peace or the strident moralisms of the Religious Right. Peace, justice, exemplary living, and evangelistic activity ought never to be denied or pushed to the side of Mennonite life, but the ways we express those concerns in the postmodern era will need to be reconceptualized. Obviously this essay will be able to sketch these themes only in outline form.

TWO MODERN MENNONITE OPTIONS:
ANABAPTIST AUTONOMY AND EVANGELICAL ENGULFMENT

Throughout the twentieth century (and even earlier) Anabaptist and evangelical themes, along with various other ideas and ideals, have been blended and contrasted in the Mennonite world. The terms *Anabaptist* and *evangelical* each have positive and negative connotations. Positively, Anabaptism stands for communal discipleship, faithfulness to the gospel commandments, peaceableness, and service. Negatively, it stands for a two-kingdom theology that sets the church against the world, for sometimes encouraging a stifling "humility," and for the sundry forms of oppression that derive from the inability or unwillingness of Anabaptists to admit their own deeply seated longings for power.

Positively, Evangelicalism stands for the experience of conversion (or new birth), heartfelt faith in Jesus, devout Bible study, and evangelism. Negatively, Evangelicalism stands for antimodernism, strident conservatism in politics, and an often egocentric individualism in faith. Focusing on the positive, many of the leading figures of American Mennonite history from John S. Coffman to Daniel Kauffman to Harold S. Bender (to trace a male-leader lineage through only one denomination) have tried with varying degrees of success to blend the best virtues of these two forms of faith in their own Mennonite worldviews. When the negative dimensions of these two orientations of faith have come to the fore, conflict has been the more frequent result.

One of the more interesting recent discussions of these two options is found in the work of J. Howard Kauffman and Leo Driedger. They describe Anabaptist Mennonitism in terms of "peacemaking, in-group identity, communalism, service to others, and less evidence of individualism." By contrast, they see evangelical Anabaptism (which they label "fundamentalist") as "much more conservative in doctrine, less accepting of equality between males and females and less open to other groups."

Kauffman and Driedger suggest that these two orientations of Mennonite faith have in recent years become more divergent and more contradictory. They thus conclude their study, *The Mennonite Mosaic*, by saying that "the tensions among Mennonites are . . . between two theologies—the original Anabaptist heritage and recent fundamentalism [e.g., evangelicalism] . . . two theologies that are contrasting, if not polar."²

Rather than pitting the strengths of one orientation against the strengths of the other, Kauffman and Driedger tend to line up Anabaptist strengths against evangelical weaknesses; they stack their academic deck against the evangelical vision. Although such an unbalanced presentation is in a certain sense unfair, Kauffman and Driedger seem more or less forced to this conclusion by their driving concern that Mennonitism continue to exist as a separate and distinct American community of faith. In my terms, they favor Anabaptist autonomy over what they fear would be an evangelical engulfment and resultant loss of identity.

Although on a certain level I dislike the unfairness of their comparison between Anabaptist Mennonitism and evangelical/fundamentalist Mennonitism, on another level I agree with Kauffman and Driedger's basic conclusion. I do so for the following reasons. Throughout this century the term *Anabaptist* (somewhat apart from any specific theological content) has been used by American Mennonites to identify themselves in terms of their historic in-group identity.

The term *evangelical*, on the other hand (and again largely apart from any specific theological affirmations), has been used by Mennonites to locate themselves on the larger map of religious faith in America. This has been necessary partly because most Americans have no idea what Anabaptism is. Used sociologically in this way, the term Anabaptist has had much more power to maintain a distinctive sense of Mennonite identity than has the term evangelical. This is because the use of the label evangelical tends to blend Mennonites into a larger homogenized religious category where their particular and distinctive orientations of faith are easily obscured.

Nonetheless, there is a downside to viewing Mennonitism exclusively in terms of Anabaptist autonomy. For Mennonites to call themselves Anabaptist as opposed to evangelical runs the risk of obscuring the numerous evangelical dimensions of historic Mennonite faith, including emphases on conversion, individual piety, and Bible-centeredness. What is more, Anabaptist Mennonitism as articulated by some scholars and activist leaders often bears strikingly little resemblance to the life and faith of Mennonite people sitting in the pews.

In ways I cannot address in full detail here, I think these two Mennonite options represent complex ways of adjusting to and resisting the structures of modernity. And one perspective they share along these lines is a heightened sense of the need for sharper, clearer communal boundaries as each Mennonite submovement has perceived the modern world to be "invading" its community. It has been precisely this heightened sense of need for clear social boundaries (reinforced by modern bipolar rationality) that has pushed so many Mennonites toward Evangelicalism while others have moved to reaffirm their Anabaptist identity.

Let me use Kauffman and Driedger's terms (which they borrow from Peter Berger) to explain the migration of some Mennonites toward Evangelicalism. These folks were worried that the Anabaptist Mennonite "sacred canopy" which formerly had protected them from the dangers of the outside world was simply no longer strong enough to survive the continuing assaults of modernity. Accordingly, they sought what they thought was a larger, more durable canopy under which to gather. The evangelical canopy seemed custom-cut for that purpose. They hoped for strength in numbers, and evangelicals seem to have the numbers on their side.

The cost of coming under the protection of the evangelical canopy was, of course, that they become evangelical Mennonites, and that involved a certain muting of Mennonitism's strange Anabaptist heritage. But these folks may have gotten more than they bargained for. When a group as small as the Mennonites enters an alliance as numerically lopsided as this one was, it is almost inevitable that the smaller movement will tend to be overwhelmed by the larger. That has been the case here. In the name of preserving Mennonite identity, numerous Mennonite distinctives have been lost in the evangelicalized Mennonite population. Kauffman and Driedger are correct: Evangelicalism as a Mennonite option tends to lead toward evangelical engulfment and hence toward weakening of the Mennonite community.

The primary alternative being offered—Anabaptist autonomy—has its own problems, however. The goal of this perspective is to preserve the distinctive heritage of the Mennonite tradition in a modern situation where such particularity is neither valued nor endorsed by the larger culture. Anabaptist Mennonites have accordingly tried to structure their separate identity around certain Anabaptist virtues and values that can be expressed in shorthand forms that are understandable by modern people—ideals such as peace, service, simple living, being "prophetic," etc.

This is a positive agenda, but it has two problems. First, this reformulation of Anabaptist identity subtly transforms older Anabaptist ways of life and faith from the idiomatic to the ideological. Second, and more to the point here, such an objective listing of characteristics and ideals begs the question of communal coherence. Many observers, Kauffman and Driedger among them, argue that Anabaptist values can only be maintained in the context of a newly invigorated sense of Mennonite community. A renewed "sense of peoplehood," they say, is the necessary social container for maintaining Anabaptist virtues and values.

This call for a strengthened sense of peoplehood, however, raises all sorts of questions about the mixed legacy of Mennonite ethnicity. I understand that a renewed Anabaptist vision of Mennonite peoplehood is not precisely the same thing as old-fashioned Swiss/Dutch/Russian Mennonite ethnicity. However, there is another sense in which a renewed emphasis on Mennonite peoplehood can create (and has to a degree already created) a new "spiritual" sense of in-group identity that can feel almost as off-putting to Mennonite "outsiders" as the barriers of older national/traditional forms of ethnicity. This raises the question: Can the Mennonite message of a universally reconciling gospel ever adequately be housed in the confines of an exclusivistic sense of Christian peoplehood?

Both these positions, the evangelical and the Anabaptist, have discovered of late that the ground under their strategic and analytic theological feet is moving. The modern age is ending, and a new, more fluid social and epistemological era is coming into being. Since recent reformulations of both Anabaptist Mennonitism and evangelical Mennonitism seem so wedded to modern/antimodern ways of thought and action, does this shifting of social and cultural realities mean an end to these perspectives?

I think not. First of all, the boundary line between modernity and postmodernity is actually often less clear than many people think. In particular, many modern/antimodern positions have shown a remarkable ability to interpret postmodern developments as extensions of certain paradigmatically modern ways of thinking and being. They see postmodernity as a radicalized form of modernity. To the degree that either Anabaptist or evangelical Mennonitism can uphold such an interpretation of contemporary developments, they will easily be able to translate their modern/antimodern sentiments into postmodern/antipostmodern sentiments and survive intact for some time to come. Some other Anabaptist and evangelical Mennonites will welcome postmodernity because they think it will be more friendly to their own particularities (more on this below).

In either case, the Anabaptist and evangelical options will remain open to Mennonites in the postmodern era. Nonetheless, I predict that numerous Mennonites will find the move to postmodernity disruptive. For these folks both the Anabaptist and the evangelical models of Mennonitism are already ringing hollow in the face of emerging postmodern realities.

POSTMODERN FAITH

Some people talk of the postmodern world as if it is a place where the particularities of communal existence denigrated in the modern era can now flourish again. Based on this vision, some Anabaptist Mennonites and evangelical Mennonites have welcomed postmodernity as an affirmation of their own particularity.

My hunch, however, is that this neat and easy vision of postmodern pluralism is mistaken. The postmodern world does affirm plurality and particularity in ways that modernity did not, but this is not a safe, mosaic-like pluralism. Instead, the pluralism of the postmodern world is fluid and porous. Particular groups may find it even harder to maintain the specificity of their identities in that context than in the older world of modernity. The postmodern world is a mixed-up/mestizaje reality, or, to use yet one more metaphor, it is at best a world of fuzzy particularity.

The fuzziness of postmodern social geography as it applies to religious groups is nowhere more evident than in the changing realities of denominational life in America. It used to be that when a local congregation bore the name of a certain denomination, this implied that that congregation was the local embodiment of a shared denominational vision of Christian faith. One can no longer, however, assume any such uniformity in denominations (or, for that matter, in local congregations which often exist as loose associations of various smaller subgroups). Denominational faith has become fuzzy both on the inside and the outside. Inside most denominations the ideas and ideals that once defined the core identities of these church bodies are no longer so neat and focused. In a similar way, the boundary lines that formerly separated one denomination from another now often seem smudged, or even erased.

A similar process of "fuzzification" also seems to be at work in the realm of individual faith. There was a time when different people knew that they were Lutheran, or Presbyterian, or Pentecostal, or Mennonite. But that is not always the case today. Many contemporary American Christians want to be known simply as "Christians." What is more, they positively dislike the notion that they or others should be able neatly to describe their faith with one unambiguous label. In terms of their churchly practice, many of these folks affiliate with several congregations and/or with a variety of Christian parachurch groups or small-group gatherings.[3]

None of this is foreign to the Mennonite world. Most Mennonite denominations are seeing the sharper edges of their identities sanded off while they watch. At the same time the internal theological diversity of Mennonite denominations tends to be on the rise as formerly external ideas and practices (from Reformed theology to charismatic worship) make their way into the Mennonite community. What is more, Mennonite believers, like many other North American Christians, often find themselves increasingly associating with different types of Christians in different kinds of settings for different purposes. Finally, Mennonite church members, again like everyone else, now increasingly split up their religious tithes and donations between their own local congregation and various other Mennonite and non-Mennonite ministries and parachurch organizations.

To make the picture even more complex, ideas and practices from within the Mennonite world are now also spreading out from Mennonitism into other churches and Christian groups. At the very least, Mennonitish ideas and ideals seem to be springing up all over, whether or not all of those developments can directly be derived from Mennonite sources.

Paul Toews had originally, I believe, intended to include this phenomenon in his *Mennonites in American Society, 1930-1970* in a final section of the book devoted to the Mennonite "diaspora" of ideas and practices into other settings.[4] Toews did not finally include a discussion of this diaspora in the volume, but the diaspora has taken place nonetheless. Along these lines, for example, I think of the writings of Stanley Hauerwas, Walter Brueggemann, Walter Wink, Nancey Murphy, and Miroslav Volf.[5] Whereas some Mennonites have enjoyed this flattery of imitation, the diaspora of Mennonite ideas and ideals has in another way made their identity struggle as a community all the more difficult. Now some of their most cherished "distinctives" are no longer all that helpful in setting Mennonites apart from other Christians.

My basic factual point is that in the postmodern world almost all religious identities seem to become fuzzy over time. In terms of their religious identity, I thus suggest that Mennonites need both to accept religious fuzziness as a fact and begin to reflect on how best to cope with, celebrate, and manage that fuzziness. Mennonites must embrace the internal diversity and external expansion of their movement and figure out what their new role can be in this fuzzy situation.

What I see needing to take place is a conceptual transition not unlike that which has occurred in the study of Mennonite history. As Mennonite historiography has moved from a theory of monogenesis to one of polygenesis, Mennonite leaders must now leave behind older monomorphic visions of what a renewed Mennonite identity can and should look like and work to develop new polymorphic visions of and for the future of Mennonite existence. In making this transition toward a polymorphic, mixed, mestizo Mennonitism, I think Mennonites will find conversation with Latino theologians crucial, since this group of Christians has struggled with a postmodern-like fuzziness of identity for many years.

Mestizaje Faith

I am borrowing the term *mestizaje* from Latino theology, particularly the writings of Arturo Bañuelas and Virgil Elizondo.[6] Literally, mestizaje means "mixed." Elizondo says that mestizaje is on one level "simply the mixture of human groups of different makeup." But mestizaje has at least two different levels of significance: the biological and the cultural. Elizondo says that "Biologically speaking mestizaje appears to be quite easy and natural, but culturally it is usually feared and threatening."[7]

As used by Hispanic people, mestizaje has a specific reference as well. The term describes Hispanic identity as formed through the mixing of Spanish/European, Amerindian, and African blood and cultures. This particular mixing of peoples was brought about through the violence of conquest and slavery, and that violence produced a mestizo community situated between the conquerors and the conquered, fitting neatly into neither of the "pure" communities that preceded it.

For Elizondo and other Hispanic theologians, mestizaje has become "a locus of theological reflection." Arturo Bañuelas says it is the "core paradigm" for Latino theology because it describes the irreducible foundation of mestizo existence.[8] Unlike the long tradition of Euroamerican Christianity, where theology has been housed in the academy, Hispanic Christians locate theology (much like historic Mennonitism) in the context of everyday life. In the words of Ada María Isasi-Diaz, Latino theology is "a community theology."[9] Elizondo says Latino theology "is a joint enterprise of the believing community, which is seeking the meaning of its faith and the direction of its journey of hope lived in the context of charity."[10]

Whereas a general conclusion can be drawn here—that theology ought to be connected to life—the Hispanic Christian community has come to a more specific conclusion as well. Bañuelas writes, "Latino theology is attempting to elaborate the link between mestizaje and God's design for humanity."[11] Elizondo is even more precise: "As a Mexican-American Christian, I am convinced that the full potential of mestizaje will be actualized only in and through the way of the Lord which brings order out of chaos and new life out of death."¹² He adds that there will be certain temptations and challenges mestizo Christians must face along the way:

> The way of Jesus to Jerusalem and the cross is the challenging task of those who are on the margins of society. Their temptation will always be to become simply the powerful themselves, as even the disciples wanted to do. But the challenge is to be willing to die so that a new way will truly be ushered in . . . God's love in and through Jesus triumphs over all the divisive hatreds and consequent violence of humanity. Jesus passes through death to life. . . . In the resurrection, God ratifies the entire way and message of Jesus.¹³

Here the specificity of Latino theology flowers into the universal message of Jesus expressed with an almost Mennonitish accent. Can Latino/mestizo Christian faith supply the Mennonite world with other images and symbols Mennonites might find helpful in their own mestizaje? I think so.

NEW IMAGES OF CHURCH FOR MENNONITE MESTIZAJE

Ecclesiology, the theology of the church, has always been central to Mennonite theology. I assume it will continue to be a central concern. Let me briefly then share images of church taken from a Hispanic context and explore their Mennonite potential. Our guide here will be Justo L. González, the well-known Cuban-American church historian and theologian. Though developed in the context of Latino mestizaje, the images he invokes can easily be adapted for use by other Christian communities in our fuzzy postmodern context.

One of the most attractive images of church that González develops is that of the church as *romería*. He writes that

> A *romería* is a combination of religious pilgrimage, community picnic, and open invitation to a festival. As the people march in *romería* toward a shrine, they stop along the way to invite others to join. A *romería* is not like an army on the march, with its sharply defined and closed ranks. It is more like a snowball rolling down a mountain, gathering more and more snow as it gathers speed. People are invited to join, in part because there is food at the end, but also because there is fun and companionship along the way . . . It is marching joyfully toward a promised future, but along the way it invites others to join the march to the fiesta, and even to have a little glimpse of the great fiesta while still along the way.¹⁴

Family is another image of church we can glean from González— Hispanic understanding of family. The Hispanic family is a much more "extended" social unit than the typical Anglo family. Using the Hispanic model as our guide, rather than the restricted nuclear model popular in the American Anglo population, we can reconceive the church as an ever-enlarging and more complex web of connections between people seeking to follow the gospel in some way or another. As González says,

> What we mean by "family" in the Latino tradition is different from what is meant by those who today in this country speak of "family values." To them, a 'family' is a tightly knit and easily definable social unit, usually living under the same roof, and composed of parents and children. . . . . When we speak of 'family' we mean a much wider group of people, of uncertain and ever expanding limits, that includes parents as well as aunts and uncles, nephews and nieces, cousins to various degrees, relatives by marriage, relatives of relatives by marriage, relatives by baptism (godparents, for example, and the relationship, unknown in the English-speaking world, of *compadres* and *comadres*), and a host of other possibilities.

González emphasizes that

> Such extended families are also interwoven, so that it is virtually impossible to belong to only one family. . . . The church as the extended family of God means that its limits are impossible to define. All who belong to God are part of this family. Some may be more distant cousins—even people whom I have difficulty understanding—but they are still part of the same family. This means that individuals and congregations must recognize each other as relatives, even though they differ in matters of practice, doctrine or culture—a shocking fact for many from the dominant culture who suddenly find themselves considered brothers or sisters of persons whom they were taught to discount.[15]

González's last discussion of the church focuses on its "catholic" identity. He contrasts the necessary catholicity of the church with the more wooden notions of unity and universality. "We know," he explains,

> that the church is not, and should never be, universal. It is not universal, not because of some lack of geographical expansion, or because some do not accept its authority. It is not universal by its very nature because it is catholic! It is not universal because it must accept into its fold many people from many tribes, languages and nations, and accept them in such a way that they each and all contribute to the whole.[16]

What holds this motley crew of disciples together for González is not some abstract commitment to unity or some neatly defined formula that defines the church's unity; it is the shared mission of the church to help see the kingdom of God established on earth. That kingdom is partly exemplified in the church, but it also extends to include all of God's overt and covert work of redemption in the world.

What this mestizo vision of the church can contribute to Mennonite consciousness is a new sense of subtlety to older Mennonite ecclesiology. In González's view, the boundary line between church and world is fuzzy, for God's activity in the world is not limited to the church alone. But this does not mean that the line between church and world is entirely obliterated (as is the case in some "liberal" ecclesiologies). The church, functioning at its best, remains the most obvious hot spot of God's actions in the world. Members of that body (even if membership cannot be as neatly defined as in the past) have certain responsibilities to live on a higher moral and religious plane than the rest of the world.

But the church must never be simply identified as the kingdom of God. The church is part of the kingdom; it is not the kingdom in its entirety, since God's active love functions elsewhere in the world. As such the church will be a community, but it must be a fluidly bounded community organized amid the world as opposed to being a precisely bounded community organized in contrast to the world. Such a vision of the church is currently present in Mennonite circles, but it needs to be enhanced and extended.

Perhaps the most difficult adjustment in ecclesiology that needs to take place in the Mennonite mestizaje is one of disposition rather than one of vision *per se*. At the core of González's description of the church is a deep sense of joy and celebration. My impression of Mennonite ecclesial practice is that it is more often motivated by a sense of duty than by an exuberance of joy. Can the Mennonite family of faith learn how to party with God and all others whom God loves? I think that such a shift is necessary in the postmodern context (while maintaining and even deepening our ability to sorrow with all those who sorrow). My hunch here is that such joy will only come through a new and renewed sense of forgiveness in the Mennonite community such as that discussed below.

Mennonite Mestizo Ethics

What kind of Christian ethic is appropriate for this fuzzy/mestizo vision of Mennonite faith where even the very line between church and world, a line that has been so important for Mennonites, is itself smudged? On this issue, rather than turning once again to Latino theology, let us look to a different source and examine the ideas of two "mainstream" scholars.

They have imbibed a good bit from the Mennonite diaspora of ideas and ideals mentioned above and also understand the mixed-up-ness of the postmodern world: Marcus Borg and Stanley Hauerwas.

In the third chapter of his interesting (though somewhat unorthodox) book, *Meeting Jesus Again for the First Time*, Marcus Borg sums up the message of Jesus by quoting the single verse Luke 6:36, which he translates as "Be compassionate as God is compassionate." Borg goes on to explain that

> The Hebrew word for "compassion" whose singular form means "womb" is often used of God in the Old Testament.... To say that God is compassionate is to say that God is "like a womb," is "womblike," or to coin a term that captures the flavor of the original Hebrew, "wombish." What does it suggest to say that God is like a womb? ... Like a womb, God is the one who gives birth to us—the mother who gives birth to us. As a mother loves the children of her womb and feels for the children of her womb, so God loves us and feels for us, for all of her children.[17]

Compassion is not, however, only a characteristic of God's being. It is part of God's command concerning how we are to live. Borg writes that "to 'be compassionate as God is compassionate' is to be like a womb as God is like a womb. It is to feel as God feels and to act as God acts: in a life-giving and nourishing way." Rather than being a safe ethic of caring, the call to live compassionately in first-century Palestine was a political act because it necessarily challenged the dominant ethical model based on purity.

As Borg says, "To put it boldly: compassion for Jesus was political. He directly and repeatedly challenged the dominant sociopolitical paradigm of his social world and advocated instead what might be called *a politics of compassion*." Continuing, Borg stresses that

> It is in the context of a purity system that created a world with sharp social boundaries between pure and impure, righteous and sinner, whole and not whole, male and female, rich and poor, Jew and Gentile, that we can see the sociopolitical significance of compassion. In the message and activity of Jesus, we see an alternative social vision: a community shaped not by the ethos and politics of purity, but by the ethos and politics of compassion.

Borg sums up, "In short, there is something boundary shattering about the *imitatio dei* that stood at the center of Jesus' message and activity: 'Be compassionate as God is compassionate.' Whereas purity divides and excludes, compassion unites and includes."[18]

Borg's presentation of Jesus' "politics of compassion" seems ready-made for a mestizo Mennonite vision of Christian faith and the world.

Compassion implies or assumes commitment to peaceful, just relations. How can one be like a womb to others if one is killing them or robbing them of the physical nourishment or material goods they deserve?

Compassion requires more, however. It requires a subjective commitment to others that goes beyond the more objective connotations of peace and justice. Compassion requires face-to-face relations with others and, in serving others, real compassion dissolves the aura of self-congratulatory *noblesse oblige* that can adhere so easily, if unintentionally, to every act of "service" that we render to those we deem less fortunate than ourselves.

Understood in Borg's terms, compassion recognizes and embraces the mixed, impure world of mestizaje. In fact, in mestizaje everyone is understood to be an impure half-breed, that the special worth of each human being as part of God's creation can most easily be discovered and affirmed.

If the politics of compassion can help us define the external ethic of a mestizo church, what should its internal ethic look like? The traditional Anabaptist and evangelical Mennonite answers have been that the church should be the pure community, a model, harbinger, and present embodiment of the coming kingdom of God. But if, as Borg suggests, we should come to see purity itself as a moral problem, where can we turn to discover an alternative moral ideal for the structuring of the community of faith?

Stanley Hauerwas has suggested that the proper place to turn is to forgiveness. In *The Peaceable Kingdom*, Hauerwas argues that forgiveness is the heart of the gospel. Who could deny this? Clearly, our salvation is based first and foremost on the fact that in Christ God has forgiven us. Just as clearly, however, our own forgiveness is somehow connected to our willingness to forgive others, as the Lord's prayer says, "Forgive us our trespasses as we forgive those who trespass against us." In forgiveness, salvation and the ethics of the redeemed community are forged into one.

It is that connection that Hauerwas explores, writing that

> We must remember that our first task is not to forgive, but to learn to be forgiven. Too often to be ready to forgive is a way of exerting control over another. We fear accepting forgiveness from another because such a gift makes us powerless—and we fear the loss of control involved. . . . It is true, of course, that in a sense to be a 'forgiven people' makes us lose control. To be forgiven means that I must face the fact that my life actually lies in the hands of others. I must learn to trust them as I have learned to trust God.[19]

Hauerwas goes on to assert that it is only when we have truly experienced what it means to be forgiven that we can begin to understand God's command to love others. Here he echoes Borg's concern about the tension between purity and compassion. Hauerwas proposes that

> This love that is characteristic of God's kingdom is possible only for a forgiven people—a people who have learned not to fear one another. For love is the nonviolent apprehension of the other as other. But to see the other as other is frightening, because to the extent others are others they challenge my way of being. Only when my self—my character—has been formed by God's love, do I know I have no reason to fear the other.

"Moreover," Hauerwas adds,

> we must be a people who have hospitable selves—we must be ready to be stretched by what we know not. Friendship becomes our way of life as we learn to rejoice in the presence of others. Thus Jesus' kingdom is one that requires commitment to friends, for without them the journey that is the kingdom is impossible. We can only know where we walk as we walk with others.[20]

Here we find a new and viable communal ethic for the Mennonite mestizaje. The goal of purity construed as moral perfection is rejected. What we are left with instead is the mutuality of forgiveness. Is this a license to tolerate sin? Of course not. Rather, it is a blunt recognition of our own continuing lack of perfection and an admission of our own need to rely on the good graces of those around us as we seek to mature in love.

I have situated Hauerwas's discussion of forgiveness under the rubric of the inner ethic of the Christian community, but, as with Borg's discussion of compassion, Hauerwas's discussion of forgiveness inevitably blurs the line between insider and outsider. It does so, however, while simultaneously reaffirming a sense of peoplehood that is distinguished from the world in general. This is precisely the kind of ethic that is called for in Mennonite mestizaje: a blurred and impure sense of peoplehood that does not mistake its own national or spiritual ethnicity for the kingdom of God itself yet truly does bind people to each other.

Could such a model ever be adopted as the working practice of the Mennonite community in its core constituency and in its diaspora? I actually think it could be adopted, largely because these themes are, in fact, part and parcel of the broader Mennonite tradition. I recall hearing Ernest Boyer Jr., former Secretary of Education and late president of the Carnegie Foundation for the Advancement of Education, who was raised in the Brethren in Christ Church, recount his experience of joining that church. He said he was asked only two questions: "Will you forgive a member of this community if someone asks you to forgive them, and will you ask forgiveness of others in this community when you need their forgiveness?" Boyer said that when he had answered each of these questions in the affirmative, he was admitted into membership in the church.[21]

The intention of the Brethren in Christ church was, in this case, to identify forgiveness as one of the internal marks of their own separate Christian community. But it is difficult to imagine that one who had truly learned to forgive others in this way could sharply curtail the practice at the social boundaries of his or her particular community. The Christian practice of forgiveness, it seems to me, must inevitably seep out to include those beyond the pall of one's own community and even those "outside" the church altogether. As that occurs, forgiveness can become one of the "foods" attracting others to the Mennonite romeria of faith which is slowly and falteringly making its way toward the fullness of the kingdom of God.

Such are the ethics of Mennonite mestizaje. We have not arrived. We are not the full embodiment of "kingdom ethics." But we do find ourselves, in the presence of many others, being willingly lured forward into the peaceable kingdom that God is, in God's own ways, bringing into being.

Conclusion

In conclusion, I return to my original question: Can I validly call myself a Mennonite, and will "real" Mennonites accept that claim? I hope so, for what lies behind that question is the much larger issue of whether the Mennonite movement will be able to open itself in the years ahead to become a postmodern fuzzy, mestizo form of faith. Such fuzziness is neither mindless eclecticism nor everything-goes relativism. It represents instead a realistic appreciation of the particular vision of the gospel cherished by the historic Mennonite community and an admission that that vision is socially "contained" (though the gospel can never really be contained) in a broken vessel. A mestizo vision of Mennonite faith will recognize that the "leakage" around the Mennonite pot is as much a part of the movement as the diverse fluids still remaining inside that old jug of faith.

A new mestizo Mennonitism will, of course, not be without its own struggles to remain faithful to the reconciliatory gospel of Jesus. The postmodern world does represent a place where "erring" may be celebrated too easily and where the meaning of discipline may be identified too quickly with authority and oppression. Although Mennonites must guard their communities against these postmodern dangers, the proper response is not to lock themselves ever more tightly into the options and oppositions currently available to them. Instead, my hope is that a renewed focus on

Christian practices like compassion and forgiveness (among other biblical virtues) will open pathways that cannot yet be seen toward new forms of community that cannot yet be imagined.

We Mennonites, inside and outside the old boundaries, are a people on romeria. Together we seek to discern God's will in the postmodern mestizaje in which we all now live.

NOTES

1. Actually I was first brought to this "Mennonite" state of faith via the writings of the Church of the Brethren scholar Arthur G. Gish. The reading of his *The New Left and Christian Radicalism* (Grand Rapids, Mich.: Eerdmans, 1970) during my first year as an undergraduate at Wheaton College changed my understanding of Christianity forever.

2. J. Howard Kauffman and Leo Driedger, *The Mennonite Mosaic: Identity and Modernization* (Scottdale, Pa.: Herald Press, 1991), 253-4. In critique of Kauffman and Driedger's work, I think no bipolar division can chart adequately the full scope of Mennonite options in twentieth-century America. Along these lines, I believe Kauffman and Driedger's heavy reliance on Peter Berger's vision of modernity and secularization skews their work, as does their easy adaptation of Robert Wuthnow's two-party description of American Protestantism. For a critique of the negative impact of the two-party Protestant paradigm, see Douglas Jacobsen and William Vance Trollinger Jr., *Re-Forming the Center: American Protestantism, 1900 to the Present* (Grand Rapids, Mich.: Eerdmans, 1998). Kauffman and Driedger's labeling of the "Anabaptist heritage" as "original" and "fundamentalism" as "recent" also seems problematic. This is especially the case given the way certain contemporary "Anabaptist" expressions of faith and life are so readily equated with forms of faith and life that flourished within various early Anabaptist communities. Modern Anabaptism and early Anabaptism are not identical. Nonetheless, the statistical findings of Kauffman and Driedger do need to be taken seriously by anyone seeking to understand contemporary Mennonitism and/or to shape the future of the movement.

3. Along these lines see David Sikkink, "'I Just Say I'm a Christian': Symbolic Boundaries and Identity Formation among Church-going Protestants" and Nancy Eisland, "Mapping Faith: Choice and Change in Local Religious Organizational Environments" in Jacobsen and Trollinger, *Re-Forming the Center*, 49-71, 404-20.

4. Paul Toews, *Mennonites in American Society, 1930-1970: Modernity and the Persistence of Religious Community* (Scottdale, Pa.: Herald Press, 1996). Toews's idea of a Mennonite diaspora seemed a wonderful, optimistic way to conclude a study of twentieth-century Mennonitism. As it was finally published, however, the book only takes the story to 1970, which is when the Mennonite diaspora was just beginning its most rapid expansion.

5. For examples of this literature see Walter Brueggeman, *The Prophetic Imagination* (Minneapolis, Minn.: Fortress Press, 1978); Walter Wink, *Engaging the Powers: Discernment and Resistance in a World of Domination* (Minneapolis, Minn.: Fortress Press, 1992); Nancey C. Murphy, *Reconciling Theology and Science: A Radical Reformation Perspective* (Kitchener, Ont.: Pandora Press, 1997); and Miroslav Volf, *Exclusion and*

Embrace: A Theological Exploration of Identity, Otherness and Reconciliation (Nashville,Tenn.: Abingdon Press, 1996).

6. See Arturo J. Bañuelas, "Introduction," and Virgil Elizondo, "*Mestizaje* as a Locus of Theological Reflection" in Mestizo *Christianity: Theology from the Latino Perspective*, ed. Arturo J. Bañuelas (Maryknoll, N.Y.: Orbis Books, 1995).

7. Elizondo, "*Mestizaje* as a Locus of Theological Reflection," 9-10.

8. Bañuelas, "Introduction," 1.

9. Ada María Isasi-Diaz, "Afterwords: Strangers No Longer," in *Hispanic/Latino Theology: Challenges and Promise*, ed. Ada María Isasi-Diaz and Fernando F. Segovia (Minneapolis: Fortress Press, 1996), 371f.

10. Elizondo, "*Mestizaje* as a Locus of Theological Reflection," 9.

11. Bañuelas, "Introduction," 1.

12. Elizondo, "*Mestizaje* as a Locus of Theological Reflection," 17.

13. Ibid., 21-2.

14. Justo L. González, "In Quest of a Protestant Hispanic Ecclesiology," in *Teología en Conjunto: A Collaborative Hispanic Protestant Theology*, ed. José David Rodríguez and Loida I. Martell-Otero (Louisville, Ky.: Westminster John Knox Press, 1997), 86-7.

15. Ibid., 91-2, 94.

16. Ibid., 88.

17. Marcus Borg, *Meeting Jesus Again for the First Time: The Historical Jesus and the Heart of Contemporary Faith* (San Francisco: HarperSanFrancisco, 1994), 46, 48-9.

18. Ibid., 49, 53, 58.

19. Stanley Hauerwas, *The Peaceable Kingdom: A Primer in Christian Ethics* (Notre Dame, Ind.: University of Notre Dame Press, 1983), 89.

20. Ibid., 91.

21. Boyer's memory of this event does not reflect the standard order for the reception of new members in the Brethren in Christ Church that was used at the time. In the Brethren in Christ *Manual for Ministers* (Nappanee, Ind.: E. V. Publishing House, 1940), seven questions are included in the ceremony. The first focuses on the authority of the Bible, the second on the Trinity, the third on holiness of life, the fourth on adherence to church practices, the fifth on stewardship, and the last two on "faults" within the community. Boyer's reference is to these last two questions. In their official form these read:

> (6) Do you promise that if any of your brethren or sisters should trespass against you, you will go and tell them their faults between them and you alone, as taught in Matthew 18:15-16? (7) Inasmuch as we are all fallible, if you should trespass against any of your brethren or sisters and they would come and tell you of your fault (according to Matthew 18) are you willing to receive it?" (*Manual for Ministers*, 15)

Rather than focusing on confronting each other about faults, Boyer's version centered on forgiveness. It could be that Boyer's own congregation used a variant order of reception for new members. More likely, Boyer himself consciously or unconsciously had altered his telling of this story to accentuate the positive virtue of forgiveness. Either way, the change represents the potential for a constructive redefinition of Mennonite moral norms from accountability to forgiveness, precisely the direction indicated by Hauerwas.

CHAPTER FIFTEEN

THE VOW OF STABILITY:
A Premodern Way through a Hypermodern World

Gerald W. Schlabach

> *One of the most significant of [monastic] vows is the vow of stability which binds a monk to one monastic community. Unless the superiors decide to send him to a foundation, the monk lives and dies in the monastery of his profession. . . . Saint Benedict, like the Desert Fathers on whom he based his Rule, had a very realistic sense of human values. He introduced this vow into his Rule precisely because he knew that the limitations of the monk, and the limitations of the community he lived in, formed a part of God's plan for the sanctification both of individuals and of communities. By making a vow of stability the monk renounces the vain hope of wandering off to find a "perfect monastery." This implies a deep act of faith: the recognition that it does not much matter where we are or whom we live with, provided we can devote ourselves to prayer, enjoy a certain amount of silence, poverty, and solitude, work with our hands, read and study the things of God, and above all love one another as Christ has loved us.* —Thomas Merton[1]

I was traveling an on-ramp to the Ohio Turnpike one weekend just as an old Carole King song came up on my tape deck. My family was with me as orange cones flashed by, for the interstate highway needs a third lane to accommodate more and more traffic in our mobile society. Just at this moment, however, Carole King voiced the unease of our hypermodern world with lines that have nagged me for some thirty years: "So far away. Doesn't anybody stay in one place anymore? . . . I sure hope the road don't come to own me."

On this particular day, however, the road was taking me to an abbey of Benedictine monks in Cleveland, where—after more than a year of reflection—I was to commit myself to a much older, premodern road by becoming a Benedictine oblate. Oblation simply means offering. Benedictine oblates are people who are not monks but who dedicate themselves, in communion with a particular monastic community, to the service of God and neighbor according to the Rule of St. Benedict, insofar as their state in life permits.[2] Specific commitments include the practice of *lectio divina*, praying the Psalms through some portion of the daily liturgy of hours, and working in the world as unto God. Benedictine values are ones Mennonites share: simplicity, hospitality, and peace.

I learned about all this soon enough once I discovered it is possible for one not Roman Catholic to become an oblate.[3] There are good historical arguments, it turns out, for considering monasticism in general—and the Benedictine sensibilities of Michael Sattler in particular—to have influenced early Swiss Anabaptism.[4] Thus the oblate option has come to seem to me a precise and concrete way to express the growing but otherwise abstract sense in which I am a "Catholic Mennonite."[5]

Writing on the sixteenth century, Sattler's biographer Arnold Snyder was surely right to avoid historical reductionism by insisting that whatever the Benedictine influence on Anabaptism, finally "There can be no Benedictine spirituality without the common liturgical prayer of the divine office, or outside the cloister, the Rule, and the Catholic Church."[6] Yet by making the oblate option possible, the Order of St. Benedict itself has decided otherwise.

To reflect on what the Rule of St. Benedict might mean for busy, non-monastic juggling of family, career, service, and solitude amid a highly mobile society is to look at juggling and mobility in the mirror. For although there is nothing inherently place-bound about monastic life generally, Benedict's rule requires a "vow of stability"—a uniquely Benedictine commitment to live in a particular monastic community for life. At first this may seem the monastic vow least likely to apply amid other ways of life. Yet precisely because it contrasts so sharply with the fragility of most commitments in our hypermodern society, the Benedictine vow of stability may speak more directly to our age, and to our churches' challenge in that age, than anything else in the Rule.

Application must be by analogy; my academic dean knows that I have yet to take a vow of stability to our college community, in anything like the technical Benedictine sense! And one cannot understand the vow of stability apart from the Benedictines' two other vows of conversion of life and of obedience, which in turn requires us to face questions of authority. Still, what I wish to argue is this: It is no use rediscovering any of our church's roots, nor discerning innovative ways to be faithful to our church's calling, if we will not slow down, stay *longer* even if we can't stay *put* indefinitely, and take something *like* a vow of stability. Slow down—because postmodernism may really be hypermodernism. Stay longer—because there is no way to discern God's will together without commitment to sit long together in the first place. A vow of stability—because it is no use discerning appropriate ways to be Christian disciples in our age if we do not embody them through time, testing, and the patience with one another that our good ideas and great ideals need to prove their worth as communal practices. As one Mennonite church leader remarked to me concerning the impact of constant mobility on our congregations: "It's getting so the Abrahamic thing to do is to stay put."[7]

POST, LATE, OR HYPER?

Postmodernism, however, seems to feast on the problem of instability rather than confront it. If there is any such thing as postmodernism, that is. Perhaps a convincing case will yet be made that phenomena that bear the name *postmodern* are distinct enough from modernity to deserve the name. My argument in this paper is simply agnostic on the matter, for the difference between late modernity and postmodernity often seems to the noncommitted observer to be more a matter of pace and presumption than of kind. Consider:

Much "postmodern" thought proceeds through "deconstruction" or a "hermeneutic of suspicion." Yet long ago René Descartes's method of reasoning was to doubt all, see what remained, and proceed from there, as did the Enlightenment in aiming to reject the authority of all traditions.

Postmodernism has now lost confidence in that very reason by which Descartes went on to seek certain foundations. Yet the Enlightenment arguably reached its high-water mark precisely when Immanuel Kant turned Enlightenment reason on itself with his own *Critique of Pure Reason*.

In reacting against Enlightenment reason, some postmodernists instead celebrate the nonrational and explore affective knowing. Yet so did nineteenth-century romanticism and twentieth-century existentialism.

All of this has purportedly led to postmodernist "decentering" of authority and knowing. Yet American individualism, at least, has always thrived by urging movement out to frontiers.

"Postmodernism" sometimes seems to celebrate the individual and sometimes community, so here things get confusing. At the extremes of modernist and "postmodernist" thought lie ontological individualism[8] and the possibility of solipsism,[9] respectively. Of course some postmodernists do locate distinct ways of knowing in particular communities, but modernists have hardly been naive about this, since it is precisely what they have feared about older traditions. In any case, it will not be clear that postmodernism has shaken the modernist bias against traditions so long as every commitment to one can be deconstructed and exposed as irrational assertion of will.

Postmodernism seems to announce the end of every "master story" of human progress. Although the "post" in postmodernism still hints at a lingering addiction to notions of progress, we are sensing the limits of human progress in a way that is distinct from the proud self-confidence of modernity. Still, if we had listened to Augustine we would have renounced proud illusions of limitless human progress long ago!

(Is there anything missing? If so, then let it be noted that one helpfully pertinent aspect of postmodernist thought is that there can be no comprehensive, encyclopedic listing of postmodernist characteristics.)

Maybe there is such a phenomenon as postmodernity, and more astute observers than I will show a way of responding to it that we may call postmodern*ism*. But they will have to forgive the skeptical for wondering a while longer whether postmodern phenomena and thought are not simply modern *phenomena* proceeding at a more frantic pace—along with a tendency for modern *thought* more intensely to gain and lose confidence in itself. In other words, they will have to forgive us for punting and simply calling it all hypermodern until convinced otherwise. And if they want to convince us they are listening to multiple voices and "others," they will have to show themselves vulnerable to the wisdom of premodern voices such as St. Benedict's.[10]

Actually, one does not even have to stretch backward that far. For at least a few of the most incisive voices on the contemporary scene are calling us to decompress, slow down, stay in place, and commit ourselves *to* places for the long haul, precisely so that the planet can provide a human home *over* a long haul. Wendell Berry and Scott Russell Sanders are among those who come to mind.

Throughout his many essays, the farmer-poet-environmentalist Wendell Berry has been arguing tenaciously that our very humanity may depend on sustaining or rediscovering the link between culture and agriculture, through local communities that recognize and nurture their relationship with the land. In "The Work of Local Culture," for example, Berry argues that a healthy local community will imitate the work of forests by improving the land and storing rather than depleting energy, while holding local memories in place like topsoil. Our national culture, laments Berry, is doing exactly the opposite. We have come to accept as a norm that our resources and our children will move away and never return home. The succession of generations tied to a place, and intrinsically learning to care for it, has been broken. Education systems prepare youth for an indeterminate career anywhere (and probably elsewhere) rather than to return home and be of use to a place and community. Berry recognizes that cycles of adolescent rebellion are necessary. However, unless adolescents have viable economic opportunities for returning to their parents and meeting them as fellow sufferers and friends, whole generations become locked into the permanent adolescence of rebellion and mere critique, untethered by a corresponding responsibility for *re*construction.

Contemporary scholarship itself reflects this permanent adolescence. Local cultures die because they cannot be stored in books but only in living communities. And without local cultures we are all the more vulnerable to exploitation. Can all this be changed? Only through local communities themselves. Berry disdains every "global" solution—even from fellow environmentalists, to say nothing of governments and corporations—as the kind of abstraction that is our problem. A single revived local community, he suggests provocatively, could do more through its example than all the government and university programs of the last fifty years.[11]

If Berry's plea for a return to rural community seems too much of a stretch for many of us, then perhaps we can hear the arguments of academic city-dweller Scott Russell Sanders of Indiana University in Bloomington. In an essay in a book only ostensibly about home ownership, Sanders challenges the voices in his own head, in North American culture, and from the admittedly eloquent emigrant writer Salman Rushdie. All these voices urge us "to deal with difficulties by pulling up stakes and heading for new territory."[12] But the national culture is wrong, argues Sanders, when it tells us that "the worst fate is to be trapped on a farm, in a village, in the sticks, in some dead-end job or unglamourous marriage or played-out game," and Rushdie is wrong to tell us that uprooted "migrant sensibility" brings tolerance while rootedness breeds intolerance.[13]

"People who root themselves in places are likelier to know and care for those places," insists Sanders, "than are people who root themselves in ideas" as Rushdie would have his permanent migrants do.[14] In our hemisphere, people rooted in ideas rather than places have been the ones who have committed the worst abuses against land, forests, animals, and human communities—hardly without shedding their bigotry. "To become intimate with your home region, to know the territory as well as you can, to understand your life as woven into the local life does not prevent you from recognizing and honoring the diversity of other places, cultures, ways." After all, those who do not value their own places are unlikely to value others' places.

Unless one is "placed," one merely collects sensations as a sightseer, lacking the local knowledge that grounds and measures global knowledge.

> Those who care about nothing beyond the confines of their parish are in truth parochial, and are at least mildly dangerous to their parish; on the other hand, those who *have* no parish, those who navigate ceaselessly among postal zones and area codes, those for whom the world is only a smear of highways and bank accounts and stores, are a danger not just to their parish but to the planet.[15]

STABILITY IN THE RULE OF ST. BENEDICT[16]

One does not have to speculate about what St. Benedict would have thought of the hypermodern propensity to move on, reinvent ourselves, and keep trying to construct lifestyle enclaves to our liking—without sticking to any one project long enough to create authentic community. Following St. Benedict's prologue, the first chapter in his rule proper describes four kinds of monks. The first two are cenobites or monks living in community (RB 1.1-2), and anchorites or hermits living alone (RB 1.3-5). Cenobitic monasticism had developed out of anchoritic monasticism in the deserts of Egypt, the mountains of Syria, and beyond, during the third and fourth centuries. At first new or prospective monks simply sought out experienced ones to guide them. They attached themselves as apprentices to these spiritual masters they called father or mother, abba or ama.

The historical process that turned clusters of hermits—who already constituted small communities despite themselves—into large and ordered communities during the fourth and fifth centuries need not detain us. Suffice to say that Benedict knew this history well enough that he commended anchorites as well as cenobites, though he seems to have preferred and obviously wrote for cenobitic communities.[17]

The third and fourth categories of monks in his typology were another matter. "Sarabaites" (RB 1.6-9) were "the most detestable kind of monks" who thought they could form small communities of two or three without the aid of either experience (i.e., an experienced master or abbot) or a rule to order their life over time.[18] They were sheep trying to construct their own sheepfolds, not the Lord's, without the aid of a shepherd.[19] Their law was their own fancy: "Anything they believe in and choose, they call holy; anything they dislike, they consider forbidden."

Yet a fourth kind of monk was even worse. This type of monk was the "gyrovagues" (RB 1.10-11), who drifted all their lives from monastery to monastery, staying only a few days. "Always on the move, they never settle down, and are slaves to their own wills and gross appetites." Though the sarabaites were "the most detestable," the gyrovagues were "in every way . . . worse," if that is possible. We might say that the sarabaites were trying to form "intentional communities" on the strength of intention alone, without accepting the need for some structure based on time-tested experience to even out the peaks and troughs of whim, passion, and mere enthusiasm for the *idea* of community. If the gyrovagues were worse, it was precisely because they were even more hyper. Think monks on MTV!

So what Benedict meant by stability, along with the other Benedictine vows of obedience and conversion of life, is clear already in chapter one. This is the case even though he initially said little about the cenobites themselves except that they "serve under a rule and an abbot" (RB 1.2).

Of course there may have been good historical reasons for insisting on stability in the early sixth century, and not all reasons may apply to our own. For centuries Christian communities had tried to find the proper way to take in itinerant Christians hospitably, without being *taken* in—as the *Didache* demonstrated already in the late first century. As monastic communities matured they had both to recognize their debt to initial forms of hermetic asceticism and to recognize the danger in some of their more extravagant practices. The political instability of the sixth century promised even more immediate dangers.[20] When Benedict associated life in the monastery with salvation itself (RB Prol. 42-44, 48), he was not necessarily pronouncing judgment on the status of Christians in ordinary parishes. However, he certainly was warning that the prospects for thoroughgoing conversion of life were not so good out where bishops were getting caught up in shifting political alliances and thus failing as shepherds.[21]

On the other hand, maybe such reasons for stability pertain more to our own century than we like to recognize. In the closing paragraph of the first edition of his book *After Virtue*, philosopher Alasdair MacIntyre baited his readers famously by suggesting that we await "another—doubtless very different—St. Benedict."²² According to MacIntyre, "the barbarians are not waiting beyond the frontiers, they have already been governing us for quite some time"—polling, managing, manipulating, and creating our consumer preferences through corporate and governmental bureaucracies alike.

Meanwhile, theorists of modern democracy fail to account for the moral life as anything more than emotivism, thus reducing moral action itself to consumeristic choice. According to MacIntyre, our hope then is in new and localized forms of community life, constituting traditions of virtue wherein Aristotelian apprenticeship, not Kantian autonomy, shapes the moral life. Such communities must divest their hope in empire, and shape their lives through narratives capable of countering its illusions in ways that discreet intermittent *decision* making fails to do. Only in such communities and traditions—which pass on their virtues through narratives and the heros or mentors who embody them—will intellectual, civil, and moral life survive the competing wills-to-power that prey on us.

MacIntyre does not quite convince me that we require a "doubtless very different" St. Benedict. But he does point to ways our own hypermodern age is more like Benedict's early medieval one than we may want to admit. Television preachers afflict conservative Christians, and theological fads afflict liberal ones. In other words, itinerant "gyrovague" Christianity cycles all around us, without the discipline of sustained community life. Further, as Stanley Hauerwas has noted, the "voluntary community" for which Anabaptists once died has degenerated—in this liberal society where most organizations are voluntary—into the marketing of churches and "church shopping" among all sectors in all traditions.²³

Thus even if these groups have far more than the two or three members that Benedict imagined, they are still "sarabaite" in their desire for community only on their own terms. All this occurs in a socioeconomic context where most days are far too like the sixth century. Marauding bands of advertisers, poll-takers, and other well-groomed MacIntyrian "barbarians" comprise a danger to Christian faithfulness far more subtle and ubiquitous than either the Roman Empire or the modern nation-state.

In this light we may begin to approach from afar the famous opening paragraph of Benedict's prologue, which to modern ears can at first sound irretrievably authoritarian and hierarchical.

> Listen carefully, my son, to the master's instructions, and attend to them with the ear of your heart. This is advice from a father who loves you; welcome it, and faithfully put it into practice. The labor of obedience

will bring you back to him [Christ] from whom you had drifted through the sloth of disobedience. This message of mine is for you, then, if you are ready to give up your own will, once and for all, and armed with the strong and noble weapons of obedience do battle for the true King, Christ the Lord. (RB Prol. 1-3)

Benedict's stated intent was to "establish a school [*schola*] for the Lord's service" (RB Prol. 45; cf. Prol. 14), or a "workshop" in which to learn to exercise the "tools of the spiritual craft" (RB 4.75-78) that were needed for Christian perfecting. As he concluded his rule he called it in fact a "little rule ... for beginners" (RB 73.8; cf. 73.1). In trust that monks had entered the monastery out of a desire to grow into the likeness of Christ by conforming their habits and practices to community life,[24] the rule conceives of their growing virtue as a paradoxical advancement in humility (RB 7).

The rule does include a worrisome number of calls for instant obedience to the commands of one's abbot and renunciation of self-will (RB Prol.1-3; 4.61; 5; 7.19-21, 31-35, 33.4). Benedictines themselves have recognized the danger of absolutist authority here.[25] But skeptics must themselves recognize a simple fact: It was not supposed to be easy to enter a Benedictine monastery in the first place. "Do not grant newcomers to the monastic life an easy entry," wrote Benedict (RB 58.1). Turn them away three or four times to test their sincerity, he continued (RB 58.3-5). Then read them the rule at least three times over the course of their novice year and generally warn them of the "hardships and difficulties" they will encounter if they resolve to seek God through life in the community (RB 58.6-16).

The obedience to authority Benedict called for, then, both requires and creates stability. Nevertheless, it is not coerced obedience. It is the obedience of an apprentice who has sought out someone who knows the life one longs to live better than one can know it oneself, at least without a master who has advanced in the craft of living this life. This master is one in a position to thwart one's favorite illusions. This is exactly what one has asked for by approaching an abbot-father (or abbess-mother[26]) in the first place.

The opening paragraph of Benedict's prologue is simply a reminder of this. The abbot is one's superior (*maior*), but the term is a play on words, for the one who has hierarchical authority is first of all to be one who is "better" or more advanced in the communal search for God to which one has committed oneself.[27] The "master" whom one must obey is a *magister*—not as in "slavemaster" but as in "master craftsperson" or "teacher."[28] No human system precludes every possibility of abuse, but the community that elects an abbot as its leader for life should be seeking someone who is already well-schooled in the virtues that *all* are seeking (RB 64.2-3).

If, as Benedict hoped, the monks identify someone with abilities for administering temporal concerns even while keeping the call to be a shepherd primary (RB 2.30-34), the monks will be freed to dedicate themselves to their own primary calling to seek God.[29] If they themselves have entered the community for the right reasons, the power of position will not be something for which they themselves are competing; if anything they will be trying to avoid it.[30]

Benedict countered some of the potential for abuse in the abbatial system, though probably only some of it. Above all, he warned the abbot and would-be abbot that they do *not* have absolute power in the community. For one thing, the abbot is himself subject to the rule (RB 3.10-11; 64.20),[31] which is in turn a distilled application of Scripture to community life.[32] All learn the rule from the very beginning of their monastic lives (RB 58.9-16; 66.8). They are to give every day to meditative reading of Scripture in rhythm with prayer and manual labor (RB 48; 4.55-56).

A thriving monastery will thus be full of people whose consciences are being formed by the rule and Scripture. Such people will know their abbot is subject to both and dare not guide or command them in ways that violate Scripture, rule, *or* conscience (RB 2.4-5). Benedict also warned the abbot or abbess repeatedly that they would have to give account on judgment day; God was the owner of the sheepfold, not they. They would be examined about those entrusted to them (RB 2.7, 11-15, 30, 39; 3.11; 64.7, 20; 65.22). If we dismiss the efficacy of this promise of transhistorical sanctions on abbots who fail to live up to their calling to make Christ himself present in the community (RB 2.1-2), this may say more about us than about the Benedictine system of authority and accountability.

In any case, Benedict also required certain procedures that favored intracommunity accountability. In guiding the lives of the monks an abbot's directions were not to come with legalistic one-size-fits-all rigidity. Rather, the abbot was to adapt directions to the need, personality, and circumstance of each monk (RB 2.23-29; 27; 37; 64:7-19). This necessarily required two-way communication. Benedict also made provision for monks to object to commands that seemed impossibly burdensome to them, though the abbot still retained the last word (RB 68).

In relation to major community matters, Benedict expected the abbot to make a final decision, but not before taking counsel from the entire community (RB 3). The main reason he gave should warn us against caricaturing the system from outside as crudely authoritarian: "The reason why we have said all should be called for counsel is that the Lord often reveals what is better to the younger" (RB 3:3).

If this were not enough, Benedict also put aside the suspicions of itinerants he had expressed in denouncing "gyrovague" monasticism. Now he not only encouraged hospitality toward visiting monks (RB 61; see also RB 53) but insisted that the abbot receive their "reasonable criticisms or observations"—for "it is possible that the Lord guided [them] to the monastery for this very purpose" (RB 61.4).

So is this system democratic? Authoritarian? Participatory? Is it perhaps what "aristocracy"—the rule of the virtuous or excellent—would mean if that term took its meaning more often from Christian virtues of humility, compassion, and vulnerability to the presence of "the least" among us? Or is it something else that we will not be able to recognize, much less name, unless we have learned to look respectfully at traditional premodern societies (both ancient and contemporary) from within?

John Paul Lederach, who has greatly advanced the field of conflict mediation by developing it for cross-cultural situations, once told me about the practices of a South American indigenous tribe. When a clan needs to make a decision, all the men in the group gather in a circle. (They do not include women; the point here is not that the procedure is perfect.) One by one, from youngest to oldest, each shares his counsel. No one loses face, since the words of those more elder are *expected* to supersede those who have already spoken. Yet all do speak and all do hear. At last the eldest speaks, having had time and opportunity to hear from all, and the word of the eldest constitutes the group's decision. End of meeting.

Here is an ocracy for which we have no prefix—and modern conceptions of democracy will not supply one. To understand, interpret, and learn from these communal practices, we had best hear the admonition of Theron Schlabach, historian of nineteenth-century Mennonites, concerning those quasi-monastic communities we more often call Old Order Mennonite and Amish.

> To understand the Old Order outlook, people with modern and progressive outlooks must, at least for the moment, set aside some of their own ingrained assumptions. They must *not* assume.... That people who accept the ideas of the eighteenth century's so-called Age of Reason are the "enlightened" ones of the world.... That the individual is the supreme unit, individual rights the most sacred rights, and human life

> richest when individuals are most autonomous. . . . That a structure of rules and explicit expectations . . . is always legalistic and at odds with the Christian idea of grace. . . .³³

In any case, Benedictines read their rule in their community, as their community's text. They do not treat it as a historical artifact, but neither do they read it like fundamentalists. What most commends the model of stability in the text—together with its accompanying pattern of authority, obedience, and measured openings for loyal dissent—is precisely that it has engendered a tradition in which flexibility, adaptation, critique, and reform are possible within the nurture of deep continuities.

The Rule of St. Benedict itself calls for flexibility at a number of points. In establishing his "school for the Lord's service," Benedict said he hoped "to set down nothing harsh, nothing burdensome," even if "the good of all concerned" required "a little strictness to amend faults and to safeguard love" (RB Prol. 45-47). At the end, he attached a chapter reminding his monasteries that "this rule [is] only a beginning of perfection" (RB 73). Benedictines have taken this to authorize careful and thoughtful adaptation as circumstance demands and communal wisdom counsels.³⁴

But the point is not really to create the perfect monastery. The Cistercian contemplative Thomas Merton once commented on the significance of the Benedictine vow of stability by stressing the very realism of Saint Benedict and the hermits of the desert before him. Benedict, he observed, "introduced this vow into his Rule precisely because he knew that the limitations of the monk, and the limitations of the community he lived in, formed a part of God's plan for the sanctification both of individuals and of communities."

In making this vow, "the monk renounces the vain hope of wandering off to find a 'perfect monastery.'" That requires deep faith, and a recognition that finally

> it does not much matter where we are or whom we live with, provided we can devote ourselves to prayer, enjoy a certain amount of silence, poverty, and solitude, work with our hands, read and study the things of God, and above all love one another as Christ has loved us.³⁵

Of course, it is clear from Merton's biography that this recognition did not come easily. Nor am I quite ready to say that just any community will do. What I am saying is that any true and sustainable community will need the virtues of mutual patience and mutual submission that the vow of stability requires and engenders. In their struggle against oppression, patriarchy, and abusive authority, some may imagine and promote radically egalitarian forms of community along liberationist, feminist, or putatively Anabaptist lines. They may assume that a premodern patriarch such as Benedict can offer little counsel. My response is simply this: *Write to me when you get halfway to your utopia, and tell me whether you do not need some vow of stability more than ever, to see you through.* That reply, however, requires unpacking.

Replies to Objections

The most obvious objection to any attempt to retrieve Benedictine stability for other communities is the one I have already had to anticipate: that the vow of stability comes linked so closely with that other vow of obedience to hierarchical authority that we had better steer clear. Let me summarize and extend my response to this objection with a chain of replies.

The vow of stability is too hierarchical: a response

1. Historical and textual studies show that Benedict significantly—even drastically—reduced the paternalistic language of the most important sources he used in redacting his own rule, especially a much longer document known as "The Rule of the Master." It is always too easy and inadequate to defend historical figures simply by calling them men or women of their times, but that is precisely because it is always true. What counts here is that a contemporary commentator such as Terrance Kardong, O.S.B., has done careful textual criticism showing that where Benedict pruned he most often removed harsh legalisms and metaphors that would make monks into the "sons" of an abbot whose fatherhood over them was that of a Roman *paterfamilias*.[36] And where Benedict inserted his own original material he most often showed great pastoral sensitivity or required abbots to be more collegial.[37]

Benedict's sparing language of the abbot as a father exhorting a son thus reflected Hebrew wisdom literature more than Roman politics.[38] He retained language that made the abbot a master because monastic life was unimaginable without the structure of apprenticeship that had first developed in the Egyptian desert.

2. What is arguably most important about democracy are the ways it holds powerful leaders accountable.[39] But if we study premodern traditional cultures carefully and respectfully, we begin to notice that modern democracy does not have a monopoly on accountability. Christian polities should strive toward the accountability of all, but in fact modern demo-

cratic processes do rather poorly at holding their *electorates* accountable. When congregationalist polities using modern democratic processes allow dysfunctional churches to run out one pastor after another, we have only exchanged one abuse of authority for another. And where congregational participation is a matter of consumer taste, we gain the accountability of the marketplace but undermine growth in Christian virtue. At minimum, then, patterns of accountability in premodern communities—such as the indigenous people of Lederach's telling, the Old Order Mennonites and Amish, and the Benedictines—deserve a second look if not a reappropriation.

3. Adding together points one and two, then, we should begin to develop a critical distance from the paradoxically authoritarian hold that modern *anti*-authoritarianism has on us. The kind of counsel taking, fear of God, and vulnerability to "the least" of those in Benedictine monasteries may or may not convince us Benedict's abbot is adequately accountable. Nevertheless, we should at least gain enough charity toward premodern texts, and enough humility about the limits of our own hypermodern sensibilities, to appropriate the wisdom in vows of stability. These can then aid us as we negotiate our way through a hypermodern world.

4. Before we pass over the wisdom of a vow of obedience, however, we might ask ourselves this: Do we really want to excise altogether the apprenticing shape of Christian life and community? Let us call our spiritual *magistri* "teachers" or "mentors" if that is more palatable than "masters." Let us remind them, as Benedict did, that the obedience of their apprentices is ultimately to Christ. Let us even spread them throughout Christian communities that are discerning God's will collectively rather than one-on-one.

Let us remind *ourselves*, however, that all learning in the Christian life involves *un*learning. To put on Christ by growing more fully into our baptism involves a putting off of old habits and illusions that die hard. For that, we need guides with enough authority and integrity to confront us with lessons we so fear to learn, that we may not learn them at all unless we obey before we fully understand or desire.[40]

No such guides are themselves free from sin; thus, none should be exempt from accountability. Furthermore, true authority bears no rightful power without the integrity that earns our trust. But unless we grant the probability that some members of the community know and embody the Christian life in fuller and more trustworthy ways than others, then there is little point in speaking of Christian growth at all—much less yearning to grow. This is because we thereby give up on the very possibility of our own growth in Christ.

5. In any case, here is the rub: Christian communities that structure their life together with polities more egalitarian than the Benedictine polity ostensibly is are going to need more protracted processes of participatory discernment as they seek to discern God's will for them collectively. For *that*, they are going to require *more, not less*, of a vow of stability! Consensus takes long to reach. Good intentions and the initial romance of community life wane. Patience frays and righteous conviction turns to anger. The elusive option of starting over with a group of ones like-minded is never absent from any non-Catholic church, is far too accessible in all Anabaptist ones, and is especially tempting in the modern milieu where voluntarism is nothing we need to die for anymore. So a figurative vow of stability is actually going to be much harder to make stick than stability in the technical Benedictine sense—yet all the more crucial! We are probably being far more modern or hypermodern than Anabaptist if we think otherwise.[41]

6. Thus as I say, write when you get halfway to utopia, because there is good reason to think you will need something like a vow of stability more than ever—to be patient and long-suffering enough with one another that God has the space to take you the other half of the way.

Seeking premodern guidance is post- or hypermodern: a second set of responses

To a second major objection, however, I cannot reply so neatly. This objection is that whether the world we are trying to find our way through is post-, late-, or hypermodern, my very attempt to find guidance in the premodern vow of stability implicates me in the dynamics of some kind of post- or hypermodern world. The very inclination, need, and possibility of looking outside of my own church tradition for wisdom to sustain that tradition may be making use of what I have called hypermodern culture. Perhaps even this paper "has been brought to you by our sponsors," a consumeristic religious economy that allows me to keep my Mennonite pacifism here, shop for a little Catholic spirituality there, and pick up a little Benedictine glue at an abbey to hold it all together.

Few things worry me more. I think, hope, and pray that what I am doing is what I hope all Christians will do—seeking to rediscover an ancient catholicity not through ecumenical shopping but by putting roots down far enough into the soil of our own traditions to discover those deep and fecund places where our roots intertwine. Even so, it is undoubtedly easier for me to think such thoughts precisely because hypermodern culture has emancipated me from precritical stay-puttedness and allowed me to make what would once have seemed very long journeys—say from Goshen to Notre Dame.

In other words, perhaps stability should *not* require looking elsewhere. I concede the point and do not know precisely what to do about it. To some extent I have to accept the so-called postmodern condition just to retrieve the wisdom of premodern sources. The churches I move among are squeamish about church discipline, but I am too well-educated to return to the Amish. So I acquire some sense of *Ordnung* in the Rule of St. Benedict while I finesse a vaguely premodern condition by doing Mennonite theology in conversation with the likes of St. Augustine. Finally my plea is simply that one cannot be stable alone. And if one's own community shows signs of instability, one must put down a stake in the longer and deeper stability that is the communion of saints.

When I first read the Rule of St. Benedict, the first note I wrote in the margin of the first paragraph went something like this: "But where to find an abbot? What if they've been abdicating?" Wendell Berry's warning about the permanent adolescence that results when the newly educated do not or cannot return home may apply all too well to our own Mennonite intelligentsia. Reacting to the alleged authoritarianism of past generations of Mennonite leadership, the last two or so generations of theological leaders in our church have been promoting an ecclesiology of participatory discernment, wherein all God's people are called to be ministers, God's will is found in the exercise of all their gifts, and every message from leadership must be tested in the gathered *ekklesia,* just as New Testament congregations were to test even the words of the prophets and apostles.[42]

Fine. In all my Mennonite years I have wanted this ecclesiology to live and breathe. But again, it takes more work, more of a vow of stability, more sitting together—long, patiently, wisely. Unless we actually and thoroughly *practice* such participatory discernment, the *theory* of participatory discernment may serve only to critique authoritarianism and will probably corrode the legitimacy even of properly accountable authority. It then risks functioning in the way Theron Schlabach says nineteenth-century revivalism functioned—as an acceptable "pipeline" into modernity.[43]

Mennonite churches have carried out important experiments in the polity of participatory discernment, but often these have happened in college towns and university fellowships. If the wider church is now experiencing a reassertion of authority that suffers unhealthy tendencies even when it is necessary, the Mennonite intelligentsia at least *shares* the blame. For too few of us have had the patience to take nascent practices of participatory discernment back into our congregations of origin. Too few of us have noticed or heeded the appeal that Guy F. Hershberger made to "Christian youth" near the close of his book on *War, Peace and Nonresistance*. In serving the host society in which Christians find themselves, he wrote, the "most constructive work which can be done is not to be found in those glamorous and spectacular enterprises associated with urban industry, military service, and the affairs of state, but rather in the quiet and more fundamental task of building the small Christian community."[44]

Because the slow and steady way of Christian faithfulness rarely offers glamour and spectacle, that is, too few of us have taken anything like a vow of stability. To do so now, we may—as Dorothy Nickel Friesen has preached in my current congregation—have to "take another path home." But return home we must.

A NOT-SO-INNOVATIVE CONCLUSION

MacIntyre's call for a new and "doubtless very different" St. Benedict[45] missed one crucial point. At least as a writer, Benedict was not very original. Most of his rule was a thoughtful redaction from earlier and often longer documents on monastic life. His innovation was simply the wise and enduring balance he struck between solitary and communal ways of searching for God, asceticism and realism, insularity and hospitality, rigor and flexibility. And if Benedict was rarely altogether original, he sensed no need to *claim* originality.

Now someone might observe that the core message of the present paper need not have referred to matters Benedictine at all. What has long been called the "second baptism" of monastic vows coincides strikingly with the meaning of first baptism as the Anabaptists believed themselves to be recovering it. My message might then have simply been this: let us take seriously our baptism, our church commitment, and the "giving and receiving of counsel" that both are supposed to entail. Let us support these primary commitments by strengthening our secondary commitments to family, neighborhood, place, and the land.

But of course that response might not sound glamorous enough to deserve a new essay. One lesson of premodern ways, however, is that we may not need to say as many new things as we think. Meanwhile, a reality of our hypermodern world is that we may need to hear old lessons from voices that are new and a bit exotic for us. Either way, the lesson is that what we need may not be a new theory or ism at all, but the virtue of patience and the practice of hunkering down to stay together through the long haul as we listen to God's voice.

The Psalm that most often begins the daily cycle of prayer in Benedictine monasteries is Psalm 95: "Come, let us sing to the Lord and shout with joy to the Rock who saves us." The Lord our God, it proclaims, is "the great king over all the gods" and bears in hand earth, mountains, seas, and dry land. Come, it urges, let us bow down, for we belong to this very God as the people of God's pasture, the flock that God leads. Then suddenly the Psalm issues a warning:

> Today, listen to the voice of the Lord: Do not grow stubborn [or hard-hearted], as your [forebears] did in the wilderness. . . . Forty years I endured that generation. I said, "They are a people whose hearts go astray and they do not know my ways.' So I swore in my anger, 'They shall not enter into my rest.'"[46]

There the Psalm abruptly ends.

The stability of the Benedictine way does not claim to be written into the fabric of the universe. But for the enabling grace of God it is a humanly made vow, and a postmodernist may well call the stability that issues from it a socially "constructed" order. Yet it renews itself each day . . . by listening. And it listens . . . from within rootedness in the living assumption that something is there beyond us to which we must listen—something beyond our every ability to construct reality.

Thus it finds its stability not in the unreliable hardness of our own hearts but in the socially embodied conviction that God has a will to voice and a hand to lead. God is the stable rock, the rock who saves. In the stability of God and God's purposes, in fact, lies our deepest freedom. As the Psalmist warns and the Benedictines repeat, hardness and unresting burden lie not in God but in hearts that go some other way.

In praying and seeking to live out the stability of God our saving rock, the Benedictines thus proclaim a freedom hypermoderns barely know. This is a freedom *not* to change everything always, a freedom even to sustain premodern ways, a freedom to conserve, to obey, to stay.

Let distant Anabaptist relatives listen too.

NOTES

1. Thomas Merton, *The Sign of Jonas* (New York: Harcourt, Brace and Company, 1953), 9-10.

2. For historical background, see Derek G. Smith, "Oblates in Western Monasti-

cism," *Monastic Studies* 13 (Autumn 1982): 47-72.

3. Like many people in recent years I first learned about Benedictine oblates from Kathleen Norris's best-selling book, *The Cloister Walk* (New York: Riverhead Books, 1987), but all I needed to decide to explore this option was the raw fact that non-Roman Catholics could become oblates, which appears in her first paragraph.

4. The following secondary sources represent a debate over the exact causal links between Sattler's Benedictinism and the Swiss Anabaptism that coalesced under his leadership at Schleitheim in 1527, but the debate itself makes clear that there was some kind of influence and suggests certain abiding affinities. See Arnold Snyder, "The Monastic Origins of Swiss Anabaptist Sectarianism," *Mennonite Quarterly Review* 67, no. 1 (1983), 5-26; *The Life and Thought of Michael Sattler* (Scottdale, Pa.: Herald Press, 1984); "Michael Sattler, Benedictine: Dennis Martin's Objections Reconsidered," *Mennonite Quarterly Review* 61 (July 1987), 262-79; Dennis D. Martin, "Monks, Mendicants, and Anabaptists: Michael Sattler and the Benedictines Reconsidered," *Mennonite Quarterly Review* 60 (April 1986), 139-64; "Catholic Spirituality and Anabaptist and Mennonite Discipleship," *Mennonite Quarterly Review* 62 (January 1988), 5-25. Also see Eoin De Bhaldraithe, "Michael Sattler, Benedictine and Anabaptist," *Downside Review* (April 1987), 111-31.

Still, my argument does not depend on the strength of the historical links between Benedictines and Anabaptists. Issuing in what may be the longest enduring communal life of discipleship that church history has seen, the Benedictine tradition would deserve our deepest respect and consideration, even if it had done nothing whatsoever to help form our own Anabaptist tradition.

5. In conversation with other Mennonites and Catholics who are exploring fresh ways of understanding the relationship between our traditions, I proposed the following definition of "Catholic Mennonites" and "Mennonite Catholics":

> We are Christians who seek to be nurtured by the fullest possible communion of Christian communities through the centuries and across the globe, even as we seek to follow Jesus Christ in life without deferring his teachings or betraying the nonviolent wisdom of his cross. We can do neither of these except in the eschatological hope that believes the peaceable kingdom he proclaimed is a present reality, and that the church for whose unity he prayed (that it might witness to that kingdom) is also a present reality. Nonetheless, for both Christian unity and God's peaceable kingdom we painfully await the gift of their fullness. We are caught, then, between the "already" of hope that calls us to live now according to both of these realities, and the "not yet" of histories that require honesty concerning the failures of our traditions to do so. Thus, no ecclesial structure feels altogether like home—and any way home is one we can only "see through a glass darkly."

6. C. Arnold Snyder, *The Life and Thought of Michael Sattler*, 192.

7. Sherm Kauffman, executive secretary of the Indiana-Michigan Conference of the Mennonite Church, and a former pastor.

8. Cf. Hobbes's and Locke's accounts of men in the "state of nature."

9. This is because a radically perspectivist epistemology has nowhere to stop posit-

ing the construction of worldviews and realities except in the ultimately unique perspective of each individual.

10. For a plea that cross-cultural understanding extend to premodern communities, see Dennis D. Martin, "Journey to a Far Country: Premodern History as Crosscultural Education," *Conrad Grebel Review* 11 (Fall 1993), 249-63. Also see the opening and closing essays in Robert L. Wilken, *Remembering the Christian Past* (Grand Rapids, Mich.: Eerdmans, 1995), 1-23, 165-80.

11. Wendell Berry, "The Work of Local Culture," in *What Are People For?* (San Francisco: North Point Press, 1990), 153-69. For a discussion of "fidelity" that parallels somewhat the practice of "stability," see Wendell Berry, "The Body and the Earth," in *The Unsettling of America Culture and Agriculture* (New York: Avon, 1977), 120-23.

12. Scott Russell Sanders, "Settling Down," in *Staying Put: Making a Home in a Restless World* (Boston: Beacon Press, 1994), 102. Sanders notes that he quarrels with Rushdie "because he articulates as eloquently as anyone the orthodoxy that I wish to counter: the belief that movement is inherently good, staying put is bad; that uprooting brings tolerance, while rootedness breeds intolerance; that imaginary homelands are preferable to geographical ones; that to be modern, enlightened, fully of our time is to be displaced" (103).

13. Ibid., 105, 103.

14. Ibid., 106.

15. Ibid., 114.

16. All quotations from the rule (abbreviated as RB) are taken from Saint Benedict, *RB 1980: The Rule of St. Benedict in English*, ed. Timothy Fry, O.S.B. (Collegeville, Minn.: Liturgical Press, 1982). I am also consulting Terrence G. Kardong, *Benedict's Rule: A Translation and Commentary* (Collegeville, Minn.: Liturgical Press, 1996), abbreviated as BR. Finally, I am indebted to Fr. Michael Brunovsky, O.S.B., the oblate director at St. Andrew Svorad Abbey in Cleveland who is well-trained in patristic and monastic history, for various clarifications concerning the rule.

17. RB 1 has provided terrain for a long and continuing debate over the conceptual relationship between anchorism and cenobitism. 1.3-5 seems to present anchorites as graduates of cenobitic communities who are now strong enough to go out and wrestle with the devil and their own vices in one-on-one combat. Yet that would seem to make monastic community life into something merely instrumental; besides, 1.13 calls the cenobites the strong or (as Kardong translates) "most vigorous" of monks. See BR pp. 31, 43, 599-600.

18. Cf. RB 1.2 where cenobites are described as "those who belong to a monastery, where they serve under a rule and an abbot."

19. Cf. RB 2.7 in which the abbot-shepherd is reminded that he is not actually the owner of the sheepfold, since the owner is rather the Lord God.

20. Political chieftains in the Latin/Germanic West had abandoned the last pretense of continuity with the Roman Empire in 476, yet the Eastern emperor Justinian attempted to regain control after 526. Whatever one thinks of that combination of political stability and militarism that the Roman Empire had once represented, its disintegration no more brought freedom from oppression and violence than the demise of

the Soviet Union has brought these to all of its regions. Whatever local improvements came from the fall of these respective empires, the improvements did not come without new dangers.

21. So, at least, suggests Fr. Brunovsky, O.S.B.

22. Alasdair MacIntyre, *After Virtue: A Study in Moral Theory*, 2d ed. (Notre Dame, Ind.: University of Notre Dame Press, 1984), 263. For a short monograph that applies MacIntyre's thought to the challenge of Christian mission in modern culture, and frames its proposals as "a new monasticism," see Jonathan R. Wilson, *Living Faithfully in a Fragmented World: Lessons for the Church from MacIntyre's* After Virtue, Christian Mission and Modern Culture (Harrisburg, Pa.: Trinity Press International, 1997).

23. Stanley Hauerwas, *In Good Company: The Church as* Polis (Notre Dame, Ind.: University of Notre Dame Press, 1995), 26, 73.

24. "Habits and practices [of] community life" approximates the initial meaning of *conversatio morum* (Prol. 49; 58.17) rather than "conversion of life," which became one of the three traditional Benedictine vows. But of course the point of conformity to the former was growth in the latter. See Kardong's discussion of RB 58.17 in BR pp. 473-74 and 483).

25. The Benedictine commentator Kardong suggested that as Benedict added to his rule over time he began to recognize the dangers in this formula, and inserted a new chapter calling for abbots to exercise their authority with gentle discretion (RB 64, in contrast to RB 2; see BR p. 541), along with a key chapter inviting monks to object to impossibly burdensome commands in a way that would elicit truly pastoral guidance from their superior (RB 68; see BR p. 572).

Even so, Kardong himself recognized that in another chapter (RB 71) Benedict abjectly failed to "take account of community life in any realistic sense," for although he began the chapter with a call for *mutual* obedience (but also see RB 72), he ended by insisting on the "capitulation and self-accusation" of junior monks to seniors, and no such system "can be said to be healthy" (BR p. 586). Still, Kardong's harsh criticism of the saintly founder of his order attests to possibilities of critique and accountability within the order that outsider observers may not always discern. See also Terrence Kardong, O.S.B., "RB 71.6-9 in the Light of Gandhi's Non-Violence," *Tjurunga* 27 (1984), 3-16.

26. Throughout this article I refer to the "abbots" of male monastic communities because this is the nomenclature in Benedict's text.

27. See BR 2.1, p. 49.

28. In any case, Kardong notes that Benedict, in redacting a more succinct and workable "rule" out of longer and harsher sources such as the anonymous "Rule of the Master," drastically reduced the number of references to the abbot as a "master" or "father," and to the monk as "son," thus reducing paternalistic overtones as well. See BR pp. 5, 66.

29. Cf. BR pp. 67-68.

30. Commenting on the first draft of this paper, Kardong noted that this in fact tends to be the case today, though not necessarily for reasons Benedict would have expected: "There is no question that Benedict makes his abbot a huge factor in the life of

the monk and the monastery. So much so, that I think it scares the daylights out of modern monks. Hence monasteries have a tough time finding anyone who is willing to be abbot! In reality, most abbots today are anything but authoritarian. American abbots tend to be rather shy and retiring; some do not do much teaching in the monastery. At any rate, the problem is the same all over society: where to find people with vision?"

31. Kardong notes that Benedict never reversed the order of the repeated pair "under a rule and an abbot," thus implying the clear priority of the rule over the abbot (BR p. 36; see RB 1.1, 6-8; 3.7-9; 23.1).

32. See RB chapters 4 and 7 for what are only the most marked examples of this distillation. Cf. BR pp. 36, 117.

33. Theron F. Schlabach, "Peace, Faith, Nation: Mennonites and Amish in Nineteenth-Century America," in *The Mennonite Experience in America*, vol. 2 (Scottdale, Pa.: Herald Press, 1988), 201-03.

34. Since Vatican II, many Benedictine congregations have been electing their abbots until age 65, rather than for life, with longer terms possible only through re-election. Another obvious example is that, according to Kardong (BR 251), "there may not be a single monastery in the world today that carries out literally [Benedict's] prescriptions for punishing monks," particularly through corporal punishment.

35. Merton, *The Sign of Jonas*, 9-10. For a more thorough exploration of the role of stability in monastic life and sanctification, see Michael Casey, OCSO, "The Value of Stability," *Cistercian Studies Quarterly* 31, no. 3 (1996): 287-301. Casey suggested that

> Solemn profession of stability means that the whole cosmic drama of salvation is transferred to the microcosm of the monastery—at least as far as the individual is concerned.... It is precisely the containment of ultimate events within the human scale that enables the monk to live more intensely.... Monastic life is not a means of escape from anything. On the contrary, it has the effect of bringing monastics into sustained confrontation with realities they might otherwise avoid, disguise, or deny. (Ibid., 29)

Likewise, Casey contrasted the lessons of stability with the lures of what I have called hypermodernism:

> The first effect of stability is that it brings lofty dreams of spiritual growth down to earth. Present opportunities are to be taken seriously since nothing much is going to change... Once the idea sinks in, there is no excuse for postponing effort under the pretext that opportunities are lacking or that the time is not ripe. In our supermarket culture it is possible to spend a lifetime toying with alternatives, convinced that one is a genuine spiritual seeker, but never committing oneself to anything beyond the first flush of enthusiasm. Stability puts an end to this sort of searching. The monk accepts to live in a microcosm, where the spiritual combat remains firmly on a human scale. (Ibid., 292-293)

36. Cf. RB 2.7, where God is decisively made the *paterfamilias* or owner of the sheepfold and the abbot is a shepherd who must give account. Those who would reject this image of God will have to excise those parables by which Jesus himself spoke of God as a land- or vineyard owner.

37. See Kardong, BR pp. 5, 8, 22, 32, 62, 75, 254-255, 403, 431-432.

38. See BR pp. 5, 66-67 on RB Prol.1. Although the filial language of the rule's opening words is prominent, it is also unique, for as Kardong points out, the only other place where the RB refers to the monk as "son" (RB 2.29) is a biblical quotation.

39. Cf. John Howard Yoder, "The Christian Case for Democracy," in *The Priestly Kingdom: Social Ethics as Gospel* (Notre Dame, Ind.: University of Notre Dame Press, 1984), 151-71.

40. Casey's observations may help us understand why.

> There is an obscurity inherent in any human commitment. When we oblige ourselves to do something, we can never know in advance whether the circumstances in which we are to render our debt will have changed. Before binding ourselves we make an assessment on the basis of both objective and subjective information, but no practical judgment can be infallible. What we decide comes into being only *after* our decision; we can never know what would have been if we had decided otherwise. Every commitment we make involves an element of risk-taking. On the other hand, once we have taken the step, we are honor-bound to a certain obstinacy not only in keeping our promises but in actively pursuing the purposes for which the promises were made. (Casey, "The Value of Stability," 298)

41. I do not have the time or expertise in sixteenth-century sources to prove my suspicion that the contentious students of Harold S. Bender's "Anabaptist Vision" have been far too quick to read their own late-twentieth-century anti-authoritarianism back into formative Anabaptism. One example, from a scholar who actually tries hard to avoid such things, may, however, illustrate the grounds for suspicion. In his biography of Michael Sattler, Arnold Snyder rightly has sought to show points of both continuity and discontinuity between Sattler's Benedictine and Anabaptist thought. Comparing Benedictine and Anabaptist processes of discernment, he argues that in the latter, the community, not its leaders, decides, and the Holy Spirit witnesses through the community's unity and unanimity. Snyder concludes that "the monastic community is obedient to Christ *via* its obedience to the Rule and its abbot" whereas "the Anabaptist community is to be obedient *directly* to Christ, his Word and his Spirit" (Snyder, *The Life and Thought of Michael Sattler*, 191-92.)

A footnote on this page, however, leads the reader to a letter of Sattler's admonishing the church of Horb to assemble constantly for prayer and breaking of bread. "In such meeting together you will make manifest the heart of the false brothers, and will be freed of them more rapidly" (John H[oward] Yoder, ed., *The Legacy of Michael Sattler* [Scottdale, Pa.: Herald Press, 1973], 62).

How? The letter does not say. But since no actual community can beg the question of who the "false brothers" are in the way that the letter *seems* to do, a more sensible reading is that someone or some party within the group has only achieved "unanimity" by deciding which voices count. The criticism here is not of Sattler, for elsewhere he in turn provides ways to make the community's shepherd accountable (see article 5 of the Schleitheim Confession in Yoder, *The Legacy of Michael Sattler*, 38-39). The criticism is of recent historiography that tends to romanticize sixteenth-century Anabaptist communities as radically egalitarian, in order to legitimize anti-authoritarian assumptions that may actually derive from late modernity. If I am right that Snyder erred at this point, his mistake was not so much egregious as symptomatic.

42. For influential monographs developing this vision, see John Howard Yoder, *The Fullness of Christ: Paul's Revolutionary Vision of Universal Ministry* (Elgin, Ill.: Brethren Press, 1987); Ross Thomas Bender, *The People of God: A Mennonite Interpretation of the Free Church Tradition* (Scottdale, Pa.: Herald Press, 1971). For counter voices, see Marlin E. Miller, "Some Reflections on Pastoral Ministry and Pastoral Education," *Understanding Ministerial Leadership*, ed. John A. Esau (Elkhart, Ind.: Institute of Mennonite Studies, 1995); Rodney J. Sawatsky, "Leadership, Authority and Power," *Mennonite Quarterly Review* 71 (July 1997), 439-51.

43. Theron F. Schlabach, "Reveille for 'Die Stillen Im Lande': A Stir Among Mennonites in the Late Nineteenth Century," *Mennonite Quarterly Review* 51 (1977), 215-16.

44. Guy Franklin Hershberger, *War, Peace, and Nonresistance*, 3d ed., reprint, 1953, Christian Peace Shelf Selection (Scottdale, Pa.: Herald Press, 1969), 252, 382.

45. Alasdair MacIntyre, *After Virtue: A Study in Moral Theory*, 2d ed. (Notre Dame, Ind.: University of Notre Dame Press, 1984), 263.

46. Translation taken from *Christian Prayer: The Liturgy of Hours* (New York: Catholic Book Publishing, 1976).

PART SIX

**PEACE WITNESS
AND POLITICAL COMMITMENT**

SIXTEEN

STICKS AND STONES, WORDS AND BONES:
The Body of Christ and the Gospel of Peace

John Stahl-Wert

Here we stand at the threshold of a new millennium. For Christians, the measure of our years of history must now be recalibrated into the plural term of *thousands*; Jesus' incarnation took place *thousands* of years ago, we must learn to say.

One would think we have had adequate time, therefore, to make our peace with this incarnation. Should not thousands of years be enough time for the church fully to incorporate the truth of Jesus' commingled humanity and divinity, both utterly complete? Apparently not. Even standing here at this heady new dawn, looking back now over thousands of years of Christian history, we still struggle with the human being, with the flesh and the blood, the skin and the bone, of our Lord.

It is arguable, I believe, that the humanity of Jesus—his very incarnation—is that which has caused the Christian church these two thousand years the greatest trouble of all.

Let me shortly provide evidence supporting this claim. Then beyond this preliminary point, I will argue that the gospel of Jesus Christ, understood by Mennonites to be a gospel of peace, is inconceivable without a more radical and thoroughgoing embrace of Jesus' flesh. Such an embrace must go beyond orthodoxy, beyond orthodogma, and even beyond orthopraxis to reach what perhaps might be called orthosomatics (right bodyhood). Finally I will say a few words about why Jesus' body—the one he had and the one he has today—deserves particular attention at this millennial moment.

THE CONTINUING CHALLENGE OF FLESH

Our Christian quest is driven fundamentally by the desire to find better ways to understand what it is that we are living and better ways to live the things we understand. To say it more simply, we want our lives to show movement toward the One in whom we still believe, whose body in this world we are called to be, yet whose person we have hardly begun to resemble, collectively or otherwise.

Who is the "we" of these last several sentences? The "we" I am addressing is a particular Christian people (Mennonite), from a certain Christian tradition (varyingly Anabaptist), at a moment in time (history's odometer having just kicked up a whole bunch of fresh zeros).

The case I am making is not relevant to this narrow "we" alone, however. If there is "one Lord, one faith, one baptism, one God and Father of all,"[1] then an Anabaptist-Mennonite reading of the gospel of Jesus Christ is pertinent to, and deserves critique in, wider Christian discourse. Given the exceptional investment Anabaptist Christians have made in the gospel of peace, I shall take up this argument about the incarnation's key to this investment with Mennonites first in mind. Other investors, to be sure, are also welcome to examine the prospectus.

I began above by saying that the humanity of Jesus is that which has caused the Christian church the greatest trouble. Indeed, from the very beginning of the story we have wanted to get his feet off the ground and place him into a more proper position for our veneration and for his exercise of Lordship. When the church was born in Jerusalem's multiethnic, Jewish Pentecost, and when the church later learned to crawl in Antioch's multicultural, Christian mission—in fact, throughout the early years of its spread and division—the humanity of Jesus was of minimal concern. Christ Jesus was the triumphant, risen, and ascended Lord of all the cosmos. From this super-elevated stage, for example, the apostle Paul proclaimed a Christ whose welcome extended beyond his own Jewishness and, indeed, completely off the map of Israel. Yes, Jesus came for the Jews, Paul's message allowed, but good news, he came also to be Christ for all.

We know what happened to this triumphant, resurrected Christ in the early decades of the church. He lost his skin, his human parentage, his particularity as Jew. The ambiguous language of Romans 8:3, for example, casts Christ Jesus (for Paul, "Christ" precedes "Jesus") as one sent by God "in the likeness of sinful flesh." Although Jesus' self-description was preponderantly in terms of his humanity—"son of humanity" was the preferred term—his earliest handlers and packagers preferred the Christly designation. The Romans 8 formulation of Jesus having existed "in the likeness of human flesh" gave easy rise and even biblical foundation to the wildfire of Docetism that made Jesus' humanness into "mere appearance." Marcion, for example, quoted that very text and exegeted the words quite decently enough when he argued that Jesus wasn't really human at all.[2]

That is the beginning of our story. Jesus ascended. Then Jesus ascended some more.

It was into this gnostic euphoria that the gospel writers stepped. Matthew and Luke through their human genealogies and birth narratives, Mark through his "son of humanity" formulation and his motif of suffering, and John through his careful language of Word made flesh (scandalous!)—each was addressing this Christological loss of skin. All four were addressing and correcting the way the human Jesus had become packaged and marketed as cosmic superman.

One might even go so far as to say that the writing of the Gospels brought about a second incarnation of Jesus. In those texts Jesus was again brought down to earth.

In the fierce debate that followed, occupying several hundred years of struggle, the fleshless, docetic Christ preferred by early Christian Gnostics was methodically re-enfleshed. At the end of the first century, Ignatius could boldly declare that Jesus Christ "was really born, and ate and drank, was really persecuted, was really crucified and really died."[3] By the time of Nicaea in the fourth century, Jesus' incarnation and human suffering had become firmly codified into the creedal formulations of orthodox Christianity.[4]

The matter was settled. Jesus was God and Jesus was human. Fully both.

And that, I assert, is the great myth. Our theological satisfaction that we have, indeed, settled this matter of Jesus' incarnation is one of our greatest delusions.

The truth, I believe, is that ever since the day Jesus ascended, the valiant effort of the gospel writers notwithstanding, we have not truly welcomed him back to the ground of our existence. Yes, our creeds say it. "Who for us and because of our salvation came down from heaven, and was incarnate by the Holy Spirit and the Virgin Mary and became human."[5] And yes, we teach it. "We have one who in every respect has been tested as we are, yet without sin."[6]

Yet regardless of these things we cite and teach, we have not made our peace with Jesus' humanity. We remain fundamentally docetic, sneaking around in our gnostic closets, forever attending our twelve-step programs of theological recovery, yet never relinquishing our craven thirst for dualism. We're dual-aholics, convinced Jesus could not in fact have been as human as we are ourselves; not and also God.

For what it's worth, I don't believe we have made peace with our *own* humanness, either. Not even close.

NO INCARNATION, NO PEACE

A colleague of mine, Mary Sage, has been a long-term member of the Western Pennsylvania Coalition Against the Death Penalty. Mary had the privilege of meeting with a widow whose husband was executed by the state of Texas just the week before. The widow told Mary a story of taking her seven-year-old son to see his father for the last time. In the car, driving toward the maximum-security facility where her husband was held, she tried to explain to him just why his daddy would be killed.

Her story came to mind as I wrestled with the incarnation of Jesus and the gospel of peace. I recalled it because the deeper my reflections went, the more I knew that the ascribed meaning that we offer for Jesus' death is the fulcrum on which the incarnation and the gospel of peace tilt. We cannot fundamentally grapple with the place of peace in Jesus' gospel until we grapple with the ancient question, "Why did Jesus have to die?"

The widow tried to explain to her why his daddy had to die. "You see," she said, "your daddy killed a man. That's a terrible thing to do, son. And so," she explained, "your daddy's punishment is that he must die for what he did."

The boy was quiet. Then he asked his question. "Mommy, who's going to kill the man who kills my daddy?"

With that simple question, a boy pulled the thread that unravels much of the garment of human history, if not also the shroud of Christian theology. How does one learn that murder is wrong through murder? We think one does, somehow, yet we are not sure how it works exactly. And not being sure, either before the execution or afterward, we always have to try it again. It is an experiment that never quite produces the expected results, yet so sure are we of its promise that we just cannot stop ourselves from repeating the trials.

Indeed, how does one learn a gospel of life through a pedagogy of judgment and death?

While we were completing our dissertations about how Jesus was both divine and human, while we were finishing our catechisms about how Jesus came to dwell among us full of grace, and while we were sitting on our mommy's laps and learning that Jesus loves me this I know—while all of that was happening—we were at the same time drinking from ancient waters. We were drinking from a pagan and worldly pool filled with justified condemnation and necessary expiation.

Is it in our bones, this "gluttony for our doom," as the Indigo Girls put it?[7] Is it coded into our DNA? Every newborn baby rushed to her baptism is a testimony to the degree to which we imagine our necks somehow poised beneath the sword of God's angry judgment. We believe that if it weren't for the fact that something somehow stops God's righteous blow, we'd be gone.

It goes deeper still. There is a great inclination not only to assume that God despises our skin, but also to despise it ourselves. Call this inclination original sin. Call it whatever you like. Just don't try to make the argument that this self-loathing died out with the ancient dualists and their certainty that flesh is evil and spirit is good. One doesn't have to reach back to third-century Clement of Alexandria, or fifth-century Augustine of Hippo, with their creatively articulated repugnance for women and sex and flesh and stinky diapers, to find evidence of our self-spite. Consider our own anesthetization of every pain, our narcotizing flights from life's every stress, our euthanization of age and infirmity, our disdain for the earth and air and water of the globe, our plastic mummification of waste products filling landfills more wondrous than the Pyramids. Consider all this and more. We can hardly claim ourselves healed of splits between spirit versus matter, mind versus body.

Why then should we believe we are healed of this dualism with regard to Jesus? It seems that from the beginning we have been uneasy at best and butcherous at worst toward human embodiment, Jesus' or ours. We have forever rearranged and trimmed and veiled and mutilated and outright killed whatever manifestations of flesh offend or shame us. In our imaginations these expiations, purifications, pogroms, and wars are necessary. They're required by a higher power who considers flesh to be anathema and in obvious need of expurgation, a cause into which we are all too ready to enlist.

So we cleanse the bloodlines, kick out the misbegotten, button high the blouses, and purge the stomach of our just-finished lunch. With gun and boot and knife and cinch, we tidy up the mess. Then we feel a little better. Until we soon feel worse again and need to do it once more.

Into this human story Jesus is born a human baby, fully God and also complete with ordinary penis and dirty pants. The Word was made flesh. Jesus came, he declared, that we might have life and have it abundantly. He shared his life with us and by all accounts allowed himself both pleasure and comfort. He bore the stripes we bear. He suffered the indignities we suffer. He knew the hunger and poverty of every low-caste child. He knew the fear and loss of every political refugee. He knew the insecurity and vulnerability of every homeless man, woman, or child. He grieved the death of those he loved. He endured even the despair of betrayal and abandonment.

What Jesus knew—what Jesus' incarnation included—are precisely those things that we do not want to know and do not want included in our own lives. It is no mystery why we are so docetic. We don't want to suffer as Jesus suffered. We don't want to lose what Jesus lost. We don't want to break. We don't want to die.

But Jesus, God, accepted this very deal of human existence. Indeed, he considered it entirely worthwhile. He responded to life's mixed conditions with a most resolute "Okay!" And in his "Okay!" he triumphed over the evil that sorely tempted him to say "Not Okay!" He triumphed over what that "Not Okay!" always does in violence to self, to others, to world, or to whatever it is that happens to be the unfortunate messenger of our so tender, so limited, and so vulnerable mortality.

I told that story of the boy because it did not take long, after the founding of Jesus' church, for new structures of condemnation and expiation, structures much like those that killed the boy's daddy, to wend their way back into our story. Juridical notions of crime and punishment, most notably in Anselm of Canterbury, put God back on the righteous throne of judgment and our fleshy necks back onto the deserving block of death.

"Why does my daddy have to die?" the boy rightly asks. Then he gets the eternally wrong answer.

If it were true that we have made peace with Jesus' humanity, then we would know he is pointing us in a new direction for our redemption. We would know that the spite we feel toward ourselves and others is not fitting, for God made us to be human just as surely as God also became human. If it were true that we're "Okay" with Jesus' humanness, with his joy and sorrow, his pleasure and pain, his loves and his losses, then we'd have a basis for being "Okay" with our own.

If we were at peace with Jesus' very human blood, then we could be at peace with each other's blood, too.

SOME REEXAMINATION IS REQUIRED

Anselm of Canterbury must be specially noted here for his role as chief progenitor of the doctrine that God required Jesus' blood. Anselm made of Jesus' blood a debt payment to "the honor of God's dignity,"[8] an idea about as original as spit. And father Abraham, progenitor of the same theme of debt and punishment, must also be noted, if not for what his story requires us to believe as much as what we have chosen to say it means.

Concerning Abraham, there is nothing discernibly meritorious about his willingness to sacrifice his son to God. Our penchant for seeing merit in his willingness with the knife shows how poisoned our skulls are with the ancient disease of blood-lust. Thousands and tens of thousands of fathers and mothers from time immemorial have been all too willing to sacrifice their baby girls and boys to God's supposed insatiable appetite for such shows of bloody devotion. Abraham just doesn't stand out on this score. He is but one more terror-driven man among the masses.

Now imagine being God in these innumerable scenes of history's horror. The devoted and terrified parent whom God loves invokes a final prayer of offering, telling God that this unspeakable thing will be done for God's sake. The child whom God loves is in a terror beyond words. And God cries "NO!" as God always cries "NO!"

Abraham's originality lies somewhere other than his participation in this scene thus far. His sacred place in holy history is irrefutable, but not because, like all his neighbors, he was sure God wanted him to kill his boy. He is so special precisely because he didn't do it. Imagine again being God in this scene. After crying "NO!" at history's every scene of terror and death, a human father finally hears your "NO!" and listens, and obeys, and spares the innocent child. Recall, as you imagine, that it was this same God much later in the story who, in Isaiah 1, broke through the deafness again. It was this same God who told the people that sacrifices and burnt offerings are nothing but an unholy stench. Why? Because, God declared, "your hands are full of blood."[9]

For Anselm, alas, Jesus' blood reflected God's continuing desire and need for such sacrifice, human even, in payment for God's wounded righteousness. What was the awful transgression that wounded God's honor so? Our humanness. Our skin. It's dirty, don't you know? It became that way right from the womb, if not unmentionably sooner.

The theory goes that Jesus could pay this required price because on the human side of the equation his lineage was clean (virgin birth, no concupiscence), and he had good blood right back to David. Likewise, on the divine side he was just plain perfect. He didn't sin. Therefore in God's court all the disgustingness of our living and breathing and bleeding and dying could be heaped up onto Jesus who, though he was human too, was a perfect sacrifice. His execution (now follow the argument closely) could satisfy the just requirement that someone must die, a requirement based on the fact that we are human, which is exactly the way God made us and the way Jesus (God) fully was, too.

What Anselm missed, alas, and what we still miss, is the real story. Just put your finger into the Gospels, point most anywhere, and you will find it. Take, for random example, the first gospel, first chapter, barely into verse 3. Matthew sticks four dirty women into Jesus' bloodline (there are quite a few dirty men there, too, as I read the account). He puts Tamar and Rahab there, both Canaanite, Tamar who sexually seduced her merciless father-in-law and Rahab who ran an escort service. Ruth of the troublesomely rebellious Moabites is there in the exalted line. And the presumably Hittite Bathsheba is there too, she who was so brazenly prone to bathe without clothes on. Oh, the purity of Jesus' blood!

We are ever so pleased, from the standpoint of the resurrected, ascended side of the equation, theologically to declare that Christ shed his blood *for* the world. But Matthew tells us something additional in the very preamble of his gospel. Jesus got his blood *from* the world. And it's not even special blood. Not pure blood. Not blue blood. His is everybody's blood, all mixed together, including that of the cursed race of the Canaanites (Tamar and Rahab), the Sodomites lineaged through the Moabite Ruth, and the hated enemy Hittites, Bathsheba.

Washed in Jesus' (mixed-race and "dirty") blood, we of human mix are marked as belonging to one another. In the ancient worlds of the Near East where blood divided according to lines of purity and proper lineage, the meaning of the words "blood" and "community" are inextricable. Whose blood are you? To what community do you belong?

But in the incarnation of Jesus,

> You who once were far off have been brought near by the blood of Christ. For he is our peace; in his flesh he has made both groups into one

and has broken down the dividing wall, that is, the hostility between us. He has abolished the law with its commandments and ordinances, that he might create in himself one new humanity in place of the two, thus making peace.[10]

Jesus' Body, Our Bodies, and the Church

There is a far better settlement to the question of the place of peace in the gospel of Jesus Christ than the one found in Abraham's willingness to sacrifice or Anselm's wantonness for blood (or in America's death row, for that matter). Theirs is a settlement that pits a flesh-hating God against a flesh-haunted humankind and requires nothing less than the death of flesh for the satisfaction of God. Theirs is an unfortunate settlement that requires us to clean the mud off of Jesus' humanity so that his pure blood can satisfy as payment for our sorrier variety. Fundamentally and unavoidably, their settlement is anti-incarnational and most difficult to square with the Jesus who was made flesh, who offered that flesh in the famous words of "this is my body," who did so that we might be made whole, bodies and all.

A far better settlement can and must be found in the very body and blood of Jesus, that which he gave and that which we are. This body and blood of Jesus, however, must be depurified *a la* Matthew 1 if it is to help us. Jesus' blood must be allowed to run back out into the streets and mix again with the "dirty" bloodlines from which it came. And while we are on the subject, our blood must be allowed to go there too. Recall the words of Jesus: "Unless a grain of wheat falls into the earth and dies, it remains just a single grain; but if it dies, it bears much fruit."[11]

This is, of course, a risky proposition. And Jesus' approach to this world *is* risky. It is not preoccupied with the defense of bloodline (or of doctrinal line, for that matter). It pushes into the crush of strangers and seeks the redemption of all, even at the risk of loss of self.

This is also, fundamentally, the approach of the early Anabaptists who walked willingly into circles of public discourse, rejected coercion and worldly defense, and entrusted the word they were given to bear fruit as the Spirit chose. Recall Conrad Grebel's letter to the revolutionary Thomas Müntzer: "The gospel and its adherents are not to be protected by the sword," he wrote, "nor are they thus to protect themselves . . . neither do they use worldly sword or war, since all killing has ceased with them."[12]

What our forbears understood, and what we must understand again, is this: when Word has a body, rather than being a disembodied edict, its proclamation is always risky. The defenseless proclamation of the gospel of peace is mustard seed confident, yeast tenacious, crushed grape efficacious, ground kernel nutritious. It affirms the victory of Jesus Christ from the ground up, from the corruptible to the incorruptible, through broken bones and shed blood. Its very foundation is incarnation, for it knows that skin must be put into the game. Why? Because skin matters. When you offer your body and blood for others, you do so because you value theirs.

The formulation that "Jesus died for me" must be transformed from a forensic strategy we use to deal with the shame and guilt of our unacceptable human existence to an affirmation of God's love for all that we are. Such affirmation must include our own willingness to die if doing so brings life to others, and otherwise to live our lives in joyful, loving fullness. "There is therefore now no condemnation for those who are in Christ Jesus."[13]

Peace has no other predicate than incarnation. Warring ways and juridical processes are the cheap escape from having to give skin. The problem is that only in giving skin is the bond of peace secured. Jesus' gospel must be defenselessly proclaimed (it needs no defense) and boldly (bodily) enacted (our bodies and Christ's body are required).

"The believing body of Christ is the world on the way to its renewal,"[14] John Howard Yoder writes.

> The Church is the part of the world that confesses the renewal to which all the world is called. The believing body is the instrument of that renewal of the world, to the (very modest) extent to which its message is faithful. It may be 'instrument' as proclaimer, or as pilot project, or as pedestal.

The body of Christ, and our bodies, are essential parts of the coin of gospel proclamation, not in their repugnant obliteration for the sake of sanitizing the soul for God, but in their determined and loving acts, sacrifice included, for the sake of providing bread, advocacy, and shield for those who suffer in their bodies. Words, likewise, are part of the coin of gospel proclamation, not in disembodied titillation and entertainment, but in embodied discourse.

Both words and bones can take redemptive position against the sticks and the stones of this world's sinful and oppressive violations. Bones can preach, words can feed, bones can comfort, words can be broken and served for the healing of many.

What the end of the second millennium has brought us, it seems to me, is only further commodification of the body as both consumer and object of consumption, guilt and shame lying at the heart of this consumptive and self-devouring appetite. Not only has our little piggy gone to market, the rest of us has made the trip as well. Our lives are played out on one side or the other of the meat case. Increasingly, we are both the buyer and the goods.

Our communities have likewise been placed onto the block and butchered into the finest and choicest cuts for sale. It is all about brand and identity and diversification and niche.

This incredible attention focused on our consuming and consumable bodies, every aspect of which is a market transaction, has emerged, ironically, precisely at a moment when the value of human life has hit an all-time low. The living and breathing, loving and thinking persons that we are have been tossed into the discount bin, there for the price of hauling away.

Jesus' birth, life, death, and resurrection are never more needed than today. We need to hear the good news afresh that God loves us beyond reason. This love is such that God joined us in skin and bone, and only too happily. This love is also such that God invites—no, requires—that we continually seek to find fresh ways to be knit together into a body of welcome that offers an alternative to the violent, denigrating, and consumptive ways of this world. That alternative, in the modest words of John, is that we should love one another.

This is the gospel of peace. And this is, in selfsame breath, good news made flesh. In days ahead, may Christ's body embrace its own incarnational calling and do so with a resounding, world-loving, and peacemaking "Okay!"

Notes

1. Ephesians 4:5-6, NRSV in this Scripture citation and those below.

2. Jaroslav Pelikan, *The Christian Tradition: A History of the Development of Doctrine, Volume 1, The Emergence of the Catholic Tradition (100-600)* (Chicago and London: The University of Chicago Press, 1971), 174. Pelikan here documents how Celsus, as rebutted by Origen of Alexandria; Marcius, as rebutted by Tertullian of Carthage; and Simonian Gnosticism, as well as the writings of Ptolemy, as rebutted by Irenaeus of Lyons—all made similarly docetic arguments that Jesus, in fact, "did not suffer."

3. Ibid.

4. John H. Leith, ed., *The Creed of Nicaea (325)* from *Creeds of the Churches* (Atlanta: John Knox Press, 1963), 31. "Who for us men and for our salvation came down and was incarnate, becoming human. He suffered and the third day he rose, and ascended into the heavens."

5. Ibid., 33. *The Constantinopolitan Creed (381)*.

6. Hebrews 4:15b.

7. Emily Saliers, *Prince of Darkness* in *Indigo Girls Live; Back on the Bus, Y'All* (New York City: Sony Music Entertainment, Inc., 1991).

8. Archbishop of Canterbury, Saint Anselm, *Why God Became Man* (Lewiston, NewYork: Edwin Mellen Press, 1980), 13.

9. Isaiah 1:15.

10. Ephesians 2:13-16.

11. John 12:24.

12. George H. Williams and Angel M. Mergal, eds., *Spiritual and Anabaptist Writers*, vol. 25 of *The Library of Christian Classics* (Louisville: Westminster/John Knox Press, 1996), 80.

13. Romans 8:1.

14. John Howard Yoder, *Body Politics: Five Practices of the Christian Community Before the Watching World* (Nashville: Discipleship Resources, 1992), 78.

SEVENTEEN

CHRISTIAN PACIFISM AS FRIENDSHIP WITH GOD:
MacIntyre, Mennonites, and the Genealogical Tradition

Chris K. Huebner

"To begin is impossible." Or so begins one recent account of the possibility of a postmodern ethics.[1] To put it less cutely, there are no pure starting points, no foundational or necessary origins of enquiry. All beginnings are provisional, constituting an aspect of a larger conversation already under way. But chapters like this one must begin somewhere.

So let me begin by suggesting that the primary question for Anabaptists with respect to postmodernity should not so much be whether to accept or reject it—whatever "it" is—but rather what it means to live amid it. Let me also suggest this: for purposes of exploring how Anabaptist theology might be understood in the network of diverse and often competing influences that go under the name *postmodernism*, there are two particularly noteworthy strands. One is the version of Thomistic Aristotelianism defended by Alasdair MacIntyre as a response to the failed Enlightenment project of providing an independent and unified foundation for ethics. The other is the Nietzschean Genealogical tradition, embodied most recently in the work of Michel Foucault and Jacques Derrida, which MacIntyre takes to be his most significant rival.

More specifically, I think it will be fruitful to recontextualize the Anabaptist understanding of Christian pacifism by locating it in the context of the debate between MacIntyre and the Genealogical tradition considered in terms of their respective accounts of the politics of friendship. But before turning to such a specifically theological reading of the debate, I shall offer a brief discussion of how the notion of *friendship* functions in their competing conceptions of politics.

FRIENDSHIP IN MACINTYRE, ARISTOTLE, AND AQUINAS

MacIntyre: Friendship, politics, and the common good

In *After Virtue*, MacIntyre attempts to overcome the excessively abstract character of modern moral philosophy by developing an account of the virtues. At that point he turns to Aristotle's discussion of friendship to clarify how ethics is to be situated in the concrete political context of the *polis*. In contrast to the ethics of modern liberalism, which is based on the notion of individual autonomy and the general principle of freedom derived from it, MacIntyre argues that Aristotelian friendship suggests an alternative conception of ethics. MacIntyre's ethic is rooted in the "shared recognition of and pursuit of the good."[2]

More specifically, he claims that the Aristotelian account of the *polis* is best understood in terms of an "interrelated network of small groups of friends," which involves the "sharing of all in the common project of creating and sustaining the life of the city."[3] Such an understanding of friendship, MacIntyre maintains, exists in sharp contrast to the characteristically modern notion of friendship. The modern understanding is not only essentially private but also primarily the name of an "emotional state" rather than a form of political organization.[4]

In an Aristotelian account of friendship, by contrast, there is no conceptual space for the distinction between public and private. Friendship for MacIntyre, as for Aristotle, is thus a fundamentally political notion. Friendship names the kinds of relationships dedicated to the common pursuit of those goods recognized as being most central to the collective life of the *polis*.

While many of these same themes are continued and further developed in his more recent work, it is noteworthy that MacIntyre's emphasis on the ethical-political significance of friendship appears to have diminished as he has made the transition from the straightforwardly Aristotelian standpoint defended in *After Virtue* to the Thomistic Aristotelian tradition he claims to represent in *Whose Justice? Which Rationality?*[5] and *Three Rival Versions of Moral Enquiry.*[6] Although he does not abandon his claim that a proper understanding of the virtues presupposes an account of the common good, he no longer develops this in terms of friendship, as he did previously, but rather in the context of a more formal discussion of justice and the good itself.

Thus in looking at the larger story MacIntyre's work is telling over time, it appears that his emphasis on friendship becomes weaker as his embrace of Aquinas becomes stronger and more thorough. This is odd, because in Aquinas's appropriation of Aristotelianism, the ethical significance of friendship was never abandoned or weakened. On the contrary, friendship appears instead to become even more central in Aquinas, insofar as it functions as the form of the virtues, describing the relationship between humans and God whereby God claims us as friends.[7] So MacIntyre's appropriation of Aquinas to supplement and complete his earlier understanding of Aristotelianism appears to run in a direction opposite to that of Aquinas himself, as least with respect to friendship.

Aquinas: From Aristotelian friendship to charity as friendship with God

To understand what is at stake in MacIntyre's apparent divergence from Aquinas on friendship, it will be instructive briefly to examine Aquinas's theological transformation of Aristotelian friendship into charity as friendship with God. Aquinas accepts the general structure of Aristotle's account of friendship, in particular his account of the friend as "another self" in which self-knowledge is subordinated to one's knowledge of others through friendship. As Aristotle himself puts it, "as then when we wish to see our own face, we do so by looking in a mirror, in the same way when we wish to know ourselves we can obtain that knowledge by looking at our friend. For the friend is, as we assert, a second self."[8]

However, Aquinas significantly transforms Aristotelian friendship, rooting it primarily in a relationship of friendship with God, a possibility Aristotle himself explicitly denied on grounds that there is not sufficient equality between humans and gods. For Aristotle there is no possibility for a meaningful relationship to develop between unequals.[9] Yet Aquinas develops a conception of friendship in which it is God who is one's other self. It is through friendship with God that we come to know ourselves and are enabled more fully to embark on the process of training and habituation into the life of the virtues.

Further, to overcome the distance between Creator and creature, Aquinas claims that such a relationship is to be christologically mediated by participation in sacramental practices in the church.[10] Thus the possibility of having such a relationship with God is, for Aquinas, not a question of abstract or conceptual achievement. Rather, the relationship is concretely embodied by developing the particular kind of character which can only be achieved by the imitation of Christ through the habitual practice of such sacraments as baptism and the eucharist. For Aquinas, then, there is no self-understanding before a relationship in which God claims us as friends. There is thus no "self" before the kind of participation which God made possible first by the incarnation of God in Christ and second by the continued presence of Christ in the church's sacramental practices.

Not only does Aquinas's account of friendship thus theologically radicalize Aristotle's understanding of the friend as another self, it also appears to call into question the strong notion of a unified and stable autonomous individual. Insofar as it makes selfhood and moral identity inseparable from one's relationships with other selves, and in particular with God, Aquinas's account of friendship might be read as suggesting the following account of the "self." The self is structurally, if not ultimately, a mix of unstable and disparate sources. It is also notably contingent, at least insofar as it is a self dependent on God's first claiming us as friends.

Yet despite MacIntyre's questions regarding the Enlightenment notion of the autonomous individual considered in abstraction from all social context, he emphasizes the unity and well-integrated character of the self to a greater degree than Aquinas's understanding of friendship in terms of interrelated other selves seems to permit. Indeed, the fact that MacIntyre can even attempt to provide an account of the self in abstraction separate from discussion of friendship with God seems to call into question MacIntyre's alleged Thomistic Aristotelianism. I say this because for Aquinas the very notion of selfhood is unintelligible apart from an ecclesial and sacramental participation with God through the imitation of Christ.

It is thus odd that MacIntyre's critique of the Genealogical tradition is not based on the hopeful possibility of friendship with God. Rather, the critique flows from the claim that "the individual human being is a *unity* in which the directedness of the different aspects of his spiritual and social existence have to be ordered hierarchically into a unified mode of life."[11] So MacIntyre does initially turn to friendship to stress the concrete political interrelationships of a community of selves (in the plural). Yet he increasingly abandons the notion of friendship for an account of the unified self (in the singular) to combat what he takes to be the destabilizing and ultimately destructive forces of the Genealogical account of difference.

DERRIDA, DIFFERENCE, AND THE POLITICS OF FRIENDSHIP

In addition to the apparent tension created by MacIntyre's turn from friendship at this point, there is another reason for disappointment. This is that the Genealogical conception of difference has itself become more explicitly developed in the context of a discussion of the politics of friendship. There are several suggestive hints in this direction in Nietzsche himself.[12] These are developed in Foucault's later work, in which friendship names an aesthetic practice of collective self-creation as an alternative to the politics of identity which he takes to be based on the "exclusion of the other."[13]

But the most extensive discussion of friendship in the Genealogical tradition is in the recent work of Jacques Derrida. In an attempt to make more explicit the politics implied by his understanding of deconstruction, Derrida seeks to develop a "democratic" politics of friendship as an alternative both to the standard understanding of democracy and to what he calls the canonical reading of friendship. Such a politics seeks to "free a certain interpretation of *equality* by removing it from the phallogocentric schema of *fraternity*" he takes to be central to the traditional understanding of friendship, including Aristotle's account of the friend as another self.[14]

In other words, Derrida is rethinking friendship without the bonds imposed by presence and proximity. He thus wants to be respectful of the possibility of "infinite difference" in friendship.[15] Derrida himself puts it in the form of a question: "Is it possible to think and to implement democracy, that which would keep the old name 'democracy,' while uprooting from it all these figures of friendship (philosophical and religious) which prescribe fraternity, the family and the androcentric religious group?"[16]

Derrida's turn to the notion of friendship is thus an extension of the general account of alterity which seeks to make room for the place or "voice" of the "other" that runs throughout his work.[17] Stated briefly, he claims that the traditional understanding of friendship is based on a "logic of opposition" characteristic of the kind of "metaphysical" or logocentric thinking he has been attempting to deconstruct throughout his career.

At the same time he claims it is beset with contradictions which turn that logic back against itself, making it unable to sustain even its most basic sets of contrasts. In particular, he claims that the traditional idea of friendship is based on a conception of unity and similarity opposed to difference and otherness, such that the friend is someone ideally similar to oneself.[18]

In contrast to such a view, although he does not deny that there is a sense of similarity in friendship, Derrida emphasizes the radical alterity of the friend. Focusing primarily on the "otherness" aspect of Aristotle's other self thesis, he claims that the friend is irreducibly other, that the otherness of the friend is "absolutely originary."[19] It is at this point that his attempt to rethink friendship as the name of a distinct kind of radical democratic politics is best understood. In short, Derrida describes the politics of friendship as one that enables a recognition of the otherness and irreducible singularity of the other: "The grace of friendship leaves the other, lets it be, gives it what it has and what it already is."[20]

Even here, however, Derrida cautions that the "grace of friendship" does not exist in the absence of conflict and discord.[21] Derridean friendship thus names a basic tension between unity and difference.[22] Although he does not go so far as to deny the very possibility of friendship, Derrida maintains that such relationships are radically unstable. Friendship is constituted at the same time by a kind of sharing and by a gap of irreducible otherness, such that there is a sense of antagonism or conflict, of *aporia* or *polemos*, which lies "at the very heart of friendship itself."[23]

This is not to suggest, however, that he marks a point of absolute rupture between the self and the other as friend. On the contrary, Derrida's discussion of friendship is designed to challenge the very distinction between self and other, such that the friend in part constitutes or enables the "self" to whom she is "other." As Derrida himself puts it, "The voice of the other friend, of the other as friend . . . is the condition of my own-proper-being."[24]

Accordingly, as with the Thomistic Aristotelian notion of the other self that MacIntyre began with but has increasingly left behind, Derrida takes the notion of friendship to suggest a kind of interdependence or interconstitution of selves in a way that challenges the idea of the stable and unified subject or self. But he does so in a much more agonistic manner, arguing that there is a more radical and pervasive sense of difference in the otherness involved in various aspects of friendship. Thus conflict and struggle are intrinsic to friendship itself.

What is perhaps even more significant about Derrida's discussion of friendship for purposes of the debate with MacIntyre is the sense in which he appears to reintroduce God into the Genealogical tradition. Whereas the Genealogical tradition is commonly traced back to Nietzsche's pronouncement of the death of God, it might be suggested that Derrida's recent work amounts to a sort of rebirth of the theological. Building on his deconstruction of the so-called "metaphysical tradition," Derrida rejects the "onto-theological" notion of God as a supreme being.[25] He nevertheless claims to be interested in the possibility of reconceiving the notion of God without the logocentrism and oppositional logic on which, he claims, it has traditionally been based.

In short, Derrida describes such a non-ontological conception of God as a transcendent alterity, a wholly and infinite other.[26]

> "Every other (one) is God," or "God is every (bit) other." . . . In one case God is defined as infinitely other, as wholly other, every bit other. In the other case it is declared that every other one, each of the others, is God inasmuch as he or she is, *like* God, wholly other.[27]

In thus attempting to free God from the ontological tendency to categorize and identify, he suggests that a relationship with God is most fully achieved at death, at the "gift of death" which is at the same time an irreducibly singular and ultimately individual experience and yet one in which one is confronted by the gaze of the absolute other which is God.[28] Thus the possibility of finally achieving friendship is, for Derrida, an endlessly delayed possibility. The politics of friendship consists in living amid this possibility.

Friendship, Discipleship, and Christian Pacifism

To sum up the discussion so far, both MacIntyre and the Genealogists attempt to develop an account of politics that provides an alternative to the liberalism of Enlightenment modernity. But MacIntyre argues that an account of the unity and continuity of the self directed toward the good is ultimately required to prevent the slide into the unconstrained conflict of will to power. This will to power he takes to be the result of the Genealogical emphasis on rupture and difference.

To move this direction, however, it appears that he has increasingly distanced himself from his earlier appeal to the notion of friendship. The Genealogists, on the other hand, claim that MacIntyre has not broken sufficiently with the universalist and objectivist assumptions of Enlightenment rationalism. Moreover, they do so by appealing to the very notion of friendship MacIntyre has apparently left behind.

It is thus a paradoxical turnaround in the debate to find MacIntyre claiming to represent the tradition of Thomistic Aristotelianism, yet seeming to move away from friendship, especially friendship with God. Meanwhile, the Genealogists are treating friendship with increasing seriousness, and Derrida is even teasing us with the possibility of theological friendship.

Instead of attempting to resolve the debate as it stands, however, I shall now turn to the more specifically theological question of what it means to embody a politics of Christian pacifism in the context of this discussion.

Milbank, charity, and the ontology of peace

Among the many possible ways of reading the debate between MacIntyre and the Genealogists, none is more suggestive for the question of Christian pacifism than that of John Milbank. In short, Milbank argues that behind their many significant differences lies a more fundamental similarity in that they both presuppose an "ontology of violence."[29] Though MacIntyre wants to avoid the kind of "irrational" conflict he takes to be characteristic of the Genealogical tradition, he claims that this cannot be settled by standards imposed from the "outside." Rather, MacIntyre advocates for a Thomistic Aristotelian version of dialectical rationality among competing traditions of enquiry. One aspect of his path involves his account of unified selves noted above, whose lives consist in the ongoing task of continuously narrating and renarrating such conflicts over time.

But Milbank argues that such an account of dialectically constrained rational conflict between competing traditions reproduces the problem MacIntyre is trying to overcome. This is because it remains rooted in an understanding of the world which takes such violence or "agonistic difference" to be ontologically basic.[30] Similarly he claims that the Genealogical tradition, including Derrida's recent gestures toward the possibility of friendship with God, is also rooted in just such an account of originary agonistic violence. This is the case, at least, insofar as it continues to presuppose a Nietzschean will to power. As Milbank himself puts it,

> Antique thought and politics assumes some naturally given element of chaotic conflict which must be tamed by the stability and self-identity of reason. Modern thought and politics (most clearly articulated by Nietzsche) assumes that there is *only* this chaos.... If one tries, like MacIntyre, to oppose antique thought to modern thought, then the attempt will fail because antique thought—as Plato already saw, in *The Sophist*—is deconstructible into "modern" thought: a cosmos including both chaos and reason implies an ultimate principle, the "difference" between the two, which is *more* than reason, and enshrines permanent conflict.[31]

As an alternative to both MacIntyre and the Genealogical tradition, however, Milbank claims that Christianity recognizes no originary violence. Christianity is instead based on an "'ontology of peace' which conceives differences as analogically related, rather than equivocally at variance."[32] That is to say, Christianity deconstructs the Genealogical assumption of the necessity of violence by embodying an "analogical coding of peace." This coding of peace denies the opposition and reduction of difference to self-identity and sustains a counter-politics of "the peaceful transmission of difference" or "differences in a continuous harmony."[33]

For purposes of the present discussion, it is also instructive to note that Milbank's account of the Christian ontology of peace is developed in terms of charity as friendship with God and the practice of forgiveness he takes to be its ethical and political instantiation. As Milbank puts it, "charity is originally the gratuitous, creative positing of difference, and the offering to others of a space of freedom, which is existence."[34] In other words, charity names the gracious self-giving of God in friendship. Then violence and difference do not have the final say but rather may be overcome through the faithful practice of forgiveness.[35]

Christian pacifism as friendship with God

Though it might be objected that Milbank is mistaken about certain important details in his treatment of MacIntyre and the Genealogists, there is a more important issue, at least from the standpoint of Mennonite theology. That issue is this: how can he provide such a powerful account of ontological peace rooted in theological charity without finally embracing a pacifist politics of nonviolence?

This concern arises because, as Milbank himself notes, "in no sense does *Theology and Social Theory* recommend 'pacifism,' and the formal specification of truth as peaceful relation cannot be applied as a criterion authorizing nonresistance."[36] Rather, in certain circumstances, such as "when a person commits an evil act,"[37] the need for "some measures of coercion" is justified. While "such action may not be 'peaceable,'" it "can still be 'redeemed' by retrospective acceptance, and so contribute to the final goal of peace."[38] In such cases, Milbank suggests, violence can actually be "beneficial" such that the "good motives of those resorting to it are recognized and recuperated by the defaulter coming to his senses."[39]

Without further clarification, however, such a claim sounds all too reminiscent of the conception of instrumental reason his polemic against "secular reason" is designed to deconstruct. At the very least, Milbank is obliged more concretely to spell out his understanding of the nature of such "beneficial violence" and the structure of retrospective justification used to support it.

In one important sense, Milbank's argument is instructive even in the face of what I take to be significant shortcomings. In particular, it is notable that his rejection of Christian pacifism is not rooted in the standard appeal to political realism, namely, that pacifism is politically naive in underestimating the widespread power of violence. Rather, I take it that by building on both MacIntyre and the Genealogical tradition, Milbank helps us get beyond the temptation to employ the simple Enlightenment dualism of real and ideal. Instead I shall suggest that Milbank finally fails to embody a politics of Christian pacifism for specifically theological reasons.

Whereas Milbank is basically correct in attempting to develop an ontology of peace rooted in charity as friendship with God, his account is at its weakest in depicting the God who claims us as friends. In particular, it appears that Milbank's theology remains insufficiently christological to the extent that it fails to pay adequate attention to the life, death, and resurrection of Jesus. In his attempt to counter the ontology of violence he takes to lie behind both MacIntyre and the Genealogists with an ontology of peaceful, harmonious difference, Milbank appears to overemphasize the creative and aesthetically expansive power of God the creator at the cost of neglecting the suffering power of the crucified God. As David Toole suggests, Milbank's mistake finally "is to stress the incarnation of the logos as the decisive moment and not to stress even more that the logos incarnate passed through the cross."[40]

In fairness to Milbank, to claim that his theology is insufficiently christological, as I have done, is admittedly somewhat of an overstatement. On the contrary, it might be suggested that it is in the two chapters on Christology in *The Word Made Strange* that some of the most important aspects of his more recent constructive position are developed.[41] Accordingly, it would be more accurate to say that his Christology is inadequate in certain specific respects. In particular, it is problematic to the extent that it appears to relativize the significance of the identity and character of Jesus.[42]

As Milbank puts it, the identity of Jesus "does not actually relate to his 'character,' but rather to his universal significance for which his particularity stands, almost, as a mere cipher."[43] Instead of focusing on the concrete unfolding of Jesus' life in the particular acts of forgiveness and healing that he performed, Milbank's Christology is based on the "logic" of "nonidentical repetition." Such a logic he claims can be derived from the event of *poesis*, or the church's aesthetic exercise of ascribing the name "Jesus" to that significant figure in the Christian story. And despite his emphasis on the aesthetic practices of the church, it appears that Milbank also relativizes the people of God, in the fundamentally related sense of both Israel and the body of Christian disciples. Further, it might be suggested that these joint relativizations are closely related to the sense in which his project appears to be devoted to the "Constantinian" task of developing a civilizational religion able straightforwardly to replace the secularism of liberal modernity in all its grand scale.[44]

Despite his gestures toward the development of a "counter-polis" in the final chapter of *Theology and Social Theory*, one gets the sense that Milbank wants the "church" simply to supplant the "world" rather than embody a concrete alternative amid it. Put differently, for all his emphasis on developing an alternative to the world, it appears there is no category of *witness* in Milbank's theology. And I am suggesting this is closely related to his inattention to the concrete details of Jesus' life, death, and resurrection.

Conversely, Mennonite discussions of Christology tend to be strongest on the question of the particulars of the story of Jesus which are at the same time a way of defining the peculiar shape of the people of God. For example, Mennonites read the Gospels, and at their better moments the Bible as a whole, as the inauguration of a radically new community rooted in the specific form of life exemplified by Jesus. Among other things, this includes the practice of economic sharing that is the Lord's Supper and the habitual training of our collective bodies as sites of resistance that need not be shaped by the sword.

It is because Milbank also emphasizes the sense in which theology concerns the formation of a counter-politics that it is so instructive to compare his work with a typically Mennonite perspective. According to Milbank, "[t]he gospels can be read, *not* as the story of Jesus, but as the (re)foundation of a new city, a new kind of community, Israel-become-the-Church."[45] If such an emphasis on politics is no more than an opposition to the privatization of theology whereby Christianity has become primarily a matter of individual salvation, then this is a welcome and in fact necessary point of emphasis. But what seems suspicious about such a claim is the implied disjunction, namely, that the Gospels are either about the formation of a new politics or the story of Jesus.

He is clearly not making the strong Troeltschian claim that "the preaching of Jesus and the creation of the Christian church were not due in any sense to the impulse of a social movement."[46] Nevertheless, Milbank does seem to suggest that with respect to the political question of the church as a counter-community, we are better off looking elsewhere than the story of Jesus.

Where he turns instead is to the category of aesthetics. In particular, he underscores his account of non-identical repetition and the related conception of the harmonious resolution of difference that he derives from the "logic" of creation and the interrelationship between the trinitarian persons. Certainly Mennonite theology could benefit from a more substantial discussion of creation and the Trinity. But it does not follow, as Milbank's work seems to imply, that such a "radically orthodox"[47] stance means one must give up the more typically Mennonite claim that the Gospels are the story of the (re)foundation of a new community *precisely because* they tell the story of Jesus.

In fact, it is only on the basis of a robust trinitarianism that such a claim is possible in the first place. That is to say, it is only on the basis of Jesus' divinity that the church can be seen as the embodied foretaste of the kingdom of God. At any rate, the particular shape of such a new Christian counter-community will look very different, depending on whether or not it is rooted in the concrete display of the character of Jesus. Or at least that is what we appear to get in the case of Mennonite theology vis-à-vis Milbank.

Milbank's account of nonidentical repetition is helpful, however, in that it avoids reification and a correlative representational account of the imitation of Christ in terms of objective mirroring of a static and external reality. Accordingly, it might be objected on Milbank's behalf that his account of the "name of Jesus" is simply an attempt to avoid the tendency toward a reified account of the identity of Jesus and the patterns of discipleship that might be identified as characteristic of Mennonite theology.

This objection is certainly justified in some cases. However, such a representational account of disciplined imitation is not a necessary characteristic of Anabaptist-Mennonite theology. In fact, it might be suggested that there are specific resources in Anabaptist ecclesiology that guard against such an interpretation. In particular, the practice of communal discernment, the ongoing task of negotiating and renegotiating the life of the community, can be seen as a way of resisting the assumption that we need to develop some fixed, once-for-all pattern of discipleship based on some final account of the identity of Jesus.

I suspect this is closely related to John Howard Yoder's characteristic reminder that we are to resist the Constantinian temptation which assumes that it is up to us to guarantee that history will come out right. Yet to avoid such temptation, it does not follow that we must give up concrete appeals to the identity and character of Jesus altogether. Rather, the church's hermeneutic practice of reading and performing the Scriptures seems precisely to require some particular account of the concrete character of Jesus, even if such an account is never taken to be absolutely "final" in and of itself.

To develop a reified Christology in this latter sense is not only to treat Jesus in abstraction from the other two persons of the Trinity, but also to treat the Bible as a depository of facts entirely intelligible apart from their instantiation in the life of the church. However, it is not clear that Anabaptist claims regarding the nonviolent character of Jesus are guilty of such problems, precisely because they are most significantly made in terms of the actual performance of embodied practices of nonviolence.

Put differently, in objecting to Milbank's aesthetic turn to christological *poesis*, I am not arguing against the appeal to aesthetics as such. On the contrary, I am questioning the sense in which his understanding of nonidentical repetition appears to be based on a lingering dichotomy between aesthetics and concrete reality. At the same time, Anabaptist accounts of discipleship sometimes privilege the latter while retaining the same dichotomous structure of the available options. But I want to suggest that it is more appropriate to understand Anabaptist-Mennonite theology as rendering the assumption that one must choose between aesthetics and concrete reality fundamentally unintelligible.

Among other things, this is exactly what the appeal to friendship with God is designed to do. For the life of discipleship is not an attempt to simply repeat or copy the life of Jesus. Rather, friendship with God names that relationship whereby God calls us to participate in God's very life through the aesthetic and embodied performance of church practices. Moreover, whereas Milbank is correct to recognize that the body of Christ is a profoundly political body, his tendency to develop this position in terms of a preference for aesthetics over against the concrete reality of the character of Jesus leads him to underestimate the possibility of a pacifist politics.

Anabaptist theology, by contrast, is best understood as an attempt to understand cross and resurrection in these terms: as the unification of an aesthetic conception of discipleship as nonidentical repetition with account of the concrete display of Jesus' life in terms of nonviolent acts of forgiveness and reconciliation. In other words, even though it has not traditionally been developed in such terms, a proper understanding of friendship with God is just another name for the traditional Mennonite understanding of discipleship. As Yoder, summarizing the Schleitheim Confession, puts it,

> The foundation of the call for nonresistance is unity with Jesus. You could of course say "unity with Christ," but the Christ it is talking about

is not some cosmic figure, and not some present mystical guide alone, but the continuation in our experience, because we are to be an undivided body. We are to be a part of what he is, and he is what he was.[48]

CONCLUSION

In conclusion, it will be instructive to summarize the main points of my argument by bringing the strands of the foregoing discussion together. To approach this debate in terms of the question of friendship with God underscores that MacIntyre's defense of Thomistic Aristotelianism is at its weakest in articulating Aquinas's theological transformation of Aristotle.

Furthermore, when set beside Derrida's version of the Nietzschean Genealogical tradition, there seems to be a "securing function." This function is designed to overcome the contingency lying behind MacIntyre's account of the unity of the self that a more thorough discussion of friendship might call into question. The recent work of Milbank, however, provides a decisive challenge to both MacIntyre and Derrida. In particular, he suggests that a properly theological understanding of creation can account for contingency and the structural instability of the human subject. Yet this understanding stops short of a Genealogical account of the will to power and the corresponding ontology of violence.

Thus it appears that Derrida's apparent theological turn to friendship with God continues to accord too great a role to the agonistic narrative of conflict and violence. At the same time, there is no need to abandon the notion of friendship as a network of interrelated selves, as MacIntyre has done, to mount a response to the Genealogical conception of originary violence. Yet Milbank's conclusions regarding pacifism can be called into question by a conception of discipleship that refuses to understand the (re)foundation of a new Christian counter-community in terms of the distinction between aesthetics and concrete reality. In other words, even Milbank's "radically theological" attempt to develop a counter-politics based on the ontology of peace is theologically deficient in that it lacks the kind of concrete specification that would be provided by a more adequate account of the person of Jesus Christ.

Taken together, it appears that despite various protests to the contrary, MacIntyre, Derrida, and Milbank all proceed in an overly theoretical and speculative manner. That is, they tend to speak in terms of abstract notions such as charity and friendship in general rather than the particular friend Jesus, "the concrete universal through whom we have perfect charity represented to us."[49]

Finally, such an understanding of Christian pacifism as friendship with God allows us to avoid such distorting conceptual dualisms as public and private, ideal and real, christocentrism and theocentrism, and self and other that have dominated the discussion of Christian pacifism in this century. Instead, this pacifist stance places the emphasis where it really matters, namely, the kind of politics embodied by the church, the very body of Christ.

For all these reasons, I think an Anabaptist account of Christian pacifism construed in terms of friendship with God is peculiarly suited to illuminate and in turn be illumined by the debate between MacIntyre and the Genealogists on the politics of friendship with which this discussion began. But this is the case only if we pose another question to the justly celebrated question, "Aristotle or Nietzsche?" that constitutes the basis of MacIntyre's project and, judging by Derrida's recent work, is central to the Genealogical tradition as well. That counterquestion is one we can imagine being asked with appropriately stubborn insistence by John Howard Yoder: "But what about Jesus?"

NOTES

1. Dawn McCance, *Posts: Re-Addressing the Ethical* (Albany, N.Y.: State University of New York Press, 1996), 1.

2. Alasdair MacIntyre, *After Virtue*, 2d ed. (Notre Dame, Ind.: University of Notre Dame Press, 1984), 155.

3. Ibid., 156.

4. Ibid.

5. Alasdair MacIntyre, *Whose Justice? Which Rationality?* (Notre Dame, Ind.: University of Notre Dame Press, 1988).

6. Alasdair MacIntyre, *Three Rival Versions of Moral Enquiry: Encyclopaedia, Genealogy, and Tradition* (Notre Dame, Ind.: University of Notre Dame Press, 1990).

7. See, e.g., Saint Thomas Aquinas, *Summa Theologiae*, trans. The Fathers of the English Dominican Province (New York: Benziger Brothers, 1948), II-II, 23, 8. See also ibid., II-II, 23, 4, ad. 1.

8. Aristotle, *Magna Moralia*, 1213a 22-24, as quoted in John M. Cooper, "Aristotle on Friendship," in *Essays on Aristotle's Ethics*, ed. Amélie Oksenberg Rorty (Berkeley: University of California Press, 1980), 320.

9. Aristotle, *Nicomachean Ethics*, trans. Terence Irwin (Indianapolis: Hackett, 1985), 1159a 7-9, 1158b 32-36.

10. Aquinas, *Summa Theologiae*, III, 79, 2; III, 79, 4, ad. 1.

11. MacIntyre, *Three Rival Versions of Moral Enquiry*, 143 (emphasis added).

12. For a helpful discussion of Nietzsche on friendship, see John Coker, "On Becoming Great Friends," *International Studies in Philosophy* 25, no. 2 (1993): 113-127,

as well as Jacques Derrida's sustained commentary on Nietzschean friendship in *The Politics of Friendship*, trans. George Collins (New York: Verso, 1997), esp. 26-45, 281-290.

13. We are told that the incomplete and unpublished fourth volume of Foucault's *History of Sexuality* was to deal more extensively with the politics of friendship. Nevertheless, some of Foucault's thoughts on friendship are available in several interviews and shorter reflections on his later work. See, e.g., Michel Foucault, "Friendship as a Way of Life" and "Sex, Power, and the Politics of Identity," in *The Essential Works of Michel Foucault, 1954-1984*, vol. 1, *Ethics: Subjectivity and Truth*, trans. Robert Hurley, et al., ed. Paul Rabinow (New York: The New Press, 1997).

14. Derrida, *The Politics of Friendship*, 232.

15. Ibid., 65, 240, 295.

16. Ibid., 306.

17. See, e.g., Jacques Derrida, "Heidegger's Ear: Philopolemology (*Geschlecht* IV)," in *Reading Heidegger: Commemorations*, ed. John Sallis (Bloomington: Indiana University Press, 1993), 164.

18. Ibid., 168.

19. Ibid., 174.

20. Ibid., 194.

21. Ibid., 196.

22. Ibid., 168.

23. Jacques Derrida, "The Politics of Friendship," trans. Gabriel Motzkin, *Journal of Philosophy* 85 (1988): 641. See also "Heidegger's Ear," 197. The related themes of *aporia* and *polemos* run throughout Derrida's discussion of friendship. See, in particular, "Heidegger's Ear," 203-216.

24. Derrida, "Heidegger's Ear," 174.

25. Jacques Derrida, *The Gift of Death*, trans. David Wills (Chicago: The University of Chicago Press, 1995), 31, 33.

26. Ibid., 2, 83.

27. Ibid., 87.

28. Ibid., 25, 33, 41.

29. John Milbank, *Theology and Social Theory: Beyond Secular Reason* (Oxford: Blackwell, 1990), 4-5.

30. Ibid., 376.

31. Ibid., 5.

32. Ibid., 279.

33. Ibid., 417.

34. Ibid., 416.

35. For a helpful discussion of the sense in which, for Milbank, a Christian ontology of peace is rooted in the practices of charity/friendship with God and forgiveness, see David Toole, *Waiting for Godot in Sarajevo: Theological Reflections on Nihilism, Tragedy, and Apocalypse* (Boulder, Colo.: Westview Press, 1998), 73-75.

36. John Milbank, "Enclaves, or Where is the Church?" *New Blackfriars* 73, no. 861 (1992): 349.

37. Milbank, *Theology and Social Theory*, 421.
38. Ibid., 418.
39. Ibid., 422.
40. Toole, *Waiting for Godot in Sarajevo*, 76.
41. See John Milbank, *The Word Made Strange: Theology, Language, Culture* (Cambridge, Mass.: Blackwell, 1997), 123-168.
42. I owe this way of putting it to Scott Bader-Saye, *Church and Israel After Christendom: The Politics of Election* (Boulder, Colo.: Westview Press, 1999), 154 n. 55.
43. Milbank, "The Name of Jesus," in *The Word Made Strange*, 149.
44. For a similar argument, though in a very different context, see Bader-Saye, *Church and Israel After Christendom*, esp. 52-69, 134-148.
45. Milbank, "The Name of Jesus," 150 (my emphasis).
46. Ernst Troeltsch, *The Social Teaching of the Christian Churches*, trans. Olive Wyon (Louisville: Westminster/John Knox Press, 1992), 39.
47. "Radical orthodoxy" is the preferred name for the "new" theological movement that Milbank and others represent. See John Milbank, Catharine Pickstock, and Graham Ward, eds., *Radical Orthodoxy: A New Theology* (New York: Routledge, 1999), esp. 1-20.
48. John Howard Yoder, *Christian Attitudes to War, Peace, and Revolution: A Companion to Bainton* (Elkhart, Ind.: Goshen Biblical Seminary, 1983), 186.
49. Frederick Christian Bauerschmidt, "The Word Made Speculative? John Milbank's Christological Poetics," *Modern Theology* 15, no. 4 (1999): 423.

EIGHTEEN

ANABAPTISTS AND POSTMODERNITY:
Two Visions of Hope

Thomas Heilke

T he titles of this book and of this chapter are odd ones: both juxtapose two nouns, the one abstract and the other concrete. *Postmodernity* is a historical symbol of sorts, whereas *Anabaptists* are real people. Both nouns evoke images of conflict and contention. When we speak of people, we can identify them by telling a story about them. To say what is an Anabaptist could be to answer the question, What is the story Anabaptists all share? But can we tell a story of an abstract noun? Postmodernity is a symbol referring to an experienced reality and implying an experience of a *modernity* it now follows. Modernity too is a symbol of meaning that sets off one period of time from another in a specific way. Whatever we make of postmodernity, it must be understood in this context.

In what follows, I briefly undertake three tasks. The first is to establish, if possible, the meaning and use of the symbol *modernity*. Following this effort, one can begin to discern the meaning of the *post-* in the still developing symbol, postmodernity. Published accounts of the scope, meaning, implications, advantages, and disadvantages of postmodernity abound. A systematic treatment is impossible here, so I will consider representative authors of the accounts of modernity and of possible postmodern responses. Third, I conclude with a brief consideration of an Anabaptist counter-vision to the postmodern responses and critiques of modernity.

The central theme of comparison in this essay is eschatology—the account of what is ultimate. The symbols modernity and postmodernity both contain such an account—either implicitly or explicitly. It is on the basis of such an account that Anabaptists may be able to engage in constructive conversation with the representatives of both. Speaking eschatologically, both modernity and postmodernity are symbols of hope. A fruitful dialogue must focus on the content of this hope, especially since the Anabaptist story is itself so strongly informed from its beginning by symbols of ultimate hope and eschatology.

The best-known historical example of Anabaptism for most people remains the Münster debacle, an event of apocalyptic eschatology gone badly awry. But an eschatological vision for this life also made possible the Anabaptist communities that followed in the aftermath of Münster. Apocalyptic expectations were widespread in the sixteenth century, closely informing Luther's Reformation outlook, for example. For Luther, however, the Reformation was more likely not the beginning of a new "modern period of history," but "the prelude to the End of all history." For Anabaptists, too, the moral disciplines that were central to their view of the church may have been "short-range holding actions to preserve the church pure for the return of its Head." When that end did not arrive, however, such an ethic of church discipline would become the new ecclesiology.[1]

This unplanned eschatological development out of an originally apocalyptic vision led to an increasingly rigorous and rigid dogmatism that centered around the ecclesiological question: What are the marks of the true church?[2] The forces of persecution, waning apocalyptic expectations amid unfulfilled predictions, and the periodic success of negotiating with political authorities to maintain autonomous and removed communities with the aim of survival led to a "decidedly separatist ecclesiological 'shape'" among the several Anabaptist traditions that survived into the late sixteenth century.[3]

These factors complicate any effort to tease out an eschatological vision in the Anabaptist tradition and to compare it with the equivalent vision in modern and postmodern accounts. For a proper understanding of modernity's eschatology, however, we must begin with an account of modernity's aspirations over against the configurations of medieval Christendom.

MODERNITY VERSUS MEDIEVAL CHRISTENDOM

The secular, John Milbank reminds us, was once not a place but a time. And in that time, "the secular was not latent, waiting to fill more space with the steam of the 'purely human,' when the pressure of the sacred was relaxed." The "secular" or *saeculum* was "the interval between fall and *eschaton* where coercive justice, private property and impaired natural reason must make shift to cope with the unredeemed effects of sinful humanity."[4] Such a notion of waiting makes sense when empire and civilization are waning, when barbarians are invading, and the social and physical infrastructure of the polity is decaying and receding, not growing and flourishing. In such circumstances, a hand-in-hand administration of spiritual and temporal powers in a sacred empire that waits for the end of all things, as was doctrinally established at the end of the fifth century by Pope Gelasius I, seems a credible interpretation of the reason the political realm and its limited possibilities exists.

This construction suffers increasing strain, however, as physical infrastructures improve, administrative competence increases, and civilizational and cultural forces (in the arts and sciences, for example) experience a new flowering. The participants in such a flowering "do not want to be a senseless appendix to the history of antiquity; they want to understand their civilizational existence as meaningful." Accordingly, "if the church is not able to see the hand of God in the history of mankind, men will not remain peaceable and satisfied, but will go out in search of gods who take some interest in their civilizational efforts."[5] The meaning the men of this new age found for themselves was rendered in the symbol *modernity*. It was an optimistic meaning, and formed by a quest for immanent human freedom as its ultimate goal.

If we were to characterize modernity in contrast to premodern sympathies and attitudes in terms of freedom, we might say that the "medieval political evocations include the spiritual personality of man, while the modern Western constitutional system leaves the spiritual personality free to become institutionalized in the churches or not at all."[6] The "spiritual self-assertion" of the modern age can be traced to a number of figures in whom we see the forces of a this-worldly spiritual personality arising that bears in its new symbolizations of meaning and order "a sentiment of the *saeculum renascens.*"[7]

These new post-Gelasian spiritual forces, come of age, express themselves in various forms of historical optimism. This historical optimism of modernity has a number of sources. It takes on a variety of shapes. In what follows, let us briefly consider three ways of telling the story of modernity with respect to optimism. In all three cases, the story ends in pessimism; the unhappy endings are the impetus for a breakout into postmodernity.

Among many possibilities, modernity may be interpreted as a working out of the problems of nominalism, as the gradual and logical development of a technocratic politics, and as the ill-fated quest for a new form of moral reasoning.

MODERNITY AS NOMINALIST NEGATION

The first interpretation of modernity recites the speculative attempt to constrain the God of nominalist theology. According to this tale, modernity begins in the collapse of the medieval scholastic synthesis between Reason and Revelation. The God "behind" revelation is revealed to be not a God who has bound himself to a rational order that can be noetically discerned, but an absolutely free and omnipotent being who, in the final analysis, is not bound in any way to a rational order found either in nature or in the soul of man.[8]

The first statement of the nominalist principles that become the touchstone of modernity was developed by William of Ockham. According to Ockham, God has neither created the world for man nor is he bound by what he creates or by the order that he creates. In consequence, God

> does not act according to human standards and cannot be comprehended by human reason. There is no immutable law or reason. Every order is simply the result of God's absolute will and can be disrupted or reconstituted at any moment.... God can [even] change the past if he so desires. Such a radical picture of God means that Ockham "not only rejects the attempts of various scholastics to subordinate God to the laws of nature, but rejects all limitations on divine action except for the law of noncontradiction."

A number of profound ontological and epistemological consequences follow from this rejection of theological rationalism in an effort to liberate "theology from the yoke of pagan philosophy."[9] We need mention only one, however: man is left alone in the universe, confronted by an essentially arbitrary God of divine will. Modernity becomes the story of the response to this profoundly disturbing situation, of various attempts "to open up a space for man, a realm of freedom invulnerable to the powers of this God."[10]

In this new vision of the world, we become "subjects opposed to a hostile world that must be conquered and subordinated to our will." This understanding is not the sum total of the modern perspective, but it is a central part. An important early response to this vision was not one of despair at the powerlessness of man, but of hope in the human possibilities available in a universe that is ruled by a sovereign, nominalist God. If, as Descartes insisted, this God loves us and has given us room to maneuver at will, then our prospects abound. This is because our technical knowledge of nature can make us her "masters and possessors," giving us the power to alleviate the ills of the human condition.[11] This sixteenth-century, technologically optimistic vision of the world and man's place in it, slated to guide several movements in modernity, will eventually receive the censure of the postmodernists.

The technological progress of the West is not, however, the only thread in this Cartesian episode. Behind Descartes's "bright dawn of reason" stands the continuing "dark and mysterious force of the omnipotent [and arbitrary] God of nominalism." The effort philosophically to come to terms with this dark force ends ultimately in failure and hence in the failure of the modern project. The failure emerges when the arbitrariness of the nominalist God is relocated in the human will itself as attempts to overcome God's inscrutable will are founded on assertion of human will.

Dislodged from its moorings in a rational cosmos, human will reveals itself to be no more rationally constrained or grounded than the dark will of the nominalist God.[12] This dark god appears not only in European literary movements, but also in the increasingly meaningless, self-referential, and unending march of technological progress as well as in the totalitarian mass murders of our century.

This description of the character of modernity seems highly abstract, trapped in a scholarly medium of philosophical speculation. Modernity is a specific epoch characterized by its own self-interpretation as an age of fulfillment or as a period of human history in which human reason attempts to constrain the radical arbitrariness of the nominalist God. Human reason increasingly reveals itself also to be grounded in sheer human will. Modernity therefore threatens to become the age not of reason, but of unreason, of nihilism, gnosticism, and arbitrary will. Beginning with an act of reason asserting itself over against arbitrary divine will and the apparently suffocating traditions that reflect that will, modernity ends up as a new realm of arbitrary will that is now human rather than divine.

If these speculative constructions of history are carried by classes of people and embodied in institutions and in ways of seeing in society at large,[13] however, we would expect to find evidence of modernity's problems in a more concrete mode. And we do in at least two distinct ways that constitute the second and third stories about modernity of which this essay takes note.

Modernity as technocratic triumph

We may point in our second telling of the modern story to the oppressiveness of the modern technocratic regimes—including the efficiency imperatives of multinational corporations, the monochromatic politics of economic housekeeping, the banalities of the mass media and mass society, and the homogenizing procedures of mass bureaucracies. In one sense, these regimes are an accidental product of the liberal portion of the Enlightenment project. In another sense, the core continuities between a technocratic politics and what at first glance seems its antithesis—the political liberalism that is the crowning political achievement of the Enlightenment—are based in the conceptions of human knowledge held by technocrats and liberals alike.

Thus, argues Thomas Spragens, several aspects of liberalism and technocracy are particularly compatible and even complimentary. Both have a positivist conception of knowledge that looks for a "secure and incontrovertible base for human knowledge" and expects the general progress in knowledge in the mathematizing sciences to be transferable to every type of knowledge. Both believe positivistic models of knowledge are available not only in the sciences of natural phenomena but also in the realm of human behavior and morals. And both groups assume that the advance of scientific progress leads to political progress.[14] The liberal project fails, however, along all these dimensions.

First, "clear and incontrovertible knowledge" is merely a particular and unself-conscious kind of mythology.[15]

Second, scientific knowledge and knowledge of human moral ends are conflated only by committing a category error—the phenomena of the natural world and of the spirit are of separate kinds that reveal themselves in distinct ways and therefore demand distinct ways of knowing.

Third, the nineteenth-century heirs of the Enlightenment myth of scientific progress encountered a "complexity and sophistication of scientific reason" that they had not anticipated, leading them to re-evaluate their optimism. Their reconsideration engendered a more elitist model of "who might be among the enlightened and therefore of how the rationalization of the political order could proceed."[16]

The result in modernity is a restricted frame of reference for political endeavors. The dream of an enlightened population that would, on the basis of its enlightenment, opt for an open and highly democratic form of rule, was traded in. It was exchanged for a conception of rule in which the enlightened few rule over the benighted many in a benevolent despotism that is in the service of all. This conception may be observed concretely in the rule of managers, technical experts, and psychotherapists. Particularly managers have developed extensive mythologies to justify their authority.[17]

Technical reason, however, cannot extend into the realm of moral reason as the Enlightenment technocrats originally anticipated it would.[18] The failure of the original Enlightenment optimism that was captured in Descartes's vision of material mastery and the gradual restriction in the technocratic moral vision developed into a technocratic political theory. Here rulership was restricted to a select few, who, on the basis of their technical expertise, could regulate the activities of the manipulable many to sustain a peaceful and increasingly perfected society of compliant "citizens." In this vision, politics as "a continual process of accommodation among contending interests and conceptions of virtue" is "an atavistic form of social organization that should properly give way to administrative regulation based on scientific principles."[19]

This interpretation of modern politics implies that contemporary ideological categories of political science and political discourse generally are insufficient for understanding how certain imperatives of rule in modernity seem to transcend ideological categories. In MacIntyre's words, they hide the modern tendency of every form of ideological rule to become Weberian.[20] Or, as Barry Cooper has shown, they obscure the similarities in the homogenizing and totalizing discourses of, say, Gulag labor camps and multinational corporations.[21] We may recall any number of contemporary slogans, including "competitiveness," "globalization," and "new paradigms."

Modernity as moral autonomy

If, finally, in our third story about modernity, we attempt to characterize modernity as a moral enterprise, we may find it appears to us as a confusion reflected in a particular set of affairs. In this story, modernity results from a series of moves toward greater moral autonomy. We hear echoes of nihilism, but the story focuses specifically on the moral enterprise of the Enlightenment—that optimistic middle-modern search for a new order of reason. The story begins with a rejection of the notion that there is a naturally given or rationally discernible state of human perfection.

This rejection does not do away with morality or ethics but only with the notion that they can be rationally directed toward a human end about which every rational human being will in principle agree. There is no discernible human telos—completion, end, or purpose—that can be universalized from rational principles as conceived by Enlightenment thinkers. On the other hand, the early moderns seemed to think there is a rationally discernible "natural" morality available to all reasonable men, even if an ultimate end for morality is not.[22] There is, in other words, no rational order of things directed toward some preordained end in either an individual human being or a collective of such beings. Nevertheless, there are naturally given norms of behavior that guide human activity in the collective.

Alasdair MacIntyre suggests the coherence of premodern ethics is premised on a claim that as we find ourselves to be and how we could be if we realized our true end is joined by a series of middle terms about how to move from the former state to the latter. If this is the case, then the rejection of a true end toward which morality aims makes orphans of both the first premise and the middle terms. Premodern ethics is premised on a philosophical anthropology of ends, on a notion of the term "man" as containing a functional component. This functional referent is not different in its essentials from more specific human functional appellations like teacher, mechanic, carpenter, or tennis player. Just as each of these can be evaluated with respect to how well or how poorly each performs his or her role, so too an individual is susceptible to a moral evaluation of how well or poorly she lives up to the role of displaying the proper functions of a "human being." Having rejected any such teleological formulation, moderns engaged in an optimistic enterprise of founding moral principles (and political order) on new nonteleological foundations.

All such modern schemata of morality fail because they

> attempt to find a rational basis for their moral beliefs in a particular understanding of human nature, while inheriting a set of moral injunctions on the one hand and a conception of human nature on the other which had been expressly designed to be discrepant with each other.[23]

All reveal themselves in the end to be incoherent because they can give no good reason, instrumental or otherwise, why any particular individual should obey any particular rule, apart from a fear of immediate consequences.

Such incoherence, coupled with the sincerity with which such claims are made, leads to the suspicion that all moral claims must ultimately be the product not of rational reflection but of will.[24] The dark forces of the nominalist God of arbitrary will appear yet again, having moved into each individual and being manifested in the universalizing moral statements of each willful individual, as Nietzsche portrayed with such penetrating effect.

The absence of rational justification for moral claims results in the belief that a mere instrumentalism underlies all of them. Moral claims become a mask for power. For this reason, modernity is more than merely a failed philosophical enterprise. That enterprise and its failings are embodied in a concrete and pervasive set of institutions that mask their arbitrary and willful use of power with a set of insupportable and seemingly arbitrarily constructed moral claims. These institutions and lifeways become the targets of the postmodern enterprise.

MODERNIST DESPAIR AND BEYOND

After several centuries, little of modernity's promise has been fulfilled: we have ended not in optimism but in despair. On the one hand, "to be modern is to adopt a specific self-understanding or self-interpretation. One sees oneself as autonomous, independent of natural constraints, independent of God, and therefore free to create meaning, equally one's own meaning and the meaning of one's society."[25]

On the other hand, despite or because of this freedom, modernity has become a madhouse ruled by the "barbarians" who administer the universal and homogenous state. It is, at best, a realm of boredom,[26] at worst an endless parade of murderous totalitarian regimes and "ethnic cleansings." Evaluations of the institutions that express power in the modern world have led to a bleak conclusion among many contemporary writers. Modernity is, in one estimation, a "historical abyss of evil" that is manifested in the tyrannical regimes of the twentieth century, a time of crisis that has devolved from "the energies of the scientific, industrial and political revolutions" of the Enlightenment to the "horror, vacuity, and mediocrity of the twentieth century."[27]

In another evaluation, we are presented in modernity with the prospect of a "global asylum" in which "the interlocking of science and social power" in a scientistic civilization reach "into every nook and corner of industrialized society." This means there may be some "possibility of personal escape into the freedom of the spirit," but "we who are living today shall never experience freedom of the spirit in society."[28]

It seems, therefore, that modernity confronts us with a seamless face: regardless of which ideology speaks, we encounter technological imperatives and epistemological nihilism. Indeed, the two seem to work hand in hand. Liberalism displays a "nihilistic logic" that the left-wing and right-wing critics of liberalism seem often to replicate in a new key. The "directionless and morally empty" prescriptions of liberalism are matched by a "spirit of weariness and wariness" in the face of the "cumulative disillusionments of recent history" that the counter-liberal ideologies have delivered.[29]

What, then, of postmodernity? This term, too, is a symbol: variously freighted, it expresses these critical assertions about modernity's hazards as true but capable of being transcended. Postmodernists attempt to refashion the modern enterprise with an acceptance that Nietzsche's critique of modernity as a defeated outcome of the Enlightenment project and its moral claims is essentially correct. What does such a refashioning look like? There are at least three potential paths.

BEYOND ENLIGHTENMENT: THREE PATHS

Henry Kariel has cogently articulated the specifically political aspects of the first of these possibilities in a happily accessible manner. Postmodernity, according to Kariel, is a situation of despair, and the "postmodernist" swims upstream against this despair. "For postmodernists, it is simply too late to oppose the momentum of industrial society." Accordingly, postmodernism becomes a practice of posture. Postmoderns "merely resolve to stay alert and cool in its midst. Consciously complying and yet far from docile, they chronicle, amplify, augment it." There is no moralism involved, nor a hope for a final end or an ultimate resolution.[30]

Despite the failed epistemological and moral enterprises that inform modern liberalism, the pervasive institutions that display these failures remain the nihilistic loci of modern power. They do so in the form of technological imperatives that bring all other human institutions to heel under the triple imperatives of consumption, efficiency, and its correlate, homogenization. These forces cause us to feel "resentful, alienated, bored, depressed." In the face of their inexorable pressure, the only recourse remaining is various forms of play. "At play, we strive for no extrinsic objectives. Not seeking to be anywhere else, we act without ulterior motives." Play suffices: "it's intrinsically satisfying," and it "detaches us from the prevailing instrumentalism."[31]

Kariel desires to avoid an "antitechnological nostalgia." He is ever-wary that his postmodern enterprise of "challenging and enlarging liberalism's model for living is to raise the specter of nihilism, of boundless permissiveness."[32] Nevertheless, he takes us through a one-hundred-fifty-page tour of forms of postmodern play by means of which we might be less bored, less dulled, and less constricted by the homogenizing effect of the modern world. In Kariel's description, postmodern play is a pessimistic struggle, a continual "whirling" that seeks to avoid excess or even dizziness. Such play relies not on fixed truths but on the "sheer consciousness" of the artist, which is all that remains to the postmodern performer.[33]

Kariel strives to avoid utopianism. His performances and his efforts to retain his balance are "desperate stopgap ventures" that continue, despite this desperation, "to demonstrate the possibility of taking an independent stand." This they can do because at least they ensure that "consumable art objects continue to be replaced by unconsumable performance art, self-destructive sculpture, and ephemeral, useless enterprises such as Christo's."[34] Ultimately, however, "nothing can deflect the nihilistic instrumentalism which, systemically promoting the expansion of its own power, seduces and extinguishes whatever remains external to it. There is no way out, no new frontier, no virgin territory."[35]

The desperate politics of postmodernism have, in sum, accepted Nietzsche's nihilism and the nihilism of liberal consumerism and capitalism. Now they simply go about their business under that bleak canopy. In the footsteps of Nietzsche, the performers of postmodernism seize "a space for action scarcely visible to those more thoroughly absorbed by their fate." They give an ironic performance that shows them to be in control, regardless of "the inconsequence of their determination, the impotence of irony." These performers "enact their sentences in a spirit of buoyant purposefulness which contradicts their victimization."[36] At best, the ironic postmodernist "maintains her independence by keeping her distance from the inescapable cultural momentum."[37]

Why, however, despair? Why distance? Why a persistent search for meaning? Why this optimistic hopelessness? What are we to make of the modern and even postmodern yearning for meaning and comfort revealed even in the self-avowed despair and ironic distance of postmodern play? And why accept a politics of irony that demands, as does Rorty's, a moral stance of doing no harm and yet accepting a confined pragmatism?[38] These curious moral injunctions amid modernity's nihilism are displayed more consistently and clearly in Gregory Bruce Smith's vision of a postmodern future. For Smith, postmodernism remains a stance of unfulfilled hope, and a politics and aesthetics of despair is not the sole response to modernity.

Smith traces a genealogy from Machiavelli through Descartes, Hobbes, Locke, Rousseau, Kant, and finally Hegel, to show how the search for autonomy, independence, and liberty defines the modern project for these three traditions of political philosophy but also in everyday understanding.[39] The usual mode of postmodernism, as displayed in Kariel's writings, is, according to Smith, "anything but postmodernism . . . it is in fact a perfectly logical extension of modernity." Postindustrial society "represents the very telos of modernity . . . an extreme manifestation of modernity's antinature animus." Smith's desire, therefore, is to move beyond modernity's prejudices and premises onto entirely new ground. The bellwethers for this project are Nietzsche and Heidegger. They, he argues, present most powerfully the final ends of modernity. They therefore help us to assess most cogently "our general, late-modern trajectory into the future, as well as possible deflections of that trajectory."[40]

Modernity, Smith contends, is ultimately a closure, a project of positing an "autonomous human Reason, both theoretical and practical," over against the world. Autonomous human reason "is active and imposes the law on the external world and itself" so thoroughly and so strongly that "modern life takes a turn toward an increasingly abstract existence." This I take to be Smith's way of describing the effects of nominalist technocracy and the hegemony of the universal and homogenous liberal state. The chief characteristic of modernity is that thought (mostly embodied in philosophy, but also in the discourses of the natural and social sciences and increasingly in the humanities) dictates to both practice and nature their assigned characteristics.[41] For Smith, to overcome modernity is to overcome this hegemony of thinking over practice. Modernity allows no reversal to earlier forms of existence, but Smith holds out the hope of a postmodern praxis that is not prefigured in a philosophical or theoretical discourse.

Despite this move beyond modernity, Smith seeks a postmodern regime with specifically "modern" characteristics. This regime will sustain "a commitment to individual dignity and the limitations of authority made possible by constitutional government."[42] It will also be a regime that respects and protects human rights, that respects and protects individualism. The regime will be "democratic" but not insist on a single, perennially determined form of rule for itself and other regimes. To make possible such a modern regime in the postmodern (postliberal, post-Enlightenment) world, however, Smith must move onto less certain ground. After all, the regime he describes is a liberal regime without its philosophical Enlightenment supports. The new postmodern regimes, Smith hopes, will avoid the "Spirit of Revenge" that still pervades Enlightenment liberalism.

Following Nietzsche, Smith interprets this "Spirit" as the desire to gain intellectual mastery over the past and theoretical and practical mastery over the present and the future. The Spirit of Revenge resents the differences of others and the open-endedness of human action. It thereby resents the indeterminacy of the future, which is to say, the indeterminacy of human existence. The Spirit of Revenge in modernity is manifested first and foremost in an exercise of theorizing by means of which we determinatively interpret the past, conceptually constrain the present, and limit options for the future. Smith therefore contends that theory and praxis must be severed in postmodernity so that praxis can regain its autonomous status. This endeavor of overcoming the spirit of revenge requires—hear the echo of Heidegger—that we let Being reveal itself without the intermediary of a preconceived perceptual (epistemological and ontological) framework.

This description of the trend from modernity to its transcendence in postmodernity tends to express uncertain hopes as credible expectations. As he replicates Nietzsche's elusive treatment of the alternative to the spirit of revenge, for example, Smith tends to neglect Nietzsche's demonstration that to overcome this spirit under secular conditions requires that we bestow grace on ourselves. Only such a self-bestowal permits us to overcome the past by affirming it in every detail and not resenting its constraining impacts on our present. Since we are mortal, the present always offers us a limited range of possibilities, even as we, in our mortality, seek for an infinity. It is this infinite striving under finite, mortal constraints that, according to Nietzsche, creates the nihilism of resentment that defines the post-theist modern age—but that also leads to the "slave morality" of Christian theism in the first place.[43]

Nietzsche was dubious that a return to so-called "premodern immediate experience" was possible, because it would require a superhuman enterprise of forgetting and an uncommon strength of spirit. His skepticism was one motive for his invention of myths of power. This led him to posit a kind of mythos of nobility that, as MacIntyre points out, does not reflect the ideas of heroic society but the needs of Nietzsche's attempted recovery from the modern "disease."

Following Nietzsche, but with insufficient attention to the "theological" problems to which Nietzsche was attuned, Smith argues that postmodernity requires that we transcend the antinature animus that is part of the modern project and (I would add) expresses the resentment of that project. Smith calls on us to "legitimiz[e] self-presenting difference," respecting it and the interactions that flow from it.[44]

But what is "difference," and what are the "types" that are differentiated naturally? Whence the accompanying moral imperatives that the heterogeneity of human reality and the "life-world," for example, "must be affirmed as the appropriate and untranscendable postmodern point of departure" or that the "interplay of an irreducible, self-presenting plurality of different types and manifestations of human beings must be respected?"[45] Who will underwrite this respect, and what will obligate us to give it? What does it mean for nature to be self-presenting? Will the self-presenting character of a virus that manifests itself in a deadly disease be treated as bad, as evil, as inevitable, as an occasion for repentance, or as an episode for medical (technological) intervention? That is to say, how will we avoid resentment of illness and the spirit of revenge it fosters that we can already observe in the aspirations of Descartes? Or, to restate the question, can technology play a nonresentful role over against seemingly natural processes and contingencies? On a different plane, will the willing concentration-camp guards of a defeated or defunct regime be censured, praised, ignored, executed, or hired for the department store security detail?

Smith argues for a "reversal of modern values" regarding our relationship to "the self-presencing Other" or to "Nature."[46] Yet he offers neither a philosophical anthropology (as Nietzsche does) nor any ontology on the basis of which we can formulate judgments that would permit us together to inhabit the world that presents itself. He tends thereby to fall into the kind of aesthetic nihilism that Nietzsche presents as the alternative to modernity (and that Kariel translates into an empirical idiom) and that Heidegger's parousiasm does not overcome.

A philosophical anthropology would give an account of human motivations able to elucidate numerous problems that surface in Smith's hopeful postmodern vision. These include the appearance of insanity (even in politics); the desire for a tolerance for diversity or a respect for difference or an openness to a variety of human ends; the desire for status and for community cohesion; the origins of a "religious mentality;" the motives of the search for excellence and of the quest for identity.

Such are a few of the politically more important aspects of human existence Smith seems largely to take for granted in his picture of postmodernity.[47] Failing a blank human slate on which nature can present itself, we may ask for the contours of a political education that will help the move from one regime to another. Again, such a request implies a philosophical anthropology. The "pretheoretical understanding of the citizen" will initiate an intracommunal dialectic. Such dialectic, because it is open to multiple perspectives and is not private, avoids the Spirit of Revenge and a return to theory that supersedes experience.[48] What sort of people can enter this world and inhabit it?[49]

In one prominent and insightful example of the kind of quasi-Nietzschean, reconstructed liberal polity Smith proposes, William Connolly argues for a liberalism that rejects both a hegemonic confessionalism and an agenda for curing "homesickness." By the first, he refers to a tendency to define oneself by negative reference toward others. The development of confession as "a cultural mechanism of power," he argues, is a product of the Christian tradition. In that tradition, confession is understood as a means of exploring the geography of the inner self and thereby coming to truth about the self.[50]

This activity takes on socially coercive and manipulative contours when accompanied by an activity of hereticization, in which one sets off the differing confession of another from one's own by declaring it "heretical" and one's own confessional claims and insights "orthodox." One's own confession is understood to be an expression of an intrinsic moral order and therefore authoritative, aligned with right order, and good. The confession of the other—the heretic—is an example of disorder, moral corruption, and retreat from an objectively given true order. The heretic becomes an object of contempt, fear, and even hatred. The orthodox confessor, in contrast, is an exemplar of rectitude and moral excellence.[51]

When confessional practices of this kind are linked to political power, they create the likelihood of coercion and other abuses of power. Such practices generate politics of identity and difference in which the adherents of the true confession deploy multiple means and powerful resources to force confessional compliance on those identified as "heretical."[52] Those who identify themselves with the true order revealed in the true confession are empowered, whereas those identified as "other" are displaced into positions of weakness and even oppression.

Connolly seeks in response a "gentle war of identity/difference" in which we can "modify liberal theory and democratic practice until they incorporate a greater degree of 'agonistic respect' into relations between incomplete, contending and interdependent identities." Such a politics would cultivate "forbearance," "toleration," "interdependence," and "generosity" in a new liberal mode more closely attuned to "'différance' as that which resides in an existing network but has not yet received stable definitions in it." Without a richer appreciation of difference, Connolly argues,

> dominant forms of liberalism remain unattuned to the crucial role new enactments of performances play, first in generating new claims to

identity, and second in retroactively crystallizing violence in previous patterns of being.[53]

The necessary accompaniment to this new appreciation of difference is a cure for "homesickness," by which he means a pervasive human tendency to seek a meaningful and universal purpose or end for political activities. Connolly shows how Hobbes, Rousseau, Hegel, and Marx each theorizes "the self first and foremost from the vantage point of its compatibility with a dream of order." He suggests that

> when we acknowledge that modern orders depend on intensive and extensive organization of the self to maintain themselves, we are in a better position to see how these opposing ideals of self can function as complementary strategies of discipline in the confines of modern life.[54]

Here again we catch the scent of confessionalism. Such selves are in each case generated in response to a "homesickness," the desire for a purpose, ultimate end, or transcendental meaning for political activity. Accordingly, each thinker "embodies the spirit of nihilism" because "each demands a definitive standard which he cannot sustain; each idealizes nothing and yearns to give it a content; each insists that life cannot go on unless the standard for which he yearns can be realized." This empty demand deserves close attention, because to overcome hereticization and a politics of oppressive difference, we must overcome "the urge to find a home in the world" that animates it.[55]

Like Connolly, Smith enjoins us to a similar Nietzschean path to overcoming this urge. Like Connolly, he calls us to resist the temptation of "pacifying existence" and to remain open to differences of character, of taste, even of merit. Such an aristocratic element in postmodernism, Smith suggests, can be "deflected in a sanguine, constitutional direction" in a situation of openness to a variety of ends.[56]

In sum, Smith seeks to overcome what he identifies as two central modern problems. He wishes, first, to avoid the abstraction of existence or the prior theorizing of experience that sets modernity on its materialistic and technological course. He wants to avoid the culmination of modernity in the totalitarian attempts of this century to reshape human and physical reality in accordance with ideological abstractions.

Second, on the one hand he seeks to re-invigorate the possibility of immediate experience that is not mediated a priori by theoretical constructions. On the other hand, he rejects the Nietzschean and Heideggerian conclusion that such a possibility requires an "epicurianizing" or privatization of philosophical thought to keep it out of the public square, where it will tend to re-impose its predeterminations.[57]

Smith's vision requires us to begin with primary experiences before theorizing its contours, but to proceed from there to a dialectic that "begins with the immediate, pretheoretical experience of reality as it reveals itself publicly to all." Such a dialectic, "freed from a Spirit of Revenge, would be political" in the sense of serving as the beginning point for a "legitimate debate as to ends."[58] To be postmodern, such debate must transcend the modern conclusion that only technical ends are accessible to consideration. It must not close off debate prematurely but recognize in the plethora of possible ends the need for consensus to make community possible.[59] Such consensus would not, it seems, be a reappearance of homesickness, because it would refuse a transcendental reference of validation.

The future Smith envisions is yet to be, of course. We remain as untutored about its contours as the apostle Paul was about the precise nature of heaven. Indeed, in many respects Smith's postmodernity stands in relation to modernity as Paul's heaven stands in relation to this earthly life. Just as this present existence contains vague hints of the life to come for Paul, so, too, the institutions of the present hold a key to the transfigured politics of postmodernity for Smith. He rejects a "simple return to primary Nature" or to past political forms. Yet Smith believes it is possible to seek a return to "immediate experience" without concocting a "romantic notion that it has recovered some primordial state that existed in the past." "A natural relation to reality in our time will open itself to a fundamentally novel, modern world of appearance." And "this relation to reality represents a reversal of modern values," which is an "opening to the postmodern."[60] We are not far from a new world, if not a new heaven and a new earth.[61]

An Anabaptist could affirm key aspects of Smith's (and Connolly's) proposals, including the need for rejection of resentment, theoretical abstraction, and modern materialism and a renewal of toleration. But what is the basis of this affirmation? A Platonist could make nearly the same argument for reversing modern values and for recovering primary experiences. And why a "novel world?" Why not the world that modernity rejected? In Smith's vision of such a novel world lies an expectation of transfiguration born of hope. It could similarly be the case that although we build an expectation born of experiences that begin in a rejection of the Enlightenment paradigms, the "ground out of which Western thinking initially grew," or the ground of "immediately lived experience"[62] has a contour not to be superseded, but recovered.

A third alternative to modernity is therefore a return to prior principles. For Anabaptists, such a recovery may seem to be the most sympathetic postmodern critique of modernity, especially when attached to standard Christian principles. If the underlying motive for the optimistic outlook of modernity and the reason for its pessimistic conclusion is that it consists in a revolt against God, then "only the grace of divine reconciliation can finally overcome" this revolt.

An assertion of the "rightness of Christianity and of its view of human nature and the political order, however, will be insufficient. Rather, as David Walsh argues, "the rightness of Christian or philosophic principles . . . must be grasped as a participation in the highest living reality that is."[63] Accordingly, he calls for a spiritual therapeutic that shifts our focus "from the level of doctrines to the experiential bases for holding them."[64] The bulk of his book is dedicated to this task.

Walsh employs the literary and philosophical efforts of a cast of characters—including Fyodor Dostoevsky, Albert Camus, Alexander Solzhenitsyn, and Eric Voegelin—to return the reader "to the primary experiences and symbols of order" that are "available to every open soul" and are the basis of a postmodern order. He calls us to an "ascent from the depths" to heal the "pneumapathological" conditions of modernity.[65] His call for a postmodern recovery of the truth of the soul against the ideological currents of the age assumes a specific role for a philosophically developed Christianity. Let us recall that modernity is in one interpretation a rejection of "Constantinian" Christianity. Turning to the civilizational role of Constantinian Christianity reminds an Anabaptist of what we should not want to reinvent as we consider the possibilities of a postmodern future.

Although Walsh takes a critical stance against the civilizational forms of Christianity that affirm only a "transcendent" eschatology, he nevertheless hesitates between three possibilities. These are a metamorphosis of Christianity; a spiritually sensitive toleration like that expressed in Bodin's *Heptaplomeres*; and a spiritually informed affirmation of a liberalism more attuned to its own spiritual and moral limitations and to its need for a "moral and religious reality" as its foundation.[66]

Walsh's ultimate project is to rescue liberalism for a postmodern order in which liberalism "break[s] free of the temptation to derive all things from the logic of the closed autonomous self" and Christianity serves largely as the best articulated content of this transcendent pole of human existence.[67] Walsh calls us to a (postmodern) renewal of the *saeculum*, not to the separatist communities of virtue of MacIntyre or the congregations of believers of the Anabaptists.

POSTMODERNITY, ANABAPTISM, ESCHATOLOGY

Anabaptists have defined themselves as a recognizable and distinct group of believers from the third decade of the sixteenth century onward. With various degrees of theological sophistication or naivete, they have articulated a vision of Christian community and existence that has stood in deliberate contrast to the articulations of medieval, Reformation, and post-Reformation Christendom. Anabaptists have also stated similar counter-positions to liberal and other twentieth-century articulations of political order.[68] We cannot here recount these articulations,[69] nor is it possible to compare along every possible avenue the connections and disconnections between Anabaptists and postmodernists. However, let us consider the position of Anabaptists over against postmodernity along the theme of eschatology.

We have seen that the meaning of the symbol *modernity* is expressed in a story with an archaic beginning, a progressivist middle, and a final, culminating end. The symbol *postmodernity* represents a challenge to this story, but it too wrestles with a conclusion. For some postmoderns, like Kariel, modernity has destroyed the possibility of any end, so that the future can only be a continuous "churning."

For others, like Connolly, the postmodern future can only be secured if we give up our eschatological aspirations in every mode. Connolly is sensitive to the basic transformations in human consciousness this rejection or sublimation would entail.

For Smith, there is the hope of a new beginning that extends the best features of modernity (liberal toleration, for example) into a new key that avoids the enveloping discourses of technobabble in its consumerist, bureaucratic, and statist forms. This new beginning opens up a new realm of freedom for the self-disclosure of the individual and of the whole. Smith calls for a this-worldly transfiguration of political discourse. He is unconvinced of Heidegger's eschatological sensitivity that declares that "only a God can save us."

Walsh takes up this theme and seeks a recovery of prior forms with a view not to re-imposing old dogma but to opening up our vision to the originating experiences that underlay them. On the bases of these experiences we can establish a spiritually attuned political order. The eschatological element of such an order is firmly transcendentalized and removed as an object of immanent aspirations. The problem in this case is how to make the story of an entirely transcendent end relevant for current, this-worldly concerns.

Given their heritage of eschatological forms, what possible response or dialogue is possible between Anabaptists and the varieties of postmodernisms? At one level, any Anabaptist response may become pre-loaded with theological banalities. After all, a version of Christianity was the original focus of Enlightenment animus, and a similar one was the target of nominalism. Nevertheless, we may offer a contrasting vision of a "heavenly city"; we may reassert the primacy of God's grace over against the self-gracing of aesthetic nihilists like Kariel and postmodern visionaries like Smith.[70]

In a moment of weakness, we may also demonstrate the spiritual arrogance of saying "We told you so." The culmination of at least two streams of modernity in the Stalinist Gulag and the Kampuchean killing fields on the one hand and the Nazi death camps on the other may point to the hubris of modernity. Yet this revelation must surely be the occasion not for celebration of an end but sorrow at its grisly form.

Similarly, the banalities of liberalism displayed in the mass consumer societies of the West, even if it is the spirit and not the body that they tend to kill,[71] hardly seem worthy of cheerful celebration. Can modern baptists and Anabaptists offer more in response than platitudes?

John Howard Yoder has indicated at least the form such a dialogue might take. And postmodernists have indicated ready-made topics for such a dialogue. As Yoder makes clear, Anabaptists cannot presume to rise above particularity in their response to the postmodern mood and its despairing or hopeful projects.[72] They can, however, adopt the eschatological terms that pervade postmodern hopes and re-deploy them to tell the story of Jesus in a newly emerging cultural context. In this way, Anabaptists can take up postmodern critiques of resentment and the desire for control as well as the postmodern injunctions to toleration. Anabaptists can then embed these themes anew in a postmodern Anabaptist eschatology.

Let us acknowledge Walsh's insight that modernity is not merely a hubristic peccadillo on the historical landscape, but the manifestation of a deeply rooted spiritual disease. Let us also acknowledge that we need not strive to become "relevant" in the clichéd sense of accepting the fundamental premises of the modern or postmodern projects. As Smith's eschatological yearnings indicate, and as Yoder's biblical examples show, we can redeploy the language of postmodernity. We can do so to articulate a different vision, just as the early Christians seized the categories, hammered them into other shapes, and turned the cosmology on its head, with Jesus both at the bottom, crucified as a common criminal, and at the top, preexistent Son and creator, and the church his instrument in today's battle.[73]

Thus, for example, the pervasive impulse among postmodernists of several stripes to overcome resentment—understood in the Nietzschean sense of rejecting the desire to master nature, the future, or the present in the variety of discursive ways that the modern enterprise attempted to do so—provides an entrée for the Anabaptist message of God's peace that sets aside all resentment. Apart from Kariel's dance of despair (which, Nietzsche might rightly suggest, may be merely a sublimated form of resentment), the other forms of postmodern rejection of resentment seem inclined toward old forms of political organization infused with new psychological content. The envisioned result is a declining of the desire for control so exemplified in the modern universal and homogenous state.[74]

To this inclination, the Anabaptist may respond with a vision of peace that calls into question the ultimate possibilities of every state or any other form of ancient, modern, or postmodern rule. Such a vision, however, with its present and future hope, could include an account of resentment and its defeat, of power and its defeat, of "homesickness" and its noncoercive fulfillment, of confessional peacefulness and charity, or of the proper relationship between practice and theory.[75]

Into the postmodern context of either irony, hope, or despair, it is not quite enough to make a call to faith. After all, "faith" is a part of the problem. It is the courage required for the adventure of faith that made the religion of faith—Christianity—increasingly tenuous as a civilizational force in the late Middle Ages.[76] To make such faith tenable, Anabaptists must present the vision of a "followable world."[77] Included in this hope-filled vision of a city yet to come and yet coming into being before our eyes, is a perspective with respect to what is ultimate. This inclusion enables those who possess it to fashion a critique of the present situation even while, on the positive side, they provide a vision of the world as it truly is.[78]

For example, postmodernity as displayed in Smith desires the benefits of liberal modernity without accepting its philosophical-anthropological premises, according to which a balance of conflicts enables a relative peace.[79] Similarly, Connolly seeks a liberalism that includes diversity and toleration, but he rejects liberalism's progressivist—its immanentist eschatological—element. In other words, he seeks the axiological component of liberalism without its teleological part, whereas Smith seeks its axiological component without its theodicy. Through artistic play, Kariel privatizes late modern liberalism's communal self-bestowal of grace (delivered in a modified market system and legal requirements for equal treatment and toleration), and he rejects liberal axiology.

Anabaptists reject the liberal norm of theoretical atheism on all three counts. "Our God reigns," they declare. They do so not in a moment of sectarian triumphalism (a charge as easily leveled against liberalism itself),[80] but in an ecumenical declaration of the coming peace of God and their present desire to live the story of that peace, given through grace, over against the self-gracing and elusive peace of the liberal dialectic of toleration and enforcement. The role of the state or any other political authority as peacekeeper, Anabaptists might say, is a legitimate intermediate role in which liberalism's promises may be affirmed. However, it is not an ultimate role, and liberalism's promises—modern and postmodern—are not an ultimate end.[81] Neither can a self-gracing and a wistful hope for peace play this role when it does not take account of sin in the way that an Anabaptist account of the ultimate things must.

In presenting their eschatological vision of hope, Anabaptists must—to repeat—resist the temptation of "relevance." Whereas we must speak in a language accessible to unbelievers, that language and the aspirations out of which it arises are not ultimate; the reality of God's present and coming reign are. It is always out of that recognition that we speak: "Thus the church's prophetic witness to the state rests on firmly fixed criteria; any act of the state may be tested according to them and God's estimation pronounced with all proper humility."[82] What is true of the state in this statement is true of any ruling authority, including the various forms of political authority envisioned by postmodernists of any stripe. It remains the case that politics is not salvation: at its best, it creates the space in which a message of salvation can be proclaimed and heard.[83] The postmodern hope is not that message.

This Anabaptist claim about the role of political authority says to the postmodernist that there will always be a potent remainder that can be filled only by God's grace and peace in this current age and in the one to come. The practical outcomes of this claim include the ability to take up a prophetic stance against the same injustices that postmodernists protest but also the ones they will themselves commit. Also needed is an ability to point out "the preference of the old aeon to the new"[84] that remains the burden of postmodernity over against the Anabaptist eschatological vision of the new kingdom—present and coming.

Anabaptists have neither more nor less a "response" to the claims and hopes of postmodernity than they had to the magisterial reformers, to the ideologies of the nineteenth and twentieth centuries, or to the idolatries of nationalism. Called to be faithful, we preserve in our way of being a "followable world." In such a world we are guided by that same hope-filled vision of the heavenly city that led those who followed before us and that stands as a counter-vision against those postmodernists who would run ahead. I have tried here only to set a reminder of some points of departure toward that city in the postmodern context.

NOTES

1. Walter Klaassen, *Living at the End of the Ages: Apocalyptic Expectation in the Radical Reformation* (Lanham: University Press of America, 1992), 117-18.

2. C. Arnold Snyder, *Anabaptist History and Theology: An Introduction* (Kitchener, Ont.: Pandora Press, 1995), 373, cf. 379-80.

3. Ibid., 375.

4. John Milbank, *Theology and Social Theory: Beyond Secular Reason* (Oxford: Blackwell Publishers, 1990), 9.

5. Eric Voegelin, *Revolution and the New Science*, ed. Barry Cooper, vol. 6 of *History of Political Ideas* (Columbia: University of Missouri Press, 1998), 56.

6. Voegelin, *The Middle Ages to Aquinas*, ed. Peter von Sivers, vol 2 of *History of Political Ideas* (Columbia: University of Missouri Press, 1997), 36.

7. Ibid., 106.

8. Michael Gillespie, *Nihilism Before Nietzsche* (Chicago: The University of Chicago Press, 1995), 14. One may note, as Thomas Hobbes made abundantly clear, that the character and possibility of modernity turns on a theological argument.

9. Ibid., 16.

10. Ibid., 28.

11. René Descartes, "Discourse on Method," ed. and trans. Donald A. Cress, *Discourse on Method and Meditations on First Philosophy* (Indianapolis: Hackett Publishing Company, 1980), 33.

12. Gillespie, *Nihilism*, 256-257.

13. Eric Voegelin, *The New Science of Politics* (Chicago: The University of Chicago Press, 1952), 127.

14. Thomas Spragens, *The Irony of Liberal Reason* (Chicago: The University of Chicago Press, 1981), 122. Cf. Frank E. Manuel and Fritzie P. Manuel, *Utopian Thought in the Western World* (Cambridge, Mass.: The Belknap Press, 1979), 461-486 and 491-505; J. B. Bury, *The Idea of Progress: An Inquiry into its Growth and Origin* (New York: Dover Publications, Inc., 1955), 153-158.

15. Alasdair MacIntyre, *After Virtue: A Study in Moral Theory*, 2d ed. (Notre Dame: University of Notre Dame Press, 1984), 79-85.

16. Spragens, *Irony of Liberal Reason*, 122.

17. MacIntyre, *After Virtue*, 75-108.

18. Spragens, *Liberal Reason*, 125.//
19. Ibid., 128.
20. Ibid., 129; Sheldon Wolin, *Politics and Vision: Continuity and Innovation in Western Political Thought* (Boston: Little, Brown and Company, 1960), 352-368; MacIntyre, *After Virtue*, 26-27, 74-75, 84-87.
21. Barry Cooper, *The End of History: An Essay on Modern Hegelianism* (Toronto: University of Toronto Press, 1984), 283-327.
22. See, for example, Thomas Hobbes, *Leviathan*, chaps. 11, 13, and 14.
23. MacIntyre, *After Virtue*, 55.
24. Ibid., 16-22.
25. Cooper, *End of History*, 283.
26. Francis Fukuyama, *The End of History and the Last Man* (New York: Avon Books, 1992).
27. David Walsh, *After Ideology: Recovering the Spiritual Foundations of Freedom* (San Francisco: HarperSanFrancisco, 1990), 3, 9.
28. Voegelin, *Revolution and the New Science*, 214-15.
29. Ted V. McAllister, *Revolt Against Modernity: Leo Strauss, Eric Voegelin, & the Search for a Postliberal Order* (Lawrence: The University Press of Kansas, 1996), 66; Walsh, *After Ideology*, 9.
30. Henry S. Kariel, *The Desperate Politics of Postmodernism* (Amherst: The University of Massachusetts Press, 1989), ix-x.
31. Ibid., xi, xii.
32. Ibid., 8, xiv.
33. Ibid., x, 49; xii; xiv, 12, 44, 74.
34. Ibid., 97-98.
35. Ibid., 179.
36. Ibid., 121.
37. Ibid., 120.
38. Richard Rorty, *Contingency, irony, and solidarity* (Cambridge, England: Cambridge University Press, 1989), 73-95, 189-198.
39. Gregory Bruce Smith, *Nietzsche, Heidegger, and the Transition to Postmodernity* (Chicago: The University of Chicago Press, 1996), 18-54.
40. Ibid., 15.
41. Ibid., 63.
42. Ibid., 284.
43. Friedrich Nietzsche, *On The Genealogy of Morals*, trans. Walter Kaufmann (New York: Random House, 1967), pt. I ; cf. Smith, *Postmodernity*, 325-26.
44. Smith, *Postmodernity*, 297.
45. Ibid., 299.
46. Ibid., 301.
47. Ibid., 335; 333, 336, 338; 334; 341; 294, 339 n.17; 330-331; 299.
48. Ibid., 313-14.
49. A philosophical anthropology need not imply a new metaphysics in order to answer such politically pertinent questions. For an example, see James Wm. McClendon's discussion of "body ethics" in *Systematic Theology: Ethics* (Nashville, Tenn.: Ab-

ingdon Press, 1986), 78-109.

50. William Connolly, *The Augustinian Imperative: A Reflection on the Politics of Morality* (Newbury Park, Calif.: Sage Publications, 1993), xvii; William Connolly, *Political Theory and Modernity*, 2d ed. (Ithaca: Cornell University Press, 1993), 177.

51. Connolly, *Political Theory*, 177.
52. Connolly, *Imperative*, 86.
53. Connolly, *Political Theory*, 177, 178 (his italics).
54. Ibid., 70.
55. Ibid., 137-8.
56. Smith, *Postmodernity*, 328, 331-333.
57. Ibid., 292-93, 302.
58. Ibid., 312, 304.
59. Ibid., 304.
60. Ibid., 301.

61. Smith is aware of potential problems in his proposal for postmodern transcendence. "That which reveals itself publicly to all," for example, "is never entirely self-evident and unproblematic." But the tendency toward excess and especially toward giving precedence to pre-formed thinking over experience can be mitigated by a self-imposed moderation (312, 316, 320). Similarly, whereas Smith's postmodern vision seems to imply an extreme historicization, it does not do so necessarily. "A variety of possibilities exist between relativism and apodictic certainty," he suggests. Accordingly, "there must be a logoi [sic] that allows one to judge between true and false prophets" (319, 320). The origins of such a logos or of moderation remain unclear.

62. Ibid., 301.
63. Walsh, *After Ideology*, 33, 34.
64. Ibid., 35.
65. Ibid., 221.
66. Ibid., 262, 240-270.
67. Ibid., 277, 270.

68. Donald Kraybill, *The Upside-Down Kingdom* (Scottdale, Pa.: Herald Press, 1978).

69. For a variety of interpretations, see the following: Harold Bender, "The Anabaptist Vision," *Church History* 12 (1944), 3-24; James M. Stayer, *Anabaptists and the Sword*, 2d ed. (Lawrence, Kans.: Coronado Press, 1976); Hans-Jürgen Goertz, *Die Täufer: Geschichte und Deutung* (München: Verlag C.H. Beck, 1980); Franklin Littell, *The Anabaptist View of the Church: A Study in the Origins of Sectarian Protestantism*, 2d ed. (Boston: Beacon Press, Inc., 1958); Snyder, *Anabaptist History and Theology*, 365-396.

70. Cf. Friedrich Nietzsche, *Daybreak: Thoughts on the Prejudices of Morality*, trans. R. J. Hollingdale (Cambridge: Cambridge University Press, 1982), 79.

71. It is worth recalling that through the machinations of their camps, totalitarian regimes seek to dehumanize their victims on the way to murdering them. Murder is more palatable when one's victims are no longer fully human. See Hannah Arendt, *The Origins of Totalitarianism*, 2d ed. (New York: Harcourt, Brace, Jovanovich, 1973), 296-300, 433-35, 437-459; and Alexander I. Solzhenitsyn, *The Gulag Archipelago*,

1918-1956: An Experiment in Literary Investigation , I-II, trans. Thomas P. Whitney (New York: Harper & Row, Publishers, 1974), 24-143.

72. John Howard Yoder, *The Priestly Kingdom: Social Ethics and Gospel* (Notre Dame: University of Notre Dame Press, 1984), 53-57.

73. Ibid., 54. C. S. Lewis once suggested that Christians can more easily speak with pagans than modern European atheists because they share a language of theism with the form that is missing in any interchange with the latter (C. S. Lewis, "Is Theism Important?" ed. Walter Hooper, *God in the Dock: Essays on Theology and Ethics* [Grand Rapids, Mich.: Eerdmans, 1970], 172). The problem for Anabaptists in postmodernity, as it was for the early Christians in the Roman ecumene, is to find common terms from which to begin a conversation and an intelligible proclamation.

74. Michel Foucault has well demonstrated the varieties of such control. See, for example, *The History of Sexuality: Volume I: Introduction*, trans. Robert Hurley (New York: Random House, 1980), esp. 135-159; *Power/Knowledge: Selected Interviews and Other Writings, 1972-1977*, ed. Colin Gordon (New York: Pantheon Books, 1980), 78-165.

75. For the latter, see especially Nicholas Lash, "Ideology, Metaphor and Analogy," in *The Philosophical Frontiers of Christian Theology: Essays Presented to D. M. MacKinnon*, ed. Brian Hebblethwaite and Stewart Sutherland (Cambridge: Cambridge University Press, 1982), 72-85; and Yoder, *Priestly Kingdom*, 28-33.

76. Eric Voegelin, *Science, Politics, and Gnosticism* (Chicago: Regnery, 1959), 108-109; Voegelin, *New Science*, 122-123.

77. The term is from Ronald Thiemann, "Radiance and Obscurity in Biblical Narrative," in *Scriptural Authority and Narrative Interpretation*, ed. Garrett Green *(Philadelphia: Fortress Press, 1987)*, 21-41, at 27.

78. John Howard Yoder, "Peace Without Eschatology?" in *The Royal Priesthood: Essays Ecclesiological and Ecumenical*, ed. Michael G. Cartwright (Grand Rapids, Mich.: Eerdmans, 1994), 157.

79. Immanuel Kant, "Idea for a Universal History with a Cosmopolitan Purpose," ed. Hans Reiss, *Kant's Political Writings* (Cambridge, England: Cambridge University Press, 1970), 41-53, esp. 47-49; and "Perpetual Peace: A Philosophical Sketch," in ibid., 102-105; Alexander Hamilton et al., *The Federalist* , no. 51.

80. Yoder, "Peace," 156.

81. Ibid., 154.

82. Ibid., 159.

83. ". . . the state is not an ideal order, ideally definable; it is a pragmatic, tolerable balance of egoisms and can become more or less tolerable. To define the point of infinite tolerability would be to define the kingdom; it cannot be done in terms of the present situation" (ibid., 160). We might add that a transfiguration of the present situation certainly seems no less incredible than Christian claims of a Resurrection, and perhaps much more so.

84. Ibid., 163.

PART SEVEN

CULTURAL CAPTIVITY AND CHRISTIAN FREEDOM

CHAPTER NINETEEN

POSTMODERN EXPERIMENTS:
Blips or New Revolution?

Leo Driedger

In a 1994 speech at Independence Hall in Philadelphia, Vaclav Havel, the playwright and president of the Czech Republic, said that "if the modern age began with the discovery of America, it also ended in America."[1] The late fifteenth and early sixteenth centuries saw the development of technology which led to land discoveries and the printing press. Spawned were the Reformation, the beginnings of capitalism, and the birth of our Anabaptist forebears, who helped launch the beginning of the modern age. Havel continued,

> The modern age has ended . . . we are going through a transitional period, when it seems that something is on the way out and something else is painfully being born. It is as if something were crumbling, decaying, and exhausting itself, while something else, still indistinct, were arising from the rubble.[2]

Havel noted previous fundamental shifts. These had happened in the Hellenistic period and the Renaissance and opened the way to the modern era. He continued,

> The distinguishing features of such transitional periods are a mixing and blending of cultures and a plurality or parallelism of intellectual and spiritual worlds. These are periods when all consistent value systems col-

lapse, when cultures distant in time and space are discovered or rediscovered. They are periods when there is a tendency to quote, to imitate, and to amplify, rather than to state with authority or integrity. New meaning is gradually born from the encounter, or the intersection, of many different elements. Today this state of mind or of the human world is called postmodernism. For me, a symbol of that state is a Bedouin mounted on a camel and clad in traditional robes under which he is wearing jeans, with a transistor radio in his hands and an ad for Coca-Cola on the camel's back.[3]

Doesn't that sound like the time of our Anabaptist ancestors who lived almost 500 years ago? And we have the privilege to go through such a time as well. We are freed to explore, to help create a new revolution! Ah, but what if it is only a blip, as one of my sociology colleagues has warned? Another psychology friend has similarly cautioned, "Postmodernism!! Well, be careful: it's a minefield!"

Alas, three exclamation marks by a respected scientist in one short sentence. Is it worth the risk? Will we get lost? Do Mennonite suburban professionals have the courage to look and observe and explore? Did Abraham? Moses? The prophets like Ruth? Jesus? Paul? Did Grebel? Did Menno? Did Harold and Elizabeth Bender, whose story we can now read?

NEW ERA, NEW STIRRINGS

Whereas my colleagues in psychology and sociology were reluctant to leave their scientific cages, there is much evidence that some 1990s Mennonites sense a new stir.

In his "Congregations and Pastors" column in the *Mennonite Weekly Review,* John Esau reported on a conference of parish clergy he attended, at which Loren Mead described the era we live in as a transition era, away from "rational empirical, logical and sequential ways" where "cause and effect are the dominant set of relationships."[4] Whereas modern science divided into smaller and smaller parts, Esau said, we are now increasingly looking for connections and relationships. Instead of causes, we observe multiple influences, where experience and intuition are given greater weight.

In the June 1998 issue of *Mennonite Life,* Lois Barrett, Secretary of General Conference Mennonite Church Home Ministries, wrote about evangelism in the context of modernity and postmodernity. "Modernity began . . . out of a desire to assert and foster individual freedom . . . an alternative to the authoritarian restraints of monarchies and church hierarchies."[5] She continued, "The postmodern world view also questions objective truth. It recognizes that there is not a neutral, objective place from which to stand and judge truth."[6]

Barrett called for a more "comprehensive understanding of the Anabaptist tradition which "recognizes some diversity, but must also clearly define a center." Although she is open to explore, she soon put on the brakes, calling for a "center," for community.[7] She said that "both Anabaptism and postmodernism have a commitment to allowing plural and diverse traditions to live peaceably side by side." Like Esau, she also stressed that "the postmodern collapse of confidence in the modern, rational, autonomous self"[8] is real, and she emphasized a common Mennonite theme of the past, namely, that new communities are needed.

In the March 3, 1998, issue of *The Mennonite*, Michael A. King, Pandora Press U.S. publisher, framed his postmodern quest around the scattering of Babel. He saw the Enlightenment as a tower of Babel, which now is in shambles. We are now "each shaped by the countless languages of the different communities, life histories, experiences, cultures and subgroups,"[9] King said. Postmodernism is one way in which we have become scattered. There is now much potential for new "rainbow" experiences of genders, races, cultures.

King also stressed the need for Christians to be part of today's postmodern discussions—along with all the other richly different peoples of the world. He pointed out that after the scattering of Genesis 11, Abraham enters in Chapter 12, leaving the first great urban civilization for a "land that God would show him." First a scattering, then a leaving, then the blessing. Risk, vision, courage clearly stand out.

In the May issue of the *Canadian Mennonite*, Margaret Loewen Reimer shared a summary of lectures she gave at Canadian Mennonite Bible College in January 1998.[10] Like King, she stressed the centrality of language for artistic imagination. There is much beauty that Mennonites must find. While Mennonites have recognized that art is dangerous, Reimer called for taking some risks. After all, our forebears were martyrs! The risk is to join with the Creator in creative work. Reimer noted the Bible is full of body language where the spirit and body must both be explored. We must experiment with new ways of seeing. "Our religious language must be adequate to embrace the many levels of our experience."[11] There is more need for "sacramental reality," which is closely bound to changing images all around us. We do not pay enough attention to the power of images.

Although leaders in church institutions have begun to sense the coming of a new era, it is our creative Mennonite writers who have followed the postmodern way for quite some time. Mennonite poets, novelists, and short story writers in Winnipeg display an extraordinary commitment to examining the iron-caged rural reserves from which they have come, the patriarchal families into which they were locked, the harshness of the religious community from which they are trying to escape, and the beauty which they are determined to find in a larger world. Di Brandt is quite open to many postmodern trends, whereas Patrick Friesen has his doubts about unstructured postmodern blips. Although some are angry and others not, most are driven to express their individual newfound freedoms. Unlike Lois Barrett, who calls for new community, many of these creative writers feel betrayed by traditional communities and structures. A question that runs through many of their writings is "where is home?"

PREMODERN, MODERN, AND POSTMODERN REVOLUTIONS

Although later than others, sociologists are also exploring this new era, illustrated by a dozen review essays of debates on postmodern experiments published in the January 1996 issue of *Contemporary Sociology*.[12] Among sociologists, views ranged from those who think postmodernism is only a blip that will soon fade like ethno-methodology to others who think it is a new major revolution spawned by the computer, similar to that of the sixteenth-century discovery of the printing press.

Lawrence Cahoone's *From Modernism to Postmodernism*, a 700-page anthology of forty-two contributors, provides one good attempt to trace changes from premodern times through the rise of modernization into the present postmodern era.[13] Cahoone's book focuses on modern civilization and its critics, including the many philosophers and early sociologists who tried to sort premodern, modern, and postmodern changes. Cahoone suggests that one reason we tend to have problems with the meaning of postmodernism is that we do not adequately understand what is modern. The remainder of this section sketches aspects of the change from premodern to modern to postmodern.

Politics of the Third Wave

In their many books, futurists Alvin and Heidi Toffler have outlined the super struggle happening in the 1990s. "A new civilization is emerging in our lives, and the blind everywhere are trying to suppress it."[14] The Tofflers describe three dramatic waves of cultural and social change in human history. The first wave—the agricultural revolution—took thousands of years, beginning some 10,000 years ago. The second wave came with the industrial revolution, which has occurred during the second half of the past millennium. The third wave—the information revolution—arrived after World War II and within a few decades has brought accelerating and enormous change.

Today, the first agricultural wave has reached almost all corners of the world, except for a few pre-agrarian peoples in South America and South Guinea. This First Wave era began around 8000 B.C. in the Middle East, identified when the first archaeological digs uncovered agricultural villages at Jarmo in Iraq and Jericho. The Amish and some conservative Mennonites have extended islands of agricultural activity into the industrial era to the present day, but even they are greatly influenced by the coming of the second, industrial wave.

The Tofflers provide some clues for distinguishing the receding Second Wave (industrial age) from an emerging Third Wave, or information revolution. The ability to distinguish is crucial.[15]

1. An apt metaphor for the second wave is the factory, which represents standardization, centralization, maximization, concentration, and bureaucratization. By contrast, customization and individualization seem to be the trend of the emerging Third Wave.

2. The Second Wave society was massified into predictable, interchangeable assembly lines. However, in the Third Wave those who think, ask questions, innovate, and risk may be more competitive.

3. Second Wave organizations tended toward a hierarchical concentration of power at the top whereas Third Wave organizations seem to push decisions down and out to the periphery, putting their eggs into many baskets.

4. If Second Wave organizations were unwieldy and overorganized, Third Wave organizations subcontract rather than adding more functions.

5. Second Wave industrialism stripped most functions from the home. Third Wave trends move functions back to the home where computers, e-mail, and the Internet can be used flexibly and part-time as needed.

The print revolution

As an agricultural revolution, the First Wave was inescapably attached to the land, where mobility was limited. The Second Wave began with the introduction of machines, which replaced human muscle power. Some associate its beginnings with the steam engine developed by 1790.

Marshall McLuhan located the beginning of the industrial era with Gutenberg's invention of the printing press in the late fifteenth century. By shifting emphasis from the ear to the eye, print technology modified our form of perception, with significant consequences for both individuals and cultures.[16] In a largely oral, agricultural Europe where few could read and write, Catholic monks in insulated monasteries had copied and recopied sacred writings by hand for centuries. Feudal Europe was an agricultural Holy Roman Empire, where lords lived in their walled castles dominating serfs who lived in subsistence on the land.

Soon after the invention of the printing press, a series of revolutions followed in the early sixteenth century. These included the Protestant Reformation, the Peasant Revolt, European discoveries of new continents, and what Max Weber called the "Spirit of Capitalism." In 1517, finding new insights in the Scriptures, Martin Luther nailed (literally or figuratively) his ninety-five theses to the Wittenberg church door, calling for a religious reformation. Luther's theses challenged the tenets of the old Catholic church, which was intertwined with the feudal economic and political system of the Holy Roman Empire. Luther's reformation cast Germanic Europe into an ideological religious struggle for decades to come. Following on the heels of this earth-shaking religious challenge, the Peasants Revolt began south of Wurttemberg in 1524 and moved northward, challenging many feudalistic economic arrangements before it was brutally crushed.[17]

Since Luther's proclamation threatened the unity of the Catholic church, it was not long before a variety of reformed religious versions appeared, with Zwingli in Switzerland and adherents of John Calvin in the northern low countries. The Anabaptists were a diverse group of radicals who wanted much greater reform of the church. They advocated a change from infant to adult baptism, separation of church from state, the priesthood of every believer, and the practice of love without violence and war.[18] Such major calls for reform threatened religious, economic, and political leaders alike. In response, Catholic counterforces crushed the Peasants Revolt in 1525 and 1526. They executed thousands of Anabaptists after the Anabaptists emerged as a movement in 1525.

In his classic *Protestant Ethic and the Spirit of Capitalism*, Max Weber portrayed the new Protestant religious ferment and ideology as the engine that changed the feudal economic system into a spirit of economic capitalism, spawning and fueling the great Western industrial revolution.[19] A torrent of suppressed anger swelled into the Peasants Revolt, which was linked to new ideas and a far-reaching Protestant Reformation, which then led to new individual economic experimentation and enterprise.

The electronic revolution

The electronic Third Wave information era first crept upon us via invention of the telegraph, telephone, radio, television, and computers. By the end of the twentieth century these early information inventions had blossomed into fax, e-mail, the Internet, and more. In the context of Third Wave brain-based economies, the mass production that characterized the Second Wave seems increasingly an outmoded form. "Demassified production—short runs of highly customized products—is the new cutting edge of manufacture."[20] Labor unions in the mass manufacturing sector have shrunk and giant TV networks shriveled as new channels have proliferated. The modern standard of the nuclear family is giving way to more demassified single-parent households, where live-alones, childless couples, and remarried couples proliferate.

The complexity of the new system requires more and more information exchange among its units—companies, government agencies, hospitals, associations, institutions, even individuals. This interchange creates a ravenous need for computers, digital telecommunications networks, and media.[21] These fast-moving changes threaten to slash many of the existing economic links between rich economies and poor. The same occurs in countries between those who try to keep up and those who cannot. For these reasons we may expect tensions among people and countries to accelerate.

Nationalism is the ideology of the nation-state, which is the product of the industrial revolution. When First Wave agrarian societies began competition in the industrialization process, they soon demanded independence and nationhood. Take the republics of the former Soviet Union, new countries of the former Yugoslavia, the Czech and Slovakia republics which have split former Czechoslovakia into two, the Palestinians and Israel, Quebec in Canada. All demanded nationalist marks that included flags, armies, and currencies to display nation-state freedoms of the industrial Second Wave.

Third Wave economies, however, are well on their way to puncturing national sovereignties, which must be changed to compete in a borderless world which McLuhan called the global village. A characteristic of the Third Wave is a reorganizing of production and distribution of knowledge and communication, interrelating data in more ways and assembling information and knowledge into larger symbols and models. This involves a change from the massive smokestack factory to the portable electronic device as the main site of economic production. Fast information and knowledge-based technologies reduce the need for massive, high-cost inventories. The result of less inventory is reduced taxes and insurance.[22]

Shakedown in the economy

Angus Reid's *Shakedown* was a frightening wake-up call to what is happening in the Third Wave economy.[23] He charted the demise of the "Spend-and-Share Era," a term he used to describe the period of national prosperity and optimism that characterized North America from the 1960s to the 1980s. Reid showed that we have entered an alarming new era of corporate downsizing, declining government services, budget cutting, shrinking incomes, and a dwindling number of blue-collar jobs. Technology and globalization seem to be killing more jobs than they are creating, while the top twenty percent are getting richer and the bottom eighty percent poorer.

Reid outlined how institutions such as governments, professions, and large corporations, which were once beacons of safety and security during the past fifty years, are no longer making our lives as predictable in an age of discontinuity. Reid named a number of myths we must face: that big is safe, that growth is good for everyone, that science and technology will save us, that a good education means a good job, and that loyalty is all. Other myths losing their plausibility are that location matters, that time is linear, that events are predictable, that culture is a sacred trust, and that the public interest still counts.[24]

What could be more threatening to Second Wave security than to say that spatial patterns are obsolete and that our time in the familiar forms of maps, calendars, and clocks can no longer be depended on for orientation? Steady state forms such as photographs, newspapers, and magazines are changing to fleeting electronic screens of the Internet and its World Wide Web. There impressions, megabytes, and messages are changed at will, with little time to think or ponder. A snowstorm of particles has rained on us. No one flake or drop remains long, but vague impressions fleetingly flit by our consciousness.

There are a host of other changes as well. In the 1960s, the new birth control pill freed youth to enter an era of experimentation without responsibility for the consequences of freer sex. During this time church attendance in Quebec dropped from eighty to twenty percent. The birth rate plunged from one of the highest to one of the lowest in the developed world. In Canada the number of households with a gas or electric stove increased from forty-eight percent in 1948 to ninety-four percent by 1968.[25]

Canada offered safe haven to draft dodgers, the Catholic Church abandoned the Latin mass, astronauts walked in space, nuclear generating plants spewed out power, new plastics created disposable packaging, and downtowns began to decline as most headed for new suburban malls. There was an air of optimism in which television became a new focus, the plastic credit card was taking hold, and manufacturing was pumping away at almost full capacity. Unemployment was less than four percent, inflation was less than three percent, and wages were growing at twice that rate. Meanwhile, governments were spending for bilingualism, multiculturalism, and the 1967 Montreal World's Fair.[26]

"In 1969, Canada had no debt . . . in 1996, the country was crippled with more than a $500 billion debt . . . ."[27] How times have changed! The spend and share era since the sixties has resulted in massive labor force growth, voracious patterns of consumption, a burgeoning public sector, and the transition from an economy based on resources and industry to one based on services. A new era is taking shape where television is fueling consumerism and computers are multiplying our capacity to store and communicate information at a level previously unimagined.

Microsoft's Bill Gates has posed a vision for what this electronic technology can do and those at the forefront of the Internet revolution constantly sing its praises. But too few ask how we got here or where we are going. E-mail and the Internet are paving the way for a popular experience of globalization that has also resulted in a stress on lower trade barriers, increasing use of global moneylenders, globalization of culture and world opinion, and the imperial reign of capitalism. Meanwhile, technological societies are aging, with increased longevity and declining fertility, pointing toward when the baby boomers will retire and swamp society's capacity to support them. We have only begun to understand the many dimensions and full implications of this morass characterized as postmodern society.

CHARACTERISTICS OF THE INFORMATION REVOLUTION

Opinion regarding the family of ideas called postmodernism is deeply divided.

> For some, postmodernism connotes the final escape from the stultifying legacy of modern European theology, metaphysics, authoritarianism, colonialism, racism, and domination. To others it represents the attempt by disgruntled left-wing intellectuals to destroy Western civilization. To yet others it labels a goofy collection of hermetically obscure writers who are really talking about nothing at all.[28]

Cahoone suggests that all of the above are misguided and that most philosophers use the word postmodernism to identify a movement that developed among intellectual circles in France of the 1960s, a movement more accurately referred to as "poststructuralism."

> They have in mind that this movement denies the possibility of objective knowledge of the real world, "univocal" . . . meaning of words and texts, the unity of the human self, the cogency of the distinctions between rational inquiry and political action, literal and metaphorical meaning, science and art, and even the possibility of truth itself.[29]

In other words, poststructuralists and postmodernists tend to reject most of the pillars of modern Western civilization. Little wonder that some people are threatened, while others ignore it as a blip that will soon go away.

Like the postmodernists, Anabaptist-Mennonites have often positioned themselves against things modern, even such pillars of Western civilization as military force and individual autonomy. So what can Anabaptists learn from all this talk about the decline of modern institutions and values? Is our fate simply to become part of the Third Wave that Tapscott calls the rise of the Net Generation—those growing up digital?[30]

Postmodern is a rather recent term. When used to distinguish "the contemporary scene from the modern, [it] seems first to have been used in 1917 by the German philosopher Rudof Pannwitz to describe the 'nihilism' of twentieth-century Western culture, a theme he took from Friedrich Nietzsche."[31] Arnold Toynbee attached the word to the post-World War I rise of mass society, in which the working class surpassed the capitalist class in importance.[32] The word appeared in literary criticism in the 1950s and 1960s as a reaction against aesthetic modernism and was used in the 1970s by scholars in architecture for the same purpose. The term entered the social sciences as a new approach to methodology, linked to trends in "post-industrialism." Let us examine further some of postmodernism's themes.

Challenging the Enlightenment and reason

Modern philosopher Immanuel Kant made reason the center of his conception of the human being.

> Enlightenment is man's emergence from his self-incurred immaturity. Immaturity is the inability to use one's own understanding without the guidance of another. This immaturity is self-incurred if its cause is not lack of understanding, but lack of resolution and courage to use it without the guidance of another. The motto of enlightenment is therefore: *Sapere aude*! Have courage to use your own understanding![33]

Kant suggested that laziness and cowardice keep people from emancipation. People remain immature for life because it is more convenient to stay immature. Dogmas, formulas, and organizations are the balls-and-chains of those who lack individual initiative and are unaccustomed to free movement. Only a few have cultivated their minds and succeeded in freeing themselves from immaturity, coldly striking out on their own way. Freedom, and its use, is the key to the enlightened way, according to Kant. Not surprisingly, however, such a valorization of reason as a means to freedom has come under critical scrutiny in postmodernity:

> A highly significant series of Western ideas starts with "providence" which is transposed to 'progress' and shifts from there into "nihilism." Providence refers to God's care for the world after creation, overseeing the process of history so that it moves forward in a line toward a specific goal. . . . The wresting of reason from medievalism and tradition prompted many to believe that further and more rapid advance was within human powers to achieve. . . . But by emphasizing the role of reason and downplaying divine intervention the seeds were sown for a secular variant of Providence, the idea of Progress.[34]

The single most significant figure in these developments was Friedrich Nietzsche (1844-1900). He announced that nihilism, where traditional beliefs and values are unfounded and existence is senseless and useless, was inevitable. He denied that there was objective ground for truth and moral values. Nietzsche devoted his life to exposing the hollowness of Enlightenment hopes and inaugurated a debate about the lack of reality or a multiplicity of realities or an anchorless sense of reality.[35] Nietzsche's slogan, "the death of God," meant that we can no longer be sure of enlightenment. He claimed that humanism found itself in crisis precisely because it replaced God with humanity at the center of the universe. He saw Western civilization as being in a twilight stage but worked at opportunities for reconstruction.

As modern society developed, the discipline of sociology appeared with Marx, Durkheim, Weber, and Simmel trying to understand the changes taking place. Karl Marx thought powerful capitalists were keeping the proletariat in bonds, Emil Durkheim was concerned about what would replace the traditional structures, and Max Weber was concerned about rational bureaucratization. Georg Simmel (1858-1918) came perhaps the closest to postmodern thinking, straddling the worlds of sociology and cultural analysis, when he saw the effects of technology on culture and the apparent loss of meaning in the world of modern industrialism.[36]

For Simmel, the social experiences of modernity were especially strongly felt in the growing urban metropolis and in the alienation of a mature money economy. These experiences were best understood in terms of the inner lives of individuals, thus providing a sort of social psychological counterpoint to Marx's analysis of capitalist society. Simmel prefigured some of the central discussions of postmodernity.[37]

Simmel thought that attachment to the world of things devalued the human world. He believed that aesthetics, culture, religion, and family, to which postmoderns seem to be returning, were means of overcoming the contradictions of modernity.

Emil Durkheim identified as major concerns an uprootedness from tradition and breaks from ties with the family, kin, and neighborhood; the absence of conventional regulation; and new mobility. These all result in a sense of uncertainty and loss of direction, leaving individuals on their own. He labeled the resulting feeling "normlessness" or "anomie."

Max Weber was perhaps the most pessimistic about technological rationality that focused on utilitarian ends while a sense of ultimate purpose evaporated. Technology, supposed to free humans, could actually enslave them and hasten the inhumane.[38] Weber saw bureaucratic technology potentially as an "iron cage" from which humanity would find it difficult to extricate itself.

Like Weber, Charles Taylor saw the Enlightenment promise of freedom as a hollow product of rationality, mocked by the machine-like systems they now inhabit. He outlined three key modern forms of malaise: first, individualism; second, instrumental reason; and third, bureaucratic political power, all of which have put humanity into the "iron cage" described by Weber. The autonomous self moves to center stage, the individual self loses a sense of meaning and purpose in a rational world, and bureaucratic politics again destines all to the dictates of the iron cage.

Skeptics of linearity and science

In his *Structure of Scientific Revolutions,* Thomas Kuhn argued that science proceeds not primarily by patient accretion of facts, but by revolutionary interpretive shifts in which one scientific "paradigm" displaces another.[39] He raised the question of the rationality of science, suggesting that scientific revolutions are noncumulative developmental episodes where an older paradigm is replaced in whole or in part by an incompatible new one.[40] Whereas science may be cumulative, it also has its revolutionary times when largely unexplained breakthroughs occur. This often happens when medical or social problems mount unsolved and scientists look elsewhere for help. Malfunction can lead to crisis, a prerequisite for revolution. For example, European medieval society in the form of a Holy Roman Empire joined religious, political, and economic forces that locked the individual into an "iron cage" of servitude. The Peasant Revolt, the Protestant Reformation, and the Enlightenment were all revolutions that drastically reformulated society into new paradigms. But if religion got trapped, so could science.[41] Science is not immune from the "iron cage."

Kuhn suggested three ways theories can be changed: first, work with phenomena already well explained by existing paradigms; second, enhance and develop already existing paradigms, as many scientists do now; and third, recognize anomalies that stubbornly refuse to be assimilated into existing paradigms and look for new paradigms with greater and broader powers of explanation. The "transition from Newtonian to Einsteinian mechanics illustrates with particular clarity the scientific revolution as a displacement of the conceptual network through which scientists view the world."[42]

In a speech at the centennial celebrations of the University of Chicago, Andrew Abbott demonstrated the volatility of science as described by Kuhn by criticizing current trends in scientific sociology and calling for a return to earlier "Chicago School" preoccupations with time and space.

> In short, sociology has degenerated into formulas—empirical, theoretical, historical. We are no longer excited enough to take risks, to float unorthodox ideas, to poach on each other's turf. We have given up writing about the real world, hiding in stylized worlds of survey variables, historical forces, and theoretical abstractions. . . . It is among people of my own age [he is 45] that I detect the sense of exhaustion, the going through of intellectual motions.[43]

Abbott suggested that "the Chicago School made a decisive advance by joining the scientific and the surveying traditions via the central idea of contextuality."[44] He sees the decline of the early Chicago School research of multiplicity in varied contexts, with the rise of monies for opinion polling and market research. Sociology followed individual preferences rather than a more complex search for why events were happening. The image of probable causality was borrowed from the physical sciences so that "by the 1970s many sociologists imagined the social world as a kind of general linear reality."[45] As Kuhn and Abbott demonstrate, such a linear understanding of scientific reality has lost plausibility for many in these postmodern times.

Critique of the metanarrative

As if challenges to enlightened reason and the hopes of science were not enough, postmodernists also attacked linear metanarrative thinking. Metanarrative thinking is ingrained in Western thought as history that has a story line moving toward goals, hopes, destiny. Jean-François Lyotard (1926-) challenged the idea of metanarrative in his treatise on postmodernism which defined postmodernism as "incredulity regarding metanarratives." Lyotard wrote that

> Science has always been in conflict with narratives. Judged by the yardstick of science, the majority of them prove to be fables. But to the extent that science does not restrict itself to stating useful regularities and seeks the truth, it is obliged to legitimate the rules of its own game. It then produces a discourse of legitimation with respect to its own status . . . I will use the term modern to designate any science that legitimates itself with reference to a metadiscourse of this kind making an explicit appeal to some grand narrative, such as the dialectics of Spirit, the hermeneutics of meaning, the emancipation of the rational . . . or the creation of wealth.[46]

Lyotard called these grand constructions "metanarratives," which are philosophical stories that legitimate their own discourse. To establish credibility a metanarrative must achieve unanimity between rational minds, according to the enlightenment attitude toward metanarratives. These narratives become incredible, however, because science attributes "progress" to itself, but it in turn presupposes it.

Borrowing from Wittgenstein, Lyotard understood this struggle for credibility to be constituted by "language games" or rules that determine attempts at legitimation. Lyotard also suggested that the notions of justification, system, proof, and unity of science no longer need to be situated in metanarratives because such notions can no longer be credibly justified by an appeal to a larger "truth." Instead, we recognize that science plays its own language game. In the postmodern era, science is neither capable of legitimating its own game nor of delegitimizing the other nonscientific language games.

As can be seen from the discussion so far, postmodernism marks a new way of viewing reality, a revolution both in our understanding of knowledge as well as our view of science. This move is from an objectivist to a constructionist outlook. Postmoderns no longer find the grand realist ideal tenable. They see it not as a world "out there" but rather as a construct of the world based on the concepts we bring to it. This is where Wiggenstein's "language games" come into play, because the various language games color and alter the way we experience our world. The "real world" is actually an ever-changing set of symbols and social creations.

Anthropologists are increasingly aware of the importance of foundational myths. Such myths embody the central core of a culture's values and beliefs and are in that sense fundamentally religious.

Postmodern thinkers speak of these systems of legitimizing myths as narratives (or metanarratives). They contend that a narrative exercises force apart from argumentation and proof and, in fact, that it provides the principal means by which every community legitimates itself.[47]

Modern thinkers claimed to have replaced myths with rational postulates, but postmodern thinkers asserted that the Enlightenment project is itself dependent on an appeal to a metanarrative which has over many years gained enormous credence in the modern Western world but is increasingly faced with problems it cannot solve. Postmoderns have given up on appealing to a central legitimating myth. In the end, all myths have become tired, including the grand narrative of science, the Enlightenment, and political ideologies. The fall of Marxism in Eastern Europe is the most recent example of a delegitimized metanarrative.

Rejection of the metanarrative is of course a challenge to the great religions of the world, which are based on metanarratives. These religions are grounded in a unified whole or "reality" involving Gods and the spirits. One agenda item for Christians, including Mennonites, is how to speak of God and spiritual reality in a time when postmodernists cast aside "objective" truth that is based in the unity of grand narratives.

Poststructuralists and deconstruction

As alternatives to metanarratives and linear thinking, postmodernists like Jacques Derrida take us back to smaller units, inviting us to examine the instability of the language we use to reconstruct reality. Derrida's "The End of the Book and the Beginning of Writing" is difficult to understand until one ponders the title that seems to reverse the way we ordinarily think about textual production. Is not writing first, before the product—the book? That, of course, is the point Derrida is making in the essay by stressing a shift from product to process: the beginning of writing. By focusing on the process of putting words together, he calls attention to their many particular combinations, their managing of context, and their hiding of origins: "'Signifier of the signifier describes . . . the movement of language" which "conceals and erases itself in its own production."[48]

Thus, writing is a "game" that we enter into, an adventure, a moving thought process that leads into new signs not seen in the same way before. Books are only end products of such processes, which have been stored in libraries as objects of knowledge. Writing, on the other hand, is a creative process that has much more potential for action, movement, thought, reflection, consciousness, experience, and affectivity beyond language itself.

According to Derrida, we in the West have become "logocentric."

> The notion of the sign always implies in itself the distinction between signifier and signified, even if, as Saussure argues, they are distinguished simply as the two faces of one and the same leaf. This notion remains therefore in the heritage of that logocentrism which is also phonocentrism; absolute proximity of voice and space, of voice and the meaning of being, of voice and the ideality of meaning.[49]

As the face of pure intelligibility, logocentrism refers to an absolute logos to which language is immediately united. This absolute logos was an infinite creative subjectivity in medieval theology: the intelligible face of the sign remains turned toward the word and the face of God. In Derrida's thought, Western thought has accepted the illusion that words—signifiers—are unproblematically tied to what they signify or point toward.[50]

Derrida did not reject logocentrism, saying that nothing is conceivable to us without it. He suggested that Nietzsche contributed a great deal toward the liberation of the signifier, except that the virulence with which he wrote often resulted in his being misunderstood. Describing the "death of God" was misinterpreted by many. What Nietzsche meant was that God as object was dead, which was a product of logocentrism rather than process or creativity.

Derrida's call for deconstruction is not an appeal for demolition as Nietzsche advocated:

> The movements of deconstruction do not destroy structures from the outside. They are not possible and effective, nor can they take accurate aim, except for inhabiting those structures. Inhabiting them in a certain way, because one always inhabits, and all the more when one does not suspect it. Operating necessarily from the inside, borrowing all the strategic and economic resources of subversion from the old structure. . . .[51]

At its heart, deconstruction concerns language. Especially with respect to written language texts, Derrida wants to wean us from too quickly assuming that we can discover the meaning of the text, because he thinks the Western philosophical tradition is hopelessly logocentric or objectivistic, fixed on an ultimate grounding. "Derrida interpreted the meaning of signifiers—words and sounds—as in a state of flux and contestation," and thus their ordering was shown to be "an act of power" related to "the capacity of a social group to impose its will on others by freezing linguistic and cultural meanings."[52]

> The logocentrism of Western culture lies in its quest for an authoritative language that can reveal truth, moral rightness, and beauty. From Plato to Russel, Western thinkers charged philosophy with the task of establishing a universal language that could disclose what is real, right and beautiful . . . Derrida detected a series of binary oppositions in Western thought that have been pivotal in efforts to establish an order of truth. Dualisms such as speech/writing, presence/absence, meaning/form, soul/body, masculine/feminine, man/woman, literal/metaphorical, nature/culture, positive/negative, transcendental/empirical, and cause/effect reappear time and again and lie at the core of Western culture.[53]

The first terms in the dualities have been considered superior. Derrida has exerted his energies toward undermining these hierarchical dualities in Western culture and giving the subordinate term its own value.

Celebrating diversity, pluralism, difference

Derrida has wanted us to examine how language locks us into power systems and has also extended this to cultural differences. He claims again that Western thought has put us into national and cultural "iron cages," as Weber would put it. Difference, diversity, and cultural pluralism surround us, a condition made clear now that the world is becoming a global village.

David Hall makes useful comparisons between China, which draws heavily from its classical premodern past, and the modern West, which abandoned too much of its past. Of the West, Hall says,

> Enlightenment rationality emerged from the idea that generic principles of logic and rationality may generate a common discourse for all cultures. Such rationalism was born from the need to connect diverse, pluralistic ideas, beliefs, and practices. Our reason was the gift of the ancient city-states, spread from Italy to the Peloponnesus, spun through the shuttles of Hebraic monotheism and Latin conceptions of *humanitas* and refined in the various furnaces of German, French, and English forms of colonialism.[54]

Hall adds that

> The desire to see essential unity among cultures is a function of our missionizing activity expressed initially through Roman and Christian ex-

pansion, and now through our rational technologies motored by an incipient economic imperialism. . . .

Then Hall points out that

Our cultural values are housed in doctrines and propositions that may be entertained as beliefs. Philosophic and scientific principles are rational in form and are therefore open to public entertainment apart from specific cultural practices.[55]

Whereas the modern West concentrated on identity, being, and permanence, the Chinese have found it easier to think difference, change, and becoming. Hall claims that Confucianism and Taoism share the desire to find a means of thinking difference, which is more postmodern than the West. "In Taoism, the sole fact is that of process or becoming—indeed Tao means 'the way,' thought of as the total process of becoming." Hall adds,

Tao is not organic in the sense that a single pattern or telos could be said to characterize its processes. It is not a whole but many wholes. Its order is not rational or logical but aesthetic—that is there can be no transcendent pattern determining the existence or efficacy of order.[56]

Chinese culture has an appreciation of difference which Western culture has not shared. The Chinese have tended toward vague boundaries of self and world. Neither dualism nor transcendence is present in the original Confucian and Taoist sensibilities. In contrast, Western political and national thinking is based on trying to develop unity, where difference is seen as chaos which must be brought into order. Diversity is worrisome, so even the many ethnic groups of many origins must be brought into one nation, dominated by one language, one culture, and one religion.

Chicago historian William McNeill agreed with Hall when he addressed scholars at the University of Toronto, saying that "polyethnicity is normal in civilized societies, whereas the ideal of one ethnically unitary state was exceptional in theory and rarely approached in practice."[57] Marginality and pluralism were and are the norm of civilized existence. He claimed that

the idea that a government rightfully should rule only over citizens of a single ethnos took root haltingly in western Europe, beginning in the late middle ages; it got into full gear and became fully conscious in the late eighteenth century and flourished vigorously until about 1920.[58]

Since then this vision of monolithic government has weakened in the West but still finds fertile ground in the ex-colonial lands of Africa and Asia.

CONCLUSIONS

We began by saying that a postmodern challenge has arrived. Cahoone, Toynbee, McLuhan, and the Tofflers see Western civilization passing through premodern, modern, and postmodern revolutions, like huge waves that have passed over Western civilization during the past. The printing press triggered the peasant revolt, the Protestant Reformation, and the spirit of capitalism five hundred years ago, moving the West from premodern feudalism to the modern Enlightenment. In the twentieth century the computer launched the electronic wave of postmodern e-mail, the Internet, the World Wide Web. Like surfers, we have mounted the postmodern Third Wave, trying to negotiate the new cross-currents that threaten us.

Opinion regarding the postmodern revolution is deeply divided. Some say it is only a blip which will soon go away. Others are threatened and are determined to fight it. Many of us recognize that new times have come. We are trying to understand what it is all about. Postmodernists challenge our preoccupation with reason and have given up on the Enlightenment. More and more skeptics are wondering whether science has caged us into the false hope of a linear line to progress. The metanarratives of evolution, science, technology, and progress, when balanced with rising crime, poverty, and family violence, also cloud our enthusiasm for an age of machines. Poststructuralists call for deconstruction and the need to celebrate difference, diversity, and pluralism.

Anabaptists emerged during the sixteenth-century revolution, during the Protestant Reformation when Gutenberg's printed word came onto the scene. They were at the cutting edge of that revolution, moving from serfdom into crafts, exploring the radical theological and economic revolt. With the coming of the computer, many are reluctant to mount this new postmodern wave, whereas others are again surfing freely, testing their skills. Anabaptist-Mennonites, for centuries agriculturalists, have only recently entered the modern scene. Thus they are unusually suited to examine the premodern, modern, and postmodern changes through which they have gone during the short span of fifty years after World War II.

NOTES

1. Vaclav Havel, "The Need for Transcendence in the Postmodern World," *Whole Systems* (World Wide Web page), http://www.worldtrans.org/whole.html, accessed June 27, 1998.

2. Ibid., 2

3. Ibid., 3.

4. John Esau, "New Era, New Ways of Thinking," *Mennonite Weekly Review* 76 (May 7, 1998), 5.

5. Lois Barrett, "Anabaptist Evangelism in the Context of Modernity and Postmodernity," *Mennonite Life* 53, no. 2 (June 1998), 32-37.

6. Ibid., 33.

7. Ibid., 34-35.

8. Ibid., 36.

9. Michael King, "Let Them be Scattered and Bless All the Earth," *The Mennonite* 1 (March 3, 1998), 10-11.

10. Margaret Loewen Reimer, "The Biblical Imagination," *The Canadian Mennonite* 2 (May 11, 1998), 6-9.

11. Ibid., 8.

12. *Contemporary Sociology: A Journal of Reviews* devoted the entire issue of January 1996 to reviews of books on postmodernity written by sociologists.

13. Lawrence Cahoone, *From Modernism to Postmodernism: An Anthology* (Oxford, England: Blackwell Publishers, 1996).

14. Alvin and Heidi Toffler, *Creating A New Civilization: The Politics of the Third Wave* (New York: Bantam Books, 1995), 19.

15. Ibid., 82-88.

16. Marshall McLuhan, *Understanding the Media: Extensions of Man* (New York, McGraw-Hill: 1964).

17. James M. Stayer, *The German Peasant's War and Anabaptist Community of Goods* (Montreal: McGill-Queen's Univ. Press, 1991), 45-92.

18. Arnold C. Snyder, *Anabaptist History and Thought: An Introduction* (Kitchener, Ont.: Pandora Press, 1995).

19. Max Weber, *The Protestant Ethic and the Spirit of Capitalism* (New York: Charles Scribners, 1904, 1958).

20. Tofflers, *Creating A New Civilization*, 3.

21. Ibid., 32.

22. Ibid., 38-40.

23. Angus Reid, *Shakedown: How the New Economy is Changing Our Lives* (Toronto: Doubleday, 1996).

24. Ibid., 14-41.

25. Ibid., 46-47.

26. Ibid., 45-50.

27. Ibid., 50.

28. Cahoone, *From Modernism to Postmodernism*, 1.

29. Ibid., 2.

30. Don Tapscott, *Growing Up Digital: The Rise of the Net Generation* (New York: McGraw-Hill, 1998).

31. Cahoone, *From Modernism to Postmodernism*, 3.

32. Arnold J. Toynbee, *A Study of History* (London: Oxford, 1954).

33. Immanuel Kant, "An Answer to the Question: What is the Enlightenment?" *Kant's Political Writings*, ed. H. B. Nisbet and Hans Reiss (Cambridge, England: Cambridge University Press, 1970), 54-60.

34. David Lyon, *Postmodernity* (Minneapolis: University of Minnesota Press, 1994), 4-5.
35. Ibid., 7.
36. Georg Simmel has never been quite as influential as Marx, Durkheim, and Weber, but he seems to have followed a different drummer that anticipated many of the features of postmodernity.
37. Lyon, *Postmodernity*, 10.
38. Max Weber, *The Protestant Ethic and the Spirit of Captialism*, trans. Talcott Parsons (New York: Scribner, 1958), 13-31.
39. Thomas Kuhn, *The Structure of Scientific Revolutions* (Chicago: University of Chicago Press, 1962).
40. Ibid., 92.
41. Ibid., 92-110.
42. Ibid., 102.
43. Andrew Abbott, "Transcending General Linear Reality," *Sociology Theory* 6 (1997): 1149-1182.
44. Ibid., 1161.
45. Ibid., 1172.
46. Jean-Francois Lyotard, *The Postmodern Condition: A Report on Knowledge* (Minneapolis: University of Minnesota Press, 1984), xxiii.
47. Stanley J. Grenz, *A Primer on Postmodernism* (Grand Rapids, Mich.: Eerdmans, 1996), 44.
48. Jacques Derrida, *Of Grammatology*, trans. Gayatri Chakravorty Spivak (Baltimore: Johns Hopkins Univ. Press, 1976), 7.
49. Ibid., 11.
50. Ibid., 13.
51. Ibid., 24.
52. Steven Seidman, *Contested Knowledge: Social Theory in the Postmodern Era* (Oxford, England: Blackwell Publishers, 1994), 202.
53. Ibid., 203.
54. David Hall, "Modern China and the Postmodern West," *Culture and Modernity: East-West Philosophic Perspectives*, ed. Eliot Deutsch (Honolulu: University of Hawaii Press, 1991), 700.
55. Ibid., 57-60.
56. Ibid., 62.
57. William H. McNeill, *Poly-Ethnicity and National Unity in World History* (Toronto: University of Toronto Press, 1986), 4.
58. Ibid., 7.

CHAPTER TWENTY

FOLLOWING CHRIST IN A POSTMODERN WORLD

J. Lawrence Burkholder

Little did we realize, as young women and men during and immediately after World War II, that when we were introduced to our tradition through Bender's *Anabaptist Vision*,[1] Hershberger's *War, Peace, and Nonresistance*,[2] Bonhoeffer's *Cost of Discipleship*, and Troeltsch's *Social Teachings*,[3] we were "moderns." We were moderns reading modern literature, even though, as men, some of us wore plain coats and our young wives and girlfriends wore coverings.

Most of us knew little about the Enlightenment and its legacy, Kant and Hegel, Marx and Mill. Nevertheless, we bore the cognitive imprint of modernity. We thought like moderns. We were self-consciously rational; our thinking was ideological; our world was structured; our philosophy was essentialist; our passion was consistency; our language was univocal; our discourse was linear; our manners were deferential; our Mennonite lives were stereotypical. We trusted our teachers. The church/world dichotomy was sharp. In those days, the church was the church and the world was the world.

We heard about cultural relativity and ambiguity. But relativity and ambiguity for us were social and moral, not linguistic. We searched for the absolute those days, and we hoped we had found it in Jesus Christ, with the help of Sunday school teachers, Mennonite doctrine, Kierkegaard's

Either-Or, and the dogmatic Christology of the Barman Confession, reinforced by the strident radicality of Schleitheim. Without Christ as the absolute, how else could one be a pacifist? Certainly not on a pragmatic basis in the face of Hitler's horrors and the rape of Nanking.

During World War II, whether from the perspective of Civilian Public Service camps or world relief, contrasts were dramatic—Europe's high culture of Goethe, Shiller, and Brahms was contrasted with death camps and ruined cities. The absolute nonresistance of Jesus was compared to the nonviolent resistance of Gandhi and Quaker pacifism. The peace of agrarian simplicities was contrasted with the contests of nations and the greed of capitalism. What were we concerned about? We were especially concerned about reality, not image; about the truth, not rhetoric; about life, not words; about meaning, not story; about decision, not speculative theology.

World War II was a crisis of such proportions as to require Mennonites, along with all major traditions, Catholic and Protestant alike, to define their reason for existence. The *Anabaptist Vision* seemed to do that as Harold Bender proclaimed that the "essence" of Christianity is discipleship *(Nachfolge Christi)*, and discipleship, according to Schleitheim (Article 6), is "to do as Jesus did."[4]

Thus the expression "following Christ" became the standard coinage by which Mennonites have represented their life and mission for over fifty years. It has epitomized Mennonite ideals and methodologies. In 1944 and thereafter, Mennonites said to themselves and to Christendom and to the World, This is who we are—we are disciples of Christ in continuity with and in some such manner as were the original twelve. The ethic of the Sermon on the Mount was not for them only but for us as well.

Our identity has been forged by confession that the Sermon on the Mount can and must be embodied by all without compromise. This distinguished us from Lutherans who claim that all should but none can follow Jesus and Catholics who claim that some can and should while most cannot and should not. And it separated us from Calvinists who say that it is a bad question; we should obey God, not just follow Jesus, while taking creation seriously as natural law.

Harold Bender never elaborated on the meaning of discipleship. But he bequeathed to us, as if by proxy, a slender volume supposed to say what the Anabaptist vision stood for. I refer to the *Cost of Discipleship* which Bender embraced without reservation.[5] He once declared, "Bonhoeffer should have been a Mennonite." The *Cost of Discipleship* became a boot camp handbook of rules of engagement for radical ethicists.

I am not sure Bender understood the subtleties of Bonhoeffer's thought or even the severity of his ethics. Bonhoeffer spoke about the Christian life as absolute insecurity, cross bearing. For "when Christ calls a man, he bids him come and die," leaving one's family and possessions and embracing the *pension*—that is, the extraordinary righteousness that exceeds the righteousness of the scribes and Pharisees, that rises above the "*justitia civilis*" of ordinary living. Such righteousness includes turning the other cheek; renouncing power, position, even one's dignity; lending without expecting repayment; becoming voluntarily poor; and going the second mile.

Bonhoeffer's ethic was typically modern in the sense that it incorporated the method of rational extrapolation of Jesus' precepts, turning them into principles of obligation. Modern Christian ethics were predominantly deontological, expressing the command—obedience and character of obligation—which was, of course, exaggerated in wartime.

Bonhoeffer's ethics presuppose European culture, which at that time was predominantly Kantian. The "categorical imperative" was written on the Western skies. This meant that ethics consisted essentially of logical extensions of premises to their universal applications—without prolegomena, without recognition of relativity, and without a sociology of knowledge, typical of later times. Bonhoeffer simply proceeded with the assumption that if Jesus, the son of God, said it, it should be done—forgiving all enemies, giving on demand regardless of merit, and living imprudently without anxiety.

Of course as young Mennonites we squirmed. We asked many practical Niebuhrian-like questions. I was especially skeptical since I had just returned from China, where I faced many problems arising from the responsible exercise of corporate power while serving as director of Church World Service and secretary of a United Nations commission. But we were products of the Great Depression as well as draftees for war and in debt. Therefore at least we need not become poor—we were poor! We were like certain contemporary Russians who said recently, and I quote, "We have no financial stress since we have no finances." Furthermore, we were conscientious objectors when pacifism presented us with an absolute dilemma—not an opportunity to witness against the obvious as during the Vietnam War.

Of course if Bonhoeffer had been in some sense open to cultural contingency, to exceptions to the rule, to subjective individualism, and selective application, we would have had less trouble with all but the most rigorous demands such as "let the dead bury the dead." But Bonhoeffer characteristically implied or employed the language of universality such as "never" or "always" rather than such conditional terms as "if" and "sometimes." That in itself makes the essential difference between the ethics of Enlightenment and the ethics of postmodernity, even though Bonhoeffer struggled against legalism as he ventured the paradoxical idea of "ordered spontaneity."

How ghastly the practical implications of being identified ideologically, spiritually, and theologically with the very same commandments and commitments that brought Christ to the cross, drove itinerants into the Syrian wilderness, sent mendicants into medieval pathways, monks into monasteries, nuns into cloisters, and Anabaptists into martyrdom. How awful were those World War II, life-and-death, ideological times to anyone who thought.

An important question we addressed in the late 1950s and early 1960s concerned the social context of discipleship. Where do the followers of Jesus belong? In response to that question, a consensus had already been formed by our own Anabaptist-Mennonite experience and confirmed by leading classical European sociologists and American crisis theologians. Our place was the sectarian community where we could develop an alternative society under the conditions of peace and purity. Were we to be involved in the world near centers of power, political decision making, economic policy, and enforced order, we would be required to compromise our principles and be lost in the ambiguity of struggles for justice. Such theologians as the Niebuhrs, J. C. Bennett, and Paul Ramsey, all realists drawing on the structural analysis of Max Weber and the typological universalism of Ernest Troeltsch, counseled us to stay where we were as sectarians. More recently Martin Marty repeated similar counsels. Anabaptist-Mennonites at that time agreed.

Recall John Howard Yoder's article in *Concern Pamphlets*, entitled "The Anabaptist Dissent," in which he contended that "the logic [sic] of the place of the disciple in society" is "to be removed from responsibility for the moral structure of non-Christian society."[6] Though he placed the key word in quotes, he nevertheless proffered the term "irresponsibility" to describe the Mennonite position vis-à-vis society. Thus what modern Mennonite scholars were saying those days was essentially in agreement with what leading sociologists and theologians were saying: "You can't have it both ways." You cannot be a Mennonite, living according to Jesus' teaching, and relate responsibly to the larger social order at the same time.

But quite to the contrary, a review of post-World War II history suggests we can have it both ways; at least we think we can. Or are we fooling ourselves? I need not review the past fifty years to prove that Mennonites have invaded the world with unexpected, almost unbelievable, energies and skills. Mennonites have taken up significant and in some places commanding positions in commerce, the professions, academics, and ecclesiological realms. We have literally relocated ourselves in society. Now we are with it—some on the fast track, some as baby boomers turning gray but savvy and rich, having achieved the American dream. In such a situation we move from modernity to postmodernity.

Postmodernism is an approach to reality as broad as culture itself, though standing for no necessary truth of a substantive nature. Above all, it is a plea for freedom to be one's own authentic self. Postmodernism is a cultural condition in which all heteronomous systems are either subjected to radical criticism or rejected all together as infractions on individual initiatives and interpretations of reality. Postmodernism is suspicious of systems, ideologies, structures, orders, institutions, and even logical constructs—especially those associated with the Enlightenment. Insofar as the Enlightenment may have fostered dialectical modes of thought such as the juxtaposition of freedom and order (Hegel), postmodernity emphasizes the former, often in a spirit of protest as would slaves to unjust treatment.

Some Mennonites find in postmodernism a philosophical presupposition by which accommodation to the contemporary culture may be helped. They see postmodernism as an ally in the quest to reject systems, typologies, laws, and the authority of bishops together with the relativising of truth to historical bias. This means that Mennonites are now free to do what was erstwhile forbidden, such as having life insurance, engaging in lawsuits, marrying outside the church, becoming wealthy, holding high public office, becoming divorced, and in general, taking on the colors of the larger culture. Postmodernism is the underlying cultural justification for individualism, situation ethics, communities of diversity, and tolerance. That Mennonite lifestyles are indistinguishable from the lifestyles of non-Mennonite neighbors may be defended in terms of appreciation for individual identity as expressions of authentic self-hood.

But postmodern freedom could express itself in ways that seem to move in the other direction as well. Postmodern individualism could express itself in a manner reminiscent of sectarian exclusivism. Postmodern nonconformist initiatives could partake of the same freedom that is employed to support conformist initiatives. Postmodernity, as such, makes no substantive demands. And so postmodern Mennonites may do what they will. Both middle-class silk garments and hair shirts may be lawful in the absence of law. "Where there is no law, there is no sin." As the lynchpin is removed, anything can happen.

If one could set forth a scenario of capitulation to the larger culture in the name of postmodern individualism, one could also set forth a scenario of sacrificial service exercised as an expression of postmodern freedom. Freedom awaits a talisman to give it character.

I suggest that for Anabaptist-Mennonites, the most significant implication of postmodernism could be its reinterpretation of service as an exercise of freedom. To serve the neighbor is no longer to respond to an extraneous authority in the form of a command but rather to express one's feeling of empathy with the neighbor's need. Love may flow from one's own internal desire to help the neighbor rather than from the authoritative decrees of a sovereign or from institutional expectations or from the "categorical imperative." In the sense that postmodern generations may exercise love in freedom rather than necessity, it may be representative more of one's experience than of repetitive constraint.

Postmodern freedom may be illustrated by the following: I have in mind a young, Mennonite, Ph.D., female scientist working for the United States government in the field of health. She is a biostatistician. Several years ago she met a Catholic who worked in the same field at the same location. They were married and were blessed with a son.

Their work had international implications insofar as they were engaged in the collection and correlation of medical information beyond national boundaries. As if by accident, they heard about a group of hospitals in south India where significant research was being carried out but where no systematic efforts were being made to conserve and correlate the results.

Such information was enough to move this young couple to request a leave of absence from their highly remunerative positions to go uninvited to India at their own expense and without pay. This they did even in the absence of church support and the concurrence of such legitimating agencies as mission boards and Mennonite Central Committee. They simply represented themselves as they made their unannounced appearance in south India. They went to India as Christians, their faith being communicated primarily through the quality of their work rather than through verbal witness. They worked hard for more than a year before returning to their posts in Washington. They made a significant contribution to the medical services and scientific research in south India.

This incident would suggest that self-reliant, unconventional, independent, sacrificial approaches to service are possible in the terms of postmodern, nonconformist self-determination. But were the whole story of this young professional couple to be told, it would include their having been rooted in traditional faith, ideological thought, authoritative structures, and stable family life as representative of modern Mennonite and Catholic communities. In reality, their postmodern independence was an extension of rather than a reaction to their upbringing. They simply outgrew modernity.

Postmodern discipleship may be related to traditional lifestyles in some such manner as a musical cadenza may be related to a classical composition. The cadenza is a musical form proposed by the composer of a concerto allowing the musician freedom to improvise spontaneously based on the composition as a whole. The cadenza represents creative freedom carried ideally in the spirit of, if not in repetition of, what has gone on before. That Beethoven would have not trusted performers enough to prompt a cadenza following his Emperor Concerto is an exception that proves the rule that a cadenza is a highly individualistic articulation most effective if the composer and performer are respectful of one another.

One may notice in the Gospel of John an articulation of Christian freedom that appears to go beyond legalistic conceptions of obedience found especially in the Gospel of Matthew. In Matthew, obedience is presented as exact conformity to the command, when, for example, a servant responds meticulously to the will of the master. The fourth Gospel, however, quite consciously elevates the relationship of Christ to the disciple as one of friendship. "I no longer call you servants because a servant does not know his master's business. Instead, I have called you friends, for everything that I learn from my father, I have made known to you" (John 15:15, NIV).

As an apprentice of Jesus, the postmodern disciple is free to live his own life rather than duplicating the life of Jesus. Postmodern discipleship is a relational ethic of teacher and pupil whose lives have been entwined by participation in a transcendent reality.

The test of postmodern discipleship will be determined by the manner and extent to which self-sacrifice is a reality. After all, the ethic of Christ culminates in the cross. One advantage of postmodernity may be the freedom by which Mennonites enter into situations in the world where danger is an inevitable consequence. Postmodern identification with the most desperate, the least desirable, and the least predictable will demonstrate how many forms the cross may take. If moderns planted land mines, postmoderns may be called to dig them out with their bare hands. The time may have come for Mennonites, having criticized Lutherans for "cheap grace," to demonstrate by heroic sacrifice that the alternative to cheap grace is not "cheap pacifism."

In conclusion, following Christ in the postmodern world must be rooted in the rigor of modern conceptions but conducted freely in the context of postmodern differentiation.

NOTES

1. Harold S. Bender, *The Anabaptist Vision* (Scottdale, Pa.: Herald Press, 1944).

2. Guy F. Hershberger, *War, Peace, and Nonresistance* (Scottdale, Pa.: Herald Press, 1944).

3. Ernst Troeltsch, *The Social Teaching of the Christian Churches*, vols. 1, 2 (London: George Allen and Unwin, 1931).

4. Bender, *The Anabaptist Vision*, 21; John Howard Yoder, trans. and ed., *The Schleitheim Confession* (Scottdale, Pa.: Herald Press, 1973), 14.

5. Dietrich Bonhoeffer, *The Cost of Discipleship* (New York: Simon and Schuster, 1995).

6. John Howard Yoder, "The Anabaptist Dissent: The Logic of the Place of the Disciple in Society," *Concern* 1 (1954), 46.

SELECT BIBLIOGRAPHY

Adam, Ian and Helen Tiffin, eds. *Past the Last Post: Theorizing Post-Colonialism and Post-Modernism*. Calgary: Univ. of Calgary Press, 1990.

Ainlay, Stephen and Fred Kniss. "Mennonites and Conflict: Re-Examining Mennonite History and Contemporary Life." *Mennonite Quarterly Review* 72, no. 2 (April 1998), 121-140.

Alison, James. *Knowing Jesus*. Springfield, Ill.: Templegate Publishers, 1994.

―――. *Raising Abel: The Recovery of the Theological Imagination*. New York: Crossroad Publishing, 1996.

Arendt, Hannah. *The Origins of Totalitarianism*. 2d ed. New York: Harcourt Brace Jovanovich, 1973.

Armstrong, Karen. *A History of God: The 4000-Year Quest of Judaism, Christianity, and Islam*. New York: Alfred A. Knopf, 1993.

Ayres, Lewis, and Gareth Jones, eds. *Christian Origins: Theology, Rhetoric and Community*. London and New York: Routledge, 1998.

Bader-Sayer, Scott. *Church and Israel After Christendom: The Politics of Election*. Boulder, Colo.: Westview Press, 1999.

Badham, Roger, and Ola Sigurdson. "The Decentered Post-Constantinian Church: An Exchange." *Cross Currents* (Summer 1997).

Bailie, Gil. *Violence Unveiled: Humanity at the Crossroads*. New York: Crossroad Publishing, 1995.

Baker-Fletcher, Garth Kasimu. *Xodus: An African American Male Journey*. Minneapolis: Fortress Press, 1996.

Bañuelas, Arturo J. Mestizo *Christianity: Theology from the Latino Perspective*. Maryknoll, N.Y.: Orbis Books, 1995.

Barbe, Dominique. *A Theology of Conflict and Other Writings on Nonviolence*. Maryknoll, N.Y.: Orbis Books, 1989.

Barrett, Lois. "Anabaptist Evangelism in the Context of Modernity and Postmodernity." *Mennonite Life* 53, no. 2 (June 1998), 32-37.

Bauman, Clarence. *The Spiritual Legacy of Hans Denck: Interpretation and Translation of Key Texts*. Leiden: E. J. Brill, 1991.

Beachy, Alvin. *The Concept of Grace in the Radical Reformation.* Nieuwkoop: B. De Graaf, 1977.

Bender, H. S. *The Anabaptist Vision.* Scottdale, Pa.: Herald Press, 1944.

Bender, Ross Thomas. *The People of God: A Mennonite Interpretation of the Free Church Tradition.* Scottdale, Pa.: Herald Press, 1971.

Bernstein, Richard. *Beyond Objectivism And Relativism.* Philadelphia: University of Pennsylvania, 1988.

Berry, Wendell. "The Body and the Earth." In *The Unsettling of American Culture and Agriculture.* New York: Avon, 1977.

——————. "The Work of Local Culture." In *What are People For?* San Francisco: North Point Press, 1990.

Best, Steven, and Douglas Kellner. *Postmodern Theory: Critical Interrogations.* New York: The Guilford Press, 1991.

Biesecker-Mast, Gerald. "Jihad, McWorld, and Anabaptist Transcendence." *Mennonite Life* 52, no. 3 (September 1997), 4-15.

——————. "Mennonite Public Discourse and the Conflicts over Homosexuality." *Mennonite Quarterly Review* 72, no. 2 (April 1998), 275-300.

——————. "Spiritual Knowledge, Carnal Obedience, and Anabaptist Discipleship." *Mennonite Quarterly Review* 71, no. 2 (April 1997), 201-226.

Blond, Philip, ed. *Post-Secular Philosophy Between Philosophy And Theology.* London: Routledge, 1998.

Bonhoeffer, Dietrich. *The Cost of Discipleship.* New York: Simon and Schuster, 1995.

Borg, Marcus. *Meeting Jesus Again for the First Time: The Historical Jesus and the Heart of Contemporary Faith.* San Francisco: HarperSanFrancisco, 1994.

Boyarin, Daniel. *A Radical Jew: Paul and the Politics of Identity.* Berkeley: Univ. of California Press, 1994.

Boyle, Nicholas. *Who Are We Now?: Christian Humanism and the Global Market from Hegel to Heaney.* Notre Dame: University of Notre Dame Press, 1998.

Brandt, Di. *Agnes in the sky.* Winnipeg: Turnstone Press, 1990.

——————. *Dancing Naked: Narrative Strategies for Writing Across Centuries.* Stratford, Ont.: The Mercury Press, 1996.

——————. *Questions I asked my mother.* Winnipeg: Turnstone Press, 1987.

Brueggeman, Walter. *The Prophetic Imagination.* Minneapolis, Minn.: Fortress Press, 1978.

Buechner, Frederick. *The Alphabet of Grace.* New York: The Seabury Press, Crossroad Books.

Burkholder, J. Lawrence. "Postmodern Dialectics." *Mennonite Quarterly Review* 72, no. 2 (April 1998), 321-326.

———. *The Problem of Social Responsibility from the Perspective of the Mennonite Church*. Elkhart, Ind.: Institute of Mennonite Studies, 1989.

Butler, Judith. *Excitable Speech: A Politics of the Performative*. New York: Routledge, 1997.

Cahoone, Lawrence. *From Modernism to Postmodernism: An Anthology*. Oxford, England: Blackwell Publishers, 1996.

Cannon, Katie G. *Black Womanist Ethics*. Atlanta, Ga.: Scholars Press, 1988.

Caputo, John D. *Against Ethics*. Bloomington: Indiana University Press, 1993.

———. *Radical Hermeneutics: Repetition, Deconstruction, and the Hermeneutic Project*. Bloomington, Ind.: Indiana University Press, 1987.

Chambers, Ian. *Border Dialogues: Journeys in Postmodernity*. London: Routledge, 1990.

———. *Migrancy, Culture, Identity*. London: Routledge, 1994.

Clapp, Rodney. *A Peculiar People: The Church as Culture in a Post-Christian Society*. Downers Grove, Ill.: InterVarsity Press, 1996.

Colas, Dominique. *Civil Society and Fanaticism*. Stanford: Stanford Univ. Press., 1997.

Cone, James H. *God of the Oppressed*. Rev. ed. Maryknoll, N.Y.: Orbis, 1997.

Connolly, William. *The Augustinian Imperative: A Reflection on the Politics of Morality*. Newbury Park, Calif.: Sage Publications, 1993.

———. *Political Theory and Modernity*. 2d ed. Ithaca: Cornell University Press, 1993.

Cooper, Barry. *The End of History: An Essay on Modern Hegelianism*. Toronto: University of Toronto Press, 1984.

Correll, Ernst. *Das schweizerische Täufermennonitum*. Tübingen: J.C.B. Mohr (Paul Siebeck): 1925.

Cupitt, Don. *Mysticism After Modernity*. Malden, Mass.: Blackwell Publishers, 1998.

Deleuze, Gilles, and Félix Guattari. *Kafka: Toward a Minor Literature*. Minneapolis: University of Minnesota Press, 1986.

———. *A Thousand Plateaus*. Minneapolis: Univ. of Minnesota Press, 1993.

Derrida, Jacques. *The Gift of Death*. Translated by David Willis. Chicago: University of Chicago Press, 1995.

———. *Of Grammatology*. Translated by Gayatri Chakravorty Spivak. Baltimore: Johns Hopkins University Press, 1976.

———. *The Politics of Friendship*. Translated by George Collins. New York: Verso, 1997.

———. "Structure, Sign, and Play in the Discourse of the Human Sciences." In *The Critical Tradition: Classical Texts and Contemporary Trends*, edited by David S. Richter. New York: Bedford/St. Martins, 1989.

Douglas, Kelly Brown. *The Black Christ.* Maryknoll, N.Y.: Orbis, 1994.

———. "Teaching Womanist Theology." In *Living the Intersection: Womanism and Afrocentrism in Theology*, edited by Cheryl J. Sanders. Minneapolis: Fortress Press, 1995.

Durnbaugh, Donald P. *Fruit of the Vine.* Philadelphia: Brethren Encyclopedia, 1996.

Eagleton, Terry. *The Illusions of Postmodernism.* Oxford: Basil Blackwell, 1996.

———. *Literary Theory: An Introduction.* Minneapolis: Univ. of Minnesota Press, 1983.

Eco, Umberto. *Postscript to the Name of the Rose.* San Diego: Harcourt Brace Jovanovich, 1984.

Edwards, James. *The Plain Sense of Things: The Fate of Religion in an Age of Normal Nihilism.* University Park, Pa.: Pennsylvania State University Press, 1997.

Ellenberger, Jacob. *Ein Lebensbild.* Frankfurt: Deutsches-Reichspost Action-Gesellschaft, 1879.

Eller, Vernard M. *Christian Anarchy: Jesus' Primacy Over the Powers.* Grand Rapids, Mich.: Eerdmans, 1987.

———. "Kierkegaard knew the Brethren-sort of." *Brethren Life and Thought* 8 (Winter 1963), 57-60.

Ellul, Jacques. *Anarchy and Christianity.* Translated by Geoffrey W. Bromiley. Grand Rapids, Mich.: Eerdmans, 1991.

Erb, Peter. *Pietists, Protestants and Mysticism: the Use of Medieval Spiritual Texts in the Work of Gottfried Arnold (1666-1714).* Metuchen, N.J.: The Scarecrow Press, 1989.

Felder, Cain Hope, ed. *Stony the Road We Trod: African American Biblical Interpretations.* Minneapolis: Fortress Press, 1991.

Finger, Thomas. *Christian Theology: An Eschatological Approach.* Vols. 1, 2. Scottdale, Pa.: Herald Press, 1985-89.

———. "Christus Victor and the Creeds: Some Historical Considerations." *The Mennonite Quarterly Review* 72, no. 1 (January 1998), 31-51.

———. "Relativity, Normativity and Imagination: A Dialogue with Gordon Kaufman." In *Mennonite Theology in Face of Modernity*, edited by Alain Epp Weaver.

———. *Self, Earth And Society.* Downers Grove, Ill.: InterVarsity Press, 1997.

Foucault, Michel. *The Archaeology of Knowledge.* Translated by A. M. Sheridan Smith. New York: Pantheon Books, 1972.

———. *Discipline and Punish: The Birth of the Prison.* Translated by Alan Sheridan. New York: Pantheon Books, 1977.

———. *The Foucault Reader*. Edited by Paul Rabinow. New York: Pantheon Books, 1984.

———. *The History of Sexuality. Volume 1: An Introduction*. Translated by Robert Hurley. New York: Random House, Vintage Books, 1977.

———. *The Order of Things: An Archaeology of the Human Sciences*. New York: Random House, Vintage Books, 1994.

———. *Power/Knowledge: Selected Interviews and Other Writings 1972-1977*. New York: Pantheon Books, 1980.

Friedmann, Robert. *The Theology of Anabaptism*. Scottdale, Pa.: Herald Press, 1973.

Friesen, Abraham. *Erasmus, the Anabaptists, and the Great Commission*. Grand Rapids, Mich.: Eerdmans, 1998.

———. "Menno Simons and the Beginnings of Dutch Anabaptism." *Mennonite Quarterly Review* 62, no. 3 (July 1998), 355-362.

Fukuyama, Francis. *The End of History and the Last Man*. New York: Avon Books, 1992.

Gadamer, Hans-Georg. *Philosophical Hermeneutics*. Translated and edited by David E. Linge. Berkeley: University of California Press, 1976.

———. *Truth and Method*. Second rev. ed. Translated by Joel Weinsheimer and Donald G. Marshall. New York: Continuum, 1994.

Gillespie, Michael. *Nihilism before Nietzsche*. Chicago: University of Chicago Press, 1995.

Girard, René. *The Girard Reader*. Edited by James G. Williams. New York: Crossroad Publishing, 1996.

———. *Job: The Victim of His People*. Stanford: Stanford University Press, 1987.

———. *The Scapegoat*. Baltimore: Johns Hopkins University Press, 1986.

———. *Things Hidden Since the Foundation of the World*. In collaboration with Jean-Michel Oughourlian and Guy Lefort. Translated by Stephen Bann and Michael Metteer. Stanford, Calif.: Stanford University Press, 1987.

———. *Violence and the Sacred*. Baltimore: Johns Hopkins, 1977.

Gish, Arthur G. *The New Left and Christian Radicalism*. Grand Rapids, Mich.: Eerdmans, 1970.

Grant, Jacquelyn. *White Women's Christ and Black Women's Jesus: Feminist Christology and Womanist Response*. Atlanta: Scholars Press, 1989.

Grenz, Stanley J. *A Primer on Postmodernism*. Grand Rapids, Mich.: W. B. Eerdmans Publishing, 1996.

Gundy, Jeff. *A Community of Memory: My Days with George and Clara*. Urbana: Univ. of Illinois Press, 1996.

———. *Flatlands: Poems*. Cleveland: Cleveland State Univ. Poetry Center, 1995.

———. "Humility in Mennonite Literature." *Mennonite Quarterly Review* 63, no. 1 (January 1989), 5-21.

Gutting, Gary. *The Cambridge Companion to Foucault*. Cambridge and New York: Cambridge University Press, 1994.

Habermas, Jürgen. "The Genealogical Writing of History: On Some Aporias in Foucault's Theory of Power." *Canadian Journal of Political and Social Theory* 10 (1986): 1-9.

———. *On the Logic of the Social Sciences*. Translated by Sherry Weber Nicholson and Jerry A. Stark. Cambridge, Mass.: The MIT Press, 1988.

Harvey, David. *The Condition of Postmodernity*. Oxford: Blackwell, 1990.

Hauerwas, Stanley. *In Good Company: The Church as Polis*. Notre Dame, Ind.: University of Notre Dame Press, 1995.

———. *The Peaceable Kingdom: A Primer in Christian Ethics*. Notre Dame, Ind.: University of Notre Dame Press, 1983.

———. *Sanctify Them in the Truth: Holiness Exemplified*. Edinburgh: T&T Clark, 1998: 191-200.

———. *Wilderness Wanderings: Probing Twentieth-Century Theology and Philosophy*. Boulder, Colo.: Westview Press, 1997.

Hauerwas, Stanley, Chris Huebner, Harry Huebner, and Mark Nation, eds. *The Wisdom of the Cross: Essays In Honor of John Howard Yoder*. Grand Rapids, Mich.: William B. Eerdmans Publishing Co., 1999.

Hebblethwaite, Brian, and Stewart Sutherland, eds. *The Philosophical Frontiers of Christian Theology: Essays Presented to D. M. MacKinnon*. Cambridge: Cambridge Univ. Press, 1982.

Hebdige, Dick. "Postmodernism and 'the other side.'" In *Stuart Hall: Critical Dialogues in Cultural Studies*, edited by David Morely and Kuan-Hsing Chen. New York: Routledge, 1996.

Hershberger, Guy. *War, Peace, and Nonresistance*. Scottdale, Pa.: Herald Press, 1946.

Holland, Scott. "So Many Good Voices in My Head." *Cross Currents* 49, no. 1 (Spring 1999), 72-83.

———. "Theology is a Kind of Writing: The Emergence of Theopoetics." *Cross Currents* 47 (Fall 1997), 317-331.

Horsch, John. *The Mennonite Church and Modernism*. Scottdale, Pa.: Mennonite Publishing House, 1924.

———. *Modern Religious Liberalism*. Reprint, New York: Garland, 1988; original pub. 1921.

Hutcheon, Linda. *The Canadian Postmodern: A Study of Contemporary English-Canadian Fiction*. Toronto: Oxford Univ. Press, 1988.

———. *The Politics of Postmodernism*. New York: Routledge, 1989.

———. *Splitting Images: Contemporary Canadian Ironies*. Toronto: Oxford Univ. Press, 1991.

Huyssen, Andreas. *After the Great Divide: Modernism, Mass Culture, Postmodernism*. Bloomington: Indiana Univ. Press, 1986.

Isasi-Diaz, Ada María, and Fernando F. Segovia, eds. *Hispanic/Latino Theology: Challenges and Promise*. Minneapolis: Fortress Press, 1996.

Jacobsen, Douglas, and William Vance Trollinger Jr. *Re-Forming the Center: American Protestantism, 1900 to the Present*. Grand Rapids, Mich.: Eerdmans, 1998.

Jameson, Fredric. *Postmodernism, or, The Cultural Logic of Late Capitalism*. Durham, N.C.: Duke University, 1991.

Jenson, Robert. "How the World Lost Its Story." *First Things* 36 (October 1993), 19-24.

———. *Systematic Theology: The Triune God*. Vol. 1. New York: Oxford University Press, 1997.

Kariel, Henry S. *The Desperate Politics of Postmodernism*. Amherst: The Univ. of Massachusetts Press, 1989.

Kasdorf, Julia. "Bakhtin, Boundaries and Bodies." *Mennonite Quarterly Review* 71, no. 2 (April 1997), 178.

Kauffman, J. Howard, and Leo Driedger. *The Mennonite Mosaic: Identity and Modernization*. Scottdale, Pa.: Herald Press, 1991.

Kaufman, Gordon. *An Essay On Theological Method*. Missoula: Scholar's Press, 1975.

———. *In Face Of Mystery*. Cambridge, Mass.: Harvard, 1993.

Keim, Albert N. *Harold S. Bender 1897-1962*. Scottdale, Pa.: Herald Press, 1998.

Keller, Ludwig. *Die Reformation und die älteren Reformparteien*. Leipzig: S. Hirzel, 1885.

Kepnes, Steven. *Interpreting Judaism in a Postmodern Age*. New York: New York University Press, 1996.

Kepnes, Steven, Peter Ochs, and Robert Gibbs. *Reasoning After Revelation: Dialogues in Postmodern Jewish Philosophy*. Boulder, Colo.: Westview Press, 1998.

King, Michael A. "Angels, Atheists, and Common Ground: Toward a Separatist and Worldly Postmodern Anabaptism." *Conrad Grebel Review* 15 (Fall 1997), 251-268.

Klaassen, Walter. *Living at the End of the Ages: Apocalyptic Expectation in the Radical Reformation*. Lanham: University Press of America, 1992.

Klassen, Pamela E. "Practicing Conflict: Weddings as Sites of Contest and Compromise." *Mennonite Quarterly Review* 72, no. 2 (April 1998), 225-241.

Kniss, Fred. *Disquiet in the Land.* New Brunswick: Rutgers Univ. Press, 1997.

Kraus, C. Norman. *An Intrusive Gospel?* Downers Grove, Ill.: InterVarsity Press, 1998.

Kraybill, Donald B. *The Upside-Down Kingdom.* Scottdale, Pa.: Herald Press, 1978.

Kristeva, Julia. *Black Sun: Depression and Melancholia.* Translated by Leon S. Roudiez. New York: Columbia Univ. Press, 1989.

Kuhn, Thomas. *The Structure of Scientific Revolutions.* Chicago: University of Chicago Press, 1962.

Levinas, Emmanuel. *Totality and Infinity.* Translated by Alphonso Lingis. Pittsburgh: Duquesne University Press, 1969.

Liechty, Daniel, ed. and trans. *Early Anabaptist Spirituality: Selected Writings.* New York: Paulist Press, 1994.

———. *Theology In Postliberal Perspective.* Philadelphia: Trinity Press International, 1990.

Littell, Franklin. *The Anabaptist View of the Church: A Study in the Origins of Sectarian Protestantism.* 2d ed. Boston: Beacon Press, Inc., 1958.

Lyon, David. *Postmodernity.* Minneapolis: Univ. of Minnesota Press, 1994.

Lyotard, Jean-Francois. *The Postmodern Condition: A Report on Knowledge.* Translated by Geoffrey Bennington and Brian Massumi. Minneapolis: Univ. of Minnesota Press, 1984.

MacIntyre, Alasdair. *After Christendom?* Nashville: Abingdon Press, 1991.

———. *After Virtue: A Study in Moral Theory.* 2d ed. Notre Dame, Ind.: University of Notre Dame Press, 1984.

———. *Three Rival Versions of Moral Enquiry: Encyclopaedia, Genealogy, and Tradition.* Notre Dame, Ind.: University of Notre Dame Press, 1990.

———. *Whose Justice? Which Rationality?* Notre Dame, Ind.: University of Notre Dame Press, 1988.

Mannhardt, Wilhelm. *Die Wehrfreiheit der Altpreußischen Mennoniten.* Maienburg: Im Selbstverlag der Altpreußischen Mennoniten-gemeinden, 1863.

Martin, Dale. *The Corinthian Body.* New Haven: Yale Univ. Press, 1995.

Martin, Dennis D. "Catholic Spirituality and Anabaptist and Mennonite Discipleship." *Mennonite Quarterly Review* 62 (January 1988), 5-25.

———. "Journey to a Far Country: Premodern History as Crosscultural Education." *Conrad Grebel Review* 11 (Fall 1993), 249-63.

———. "Monks, Mendicants, and Anabaptists: Michael Sattler and the Benedictines Reconsidered." *Mennonite Quarterly Review* 60 (April 1986), 139-64.

McAllister, Ted V. *Revolt Against Modernity: Leo Strauss, Eric Voegelin, & the Search for a Postliberal Order.* Lawrence: The Univ. Press of Kansas, 1996.

McCance, Dawn. *Posts: Re-Addressing the Ethical.* Albany, N.Y.: State Univ. of New York Press, 1996.

McClendon, James Wm. Jr. *Doctrine: Systematic Theology, Volume II.* Nashville: Abingdon, 1994.

———. *Ethics: Systematic Theology: Volume I.* Nashville, Tenn.: Abingdon Press, 1986.

McLuhan, Marshall. *Understanding the Media: Extensions of Man.* New York: McGraw-Hill, 1964.

Milbank, John. *Theology and Social Theory: Beyond Secular Reason.* Oxford, UK: Blackwell, 1993.

———. *The Word Made Strange: Theology, Language, Culture.* Oxford, UK: Blackwell, 1997.

Milbank, John, Catharine Pickstock, and Graham Ward. *Radical Orthodoxy: A New Theology.* New York: Routledge, 1999.

Miller, Caleb. "Why Mennonites Should be Wary of Postmodernism." *Mennonite Quarterly Review* 72, no. 2 (April 1997), 326-332.

Miller, James. *The Passion of Michel Foucault.* New York: Simon & Schuster, 1993.

Muller, John P., and William J. Richardson, eds. *The Purloined Poe: Lacan, Derrida, and Psychoanalytic Reading.* Baltimore: Johns Hopkins Univ. Press, 1988.

Murphy, Nancey. *Beyond Liberalism and Fundamentalism.* Valley Forge, Pa.: Trinity Press International, 1996.

———. *Reconciling Theology and Science: A Radical Reformation Perspective.* Kitchener, Ont.: Pandora Press, 1997.

Murphy, Nancey, and James McClendon. "Distinguishing Modern from Postmodern Theology." *Modern Theology* 5 (April 1989): 191-214.

Nealon, Jeffrey T. *Alterity Politics: Ethics and Performative Subjectivity.* Durham, N.C.: Duke Univ. Press, 1998.

Nietzsche, Friedrich. *Beyond Good and Evil: Prelude to a Philosophy of the Future.* Translated by Walter Kaufmann. New York: Vintage, 1966.

———. *On the Genealogy of Morals.* Translated by Walter Kaufmann and R. J. Hollingdale. New York: Vintage Books, 1989.

Norris, Kathleen. *The Cloister Walk.* New York: Riverhead Books, 1987.

Nussbaum, Martha. *Cultivating Humanity: A Classical Defense of Reform in Liberal Education.* Cambridge: Harvard University Press, 1997.

Philips, Dirk. *The Writings of Dirk Philips*. Translated and edited by Cornelius Dyck, William Keeney, and Alvin Beachy. Scottdale, Pa.: Herald Press, 1992.

Pickstock, Catherine. *After Writing: On the Liturgical Consummation of Philosophy*. Oxford: Basil Blackwell, 1998.

Pipkin, H. Wayne, ed. *Essays in Anabaptist Theology*. Elkhart, Ind.: Institute of Mennonite Studies, 1994.

Poulakos, John. *Sophistical Rhetoric in Ancient Greece*. Columbia, N.Y.: Univ. of South Carolina Press, 1995.

Prado, C. G. *Beginning With Foucault: An Introduction to Genealogy*. Boulder, Colo.: Westview Press, 1995.

———. *Starting with Foucault: An Introduction to Genealogy*. Boulder, Colo.: Westview Press, 1995.

Radner, Ephraim. *The End of the Church: A Pneumatology of Christian Division in the West*. Grand Rapids, Mich.: Eerdmans, 1998.

Reeder, Hermann. *Predigten zu Festtagen und bei besonderen Veranlaßischen Mennoniten*. Leipzig: Karl Tauchnitz, 1843.

Rorty, Richard. *Achieving Our Country*. Cambridge: Harvard Univ. Press, 1998.

———. *Contingency, Irony, and Solidarity*. Cambridge, England: Cambridge Univ. Press, 1989.

Roth, John D. "Community as Conversation: A New Model of Anabaptist Hermeneutics." In *Essays in Anabaptist Theology*. Elkhart, Ind.: Institute of Mennonite Studies, 1994.

———, ed. *Refocusing a Vision: Shaping Anabaptist Character in the 21st Century*. Goshen, Ind.: Mennonite Historical Society, 1995.

———, ed. and trans. *Letters of the Amish Division: A Sourcebook*. Goshen, Ind.: Mennonite Historical Society, 1993.

———, and Ervin Beck, eds. *Migrant Muses: Mennonite/s Writing in the U.S.* Goshen, Ind.: Mennonite Historical Society, 1998.

Said, Edward. "The Text, the World, the Critic." In *The Critical Tradition: Classical Texts and Contemporary Trends*. Edited by David S. Richter. New York: Bedford/St. Martins, 1989.

Sanders, Cheryl J. *Living the Intersection: Womanism and Afrocentrism in Theology*. Minneapolis: Fortress Press, 1995.

Sawatsky, Rodney. "Leadership, Authority, and Power." *Mennonite Quarterly Review* 71, no. 3 (July 1997), 439-51.

———. "The Quest for a Mennonite Hermeneutic." *Conrad Grebel Review* 11 (Winter 1993), 1-21.

Schlabach, Theron. *Gospel Versus Gospel*. Scottdale, Pa.: Herald Press, 1980.

———. "Peace, Faith, Nation: Mennonites and Amish in Nineteenth-Century America." In *The Mennonite Experience in America*. Vol. 2. Scottdale, Pa.: Herald Press, 1988.

Smith, C. Henry. *The Story of the Mennonites*. Berne, Ind.: Mennonite Book Concern, 1945.

Smith, Gregory Bruce. *Nietzsche, Heidegger, and the Transition to Postmodernity*. Chicago: The Univ. of Chicago Press, 1996.

Snyder, C. Arnold. *Anabaptist History and Theology: An Introduction*. Kitchener, Ont.: Pandora Press, 1995.

———. *The Life and Thought of Michael Sattler*. Scottdale, Pa.: Herald Press, 1984.

———. "Michael Sattler, Benedictine: Dennis Martin's Objections Reconsidered." *Mennonite Quarterly Review* 61 (July 1987), 262-79.

———. "The Monastic Origins of Swiss Anabaptist Sectarianism." *Mennonite Quarterly Review* 67, no. 1 (January 1983), 5-26.

Snyder, C. Arnold, and Linda A. Hecht., eds. *Profiles of Anabaptist Women*. Waterloo, Ont.: 1996.

Spragens, Thomas. *The Irony of Liberal Reason*. Chicago: The Univ. of Chicago Press, 1981.

Stayer, James M. *Anabaptists and the Sword*. 2d ed. Lawrence, Kans.: Coronado Press, 1976.

———. *The German Peasant's War and Anabaptist Community of Goods*. Montreal: McGill-Queen's Univ. Press, 1991.

Stayer, James M., Werner O. Packull, and Klaus Deppermann. "From Monogenesis to Polygenesis: The Historical Discussion of Anabaptist Origins." *Mennonite Quarterly Review* 49 (April 1975), 83-122.

Swartzentruber, Elaine K. "Marking and Remarking the Body of Christ: Toward a Postmodern Mennonite Ecclesiology." *Mennonite Quarterly Review* 71, no. 2 (1997), 243-265.

Sweet, Leonard. *Faithquakes*. Nashville, Tenn.: Abingdon Press, 1994.

Taylor, Charles. *Sources of the Self: The Making of Modern Identity*. Cambridge, Mass.: Harvard Univ. Press, 1989.

Tiessen, Hildi Froese and Peter Hinchcliffe, eds. *Acts of Concealment: Mennonite/s Writing in Canada*. Waterloo: Univ. of Waterloo Press, 1992.

Toews, Paul. *Mennonites in American Society, 1930-1970: Modernity and the Persistence of Religious Community*. Scottdale, Pa.: Herald Press, 1996.

Toole, David. *Waiting for Godot in Sarajevo: Theological Reflections on Nihilism, Tragedy, and Apocalypse*. Boulder, Colo.: Westview Press, 1998.

Toulmin, Stephen. *Cosmopolis: The Hidden Agenda of Modernity*. New York:

Free Press, 1990.

Townes, Emilie M. *In a Blaze of Glory: Womanist Spirituality as Social Witness.* Nashville: Abingdon, 1995.

Townes, Emilie M., ed. *A Troubling in My Soul: Womanist Prospectives on Evil and Suffering.* Maryknoll, N.Y.: Orbis, 1993.

Tracy, David. "The Hidden God." *Cross Currents* 46 (Spring 1996), 5-16.

———. "The Return of God." *Naming the Present.* Maryknoll, N.Y.: Orbis Books, 1994.

Troeltsch, Ernst. *The Social Teaching of the Christian Churches.* Vols. 1, 2. London: George Allen and Unwin, 1931.

Van Braght, Thieleman J. *The Bloody Theater or Martyrs Mirror.* Scottdale, Pa.: Herald Press, 1985.

Vickers, Brian. *In Defence of Rhetoric.* Oxford: Clarendon Press, 1988.

Volf, Miroslav. *Exclusion and Embrace: A Theological Exploration of Identity, Otherness, and Reconciliation.* Nashville: Abingdon Press, 1996.

Voolstra, Sjouke. "'The colony of heaven': The Anabaptist aspiration to be a church without spot or wrinkle in the sixteenth and seventeenth centuries." In *From Martyr to Muppy*, edited by Alastair Hamilton, Sjouke Voolstra, and Piet Visser. Amsterdam: Amsterdam Univ. Press, 1994.

Walsh, David. *After Ideology: Recovering the Spiritual Foundations of Freedom.* San Francisco: HarperSanFrancisco, 1990.

Waltner, Erland, ed. *Jesus Christ and the Mission of the Church: Contemporary Anabaptist Perspectives.* Newton, Kans.: Faith and Life Press, 1990.

Waltner, Gary. "Aus der Pfalz nach Nordamerika." *Mennonitische Geschichtsblätter* (1976), 13-23.

Weaver, J. Denny. "The Anabaptist Vision: A Historical or a Theological Future?" *Conrad Grebel Review* 13 (Winter 1995), 69-86.

———. *Becoming Anabaptist.* Scottdale, Pa.: Herald Press, 1987.

———. "Confessing Jesus Christ from the 'Margins.'" *Direction* 27, no. 1 (1998), 28-40.

———. "Is the Anabaptist Vision Still Relevant?" *Pennsylvania Mennonite Heritage* 14, no. 1 (January 1991), 2-12.

———. "Reading Sixteenth-Century Anabaptism Theologically: Implications for Modern Mennonites as a Peace Church." *Conrad Grebel Review* 16 (Winter 1998), 37-51.

Weaver, Alain Epp, ed. *Mennonite Theology in Face of Modernity: Essays in Honor of Gordon D. Kaufman.* North Newton, Kans.: Bethel College, 1996.

Westphal, Merold. "Taking Paul Seriously: Sin as an Epistemological Category." In *Christian Philosophy*, edited by Thomas Flint. Notre Dame, Ind.: University of Notre Dame Press, 1990: 200-226.

White, Stephen. *The Recent Work Of Jürgen Habermas.* New York: Cambridge, 1998.

Wiebe, Dallas. *Our Asian Journey.* Waterloo, Ont.: MLR Editions Canada, 1997.

Wiebe, Rudy. *The Blue Mountains of China.* Grand Rapids, Mich.: Eerdmans, 1970.

———. *Playing Dead: A Contemplation Concerning the Arctic.* Edmonton: NeWest Press, 1989.

———. "The Skull in the Swamp." *Journal of Mennonite Studies* 5 (1987): 8-20.

Williams, Delores S. "The Color of Feminism: Or Speaking the Black Woman's Tongue." *The Journal of Religious Thought* 43, no. 1 (Spring-Summer 1986): 42-58.

———. *Sisters in the Wilderness: The Challenge of Womanist God-Talk.* Maryknoll, N.Y.:: Orbis Books, 1993.

Williams, George H., and Angel M. Mergal. *Spiritual and Anabaptist Writers*, vol. 25 of *The Library of Christian Classics.* Louisville: Westminster/John Knox Press, 1996.

Williams, James G. *The Bible, Violence, and the Sacred: Liberation from the Myth of Sanctioned Violence.* Valley Forge, Pa.: Trinity Press International, 1994.

Wilson, Jonathan R. *Living Faithfully in a Fragmented World: Lessons for the Church from MacIntyre's After Virtue.* Christian Mission and Modern Culture. Harrisburg, Pa.: Trinity Press International, 1997.

Wink, Walter. *Engaging the Powers: Discernment and Resistance in a World of Domination.* Minneapolis, Minn.: Fortress Press, 1992.

Winquist, Charles. *Desiring Theology.* Chicago: University of Chicago Press, 1995.

Wyschogrod, Edith. *Saints and Postmodernism.* Chicago: University of Chicago Press, 1990.

Yoder, John Howard. "'Anabaptists and the Sword' Revisited: Systematic Historiography and Undogmatic Nonresistants." *Zeitschrift für Kirchengeschichte* 85, no. 2 (1974).

———. "The Anabaptist Dissent: The Logic of the Place of the Disciple in Society." *Concern* 1 (1954), 46.

———. "Armaments and Eschatology." *Studies in Christian Ethics* 1 (1998): 43-61.

———. *Body Politics: Five Practices of the Christian Community Before the Watching World.* Nashville: Discipleship Resources, 1992.

———. *Christian Attitudes to War, Peace, and Revolution: A Companion to*

Bainton. Elkhart, Ind.: Goshen Biblical Seminary, 1983.

———. *The Christian Witness to the State*. Newton, Kans.: Faith and Life Press, 1964.

———. *For the Nations: Essays Public and Evangelical*. Grand Rapids, Mich., and Cambridge, U.K.: William B. Eerdmans Publishing Company, 1997.

———. *The Fullness of Christ: Paul's Revolutionary Vision of Universal Ministry*. Elgin, Ill.: Brethren Press, 1987.

———. *The Legacy of Michael Sattler*. Scottdale, Pa.: Herald Press, 1973.

———. "On Not Being Ashamed of the Gospel: Particularity, Pluralism, and Validation." *Faith and Philosophy* 9 (July 1992): 285-300.

———. *The Politics of Jesus*. 2d ed. Grand Rapids, Mich.: Eerdmans, 1994.

———. *Preface to Theology: Christology and Theological Method*. Elkhart, Ind.: Goshen Biblical Seminary; distributed by Co-op Bookstore, 1981.

———. *The Priestly Kingdom: Social Ethics as Gospel*. Notre Dame, Ind.: University of Notre Dame Press, 1984.

———. *The Royal Priesthood*. Grand Rapids, Mich.: Eerdmans, 1994.

Zercher, David L. "A Novel Conversion: The Fleeting Life of *Amish Soldier*." *Mennonite Quarterly Review* 72, no. 2 (April 1998), 141-160.

Zornberg, Avivah Gottlieb. *Genesis: The Beginning of Desire*. Jerusalem: The Jewish Publication Society, 1995.

———. "Reveille for *Die Stillen Im Lande*: A Stir Among Mennonites in the Late Nineteenth Century." *Mennonite Quarterly Review* 51, no. 3 (July 1977), 215-16.

Schowalter, Paul. "Die Ibersheimer Beschlüße von 1803 und 1805." *Mennonitische Geschichtsblätter* (1963), 29-36.

Seidman, Steven. *Contested Knowledge: Social Theory in the Postmodern Era*. Oxford, England: Blackwell Publishers, 1994.

Simons, Menno. *The Complete Writings of Menno Simons*. Translated by Leonard Verduin and edited by J. C. Wenger. Scottdale, Pa.: Herald Press, 1984.

Smart, Barry. *Michel Foucault*. London: Routledge, 1988.

THE INDEX

A

Abbott, Andrew, 397
ABC, 20/20, 26-30
abortion, 48
Abraham, 263-264, 303, 333, 335, 386-387
absolutes, 51, 77, 117, 274
Acker, Kathy, 184
Afrocentricism, 264-265
Ainlay, Stephen, 92-93, 100
Althusser, Louis, 94, 205
Amish, 19, 25-31, 62, 92-93, 201, 204, 311, 314, 316, 389. *See also* Mennonites: Amish
    religious doctrines, 135
Ammann, Jakob, 201
Anabaptists. *See also* Amish, Mennonites, theology
    eschatology, 36, 374-378
    Christendom, 50, 91
    Dutch, 196
    fanaticism, 194-195
    history, 94-95, 101, 176
    martyrs, 20-21, 131, 136, 208-209, 387, 409
    modernity, 20, 23, 62, 121, 288, 356
    politics, 36
    polygenesis, 61, 290
    salvation, 36
    sixteenth-century, 21, 30-31, 71, 78, 91, 194, 214, 252, 254, 385-386, 390, 403
    spiritual formation, 243
    Swiss Brethren, 122
    church, 23
Anabaptists and Postmodernity conference, 13, 16-17, 31
Anabaptist Vision, The, 148, 177, 406-407
Angas, William Heinrich, 132-133
Anselm of Canterbury, 252, 254, 332-335
Anthony, Susan B., 263
antifoundationalism, 76, 79-85
apocalypse, 42, 50, 134
    characters, 49
    vision, 257

aporia, 344
Aquinas, Thomas, 44, 339, 341, 352
Arac, Jonathan, 95
Aristotle, 340-341, 343-344, 352-353
Armstrong, Karen, 243
Arnold, Gottfried, 151-152
Asante, Molefi Kete, 264
Augustine of Hippo, 62, 194, 196, 304, 316, 331
August, Ludwig Wilhelm, 136
Ausbund, 123, 136-137
Bádham, Roger, 149

B

ban, 200-201
Bañuelas, Arturo, 291
baptism
    infant, 19
    believer's, 22, 123, 125, 195 199, 204, 317
Barbe, Dominique, 222
Barrett, Lois, 198, 386-388
Barth, Karl, 16
Basil of Caesarea, 258
Bauman, Clarence, 151
Beachy Amish, 141. *See also* Amish, Mennonites
Beckett, Samuel, 42
Believers Church Conference on Christology, 270
Bender, Elizabeth, 386
Bender, Harold S., 148, 151, 176-181, 198, 285, 386, 406-408
Benedict, 301, 304, 306-318
    Rule of St. Benedict, 302-318
    vow of stability, 306-318
Benedictines, 302-303. *See also* Benedict
Bentham, Jeremy, 179
Berding, Helmut, 121
Berger, Peter, 67, 287
Berry, Wendell, 304-305, 316
Bethel College, 11, 108
Bible, 45, 75, 96, 100, 110, 114, 124, 131, 153-154, 169, 215, 217-219, 223-229, 286, 349, 387

interpretation, 262-264
  Scripture, 310
Biesecker-Mast, Gerald, 13, 20, 34, 94, 101
Biesecker-Mast, Susan, 14, 19
Bloch, Ernst, 34, 149
Blond, Philip, 44
Bluffton, Ohio, 25
Bluffton College, 3, 11-14, 16-17, 25, 50, 270
Blum, Peter, 32
Bonhoeffer, Dietrich, 16, 406-409
Borg, Marcus, 295-297
Boyer Jr., Ernest, 297-298
Boyle, Nicholas, 41-52
Brandt, Di, 34, 162-170, 178-182, 388
Brethren, 151-153, 183
Brethren in Christ, 281, 298
Brown, Raymond, 153
Brueggemann, Walter, 290
Buechner, Frederick, 95-96
Burke, Edmund, 67
Burkholder, J. Lawrence, 36, 198
Burkholder, John Richard, 34
Burt, John, 148
Butler, Judith, 205

C

C. Henry Smith Series, 3, 11-14
Cahoone, Lawrence, 388
Calvino, Italo, 180
Calvin, John, 390
Cambridge University, 44, 221
Canadian Mennonite Bible College, 387
Cannon, Katie, 260-266
capitalism, 22, 32, 48, 366, 385
  consumer, 86
  global, 46-51, 203, 362
  industrial, 23
  third-wave economies, 391-394
Catholics, 22, 51, 91, 123, 139-140, 168, 214-215, 252, 282, 302, 390, 393, 407, 412
  First Vatican Council, 51-52
Chambers, Iain, 162
Christendom, 34, 92, 149-150, 215, 252
Christliches Gemüths-Gespräch, 138
Christliches Gesangbuch, 137
Christliche Lehre zunächst zum Gebrauch der Taufgesinnten in Deutschland, 138

church, 189, 193-194, 199, 202-203, 206, 252, 254, 285, 289, 293-294, 349, 357. *See also* theology: ecclesiology
  African-American, 260, 267
  catholicity, 293
  discipline, 70, 121, 123, 125, 130, 135, 138, 140, 200-201, 203, 316
  early, 78
  leadership, 128-130
  polity, 136, 199, 313-316, 358
  universal, 51
  without spot or wrinkle, 200-201
Clapp, Rodney, 210
Clement of Alexandria, 331
clothing, 207
Coffman, John S., 285
Colas, Dominique, 194-195
Collegiants, 197
Concern group, 216
confession, 62, 67-70
conflict, 92-94, 101, 121-122, 128, 140-141, 197, 199, 344
Confucianism, 402
Connolly, William, 370-374
conscientious objection, 207
Constantinianism, 50, 91, 149, 224, 253, 255, 257, 272-273, 350, 373
consumerism, 23-24, 32, 35, 46, 86-97, 203, 308, 336-337, 366
  culture and, 26
  commodities and, 12, 336-37
  information revolution and, 393-394
  media culture and, 25 28-30, 52, 205, 361, 391. *See also* media: religious, 315
consumption, 28, 183, 205-206
Cooper, Barry, 362
Cost of Discipleship, The, 406-408
countercultural, 148, 183, 197-198, 207, 217
covering (women's), 206-207
cultural. *See also* countercultural
  contexts, 83, 228
  experience, 81
  factors, 75
  industries, 206
  pluralism, 401
  religion, 222
  studies, 113, 160
  values, 401-402
  work, 182

culture, 187, 305-306

D
Dahlem, Valentin, 129
Daniel, 271
Dante, 45
de Toqueville, Alexis, 67
death penalty, 330-331
deconstruction, 47, 113, 117, 221, 271, 303, 347, 399-401
Deknatel, Johannes, 124, 138-139
Deleuze, Gilles, 149-150, 185-186
Denck, Hans, 150-151
denominational faith, 289-291
Derrida, Jacques, 16, 30, 61, 176-179, 339, 343-346, 352-353, 399-401
Descartes, René, 303, 360, 369
Dettweiler, Christian, 125
Dewey, John, 48
Didache, 307
discipleship, 148, 150, 198, 207-209, 227, 303, 350, 412
Donatists, 194
Douglas, Kelly Brown, 260, 268-269, 273
Driedger, Leo, 36, 285-287
Friesen, Abraham, 195, 197
dualism, 195, 200, 348
Durkheim, Emil, 395-396

E
Eagleton, Terry, 47-48
Eastern Mennonite University, 235
Eckhart, Meister, 154
economy, 47, 93, 391-393, 396
    market, 48
Eco, Umberto, 221
Edwards, George, 26
Elizabethtown College, 16
Elizondo, Virgil, 291
Ellenberger, Jakob, 126
Emerson, Ralph Waldo, 154-155
Enlightenment, 43, 46, 61, 63, 92, 112, 121, 339, 342, 345, 348, 361-367, 372, 375, 387, 394-403, 406, 410
Environmental pollution, 86
Episcopalians, 268
Erasmus, 195-196
Esau, John, 386-387
eschatology, 33, 36, 86, 357, 373-378
    Augustinian eschatology, 194, 196
Esther, 271
European Heritage Tour, 20

evangelicalism, 285-289
excommunication, 201. *See also* ban
exile, 271
Eymann, Christian, 130
Faith and Life Press, 110
feminists, 166, 282, 313
feudalism, 22, 51, 403
Finger, Thomas, 33, 198
forgiveness, 35, 154, 294, 296-299, 347
foundationalism, 75, 77, 272. *See also* antifoundationalism
Foucault, Michel, 16, 32-33, 42, 60-71; 92-101, 112, 179, 181, 204-205, 339, 343
Franck, August Herman, 124
Franklin, Benjamin, 152
French Revolution, 121
    French Civil Code, 127
    reforms, 121, 140
Freud, Sigmund, 224
Friedelsheim congregation, 134, 137, 139
Friedenreich, Lorenz, 124
Friesen, Abraham, 195, 197
Friesen, Patrick, 388
fundamentalism, 150-153, 285, 312
Funk, John, 150

G
Gadamer, Hans-Georg, 16, 98-101
Galle, Johannes, 128, 130, 134-141
Galle, Joseph, 132-133
genealogy, 63-66, 69, 97, 339-348, 352-353
Germantown Mennonite Church, 94
Ghent, Henry of, 44
Girard, René, 34, 217, 221-227
Goethe, 120
González, Justo L., 292-294
Goshen, Indiana, 25
Goshen College, 11
Gramsci, Antonio, 94
Grant, Jacqueline, 265
Grebel, Conrad, 335, 386
Grimsrud, Ted, 81
Guattari, Félix, 149-150, 185-186
Gundy, Jeff, 34

H
Hagar, 263-264
Hall, David, 401-402
Hall, Stuart, 171

Hanson, R. C. P., 258
Harvey, David, 46-47
Hauerwas, Stanley, 32, 41, 50-51, 85, 206, 217, 224-225, 290, 295-297, 308
Havel, Vaclav, 385
Hayek, Friedrich, 67
headship, 206-207
Hegel, G.W.F, 43, 224, 366, 371, 406, 410
Heidegger, Martin, 367, 371, 374
Heilke, Thomas, 36
Herald Press, 92-93, 96, 101
Herbert, George, 243
Hershberger, Guy F., 198, 317, 406
Hirschfield, Jane, 186-187
Holland, Scott, 15, 34, 203, 206, 209
Holmes County, Ohio, 26
holy kiss, 148, 154
homosexuality, 94
Horsch, John, 150-153
Hostetler, Beulah Stauffer, 198
Howells, Coral Ann, 165
Huebner, Chris, 36
Huebner, Harry, 217
humility, 121, 179, 185-188, 285, 309, 377
Hunzinger, Abraham, 135
Hurston, Zora Neal, 261
Hutcheon, Linda, 162-163, 165, 168-170
Huyssen, Andreas, 161

I
Ibersheim
 conference, 125
 congregation, 132, 139
identity
 Anabaptist-Mennonite, 19, 35, 108-109, 122, 280-299, 407-410
 countercultural, 24
 social, 94
Ideologies: political, 20, 370
Ignatius, 329
incommensurability, 114
industrialism, 364, 394-395
Industrial Revolution, 388-389, 403
intellectuals, 41-42, 46
Ishmael, 263

J
Jacobsen, Douglas, 35
Jansen, Sue Curry, 92-93

Jansz, Anna, 199-200, 203, 209
Janzen, Jean, 182
Jameson, Fredric, 46
Jenson, Robert, 35
Jermann, Rosemary, 258
Jesus, 42, 49, 64, 68-69, 85-87, 153, 168, 193, 209, 214-215, 219, 227, 251-252, 254, 256-259, 261-262, 268-274, 285, 295, 328-337, 348-353, 375-376, 386, 406, 408, 412. *See also* theology: christology
 blood, 334-335
 Christ, 314, 328-329, 342, 413
 humanity, 259, 327-335
 divinity, 259, 331.
John Paul II, 50
Joseph, 271
Judaism, 149-151, 154, 271-273
Jung-Stilling, Heinrich, 124
justification, 153

K
Kafka, Franz, 150, 185
Kägy, David, 125, 128, 130, 135, 139-141
Kampen, John, 14, 17
Kant, Immanuel, 303, 394-395, 406
Kardong, Terrance, 313
Kariel, Henry, 365-369, 374-377
Kasdorf, Julia, 182-183
Kauffman, Daniel, 151, 285
Kauffman, J. Howard, 285-288
Kaufman, Gordon, 81, 284
Keen, Sam, 233-234
Keller, Ludwig, 150
Kierkegaard, Søren, 30, 152-153, 406-407
King, Michael A., 14, 16, 33, 387
Kirk, Russell, 67
Klassen, Pamela, 93-94
Kniss, Fred, 92-93, 100
knowledge and power, 67-68
Krahn, Cornelius, 110-111
Kraus, C. Norman, 198, 209, 217
Kraybill, Donald, 198
Krehbiel, Adam, 125
Krehbiel, Heinrich, 126
Krehbiel, Jakob, 126, 136
Krehbiel, Katharina, 138
Kristeva, Julia, 188
Kroetsch, Robert, 162, 165-166
Kropf, Marlene, 35
Kuhn, Thomas, 396-397

L

Lacan, Jacques, 177
Laclau, Ernesto, 94, 101
Lapp, Johannes, 135-137
Lapp, John, 131
Lederach, John Paul, 311-314
Lehman, Whitney, 17
Levinas, Emmanuel, 154
Lewis, C. S., 221
liberalism, 48, 67, 364-367, 370-377
Liechty, Daniel, 81
literature
   contemporary, 217
   Mennonite culture, 162-164, 169, 171, 179
   Mennonite fiction, 107, 163, 172
   Mennonite narratives, 165, 167, 181
   Mennonite writers, 171, 175, 183-188, 387-388
   narratives of history, 162
   narrative systems, 167
   of the visible church, 209
   style, 161
Luther, Martin, 195, 357, 390
   Lutheran belief, 141, 197, 199
   Lutheran reformation, 196, 357
Lutherans, 129, 132, 138-139, 282, 289, 407, 413
Lyotard, Jean-François, 16, 43, 91, 109, 398

M

MacIntyre, Alasdair, 36, 307-308, 317, 339-353, 362-363, 374
Manchester College, 155
Marty, Martin, 409
Martyrs Mirror, 20, 137, 208, 244
Marx, Karl, 224, 371, 395-396, 406
McClendon, James, 217
McLuhan, Marshall, 389-391
McNeill, William, 402
media, 24, 26-31, 205-206, 210. *See also* consumerism: mass media
Menno, Menno Simons, 165-166, 386. *See also* Simons, Menno
Mennonite Central Committee, 281, 411
Mennonite Publishing House, 151
Mennonites
   Amish, 141
   architecture, 131-133
   Mennonite Brethren, 141
   Canadian, 164
   catechism, 128, 138-140
   Catholic, 35, 302
   communities, 183, 197, 288, 298
   conservative, 131, 135, 137-140, 207, 285, 389
   Dutch, 133, 197, 284
   Eastern District, 136
   European, 129, 140
   evangelical, 284-292
   fiction, 107. *See also* literature: Mennonite fiction
   Franconia Mennonite Conference, 94
   General Conference Mennonite Church, 141, 386
   history, 108-112, 181-182, 196
   leadership, 316
   ministerial authority, 130
   ministerial training, 129
   (Old) Mennonites, 141, 206
   Old Order, 207, 283, 311, 314
   Russian, 33, 167
   South German, 33, 121-124, 127-128, 133, 135, 140, 150
   Swiss, 169-170, 284
   Swiss Brethren, 151, 195-196
   theology of, 36, 124, 129-30, 182. *See also* theology
   tithing and, 130
   worship and, 123, 128, 136. *See also* theology, worship
   hymn singing and, 234-247
Merton, Thomas, 282, 301, 312
Mertz, Johannes Baptist, 149
Merwin, W.S., 155
Messiah, 239-240, 245
Messiah College, 281
Middle Ages, 20, 52, 221
Milbank, John, 217, 227-228, 346-352, 357
millennium, 36
Miller, Caleb, 98-99
Miller, James, 95
mission movement, 128, 133-135, 140, 194
Möllinger, David, 123
Möllinger, Martin, 125
Monsheim congregation, 123, 130, 132, 134, 137, 139
Montaigne, 43

Morgenthaler, Sally, 234
Moses, 386
Mouffe, Chantal, 94, 101
Münster, 34, 137, 147-148, 195, 357
  St. Lamberti's Church, 29, 149
Müntzer, Thomas, 335
Murphy, Nancey, 290
mutual aid, 130, 203

N

Nafziger, Ken, 235
nationalism, 51-52
Nealon, Jeffrey, 207
Neuman, Shirley, 163
Neuwied congregation, 124, 132
Newton, Kansas, 108, 110, 113
Nicaea, 253-259, 270
Niehbur, Reinhold, 16, 217
Niehbur, Richard, 16
Nietzsche, Friedrich, 42, 60-64, 97, 155, 181, 186-187, 224, 343-344, 364-371, 376, 394-395, 400
nonconformity, 25, 27, 29, 37, 151, 198-199, 288
noncreedalism, 151-152
nonresistance, 68, 123, 136, 148, 150, 178-179, 181, 189, 200, 407. *See also* pacifism
nonviolence, 223, 252, 297, 351
nostalgia, 180

O

Oakeshott, Michael, 67
oaths, 123, 195
Oberholtzer, John, 136
Ockham, William of, 359
O'Brien, Conor Cruise, 215
Oetinger, Friedrich, 124
Onesimus, 263
oppression, 76, 85-86, 262-263
Ordnung, 26, 123, 129, 135, 139, 316
orthodoxy, 148, 152, 256, 266, 328-329, 370
Our Asian Journey, 106-109, 113-117, 187
Oyer, John, 181

P

pacifism, 19, 34-36, 49-50, 126, 139, 148, 183, 194-196, 206, 223, 254, 257, 271, 281, 315, 317, 340, 346-353, 407-409, 413. *See also* nonresistance

Palatinate, 122-124, 133
Pandora Press, U.S., 14, 16, 387
Pannwitz, Rudof, 394
panoptican, 179
particularity, 62, 64, 69, 94, 116, 260, 265, 298. *See also* truth
  Anabaptist, 78-78, 254, 289
  classic orthodoxy and, 252-255
Paul, 97, 199-200, 219, 256, 328-329, 372
Peace Shall Destroy Many, 163, 167, 176
Pelagians, 194
Pentecostal, 282, 289
performance, 206-210, 350
persecution, 20-21, 123, 136, 139, 152, 244, 247, 260
Peterson, Eugene, 243
Pietism, 151
Pittsburgh, 15-16, 155
Plato, 198, 209, 346
Platonism, 34, 194-196, 199, 372
pluralism/relativism, 13, 68-70, 221, 252, 270-271, 284, 289
Poe, Edgar Allen, 177
poetry, 45
politics, 70
  alterity and, 207
  compassion and, 295-299
  cross and, 68-69. *See also* theology: atonement
  friendship and, 340-348, 351-353
  pacifist, 351
  power, 67-68, 91-102, 106, 113, 182-183, 252, 345-346
  biblical, 96
  economic, 92-94, 96, 261
  of language, 204-205
  of the gospel, 69
  political, 261, 370-377
  power-knowledge and, 65-67, 92, 100
  social, 179, 205
Prado, C.G., 95
Presbyterians, 289

Q

Quakers, 183, 407
Reed, Kenneth, 92
Reeder, Hermann, 125, 132
Reformation, 51, 78-79, 196-197, 374, 385
  Protestant, 390, 397, 403
  Radical, 149-152. *See also* Anabaptists

INDEX 435

R
Reformed church, 123, 129, 132, 139
Reid, Angus, 392
Reihl, Wilhelm Heinrich, 127
Reimer, James, 284
Reimer, Margaret Loewen, 387
Reitz, Johann Heinrich, 124
relativism, 62, 76-78, 82. *See also* pluralism/relativism
Richard, Wesley, 17
Risser, Johannes, 128, 133-136, 140-141
Roosen, Gerrit, 138-139
Rorty, Richard, 47-48
Roth, John D., 15, 33
Rousseau, Jean-Jacques, 62
Rushdie, Salman, 305-306
Ruth, 334, 386
Ruth, John, 20

S
sacraments, 216, 234, 236, 246, 342
Sage, Mary, 330
Said, Edward, 181
Sanders, Scott Russell, 304-305
Sarah, 263-264
Sattler, Michael, 199-201, 301-302
scapegoat, 222-223
Schell, Jonathan, 182
Schlabach, Gerald, 16, 35, 50-51
Schlabach, Theron, 16, 198, 311, 316
Schlegel, 43
Schleitheim *Brotherly Union*, 202, 204, 351, 407
Schwager, Raymund, 227
Scottdale, Pennsylvania, 151
Scotus, Duns, 44
Sembach congregation, 132, 134, 137, 140
separation, 199
  of church and state, 19-23, 140, 204, 255
  from the world, 134, 196-210, 286
sexuality, 48, 184-185, 331, 392
Silverman, Hugh, 99
Simmel, Georg, 395
Simons, Menno, 25, 29, 34, 150, 199-201. *See also* Menno
Sinsheim congregation, 139
Smith, C. Henry, 106, 109-114. *See also* C. Henry Smith Series
Smith, Gregory Bruce, 366-376
Snyder, C. Arnold, 94-95, 101, 302

Snyder, Lee, 7, 14, 17
social boundaries, 287, 299
social order, 251-259, 271
Sowell, Thomas, 67
Spirit, 31, 68, 186, 242, 244, 330
Spragens, Thomas, 361
Stahl-Wert, John, 15, 35-36
Stahl-Wert, Milonica, 15
Stanton, Elizabeth Cady, 263
The Story of the Mennonites, 109-110
Studies in Anabaptist and Mennonite History, 12
survival, 49, 264
Swartzentruber, Amos Orley, 216
Swartzentruber, Elaine, 185
Sweet, Leonard, 244
sword, 123, 126, 195, 199, 258, 335

T
Taoism, 402
Tauler, Johann, 150
Taylor, Charles, 396
Technology, 27-30, 391-392, 403
Tersteegen, Gerhard, 124
The Blue Mountains of China, 225-228
theology
  African-American, 260-269
  Anabaptist, 77-81, 148-149, 154, 217
  atonement, 124, 222-225, 227-228, 252, 269, 332-337
  black womanist, 260-274
  Christology and, 35, 252-259, 268-270, 348
  conversation and, 82-84
  Constantinian, 259, 273
  desire and, 154
  ecclesiology and, 141, 199, 292-294, 316, 350, 357
  eschatology and, 374-378
  Latino, 291-295
  love, 151-152
  mainstream, 95
  Mennonite, 36, 81, 198, 347-351. *See also* Mennonite
  natural, 44
  normative, 151, 252
  of worship, 34, 218-229
  Reformed, 290
  sacrificial, 218-229
  sacramental, 216, 246-247
  salvation, 124, 152, 154

sanctification, 227
systematic, 34
womanist, 259-274
Thirty Years War, 20
Thomistic Aristotelianism, 339-346, 352
Tiessen, Hildi Froese, 34, 188
Tiessen, Paul, 33
Toews, Paul, 290
Toffler, Alvin and Heidi, 388-389
Toole, David, 42, 348
Toronto Mennonite Theological Center, 281
Tourism, 12, 19-20
Townes, Emilie, 266-267
Toynbee, Arnold, 394
tradition, 77, 80, 121, 252-255
    historic, 78, 82
    biblical, 81, 217
    orthodox, 256-259. *See also* orthodoxy
Troeger, Thomas, 245
Troeltsch, Ernst, 16, 217, 349, 406, 409
truth, 32-34, 176-178, 180
    particular, 64-65, 69
    Platonic, 63-66, 69
    universal, 12-13, 33, 65, 75-76, 80-85, 208, 266-267, 273

U

United Church of Christ, 281
university, 42, 46, 49, 127, 131, 161

V

van Braght, Thieleman, 20, 208
Vietnam War, 183, 281, 408
violence
    linguistic, 99
    religious, 222
von Mises, Ludwig, 67
Voolstra, Sjouke, 196-197
Volf, Miroslav, 290

W

Walsh, David, 373-375
Waltner-Toews, David, 171
War, Peace, and Nonresistance, 317, 406
Weaver, J. Denny, 14, 16, 35, 94-95, 101, 198, 217
Weber, Johann, 137
Weber, Johannes, 125
Weber, Max, 395-396, 409
Weber, Peter, 124, 129
Weem, Renita J., 262-263

Weierhof congregation, 125-126, 132-134, 138-140
Westminster Theological Seminary, 281
Weydman, Leonhard, 128-133, 137-141
Wheaton College, 281
Whitman, Walt, 155, 187
Wiebe, Armin, 107
Wiebe, Dallas, 33, 106-117, 187
Wiebe, Rudy, 34, 162-164, 167-168, 176, 225-226
Wilde, Oscar, 188
Williams, Daniel H., 255-258
Williams, Delores S., 263-264, 269
Williams, James G., 224
Wilson, Robert, 161
Wink, Walter, 290
Wittgenstein, Ludwig, 398
Wolfart, Michael, 152
worship, 123, 133, 189, 197, 210, 216-229, 290. *See also* theology: worship
    singing, 234-247

Y

Yoder, John Howard, 22-23, 32, 42, 49-50, 197-198, 202, 217, 225, 253, 270-272, 336, 350-353, 375, 409
youth, 23-24, 126

Z

Zercher, David L., 92, 94, 101
Zornberg, Aviva, 154
Zwingli, Ulrich, 195

THE CONTRIBUTORS

Peter Blum is Associate Professor of Sociology and Social Thought at Hillsdale College. He has published and lectured in the areas of philosophy, ethics, social theory, and Amish-Mennonite culture.

J. Lawrence Burkholder is President Emeritus of Goshen College, where he was president 1972-1984. A respected church leader and scholar, he has worked at the forefront of numerous movements for human relief and civil rights, and has lectured and published in the areas of Christian theology and social ethics. *The Limits of Perfection* (Pandora Press, 1993) contains an extended autobiographical sketch by Burkholder and numerous responses to his *The Problem of Social Responsibility From the Perspective of the Mennonite Church* (Institute of Mennonite Studies, 1989).

J. R. Burkholder is Professor Emeritus of Religion at Goshen College. He has served the church as pastor, missionary, scholar, and teacher. Among his works is a book entitled *Children of Peace* (Brethren Press, 1982, co-authored with John Bender) and the well-known festschrift for Guy Hershberger, *Kingdom, Cross, and Community* (Herald Press, 1976, co-edited with Cal Redekop).

Leo Driedger is Professor of Sociology at the University of Manitoba, where he specializes in ethnic relations. He has published numerous books in Anabaptist-Mennonite studies, including *The Mennonite Mosaic* (Herald Press, 1991, co-authored with J. Howard Kauffman) and *Mennonite Peacemaking* (Herald Press, 1994, co-authored with Donald Kraybill). Among his many significant contributions to the Mennonite churches have been his roles as executive secretary of the General Conference Mennonite Church Peace and Social Concerns Committee (1957-1961) and chair of Mennonite Central Committee Manitoba.

Tom Finger has most recently been Professor of Systematic and Spiritual Theology at Eastern Mennonite University and has taught in many other settings as well. His theological writing includes *Systematic Theology: An Eschatological Approach* (vols. 1 and 2; Herald Press, 1985, 1989) and

Self, Earth, and Society (InterVarsity Press, 1997). He is an ordained minister in the Mennonite Church.

Jeff Gundy is Professor of English at Bluffton College. He is a widely published and accomplished poet whose recent book entitled *A Community of Memory* (University of Illinois Press, 1995) is a creative nonfiction account of his Gundy ancestors.

Stanley Hauerwas is the Gilbert T. Rowe Professor of Theological Ethics at the Divinity School of Duke University and will be the Gifford Lecturer at the University of St. Andrews in Scotland in 2000-2001. A prolific author, his most recent works include Wilderness Wanderings (Westview Press, 1997) and Sanctify Them in Thy Truth (Abingdon Press, 1999).

Thomas Heilke is Associate Professor in the Department of Political Science at the University of Kansas. He is most recently author of *Nietzsche's Tragic Regime: Culture, Aesthetics, and Political Education* (Northern Illinois University Press, 1998) and of *Eric Voegelin: In Quest of Reality* (Rowman & Littlefield, 1999), as well as several essays on Anabaptist political thought and other topics.

Scott Holland is Associate Professor of Peace and Cross Cultural Theologies, Bethany Theological Seminary. He has pastored congregations in the Mennonite Church and the Church of the Brethren. He is author of many essays on Anabaptist public theology and aesthetics, co-editor of *The Limits of Perfection* (Pandora Press, 1993), and contributing editor for *Cross Currents: The Journal of the Association for Religion and Intellectual Life*.

Chris Huebner is a graduate student in Theological Ethics at Duke University and co-editor of the recent festschrift for John Howard Yoder entitled *The Wisdom of the Cross* (W.B. Eerdmans, 1999).

Douglas Jacobsen is Professor of Church History and Theology at Messiah College. He has lectured and written on numerous aspects of American evangelical and Protestant identity. He is the author of *An Unprov'd Experiment: Religious Pluralism in Colonial New Jersey* (Carlson Pub., 1991) and co-editor of *Re-Forming the Center: American Protestantism, 1900 to the Present* (W. B. Eerdmans, 1998).

Michael A. King is pastor of Spring Mount (Pa.) Mennonite Church as well as publisher, Pandora Press U.S., and editor, InterLink Communication Services He is the author of numerous articles and has had published two books, *Preaching about Life in a Threatening World* (co-authored with Ronald J. Sider, Westminster, 1987) and *Trackless Wastes and Stars to Steer By: Christian Identity in a Homeless Age* (Herald Press, 1990).

Marlene Kropf is Assistant Professor of Spiritual Formation and Worship at Associated Mennonite Biblical Seminary and Minister of Worship and Spirituality for Mennonite Board of Congregational Ministries. She is co-author of *Praying With the Anabaptists* (Faith & Life Press, 1994).

John D. Roth is Professor of History at Goshen College where he also is director of the Mennonite Historical Library and editor of *The Mennonite Quarterly Review*. He has written many articles on Anabaptist-Mennonite related themes and is editor and translator of *Letters of the Amish Division* (Mennonite Historical Society, 1993).

Gerald W. Schlabach is Associate Professor of History and Religion at Bluffton College. He worked as a writer and program adminstrator for Mennonite Central Committee during the 1980s and is the author of numerous essays and books, including *And Who Is My Neighbor?* (Herald Press, 1990) and the forthcoming title, *For the Joy Set Before Us: Augustine and Self-Denying Love* (Univ. of Notre Dame Press).

John Stahl-Wert is director of the Studies Institute at the Pittsburgh Leadership Foundation and executive director of the Pittsburgh Urban Leadership Service Experience (PULSE), a voluntary service program for Mennonite college graduates. An ordained minister in the Mennonite Church, he has co-authored the book *Welcoming New Christians* (Faith and Life Press and Mennonite Publishing House, 1995) and many articles in the areas of narrative theology and Christian hospitality.

Hildi Froese Tiessen is Associate Professor of English and Peace and Conflict Studies at Conrad Grebel College, the University of Waterloo. She has edited five volumes of work by and about Mennonite writers/writing, including *Liars and Rascals: Mennonite Short Stories* (University of Waterloo Press, 1989).

Paul Tiessen is Professor in the English Department at Wilfred Laurier University. He has edited and co-edited numerous books on literature, film, art, and photography, most recently, *A Darkness That Murmured: Essays on Malcolm Lowry and the Twentieth Century* (University of Toronto Press, 1999).

J. Denny Weaver is Professor of Religion at Bluffton College and editor of the C. Henry Smith Series. He has published widely in the field of Anabaptist-Mennonite historical theology, including the books *Becoming Anabaptist* (Herald Press, 1987), *Keeping Salvation Ethical* (Herald Press, 1997), and the forthcoming *Anabaptist Theology in Face of Postmodernity: A Proposal for the Third Millennium* (Pandora Press U.S., 2000).

THE EDITORS

Susan Biesecker-Mast has been Assistant Professor of Communication at Bluffton (Oh.) College since 1996. She received her B.A. from the University of Wisconsin, Madison, where she studied communication arts. Her graduate degrees are from the University of Pittsburgh in the areas of rhetoric and communication. Since completing her studies she has published many articles in classical rhetoric, American feminism, and tourism in Amish-Mennonite communities.

Susan was baptized as a Catholic and grew up near Chicago, where as a young person she became involved with the Willow Creek Community Church youth group. While studying in Pittsburgh, she began attending Pittsburgh Mennonite Church, where she was rebaptized in 1991. That same year she was married to Gerald Mast, after two years of courtship originating in intense conversations about postmodernism, Derridian deconstruction, and God. She belongs to First Mennonite Church, Bluffton.

Gerald Biesecker-Mast has been Assistant Professor of Communication at Bluffton College since 1996. He completed a B.A., with a major in communication arts, at Malone College, Canton, Ohio. He received his graduate degrees in rhetoric and communication from the University of Pittsburgh. He has published a number of essays on religious communication, social conflict, and Anabaptist persuasion.

Gerald grew up in Holmes County, Ohio, and was baptized into the Zion Conservative Mennonite Church in Benton at age sixteen. While studying in Pittsburgh, he met Susan Biesecker in a graduate seminar, and after many long and wide-ranging discussions, he and Susan were married in 1991 at Heinz Chapel. He is a member of First Mennonite Church, Bluffton.